Medicating Schizophrenia

Medicating Schizophrenia

A History

SHELDON GELMAN

RUTGERS UNIVERSITY PRESS
New Brunswick, New Jersey, and London

Library of Congress Cataloging-in-Publication Data

Gelman, Sheldon, 1946–
    Schizophrenia and medication : a history / Sheldon Gelman.
        p.   cm.
    Includes bibliographical references and index.
    ISBN 0-8135-2642-6 (alk. paper). — ISBN 0-8135-2643-4
(pbk. : alk. paper)
    1. Schizophrenia—Chemotherapy—History. 2. Antipsychotic drugs—
History. I. Title.
RC514.G44   1999
61.89′82061—dc21   98-47002
                                                         CIP

British Cataloging-in-Publication data for this book is available from the British Library

Composition by Colophon Typesetting

Manufactured in the United States of America

Contents

For my teachers
Alexander Brooks and Raymond Fogelson
and, in memory,
Albert Blumberg and Warren I. Susman

Acknowledgments

I OWE THANKS to Alexander Brooks and Judy Cracker, who introduced me to the subject of this book; Steven Smith, who encouraged me to write it; David Goshien, who supplied moral support; Sally Goodwin, who read it; and James Wilson, who discussed it with me for almost a decade and commented on numerous drafts.

I am also grateful for the research support and class release time that allowed me to write. The dean of the Cleveland-Marshall College Law, Steven Steinglass, gave me both; so did his predecessor, Steven Smith. Grants from the Cleveland-Marshall Fund (David B. Goshien, chair) enabled me to work on the manuscript during three summers. Cleveland State University allowed me a year-long sabbatical in 1995–96 for research.

The Cleveland-Marshall Law Library lent me able assistance and obtained hundreds of medical journal articles for me. Eric Domanski, Leon Boyd, and Laverne Carter kept the computers and the printers running. Janice Aitken, Amy McGrory, and Tava Slone-Young contributed excellent research and editorial assistance.

My family now understands why book authors express profound gratitude to anyone who lived with them through the writing. I understand why too. My deepest thanks to Jean Lifter, Hannah Gelman, and Jacob Gelman.

Medicating Schizophrenia

Introduction   Medication and Progress

NEW MEDICATIONS became available for psychiatric use during the early 1950s. Chlorpromazine appeared in the United States under the name Thorazine; other drugs with similar actions and effects quickly followed. Within a decade, psychiatrists had centered their hopes for their patients and institutions, even for their profession, on the new treatment.

At the outset, psychiatrists used the medications for a variety of mental conditions. It soon became apparent, however, that patients suffering from schizophrenia—a chronic disease marked by disordered thinking, hallucinations, social withdrawal, and, in severe cases, a deterioration in the capacity to lead a rewarding life—profited the most. Schizophrenia was a scourge; it produced more hospitalization, and probably more suffering, than any other mental illness.

Medication gave psychiatrists reason to hope. The drugs ameliorated florid psychotic symptoms, often dramatically. Institutions housing medicated patients became calmer—more like "hospitals," less like "madhouses." Yet the hopes surrounding medication arose not just from patient responses and institutional changes but also from psychiatrists' own professional wants and needs. The 1950s and early 1960s were a time of notoriously bad mental hospitals, declining public trust in psychiatry, and plummeting professional standing. Psychiatrists needed—and outside forces demanded—a change.

Treatments in 1950s mental hospitals included lobotomy, which surgically severed connections between the frontal lobes and the rest of the brain; insulin coma therapy, which sent patients into comas by manipulating insulin levels; and electroconvulsive therapy, which produced convulsions powerful enough to break patients' bones and which psychiatrists employed for a variety of conditions, including schizophrenia. Although drastic, these treatments produced generally disappointing results, especially in schizophrenia. Despite the treatments, patients often remained hospitalized for years, if not the rest of their lives. As state hospitals expanded to the size of small cities, conditions within them deteriorated. After World War II, critics compared them to Nazi concentration camps.

Once, state hospitals had represented a source of state pride—something comparable to a major public university today. For seventy-five years, they had commanded a major part of the states' social welfare spending. By the early 1950s, however, recurrent scandals over conditions, a long record of apparent failure, and a growing desire by states to fund other public projects—including universities—undermined their position.

Psychiatric treatments, and not just psychiatric institutions, were losing stature. Before World War II, coma and convulsive therapies had received favorable public attention, as had lobotomy. Some regarded the treatments as a biological revolution in psychiatry. Egas Monitz, the inventor of lobotomy, even received the 1949 Nobel Prize in Medicine. By the early 1950s, however, many physicians and much of the public regarded psychiatric treatments warily. Despite Monitz's Nobel Prize, lobotomy in particular was reviled and feared. And as the products of its "biological revolution" lost their luster, psychiatry itself seemed to decline.

Within a decade and a half, medication changed all that. The coma therapies and lobotomy had virtually disappeared by the 1960s, while electroconvulsive therapy, significantly modified, survived largely as a treatment for depression. The century-old network of state hospitals began giving way to a new public mental health system. Maintained in the community on medications, people with schizophrenia would return to hospitals only briefly, and then only to have a medication regimen adjusted or reinstituted. Medication and community care were supplanting the hospitals; the 1950s idea of the hospitals as concentration camps was giving way to a picture of people being restored to human and legal freedom.[1]

Those developments underlie the standard version of the history of medication—the implicit history carried about by many psychiatrists in their heads, invoked by them on ceremonial occasions, and conveyed by the profession to the public. By this account, medication constituted a revolutionary treatment, a biological advance that produced clinical, medical, and social advances in its wake. Patients gained an effective treatment. That in turn led to the demise of the state hospitals and the rise of community care. And as patients rejoined the community, psychiatry rejoined the mainstream of medicine, no longer a profession that administered terrifying treatments in inhumane institutions.

This account of medical progress rarely receives a lengthy defense; its validity is usually considered self-evident. It cannot owe very much to investigation, for few relevant studies exist. Judith Swazey's exhaustively researched history of medication appeared in 1974 and remains the leading account. Swazey's book appeared too soon to cover pivotal events, however, and it relied upon a picture of the actions and side effects of medication that was unraveling even as she wrote. Little else has appeared on the general subject.[2]

Despite its lack of scholarly support, the standard version's influence has been widely felt. Because of it, many people assume that the ethical and social issues that surrounded somatic psychiatric treatments prior to the medication era have become moot. By the mid-1990s, for example, leading bioethicists viewed as paradigms of unethical research experiments that *withheld* these medications from patients who did not want them—the way one might regard an experiment that *administered* lobotomy.

Psychiatry's severest critics reflect the standard version's power by offering a mirror image of it. They suppose that nothing fundamental has changed in the field and no significant progress has occurred. Indeed, they regard progress in psychiatry not as self-evident, but as virtually inconceivable. For example, an influential 1978 law review article portrayed psychiatry as a "therapeutic orgy," with lobotomy and medications among the featured amusements. "Progress" could never characterize that activity. Or consider the work of Thomas Szasz, who maintains that mental illness is a "myth" and that it does not really exist. Since one cannot devise improved treatments for a nonexistent condition, it follows that therapeutic progress is impossible. Szasz portrays every era's somatic treatments as the result of the same mistaken belief about mental illness. His historical studies are revealing, but every event in them illustrates the same timeless error—the belief in an "illness"—over and over again.[3]

The standard and critical accounts of psychiatric history reflect general tendencies in historiography. Steven Jay Gould has described two models. The first posits forward movement or historical progress; the second, recurrent historical cycles, or movement in place. These models fit the standard and Szaszian accounts perfectly.[4]

A simple preference for one model or the other tells us nothing about the psychiatric (or any other) past. Yet little more than such a preference often seems at work in accounts of the medication era. Conveying nothing about the past, these models often reflect attitudes toward present developments instead. Defenders of current psychiatric practice usually favor the "progress" model; critics, the cyclical one. One can imagine other possibilities: a critic, for example, who recognizes progress everywhere in medicine except psychiatry (a view some physicians hold); or a psychiatrist who subscribes to a cyclical view but aligns medications with humane interventions in earlier periods—like breaking mental patients' chains in the eighteenth century—rather than with things like lobotomy. Yet the general correlations—defense of current practice and belief in psychiatric progress, criticism of current practice and belief in historical cycles—usually hold.

In fact, the events of the medication era are more interesting than abstract models. Moreover, if a model must be chosen, its selection should follow rather than precede historical investigation. What has resulted from inadequate inquiry is psychiatric history as morality tale, with progress often reduced to a guiding dogma. But the history of the medication era includes intellectual zigzags, improbable events, and sudden reversals. It bears little resemblance to any morality tale, or to any simple model of progress.

Although events do not conform to a simple historical model, they do conveniently fall into four more or less distinct periods.

The First Period: The 1950s and Early 1960s

The first period of the medication era began with the appearance of chlorpromazine and lasted about a decade. The effectiveness of medication against psychotic symptoms impressed most psychiatrists, as did the resulting changes in the atmosphere on wards. Still, psychiatrists entertained diverse views about medications' benefits, effects, and public health implications.

Many considered medications to be "major tranquilizers" that powerfully calmed patients. Psychological accounts of drug actions enjoyed more support than neurological explanations did, although each had its adherents. Proponents of the "major tranquilizer" idea examined the effect of tranquilization on patient psychology; more neurologically oriented psychiatrists traced the benefits of medication to a neurological syndrome of drug-induced "psychomotor indifference" that supposedly produced therapeutic advantages. Some psychiatrists combined the two approaches. Still others, although a minority, suggested that medications acted directly on the physical or neurological causes of schizophrenia, without inducing any intermediate disease.

Pierre Deniker, a discoverer of chlorpromazine, supplied one of the leading neurological accounts. Deniker theorized that psychomotor indifference and other common medication effects, including an array of purposeless mouth and jaw movements, resulted from a medication-induced brain disease that resembled encephalitis. This disease, he believed, ameliorated the effects of a patient's naturally occurring illness. Nor were explanations linking therapeutic effects to pathology uncommon in psychiatry; similar accounts had appeared for lobotomy and insulin coma therapy, among other treatments. Some psychiatrists explicitly likened medications to these older therapies, describing them as "chemical lobotomies" or the "insulin of the nervous system."

Psychiatrists disagreed about other matters, besides the actions of medications. If some regarded drugs as near cures, others viewed them as being frequently less effective than insulin coma or lobotomy. Not least of all, psychiatrists differed over the likely effects of medication on the public health system. Most supposed that the use of medication would simply improve the operation of state hospitals. With greater foresight, a minority envisioned the virtual dismantling of state hospitals.

The Second Period: The Early 1960s to 1980

In early 1963, President Kennedy urged a shift away from hospitals toward "community" care. Kennedy cited medications and a general moral advance in American society as making the change possible. Congress responded by funding a system of community mental health centers. Deinstitutionalization began in earnest by the end of the 1960s, and accelerated throughout the 1970s.

Views of medication changed dramatically at about the time of Kennedy's proposal. A 1964 National Institute of Mental Health Collaborative Study demonstrated that medication produced significantly more improvement in symptoms than a placebo. The Study also declared medications "safe," side effects generally "trivial," and drug actions truly "antischizophrenic" in nature. Other research reported that patients withdrawn from medications relapsed more quickly than those maintained on the treatment: about 60 to 80 percent of the withdrawn patients and 30 to 40 percent of those continuously medicated relapsed over a two-year period.

Earlier ideas about medications dropped from view suddenly, as if through a trap door. Medications were no longer "major tranquilizers," indifference-producing agents, or causes of encephalitis-like syndromes. Psychological explanations faded; in their place, psychiatrists soon hypothesized a "chemical imbalance" of neurotransmitters in the brain that medications supposedly redressed. And the medication-produced symptoms that underlie the older ideas—psychomotor indifference and encephalitis-like movements, in particular—also largely disappeared from psychiatrists' awareness. This process went so far that the effects virtually had to be rediscovered later; in the case of encephalitis-like movements ("tardive dyskinesia") they received wide recognition only after a long and bitter controversy.

Swazey's 1974 history captured the prevailing ethos, and the resulting sense of triumph in psychiatry. Yet the picture she drew of medication as something akin to a "magic bullet" against schizophrenia had begun to dissolve almost as soon as the NIMH Study gave it form. By the time Swazey's book appeared, the vision was verging on disintegration.

The claim of "trivial" medication side effects went first, and the rest followed. Even before 1960, a few European psychiatrists had reported cases of medication-induced "dyskinesias" (repetitive, purposeless movements) persisting after patients stopped taking the drugs. These dyskinesias affected various parts of patients' bodies, but especially their mouths, jaws, and tongues. Deniker had described similar movements as a common effect of chlorpromazine, but his observations had not caused alarm. The reports about tardive dyskinesia did; the persistence of the movements suggested long-lasting and probably permanent neurological damage.

At first, American psychiatrists largely ignored the problem. In 1967, however, an NIMH research psychiatrist named George Crane announced a startling finding: 25 percent of patients on NIMH research wards manifested the symptoms of tardive dyskinesia. Both Crane and his critics perceived enormous implications if his finding held up; one critic said that the previous fifteen years of progress—the medication era—would be undone if Crane were correct.

If anything, Crane had underestimated the true extent of tardive dyskinesia. Yet his early critics insisted that he had reported something that was not there, and they attacked his professionalism. Over the next half-decade, leading psychiatrists either dismissed Crane's findings or ignored them, and clinicians continued to prescribe medications as if tardive dyskinesia did not exist.

By the mid-'70s, an accumulation of research results and legal developments undermined the rejectionist position. More investigators reported high rates of tardive dyskinesia. In 1978 a federal judge heard George Crane's testimony and took state psychiatrists to task for their refusal to acknowledge the disorder. The criticism made it clear that tardive dyskinesia could no longer be ignored.

By 1980, the psychiatric consensus about tardive dyskinesia changed. Psychiatric leaders now acknowledged prevalence rates in the range of 10 to 20 percent, but they deemed permanent side effects less significant than psychiatrists had once thought. Tardive dyskinesia constituted a serious side effect in this view, but almost all patients should continue to receive medications nonetheless.

Other negative side effects also received renewed attention. Columbia University researchers basically rediscovered the syndrome of drug-induced "psychomotor indifference" in 1975. Calling it "akinesia," they reported that it occurred frequently and that psychiatrists—including themselves, in earlier work—rarely recognized it as a drug side effect. At about the same time, researchers at UCLA reported that medications produced psychological distress in almost half of patients, and that psychiatrists rarely noticed the problem.

Leading psychiatrists also expressed disappointment with the benefits of medication. Jonathan Cole, who had described medications as "anti-schizophrenic" in the NIMH Collaborative Study, offered a rather different picture ten years later. He observed that medication usually failed to affect schizophrenia profoundly and that a sizable minority of patients seemed to derive no benefit. With other prominent investigators, Cole turned his attention to identifying patients who should *not* receive the drugs; in 1976, he suggested that nearly half of patients fell into this category.

Portrayed in 1964 as antischizophrenic and free of serious side effects, medication emerged from the 1970s as a treatment with alarming side effects, nonprofound benefits in most cases, and no benefit at all in many. The picture of antischizophrenic actions and trivial side effects had become untenable. The new understanding did not penetrate clinical practice or public consciousness, however. To a remarkable extent, clinicians used—and the public regarded—medications exactly as they had before. Deinstitutionalization continued apace.

The Third Period: The 1980s and Early 1990s

During the medication era's third period—the 1980s through the early 1990s—psychiatrists and society settled on a series of practical justifications for continuing the clinical practices and mental health policies that the old vision had supported. A notable example occurred in 1980, when Cole retracted his earlier advice about withholding medication. Without suggesting his earlier analysis had erred, Cole now portrayed withdrawal as impractical because medication constituted the "cornerstone" of the public mental health system.

Researchers occasionally offered clinical recommendations, but few went as far as Cole's in 1976. And whatever the recommendation, it produced little effect on clinical practice. Clinicians continued to prescribe medications for almost all their patients with schizophrenia (albeit with more references to "balancing" benefits and risks of the treatment), regardless of what researchers thought. Nor did public mental health policy change in light of the new understanding of medication. Deinstitutionalization had acquired a logic of its own; its wisdom and morality no longer depended on the properties of medications.

With research conclusions largely disconnected from clinical practice and public policy, psychiatric investigators produced varied findings about medication. They disagreed with each other, but the disagreements did not run as deep as those of the 1950s, when psychological and neurological approaches vied for support, or those of the late 1960s and 1970s, when psychiatrists battled over the Study vision. Theories and findings were stated more cautiously; and less of consequence turned on them.

For example, few researchers still regarded schizophrenia as an identifiable neurochemical imbalance in the brain. During the second period, the validity of "chemical imbalance" theory had seemed to matter greatly; clinicians and proponents of deinstitutionalization cited it to support their positions. Now that the theory seemed wrong or vague, it had only academic significance. No one argued that the clinical and public health practices the "chemical imbalance" theory had supported should be rethought in light of the theory's decline.

The pattern repeated itself in other areas of inquiry. Medication's long-term benefits, effects on "negative" symptoms such as social withdrawal, and side effects such as tardive dyskinesia all seemed to lack practical importance, either for prescribing or for public health—unlike the earlier issues of how well medications worked (in the 1950s and 1960s) or the existence of permanent side effects (in the 1960s and 1970s). Even within the world of research, less of consequence seemed to turn on particular results. For example, some investigators found that medication affects certain brain regions by exacerbating local neurochemical abnormalities associated with schizophrenia, yet the investigators failed to consider the obvious possibility that medication might worsen some aspects of the disease.

A similar disconnectedness took hold outside of psychiatry. Like psychiatrists, judges and policymakers no longer linked the best understanding of the benefits, actions, and side effects of medication to conclusions about public health or patient rights. Thus, states pursued deinstitutionalization, and most courts defined patient rights, as if medications really countered schizophrenia in the brain and tardive dyskinesia barely existed.

The Fourth Period: The Mid-1990s Onward?

As the medication era entered its fifth decade, renewed optimism stirred psychiatrists. For one thing, "atypical" antipsychotic medications became a clinical option in the early 1990s. Compared with standard medications, atypicals produced somewhat different neurochemical effects and, for many, significantly less troublesome side effects. Moreover, some people with schizophrenia who do not respond to standard medications do improve on atypicals. Many psychiatrists consider them the most important treatment innovation in schizophrenia since chlorpromazine.

The first atypical, clozapine, appeared originally in the 1960s. Clozapine's side effects included a rare but sometimes fatal blood disorder, however, and it was withdrawn from the market as a result. Clozapine now has been reintroduced, and newer atypicals, which do not cause the same problem, have appeared. More seem to be on the horizon.

Many researchers are reserving judgment about atypicals, which may or may not live up to the hopeful expectations. Yet the new optimism among psychiatrists—and the case for recognizing a new period in the medication era —does not rest on atypicals alone. More generally, prominent researchers have declared psychiatry the leading medical field in a much heralded "decade of the brain." According to these writers, cutting-edge research into the brain has transformed psychiatry, even though, as yet, few clinical innovations have resulted. In a mirror image of that approach, one prominent psychiatrist has turned to the past. Based on decades-old charts that supposedly showed unmedicated patients suffering from dyskinesias, Richard Jed Wyatt concluded that much tardive dyskinesia results from schizophrenia, not drugs. He also argued that medication prevents the "brain damage" that results from untreated schizophrenia. Taken together, his positions revived something like the Study vision of a safe, profoundly antischizophrenic treatment.

Wyatt's theorizing had much less influence than future-oriented claims did. Like its forward-looking counterparts, however, it suggested that the third period of the medication era had run its course. Psychiatrists were searching for something meaningful to replace the third period's practical but uninspiring justifications for existing practice.

Other signs pointed to the end of a stage in the medication era. Deinstitutionalization probably went as far as it could, culminating thirty years of public health reform. The U.S. Supreme Court made explicit what it had only implied before: the federal courts would not significantly interfere with the use of medication. Nor would legislatures or, for that matter, any agency of government.

Finally, there were the bioethicists who likened experiments that *withhold* medications from patients who do not want them to notorious Nazi medical experiments. Such an analogy would have been unlikely at any earlier time, even during the heyday of the Collaborative Study. Thus, as psychiatrists heralded the arrival of new atypical medications, nonpsychiatrists treated the widespread use of antipsychotic drugs as the only conceivable course—ethically, politically, and legally. In these respects, at least, the medication revolution had run its course.

Models in the History of Medications

The two historical models, progress and cycles, both describe regular, predictable movement; they differ only about its direction. Yet developments in the medication era were strikingly irregular and unpredictable, as the preceding sequence shows. Neither model fits particularly well.

Consider the shifts. During the first period, many psychiatrists counted psychomotor indifference or oral-facial movements as something like a biological signature of medication. During the second period, the same effects faded so thoroughly from awareness that psychiatrists had to rediscover them later. In the third period, a consensus emerged that the effects existed, but were relatively unimportant. In the fourth period, many psychiatrists simply shifted their gaze elsewhere.

Ideas about the benefits of medication underwent parallel change. From the idea that medication worked effectively, but usually without any profound effect on the underlying illness (the first period), many psychiatrists moved to the idea that medications did work profoundly (the second period). Then, in the third period, researchers returned to a view like the first one. A cyclical model might account for that—but not for the fact that clinicians' views of medications did not change, not even when research results undercut them. Finally, the idea of profound medication-induced changes *in* patients' brains would be partly supplanted by the idea of medication contributing to a profound understanding *of* the brain *by psychiatrists* (the fourth period).

Ideas about the relationship between psychiatric understanding and public health policy also shifted. In the second period, leading psychiatrists urged a transformation of the public health system because of research findings about medication. In the third period, leading psychiatrists took the opposite position, arguing that research conclusions about tardive dyskinesia and limited drug benefits should yield to the needs of the new system of community care. A comparable argument, made in the early 1960s, would have insisted that the existing network of state hospitals—the then prevailing system—should survive no matter how well medications worked.

Concepts disappeared too quickly, and inversions in thought occurred too often, for any simple model of historic cycles or progress to succeed. A "house of mirrors" might be the better metaphor. In particular, the zigzags of the medication era do not comport well with standard accounts of psychiatric progress. As side effects and benefits fell in and out of fashion, processes other than pure medical discovery seemed to be at work.

In fact, at crucial junctures—and especially at the outset of the second period—researchers went far beyond their data or ignored obvious facts when arriving at important conclusions. Chapter 3 of this book examines how antischizophrenic effects arose largely from new linguistic usages, redefinitions of old concepts, and rhetoric manipulation. Chapters 4 and 5 describe a series of seemingly arbitrary theoretical and historical presumptions devised by George Crane's critics; these made it all but impossible for tardive dyskinesia to exist. Chapter 6 shows how leading researchers changed their minds about tardive dyskinesia in problematic ways.

Despite the zigzags and reversals, events did not unfold randomly. Many psychiatrists changed their minds at about the same time, and in about the same way. Those shifts largely define the periods within the era. Moreover, clinical practice remained constant from the second period onward, as did the course of deinstitutionalization. Thus, it seems possible to generalize about developments.

Social Progress

According to standard views, psychiatric advance fueled social and moral progress during the medication era. Patients gained liberty and meaningful lives. Society relieved itself of the moral burden of state institutions.

Such ideas enjoy wide support, but they are more controversial than the idea of pure psychiatric progress. Some consider deinstitutionalization a major failure. Everyone concedes that it gave rise to major problems, including homelessness, revolving door hospitalizations, and inadequate treatment—a sharp contrast to the supposedly unsullied progress of psychiatry itself.

By most accounts, the problems resulted from lapses in planning, funding, public education, or law, and not because of any failing of psychiatry. Because of such lapses, psychiatric progress did not yield as much social progress as it might have. Clinicians, too, may have mistranslated psychiatric research advances into practice. These views allow one to subscribe to psychiatric progress fully, while hedging about social and/or clinical progress.[5]

Such accounts presuppose a one-way relationship between psychiatric knowledge or understanding and social or clinical developments. New psychiatric knowledge impels beneficial social and clinical change, unless misfeasance, malfeasance, or, according to some angry commentators, malevolence interferes. Yet during the medication era, a countercurrent or reverse effect operated, which the standard views miss. That is, ideas about beneficial social and clinical change influenced and at times shaped basic psychiatric understandings of medication and schizophrenia.

In particular, psychiatric understanding shifted during the early 1960s in precisely the ways required to expedite hoped-for changes in public health policy. Medication benefits suddenly materialized, and side effects suddenly disappeared. Later, unwelcome facts received only grudging and incomplete acknowledgment, and that only when absolutely necessary—a feature more akin to a lawyer's calculated arguments than to medical science. Leading journals did publish damaging findings about medication, and some psychiatrists explored sensitive areas; their work generated the unwelcome facts that psychiatry had to contend with. Yet at critical junctures, desired social or professional outcomes prompted leading psychiatrists to ignore data, go beyond it, or artificially limit their inferences.

This picture conflicts with standard views of psychiatric and social progress during the medication era. Psychiatric progress, supposedly the engine of social progress, seems a smaller and less capable engine. At times, nothing like psychiatric progress drove developments.

Progress and Psychiatry

Modern psychiatry is hardly alone in its avowals of historic advance. Progress puts many things in a better light. It makes the future appear promising, the present look better, and the past seem less troublesome. For those reasons, governments and businesses, even individuals, often claim the mantle of progress.

Yet psychiatry has an unusually intense concern with progress. Much of the reason for this lies in psychiatry's past, a past marked by reputed overreaching. Deserved or not, this historical reputation affects present perceptions. Today, for example, many people think of 1950s lobotomists and insulin coma therapists more as menacing figures than as medical ones—practitioners more dated, yet somehow having more contemporary relevance, than nonpsychiatric physicians of the same era—or, for that matter, than 1940s political figures or captains of industry.

The felt distinction between psychiatry and medicine (or politics or business) does not rest on its lack of effective treatments, or at least not on that alone. Other branches of medicine have lacked effective treatments but still fare better than psychiatry in memory. And psychiatric treatments like insulin coma therapy or lobotomy may in fact have worked: the distinction does not generally rest on someone's considered judgments or informed comparisons. People who draw it often know almost nothing about psychiatry or other medical specialties.

Because of its historical reputation—what might be called psychiatry's "lobotomy problem"—the profession stands to benefit more than most from a radical break with the past. Progress in general, and the idea of a medication revolution in particular, accomplish that break. They create a historical gap that makes modern-day psychiatrists and 1940s lobotomists incomparably different.

Progress does more than effect a break with the past. It also imparts a sense of momentum, which makes the present seem better than it otherwise would. In psychiatry, this puts the often mixed outcomes of using medication in a better light. Progress also makes the future appear promising, a perception that encourages optimism about—and research funding in—the field.

These temporal implications of progress reinforce one another. The future seems brighter because of the added luster of the present, and because the past casts no shadow. The past seems more dismal compared to the bright present and the shimmering future; that makes the revolution separating past from present appear more momentous. The present seems better because it presages a bright future, and because of the absence of taint from the past.

To appreciate these effects, imagine that treatment outcomes in schizo-phrenia today resulted not from medication, but from a form of lobotomy, a pro-cedure with a dismal past and unpromising future. Would not the same side effects as those produced by medication appear more menacing, and the same benefits appear more questionable? Some psychiatrists in the 1950s had described medications as "chemical lobotomies" or the "insulin of the nervous system." Given those characterizations, a policy of medication and deinstitu-tionalization in the 1960s might have seemed comparable to lobotomizing pa-tients or making them comatose on a massive scale and then discharging them from hospitals. Public support for such a measure seems unlikely. Conversely, one needs no imagination to gauge the implications of "progress": the progress view prevailed in the '60s, and we know what happened.

Assessing Progress

On the face of it, progress in psychiatry looks like a question that has a tech-nical, psychiatric answer. What results did lobotomy achieve, or insulin coma therapy, or moral therapy, compared to medication? Those issues are psychi-atric, and they may appear decisive. Better results equal psychiatric progress; dramatically better results, revolutionary psychiatric progress. Progress, or its absence, becomes self-evident once the results are in.

Yet the matter is not that simple. Assessments of therapeutic outcome often provoke hopeless, apparently irreconcilable disagreement. The effectiveness of nineteenth-century moral treatment (humane care in an intensely regulated setting) remains sharply disputed; lobotomy garnered powerful endorsements, including the Nobel Prize, as well as opprobrium; some distinguished psychia-trists of the 1950s regarded insulin coma as better than medication. Today, many psychiatrists believe that insulin coma produced benefits only because it focused intense staff attention on patients undergoing it, but that judgment raises fur-ther assessment difficulties. If a powerful placebo effect produces the best out-come, does it represent progress or not?

Even evaluations of medication remain problematic. A large body of research has found medication significantly more effective than a placebo. Yet much of this work measures reduction in symptoms—hallucinations, delusions, and the like—rather than improvement in someone's quality of life. The work bears importantly on the value of medication, but it does not preclude the pos-sibility that someone may hallucinate less and still be worse off overall.

In fact, the effects of medication on the course of patients' lives remain largely unknown, or controversial. Contemporary studies of the issue report con-flicting results, as do studies of the effects of medication on the ability to work or sustain social relationships. Lobotomy research fell short in precisely the same areas. Thus, the modern research consensus about medication does not extend to issues highly relevant to assessing progress in the field.

Two special difficulties contribute to the uncertainty in psychiatry. Psychiatric outcomes notoriously resist assessment because human personality is complex, and serious mental diseases have so many manifestations. Beyond that, gauging psychiatric success often requires a value judgment about a human action, capability, or danger. To take an extreme example, was a woman in the 1940s better or worse off after a lobotomy had diminished her fears of sexual assault from her husband and, in the process, rendered her unfit for any vocation except housewife, if that? Lobotomists considered her better off; some later evaluators agreed. Yet such assessments inescapably require judgments about values and social roles—a feature that becomes particularly clear when, as in this case, we may disagree with someone else's conclusions.

Psychiatric assessment usually entails judgments of this kind, although not always so obviously. Complicating matters, the self-evaluations and judgments of persons with serious mental illness often seem problematic. And the objective measures often available elsewhere in medicine—length of life, volume of blood, the presence or absence of a virus—are typically unavailable. Psychiatrists themselves often insist on the ineffability of treatment decisions in clinical settings.

The difficulties multiply when comparing treatments from different eras. One can neither see patients from the past nor include them in rigorous comparative studies. Data are forever lost to time. Nor can one necessarily determine whether circumstances distorted contemporary assessments of a discarded therapy; some argue that gross overcrowding in state hospitals interfered with a fair trial of moral therapy, for example. Morals and social roles change over time, immeasurably complicating the moral and social dimensions of the puzzle.

Beyond that, determining what constitutes the proof of "progress" raises problems. Because medications work better than lobotomy, does it follow that the next treatment will be better still? Or that the later part of the medication era is better than the earlier part? Carried too far, "progress" becomes a kind of crude historical determinism.

Supposing "progress" is not taken too far, its implications still do not emerge as clearly, or include as much, as adherents of the standard history often suppose. For one thing, the existence of a superior treatment does not necessarily mean that professional processes and clinical decision making also improved. Perhaps researchers discovered the treatment not because of any fundamental breakthrough in technique, but serendipitously. Even if a breakthrough occurred, its influence might remain confined in research settings. The emergence of a superior treatment may make surviving professional practices less defensible, but that does not mean the old practices will change. It does not guarantee that patients, society, or the profession will be better off.

Claims of social progress in the medication era present similar problems. Insofar as these claims depend on the arguments for the superiority of medication to other therapies, they involve the same uncertainties. Beyond that, the same types of technical, historical, and moral complication that befog any judgment about treatments also loom over judgments about public mental health systems and social conditions.

Nor does a superior treatment necessarily mean that courts and legislatures should always defer to psychiatrists' judgments about it, as is often claimed. If objective standards of therapeutic success accompany the new treatment, its existence may point in the direction of less deference, not more. Judges and legislators, as well as the public, will have a better handle on the psychiatric issues because of the objective standards; hence, they can arguably make their own judgments.

Methods and Objections

Despite the numerous unresolvable questions, significant parts of the progress puzzle can yield to historical inquiry. Difficulties that beset comparisons of different treatment eras, for example, can be avoided by focusing on a single era, such as the era of medication. One can examine how psychiatric understanding and knowledge developed during this time, and how they related to other developments. The preceding account followed that approach, and the remainder of the book expands upon it.

One can also assess—and, I believe, refute—the most detailed historical claim that psychiatrists make about the medication era. The delayed recognition of tardive dyskinesia represents an obvious challenge to ideas about steady, global progress in the field. For this reason, psychiatrists have singled out tardive dyskinesia for historical attention; here, a need is perceived to demonstrate progress, not just celebrate it. Thus, the place of this disorder in historical analysis resembles its role in clinical assessment. Just as psychiatrists assume that if tardive dyskinesia does not preclude widespread use of medications nothing does, they also assume that if the history of tardive dyskinesia comports with progress everything else does too. Yet, as later chapters demonstrate, tardive dyskinesia hardly comports with psychiatrists' ideas about progress.

Historical inquiry can also influence thinking about unresolvable issues of medication-era history, including other aspects of the progress problem. No conclusion regarding such matters can presently compel assent. Yet people still may change their minds about them in light of historical evidence, and do so rationally. Many people already hold a position and may reasonably change it in light of new information or argument. Explaining how may prevent misunderstandings about my own arguments.

Much depends on one's starting position. Standard accounts, for example, link medication and the transformation of psychiatry into a full-fledged branch of medicine. Those developments supposedly reinforced one another: a transformed psychiatry produced treatment advances; treatment advances helped transform psychiatry. Thus, arguments that weaken one's belief in a transformed psychiatric profession—and I make such arguments, in connection with side effects and other matters—may also weaken one's belief in medication as an unprecedented advance. Yet if my arguments bear on the issue of the superiority of medication in this way, it is only because of the supposed link—which is not mine—between the stature of psychiatry and the quality of medication.

This works in the opposite direction, too. A description of the current research consensus about medication, such as the one in this book, may change someone's mind about the stature of medication as a treatment. Given the supposed link between medication and the character of psychiatry, that may also change someone's thinking about psychiatry itself.

In fact, many people overestimate medication, including a large number who work in clinical settings. They consider the drugs almost cures; suppose that medications nearly always prevent relapse; and regard side effects (except for tardive dyskinesia) as generally unimportant. Those qualities would make medication a superior treatment, but they do not conform to what researchers have long known. In this instance, the considerations that might change someone's mind originate with psychiatric investigators, and the disclaimer noted earlier also applies: the supposed link between medication and the character of psychiatry is not mine.

Other misunderstandings may result from reading my arguments too generally, or supposing that certain assumptions underlie them. I reach some unflattering conclusions about the medication era, but I do not presume that psychiatry is therefore unique among medical specialties. Nor do I assume that psychiatry's performance typifies medicine or science. Other scientists and physicians may well have acted as psychiatrists did; indeed, some historians suggest that social factors generally influence or distort scientific and medical conclusions. Those possibilities have no bearing on my account of developments in the medication era, however. I do not think that psychiatrists had to perform as they did; it is enough that they did so.

This stance distinguishes me both from supposed antipsychiatrists like Thomas Szasz and from adherents of the standard version of medication-era history. Both suppose that a deep-seated, persistent feature of modern psychiatry underlies developments in the medication era. Psychiatry necessarily performed badly in one version, and necessarily well in the other. According to Szasz, a basic cognitive mistake—the belief in mental illness—shaped events, with inevitable and predictable consequences for patients and society. According to standard accounts, a fundamental discovery (medication), a new research program (into the brain), or some other professional transformation reshaped psychiatry—again, with inevitable and predictable consequences for patients and, less predictably, for society.

Both positions produce premature judgments and slight the facts. Before one can say how physicians or psychiatrists performed, detailed inquiry is necessary. The issues are empirical ones, and I have tried to approach them in that way. The presumption that historical actors always and inevitably perform in a certain way only stifles inquiry.

The Szaszian and standard approaches differ in one respect. Szasz, a critic of established institutions and received understandings, thinks that insights emerge from analyzing the past. To strong adherents of the standard account, however, analysis appears unnecessary. Progress is self-evident and not debatable; one simply celebrates it. In that view, raising historical questions about modern psychiatry probably reflects bad intentions toward the profession.

Obviously, I take the side of analysis and extended discussion. Yet I do not agree that any deep and inherent flaw bedevils psychiatry. Instead, my analysis presumes the accuracy of the present research consensus about medications. I begin with the idea that this consensus affords the best available understanding of the treatment.

Reliance on the current research consensus raises other issues, since it examines thinking from other periods through the lens of present-day understanding. That may seem analogous to using current moral or political conceptions to judge past actors or eras unfairly. Yet a history of medication has but three choices: it may accept present findings about medications; it may reject present findings, and defend different ones; or it may proceed as if no findings, present or past, were more accurate or better than any others.

The last approach is misguided. If findings cannot qualify as right or wrong, then George Crane's critics, who ignored tardive dyskinesia, become analytically indistinguishable from Crane, who put his career on the line and who was right. Scientifically—and morally—that seems absurd. It is equally absurd historically. It suggests that Crane's acknowledgment of tardive dyskinesia requires the same type of inquiry and explanation as his critics' refusal to do so. If no account is right or "privileged" with respect to truth, one cannot not say that Crane reported tardive dyskinesia because it was there, or that his critics ignored the obvious. Nothing useful can come from such limitations on inquiry.

The second approach—defending nonconsensus views about medications —is simply not mine. I am not a psychiatric researcher, and this is not an investigation into substantive psychiatric issues. Studies that combine history with science or medicine do exist, but this is not one of them. Instead, it accepts the present research consensus and takes the first approach.

That approach raises yet another question. Would a different present consensus about medication produce a different history of the medication era's past?
The answer, unavoidably, is yes. Consider the year 1967. Psychiatrists still de-
bated the existence of tardive dyskinesia then, so a pure work of history could
not have treated Crane as correct and his critics as mistaken. Someone qualified to do so might have combined history and psychiatric research into a single work; Crane himself produced an article of that kind later. Yet a purely
historical study either would have had to treat Crane and his critics as equally
likely to be correct in 1967, or, more likely, would have accepted the strong 1967
consensus that tardive dyskinesia occurred rarely if ever and had only marginal
importance. In that context, a 1967 history might have asked why Crane went
wrong, and perhaps developed his critics' suggestions that he had acted in bad
faith. That historical inquiry might have turned up something interesting; at a
minimum, it would have preserved the prevailing—and highly unlikely—
assumptions of the day. Given our present knowledge of tardive dyskinesia,
however, the resulting historical analysis would have been worthless.

History's dependence on present medical knowledge does not make it
unique. Clinicians depend upon present medical knowledge, too; at least, they
should. Even researchers, who create new knowledge, use the present medical
consensus as a starting point. No worse off than psychiatrists in this regard, historians also enjoy the advantage of latitude in choosing when to investigate
their subject.

If the late 1960s represented a bad time to write a history of the medication era, the present seems like an especially good one. With the era in its fifth
decade, psychiatrists know much about medication; the present consensus appears viable. Moreover, a number of the era's major developments—including
deinstitutionalization and the tardive dyskinesia controversy—seemingly have
run their course.

Regardless of when they are written, histories based on a present medical
consensus are subject to a unique temptation. They can treat the differences
between past and present conclusions as errors resulting from inferior science—
as if past and present answers were being submitted for review at the same time.
Succumbing to that temptation produces incoherence, however. It leads to the
conclusion that all science—including today's—is corrupted, since tomorrow's
results will surely differ. Usually, the appropriate historical question concerns
how somebody managed to discover something, not why someone else failed
to discover it sooner.

Yet one cannot simply dismiss all possibility of bad science or improper influence in the past. Those things happen, and historiographic approaches that
dictate unvarying sympathy for past errors make it impossible to discover them.
Historians' methodology should not rule out such events. Why psychiatrists

failed to notice, acknowledge, or remember something are fair questions, and I ask them.

I have tried to make the answers fair by examining the reasons psychiatrists offer for their conclusions, as well as the intellectual or social context. Comparisons to older positions have also proved useful. For example, I examine prevailing views of the 1960s in light of earlier understandings and observations from the 1950s. When psychiatrists went beyond their data in the 1960s to adopt positions that we now know to be mistaken—and, in doing so, discarded observations and findings from the 1950s that we now know to have been correct—close scrutiny seems in order, and the dangers of unfair, post hoc criticism appear diminished. If those mistaken positions were also expedient or consistent with larger political and policy developments it also seems fair to inquire about possible motivations.

Psychiatrists' changing positions often emerge from subtle variations in statements by the same figure at different times, or in variations from frequently repeated expressions or verbal formulas in the literature. For example, in the 1950s a prominent psychiatrist observed that side effects that disrupted patients' lives in the community constituted mere "annoyances" within mental hospitals. The difference presumably arose from the minimal demands of the hospital, where patients had no need to work or live independently. As deinstitutionalization gained momentum during the 1960s, the "annoyances" phrasing reappeared; but references to lives being disrupted outside hospitals did not. In the new formulation, side effects became mere "annoyances" everywhere because of the benevolent chemical attributes of medication—virtually the opposite of what was originally meant. The variation in phrasing captures a movement in thought that might otherwise escape notice, and examining it reduces the risk of unfair, post hoc criticism. Characterizing side effects as mere "annoyances" is mistaken in light of present knowledge—but it is not current knowledge that makes the deletion of the "mental hospital" reference in the 1960s wording so questionable.

The examination of such changes in phrasing is a method that historians of political philosophy employ. Some may see the specter of "soft science" in it, or even a hint of sympathy on my part for the old analytic traditions in psychiatry. I would not argue with the "analytic" characterization, but ideas of "hardness" and "softness" seem to me beside the point. I simply know of no better way of approaching these dimensions of the historical problem.[6]

The "softness" issue has a parallel within medication-era psychiatry. Psychiatrists often ignored qualitative aspects of their patients' response to treatment, such as how medications made people feel or affected social capacities. Instead, psychiatrists focused on things that better lent themselves to "hard" data, such as the number of days a patient spent hospitalized. William T.

Carpenter has pointed out that important aspects of mental disease and treatment were obscured because of this methodological preference. I see no reason for a similar mistake, or a comparable distinction between "hard" and "soft" data, in writing medication-era history.[7]

Throughout, I have attempted to provide a "feel" for the issues and debates of the era. The book emphasizes depth more than breadth of coverage. Psychiatric articles and statements that constructed new viewpoints or that put old views to rest supply the focal points. I have also tried to avoid losing any part of medication-era history because of a premature resort to causes. If the power of pharmaceutical companies or politics explains aspects of psychiatrists' thinking—as some have suggested, accurately in my opinion—it remains essential to describe the psychiatric thinking, the thing that supposedly bears those marks of outside influence. Capturing that thinking has been my first goal.

959 44

From Chlorpromazine to the NIMH
Chapter 1 *Collaborative Study*

Psychiatry has long sought a true "antipsychotic" treatment—one that would cure, partially or completely, serious mental illness. An antipsychotic treatment would relieve millions from the scourge of some of the worst diseases known to humankind. It would also answer any lingering questions about whether psychiatric conditions constitute diseases in the first place, for only diseases can be cured. It would firmly establish psychiatry's place within medicine.

For similar reasons, an antipsychotic therapy would alter the perception that psychiatry threatens people's rights. A cure would render extended psychiatric hospitalization unnecessary. Even if mental illness still required brief intervals of unconsented-to treatment, an antipsychotic therapy would bring psychiatry's moral profile into line with that of the rest of medicine. When physicians treat unconscious persons who cannot consent, for example, ethical and legal issues arise, yet few regard such treatment as a serious threat to "liberty." Psychiatric interventions that qualified as "antipsychotic" would appear like that, losing their former political and constitutional dimension. Psychiatry would jeopardize rights no more than internal medicine does.

Until the advent of chlorpromazine, no therapy had lived up to the antipsychotic ideal. Psychiatrists had entertained high hopes for many new treatments and sometimes described them in "antipsychotic" terms. Yet their hopes were always dashed. During the mid-nineteenth century, for example, psychiatrists perceived antipsychotic properties in the institution of the mental hospital itself. One theory deemed urbanization or social decay the causes of mental illness; mental hospitals, with their bucolic, nonurban environments, reversed those causes. If a lack of moral discipline produced mental illness, hospitals could instill that discipline and, again, reverse the course of disease. Thus, mental hospitals themselves qualified as antipsychotic.

The ideal of an antipsychotic hospital never died completely, but it steadily lost ground to an opposite view. In this countervision, mental hospitals represented antitherapeutic institutions that *caused* mental dysfunction. By the late 1960s, for instance, many observers concluded that mental patients required above all a remedy for the dysfunctions caused by hospitalization—a cure, as it were, for the condition of "institutionalization." The remedy might involve teaching patients to shop and cook for themselves, skills that had atrophied with years of regimented hospital routine. Whatever else it entailed, of course, a remedy for "institutionalization" ultimately required the patient's release from the hospital. Thus, "liberty" became antipsychotic too.

Such views came to the fore during the Progressive Era of the 1890s and again in the Great Society of the 1960s and 1970s. These periods produced legal reforms that made it harder to commit people. At the same time, some people continued to view hospitalization in purely medical terms; they focused on the patient's illness, rather than on the fact of confinement, and perceived no real threat to liberty.

Occasionally, the debate over liberty encompassed measures other than hospitalization. In the late nineteenth century, for instance, a controversy arose between those who opposed all physical restraints in a mental hospital and those who thought restraints were occasionally humane. The hospitals had begun using narcotics in place of physical restraint, a substitution rarely mentioned in the debates. Although this controversy unfolded within psychiatry, not in the law, it seemed at least as much a debate about liberty as about optimal treatment. Confusing antipsychotic measures with constitutional liberty became a real possibility.

Through the 1930s, state hospital care continued to deteriorate, and psychiatric interventions—including putting patients to sleep for extended periods or removing body parts such as teeth or ovaries—remained highly suspect. During the 1930s, however, new somatic therapies appeared—the convulsive therapies, coma therapy, and lobotomy. All of them required hospitalization: mental hospitals, like general hospitals, were becoming places where physicians performed elaborate medical operations.

Some psychiatrists claimed the new measures qualified as antipsychotic— the inventor of electroconvulsive therapy' spun out a convoluted theory of disease and electrical balances, for example—but practitioners generally used them without presuming to understand how they worked or considering them cures. Despite that, many regarded the "biological therapies" as marking a new era in psychiatric history. The award of the 1949 Nobel Prize in Medicine to the inventor of lobotomy seemingly vindicated such views. Lobotomy received the honor even though it obviously involved a kind of brain mutilation; the operating premise was that mentally ill persons with surgically damaged frontal lobes functioned better than mentally ill persons with their frontal lobes intact. No one supposed that functioning frontal lobes represented a "pathological" condition, so few regarded lobotomy as "antipsychotic" in nature—though many considered it highly effective and useful. Moreover, lobotomy treated many different conditions, and one could hardly regard it as a specific cure for each. Yet the fact that its inventor received the Nobel Prize suggested that the treatment represented an enormous advance.

Nonetheless, American psychiatry lost prestige after World War II. The public came to think of lobotomy, in particular, as brutal. With the ethical taint growing, the number of operations fell off dramatically in the early 1950s. Electroconvulsive therapy and insulin coma therapy seemingly lost ground with the public as well, although they never produced quite the same revulsion that lobotomy did.

These therapies were not the only problem that faced American psychiatry. State hospitals had long attracted criticism because of their deplorable conditions. After World War II, this criticism escalated, with some people comparing the hospitals to Nazi concentration camps. And despite the use of increasingly controversial somatic treatments, mental hospital populations had continued to grow.[1]

The size of the hospitals itself became a liability. Since the late nineteenth century, mental hospitals had received a large part of states' budgets. Institutional construction afforded prime public works projects, and—to an extent difficult to appreciate today—operating the hospitals represented a major social welfare program. In the 1950s, however, a state university or a highway came to appear a far more attractive project for states. Yet the hospitals still consumed large parts of states' budgets. It did not help that psychiatry carried so little prestige, and that recurrent scandals dogged the institutions.[2]

The psychiatric profession did not unify around a single response to these difficulties. Many psychiatrists affirmed the value of convulsive and surgical therapies. Some talked of better mental hospital management. Interest grew in preventing the development of mental illnesses through community interventions —reflecting a tendency to shift professional attention away from mental hospital patients and toward less disturbed individuals.[3]

One of the most influential responses came from Harvard psychiatrist Milton Greenblatt, who proposed a change in direction. Known as an expert on the biological therapies, during the early 1950s Greenblatt turned his attention toward sociology and anthropology, old-style "moral therapy," and democratic political theory. Along with his collaborators, he revived mid-nineteenth-century claims about antipsychotic social arrangements and late-nineteenth-century concerns about political liberty.[4]

Greenblatt argued that mental hospitals failed because of their undemocratic features and their totalitarian institutional structures. He urged that they become more democratic. Where nineteenth-century theorists often emphasized discipline and authority, Greenblatt favored a breakdown of the hospitals' hierarchical structures; for example, he opposed rules that discouraged socializing among nurses and doctors. His animating idea was not that mental health would restore patients to liberty, but that liberty would restore patients to health. Political liberty came first in this view; it virtually qualified as antipsychotic.[5]

At the same time, Greenblatt retained a sense of ease about biological interventions that seems almost unimaginable today. He argued, for example, that insulin coma therapy remained worthwhile even if it produced no therapeutic benefits except for a placebo effect. A potentially life-threatening procedure, the treatment necessitated close monitoring of patients by hospital staff. Greenblatt thought the resulting staff attention was so therapeutic that it justified the risks.[6]

This kind of comfort with biological intervention survived into the first decade of the medication era. Psychiatrists initially thought of medication as an intervention like insulin (in the nonplacebo view, insulin coma therapy) or lobotomy: a generally noncurative, sometimes dangerous measure that often produced benefits in cases of serious mental illness. When that view changed—when psychiatrists came to regard medication as more like insulin in the maintenance of diabetics and less like insulin in the production of comas—visions of liberty again came to the fore. These new visions were grander than Greenblatt's, however. Restored to liberty with medications, the mentally ill would become free of hospital hierarchy and restraint by becoming free of the hospital itself. The mental hospital would not be democratized; it would be swept away.

Chlorpromazine: The 1950s

Chlorpromazine, the first of the new medications, became available in American mental hospitals during the early 1950s. Chlorpromazine was undergoing tests as an agent for enhancing the effects of anesthetics when French researchers noticed that it calmed, or "tranquilized," patients. Preliminary psychiatric tests of its psychiatric uses began in 1951. By May 1954, the American pharmaceutical company Smith, Kline & French had begun marketing chlorpromazine in the United States under the trade name "Thorazine."[7]

The name "Thorazine" suggested continuity with existing somatic therapies. In classical mythology, Thor was the god of thunder. "Thorazine" conjured up a measure that resembled electroconvulsive therapy but lacked the flash of lightening or electricity. The drug's European name, "Largactil," also suggested sheer power—"large action"—rather than any profoundly new mechanism of action.

In the first decade of the medication era, psychiatrists often likened the new treatment to older therapies. In 1961, for example, the head of St. Elizabeth's Hospital in Washington, D.C., informed a congressional committee that lobotomy had all but disappeared because "you can get pretty much the same effect by giving . . . [patients] these drugs." For the same reason, he said, electroconvulsive therapy "ha[d] . . . pretty much gone out" too; so had "padded cells," since medications "might be termed chemical restraints." According to a leading text of the 1950s, chlorpromazine was also considered "the insulin of the nervous system."[8]

Some psychiatrists deemed such comparisons unfair—not to medication, but to the older therapies. Noting the "claims" that "chlorpromazine acts as a chemical lobotomy" and therefore "dispenses with the need for psychosurgery," Paul H. Hoch and his collaborators wrote in 1956 that they "wish[ed] . . . [it] were true." Yet they believed otherwise. Chlorpromazine could keep many "hyperactive patients . . . tranquilized almost indefinitely," they reported, but the drug appeared inferior to lobotomy in cases of "anxiety and motor tension." Similarly, the text that Hoch coauthored with Lothar Kalinowsky reported numerous studies that found insulin coma superior to chlorpromazine in cases of schizophrenia. According to Kalinowsky and Hoch, even the psychiatrists "who introduced chlorpromazine" considered medication inferior to insulin in certain instances.[9]

The comparisons to older therapies were not surprising. Lobotomy had given psychiatry medical respectability and a Nobel Prize. The convulsive and coma therapies supposedly had marked major advances as well, and they remained in wide use. Such comparisons seem remarkable today because standard accounts of psychiatric history color our vision; we forget that a previous standard version had hailed a biological revolution in the 1930s. During the 1950s, the idea of chlorpromazine as a radically different kind of therapy constituted a minority view; it probably enjoyed no more support than the notion of lobotomy as an epoch-making therapy did during the 1930s.

Explicit comparisons between lobotomy and medication fell into disuse quickly; a younger psychiatrist probably would not have given the 1961 testimony likening the two treatments. Some physicians had always regarded lobotomy as crude and brutal, the view that the public came to share after World War II. Because of the change in public attitude, lobotomy entered its dramatic decline before chlorpromazine ever appeared; according to Peter Sterling, the number of lobotomy operations began to fall off "around 1948" and "no evidence . . . support[s] the oft-quoted dogma that lobotomy declined only after the introduction of [medications]."[10]

If explicit comparisons faded, a theory that implicitly linked old and new treatments remained influential. According to this conception, medications induced an encephalitis-like brain disease that, in turn, produced clinical improvement. Lobotomy had induced brain damage by design, and according to this theory, so did medications.[11] This chief proponent of this theory was Pierre Deniker, one of the French physicians who discovered chlorpromazine's psychiatric uses. Deniker had noticed "striking similarities" between drug effects and the "sequelae" of "encephalitis lethargica," or sleeping sickness. In particular, a drug-induced syndrome of "psychomotor indifference"—diminished physical and mental activity, physical stiffness, a "mask like" facial expression, and a weakening of the desire to act—closely resembled the aftereffects of that brain disease. Deniker came to regard that syndrome as chlorpromazine's biological signature in the body and a desirable sign that the drug was working.[12]

Deniker did not recoil at treating mental illness by inducing a brain disease. "[T]he somatic disease may be necessary to cure the mental illness," he wrote. Ample precedent existed for his view. The "most successfully used biologic therapies in psychiatry," Deniker pointed out, "produce artificial somatic diseases." He had in mind malariotherapy, a procedure in which neurosyphilis patients received injections of malaria-infected blood and then, weeks later, received drugs to cure the malaria. This had proved a somewhat effective treatment for neurosyphilis. Insulin coma therapy and electroshock fit the same mold, Deniker thought, because they produced a state like "epilepsy." He did not mention lobotomy at this point—the year was 1961—but, of course, it too involved artificially induced brain damage.[13]

In a reminiscence nine years later, Deniker observed that "[a]gents used for biological treatment in psychiatry are precisely those that cause 'therapeutic diseases.' " Now he counted lobotomy as well as malariotherapy in that category, noting that the discoverer of each had "received the Nobel Prize." Swazey traced similar ideas in French medicine back to the 1840s, when some physicians supposed that mental illness "could be treated best by substituting for its symptoms similar but more controllable symptoms induced by . . . drug[s]."[14]

In light of his theory, Deniker readily accepted the symptoms of drug-induced brain disease. In fact, he recommended increasing the dosage until they appeared; in his view production of "neurologic symptoms" was "necessary" for the best results. Other researchers agreed, based on theoretical considerations like Deniker's, their own clinical observations, or both. For example, Herman Denber and John Travis suggested increasing dosages in order to produce "the appearance of most reactions, particularly the extrapyramidal syndrome [e.g., tremor and rigidity]" because such effects "are often the precursors of a clinical remission." Jesse L. Bennett and Kenneth A. Kooi observed a "high relationship . . . between [drug-] induced parkinsonism, induced abnormality of EEG and clinical remission." George Brooks noted that all patients on high doses showed evidence of "basal ganglion dysfunction" or parkinsonism and thought that "the greatest improvement coincided with the development" of such dysfunction; Frank J. Ayd wondered whether doctors "should deliberately produce basal ganglion symptoms" in order to increase "the improvement rate." John Denham and David Carrick concluded that the encephalitis-like symptoms "are of value because of the associated therapeutic benefit."[15]

There were other theories about how medication affected patients and produced clinical improvement. Many psychiatrists considered the drugs powerful stimulus-reducing agents or "major tranquilizers," a term that became the most common name for the treatment. The concept paralleled Deniker's. He posited a drug-induced brain syndrome that produced clinical benefits; adherents of tranquilizer theory posited a drug-induced psychological state, one normally considered pathological, that did likewise. Thus, William Winkelman compared the effects of chlorpromazine to a "conversion hysteria . . . characterized by a state of indifference and complacency, and . . . pathological tranquillity of mind." Deniker regarded mental (and physical) "indifference" as chlorpromazine's trademark; Winkelman thought the drug "could be called an indifference-producer." Deniker noted that medications "produce a disinterest in the patient for his own delusion"; Winkelman observed a "disinterest or indifference to exogenous or endogenous painful stimuli." The difference between them lay in Deniker's penchant for neurological explanation and Winkelman's penchant for the psychological. Both accounts agreed with Sidney Malitz's claim that "it is well known that the great advantage of the tranquilizers is their ability to produce a calming effect with a minimum of drowsiness and absence of confusion."[16]

Another theory portrayed medications as "chemical restraints" that exerted a chemical "holding down" action. The word "neuroleptic" described this effect, and the medications became known as "neuroleptics" as well as major tranquilizers. Reviewing the origin of "neuroleptic" forty years later, Colonna pointed out that it was chosen because the "suffix *lepsis* signified a taking hold or seizure, in contrast to *analepsis*, which meant a repairing."[17]

These theories did not necessarily conflict. Medications could "tranquilize" and also work as "chemical lobotomies," for example. After all, lobotomy produces a person who "does not perceive difficulties any more, is no longer disorganized by them, and is thereby enabled to function"—much the same as tranquilization. Nor were the "tranquilizer" and "chemical restraint" ideas inconsistent. A restraint could calm a patient, and a tranquilizer could restrain one. Moreover, many psychiatrists seemingly had little interest in elaborate theories about how medication worked. The convulsive and coma therapies never received satisfactory explanations, yet they had enjoyed wide use. Why should medication prove different?[18]

For that matter, many psychiatrists considered the use of medication an auxiliary measure that simply made patients more amenable to other interventions, such as the hospital milieu, psychotherapy, or electroconvulsive therapy.

Benjamin Pollack, for example, observed that chlorpromazine "seems to make the patient so much more receptive to other therapy, breaking down . . . many emotional barriers which formerly produced resistance." Herman Denber and John Travis reported that the drug was transforming custodial institutions into "dynamic therapeutic environment[s]"; that happened, as another psychiatrist explained, because chlorpromazine was "useful in converting acutely disturbed psychotics into tractable, accessible patients who could then participate more actively in the hospital rehabilitation program." Paul Hoch saw "the integration of chemotherapy and psychotherapy" as a crucial task, while a New Jersey mental hospital official thought that the calming effects of medication "prepare[d]" patients "for electroshock and other established forms of treatment." Even Pierre Deniker, with his theory of a medication-induced encephalitis-like disease, wrote in 1956 that the "most important" advance that chlorpromazine brought to schizophrenia treatment was "the improvement in the rapport of the patients which opens up new possibilities for psychotherapy."[19]

These psychiatrists saw important benefits but did not think medications cured or even profoundly affected schizophrenia. That made theory about the action of medication seem even less important. Other psychiatrists, however, perceived something profound. They discerned a "specific" or antipsychotic effect that affected the very process of disease. Such claims were usually limited and cautious. One doctor, for example, observed that medications "appear to have a specific effect on early schizophrenia . . . apart from their ability to make the patient tranquil." Offering a different version of the claim, Donald Blair and Desmond Brady argued that while insulin coma "perhaps" benefited more patients, medications were "therapeutically a distinct advance" in long-term cases because they "attack[ed] the schizophrenic process more radically and potently." According to the first account, medications demonstrated a specific effect in "early" schizophrenia; according to the second, the "potent" effect appeared in long-term cases. These physicians agreed that medication did not universally produce the effect; Blair and Brady even suggested that more patients might respond well to insulin coma treatment.[20]

Others added different caveats. Julian Abrams claimed that chlorpromazine "has the effect of starting a reversal" of some parts "of the schizophrenic process" but that it did not ameliorate withdrawal from the world, a key schizophrenic manifestation or symptom. Another psychiatrist noted that despite "specific effects," at least half of medicated patients did not benefit and the side effects sometimes reached dangerous levels. Deniker himself suggested that chlorpromazine had a "real curative effect" in some instances—but not, as noted already, in schizophrenia.[21]

Even with the caveats and qualifications, the 1950s proponents of a "specific effect" remained in the minority. Most researchers made no such claims; instead, they emphasized that schizophrenia endured despite treatment. For example, Ivan Bennett noted that while medications reduced "psychomotor excitement" the "patients remain schizophrenic." John Donnelly reported that even when medications produce "remarkable social improvement . . . our findings are that underneath this the ideation, and often the affect, is not fundamentally changed"; rather, "[t]here is [simply] . . . less overt verbalization of the psychotic delusions when the patient is on the drug." Herman Denber and Etta Bird reached similar conclusions about chronically ill patients: on medication, they "become disinterested in their persecutors" and, as a result, either stop hallucinating or say such things as "I hear them [the hallucinations] but they don't bother me anymore." Looking back on the period, Garfield Tourney noted that psychiatrists considered chlorpromazine "a valuable therapeutic agent" but that "exaggerated claims were not so often made regarding its curative powers as with treatment measures in the past; it was regarded as being palliative rather than curative by most investigators."[22]

These researchers knew that medications "can at times produce dramatic improvements in cases that have been completely refractory to other forms of somatic therapy," yet that did not mean the treatment was truly curative. Today, for example, "atypical" antipsychotic medications such as clozapine sometimes "produce dramatic improvements in cases that have been refractory" to treatment with other medications, but most psychiatrists do not, on that account, count the "atypicals" as cures. During the 1950s, many psychiatrists appear to have thought of medication in a similar way.[23]

Side Effects

Prevailing theories comported with and often depended upon the existence of significant drug side effects. The "brain disease," "chemical lobotomy," "tranquilization," and "chemical restraint" notions presupposed diffuse drug actions and drug-induced pathological states. No psychiatrists condemned such ideas as unethical or transparently false. Nor did anyone deny that the effects of medication commonly mimicked the symptoms of brain diseases like encephalitis or Parkinson's.

Many psychiatrists even objected to the terms "side effect" or "complication" when applied to "basal ganglion dysfunctions" or "encephalitis-like" signs. Those things were inherent in drug actions, according to these psychiatrists, and even desirable. Thus, Fritz Freyhan wrote that medication-produced tremor and stiffness, "[f]ar from being complications" were in fact "closely related to the drug's psychiatric effectiveness." In 1955 Lomas distinguished "side-effects"—parkinsonism, for example—which "are usually due to the pharmacological action of Chlorpromazine on the autonomic nervous system and are therefore necessary concomitants of the treatment" from "toxic reactions," such as hepatitis, which "are observed in relatively few patients and are due to idiosyncrasy."[24]

Other psychiatrists disagreed. They held that the use of medication produced benefits in the absence of neurological dysfunction. Writing in the *Journal of the American Medical Association*, Robert Hall reported in 1956 "only a weak and equivocal association of neurotoxic reactions with psychiatric improvement." Some found no connection at all.[25]

In any event, the recognized "side effects," "complications," or "concomitants of treatment" were numerous. By 1957, Deniker's inventory included "the akinetic syndrome [that is, diminished mental and muscular activity] in all its intensity," parkinsonism, akathisia [an inability to remain still, usually accompanied by subjective distress], and oculogyric crises (that is, crises affecting the eyes). Most psychiatrists thought these effects usually diminished with continued treatment, responded well to "anti-parkinson" medications, and disappeared when medication stopped.

Yet the alarming possibility existed that some effects of medication would persist or become permanent. In 1961, Deniker noted a drug-induced syndrome characterized by

> attacks of trismus [lockjaw-like spasms of the chewing muscles] . . .
> and attacks called "hysterical" or "hysteria-like" by the early
> observers . . . [both of these resembling] manifestations . . . of the
> "syndrome excito-moteur" of postencephalitic patients. . . . The
> trismus, sometimes violent, but always reducible by will-power and
> suggestion, is part of the "syndrome linguo-fascio-masticateur" . . .
> characterized by involuntary opening of the mouth, movements of the
> lower jaw and tongue and by various types of protrusion of the
> lips. . . . The "syndrome excito-moteur" also includes the various types
> of tremors, jerky movements, akatisia [sic], akinesia and the
> choreoathetotic phenomena.[26]

Some psychiatrists were reporting that this "syndrome linguo-fascio-masticateur" persisted after drugs were withdrawn; they feared that it became permanent. Sporadic reports about the condition—called "tardive dyskinesia" (because it appeared relatively late in treatment) or "persistent dyskinesia"—began appearing in European medical journals by the late 1950s.

Leading researchers had expected to discover irreversible, neurological side effects. George Crane later recalled that tardive dyskinesia surprised researchers only because they had focused on a different possibility: medication-induced Parkinson's syndrome (Deniker's "psychomotor indifference") persisting or becoming permanent. In 1959, George Paulson observed that the issue of medication-caused permanent brain damage remained unresolved, but he noted provocatively that "most of the neurologic complications from . . . [medications] are within the range of post encephalitic Parkinsonism"—a permanent condition.[27]

At the outset the evidence had appeared that drug-induced Parkinson's symptoms and other effects could persist after medication stopped. Hall reported that result in a 1956 *Journal of the American Medical Association* article, "Neurotoxic Reactions Resulting from Chlorpromazine Administration." One of the first studies of chlorpromazine in a major American publication, the article included these findings: thirty-six out of ninety medicated subjects developed "neurotoxic reactions" such as rigidity, tremor, and akinesia; 44 percent of the affected patients still showed toxic signs twenty-nine days after discontinuation of the drug; and 17 percent, or six out of the thirty-six, continued to show definite neurological abnormalities sixty days after discontinuation of the drug, when the study stopped. Thus, relatively brief chlorpromazine exposure could produce neurological changes that persisted.[28]

Psychiatrists generally ignored "Neurotoxic Reactions," particularly in the United States. Yet it would have been easy to test its conclusions. One only had to observe patients after they discontinued medication, and in this period psychiatrists did remove patient from drugs. Some psychiatrists surely possessed enough curiosity to examine such patients. Yet American psychiatrists did not confirm or refute Hall's claims, at least not in print. Nor did they examine the possible persistence of side effects more than sixty days after drugs were discontinued, the issue Hall had left open. Instead, most continued describing side effects as completely reversible, despite the evidence.[29]

Another "complication" or "concomitant" of treatment involved patients' subjective feelings or states of mind. These had interested psychiatrists very early. In 1952, a French psychiatrist, Quarti, took a test dose of chlorpromazine and reported her subjective states on medication; according to Swazey, her report spurred other physicians to investigate chlorpromazine's psychiatric uses. Yet some of the changes were quite distressing:

> I began to have the impression that I was becoming weaker, that I was dying. It was very painful and agonizing. . . .
>
> I experienced an illness more pronounced than depression. . . .
>
> [About an hour later] the painful feeling of imminent death disappeared to make room for a euphoric relaxation. I had felt all along that I was going to die, but this new state left me indifferent . . . I felt incapable of being angry about anything, irresistibly optimistic, and full of love for the whole world. Although very much in touch with my surroundings, I was more and more overcome by an extreme feeling of detachment from myself and . . . others. My perceptions

were normal, but their tone had changed; everything was filtered, muted. . . .

The affective changes lasted for about a week. . . . The mood was of perfect euphoria, unaffected by all the little traumas of daily life.[30]

Mental distress of the sort that Quarti experienced early in her experiment, received occasional attention during the 1950s. Reports noted that patients frequently disliked how medication made them feel and sometimes became anguished as a result of treatment. "[M]any patients" discontinued medication, according to one psychiatrist, because of "an increase in their anxiety associated with marked weakness, drowsiness, aches and pains, or feelings of depersonalization and depression"; a few even developed "acute psychotic reactions . . . characterized by intensification of unreality feelings . . . and the development of hallucinations and delusions." In 1955, Vernon Kinross-Wright observed that "[m]ost patients, when questioned, report they dislike the way the drug makes them feel."[31] Another study of 125 medicated patients, by Paul Hoch, reported, "Twelve . . . complained of feelings of depersonalization; of feeling strange, peculiar and out of contact. Eight patients developed a marked lethargy and weakness. Nine patients had a feeling of depression of [sic] not being able to function; a peculiar sensation of being driven and restless. In all these instances the drug had to be withdrawn because the patient requested it. If the drug was reintroduced these psychic complications reappeared in all but a few patients."[32] Hoch regarded these complications as real but deemed them important mostly because they made it difficult to "induce" the afflicted patients to accept medications again. He recommended "psychotherapy" as a way of preventing patients from having "their faith in the therapist shaken" by the "very disagreeable psychological effect" of medications.[33]

PSYCHIATRISTS' REACTIONS TO SIDE EFFECTS

Psychiatrists in the 1950s freely acknowledged the nonpersistent side effects of medication. Theories like Deniker's even made a virtue out of necessity, portraying stiffness, lethargy, and dyskinesia as signs of the effectiveness of medication. Persistent or permanent effects were a different story, however. Psychiatrists ignored Hall's report about the persistence of side effects even though it appeared in one of America's premier medical journals.

Had Hall reported a new medication benefit, or something that made side effects appear less serious, it seems unlikely psychiatrists would have ignored it. Indeed, Hall's other principal finding—that the benefits of medication apparently did not depend on concurrent side effects—soon carried the day. Evidently, psychiatrists simply did not want to acknowledge persistent effects. The only other possibility—that no physicians cared, or had any curiosity about the issue, even in private—seems both less likely and even less flattering to the profession.

Why did psychiatrists resist findings of persistent side effects? The answer lies with psychiatry's "lobotomy problem." If medications induced long-lasting neurological damage, they would resemble lobotomy. Yet lobotomy's disrepute already threatened psychiatry's stature by 1956. Clearly, medications could produce lobotomy-like indifference; indeed, Quarti's experiment with taking chlorpromazine yielded a mental state that resembled the aftermath of a lobotomy in numerous ways, including the "extreme feeling of detachment," the altered emotional "tone" of experience, the sense of "everything [being] . . . filtered, muted," and the almost mindless "euphoria." If medications also produced irreversible neurological changes, they might become indistinguishable from lobotomy in the public's mind—with grave consequences for the future of the treatment.

What of the side effects, those that psychiatrists freely acknowledged? Opinions about the clinical and ethical significance of these effects varied. Some disagreements rested on apparent differences in observation. For example, there were psychiatrists who noticed patients' feelings of depersonalization or depression while on medication, and there were other psychiatrists who did not—or, at least, who did not consider those feelings worthy of comment in reports. Equally important, psychiatrists characterized patients' subjective reactions in different ways.

Compare, for example, Hoch's account of patients' feelings—"depersonalization," "depression," and "not being able to function," which led to drugs being withdrawn—with Winkelman's version of similar patient reactions: "[Eighty five] patients . . . spontaneously stopped the drug in less than one week, owing to what might be called a negative psychological response. . . . These patients were severely hypochondriacal with bizarre symptoms and interpreted subjectively-experienced reactions during chlorpromazine therapy as serious manifestations of disease, or as serious effects of the drug. . . . [T]he same patients showed similar unexpected subjective reactions in trials with other drugs. They did not show normal response to any treatment. When some were given chlorpromazine in an unrecognized form, in smaller or often in the same dosage, the response was not seen."[34] Hoch attributed the distressing subjective feelings to the medications. Winkelman made patients responsible. In his version, pre-existing mental conditions led patients to misinterpret "subjectively-experienced reactions during chlorpromazine therapy" as "serious effects" of the drug or their illness. Thus, the patients (and presumably Hoch, who made a similar mistake) failed to "show normal response."

Winkelman never tried to establish the parameters of a "normal" response to medication; he simply assumed it would be favorable. Yet psychiatrists later observed that normal persons respond to medication with distress; and Quarti did so during her 1952 experiment. That makes Winkelman's patients "normal" in their reactions as well.[35]

Aside from that basic error, Winkelman's reaction to his patients' distress seems surprising. He presumed that "subjectively-experienced reactions" could never represent "serious effects of the drug" because patients themselves were at fault. Psychiatrists try to ease mental suffering, yet Winkelman seemingly discounted distress because he supposed the patients to be responsible it. But even if the distress was not "normal," as Winkelman claimed, that was hardly a reason to dismiss it.

Throughout the medication era, psychiatrists frequently laid the blame for drug reactions on supposed preexisting patient conditions, physical or mental. Winkelman's response seems mild, for example, compared to psychiatrists who later attributed tardive dyskinesia to "non-diagnosable, pre-existing brain damage" or ignored distressing drug reactions altogether. He at least acknowledged *something* and tried to explain why patients, rather than chlorpromazine, bore responsibility for it. Yet Winkelman's approach shows how rationalizations, not patient responses, could dictate conclusions. He conceded that his patients felt distress on medications, yet he still managed to avoid counting distress as a medication side effect. Nor was this phenomenon restricted to distress. Winkelman found an incidence of parkinsonism-like syndrome of less than 0.2 percent, yet he also observed that "the drug causes disinterest or indifference to exogenous or endogenous painful stimuli"—phenomena that, according to Deniker and others, reflected a drug-induced Parkinson's syndrome. Characterizing the condition as they did, the rate of drug-induced parkinsonism would rise to a figure approaching 100 percent.

Thus, psychiatrists' characterizations greatly influenced what they wrote and said. Indifference could be a side effect, as Hall thought; part of a drug-induced pathological syndrome inseparable from drug benefits, as Deniker imagined; or neither of those things, as Winkelman somehow supposed. At the same time, general questions of characterizing patient reactions rarely received explicit attention, and when they did, the discussion could become angry.

In one discussion of the issue, Herman Denber praised foreign doctors who "approached . . . [side effects] in a medical fashion"—unlike the "rather curious, anxiety-ridden, almost hysterical tone [that] has permeated case reports of such effects in this country." Denber cited no examples, but his rhetoric was striking. He had attributed to *psychiatrists* symptoms, such as anxiety and hysteria, typical of psychiatric *patients*. The reversal came about gradually, as Denber cited the progression of American psychiatry's symptoms from "curious," to "anxiety-ridden" to "almost hysterical." It all began with psychiatrists' "curious" tone; read literally, Denber might have been objecting to psychiatrists' curiosity about side effects. In the end, he portrayed "hysterical" American psychiatrists as in need of something like a major tranquilizer.[36]

Obviously, psychiatrists disagreed about how seriously—or "hysterically"—to regard side effects. Relatively little of the disagreement survives in the printed literature; it must have unfolded mostly in private discussions or exchanges at conferences. Nathan S. Kline, an eminent American psychiatrist, did address the subject for publication, however. Like Denber, he clearly resided outside the "hysterical" camp. In 1956 Kline wrote, "The widespread use of . . . [chlorpromazine and reserpine, a drug in a different class that Kline helped introduce] has brought to attention the need for handling the side effects which these drugs sometimes induce. The greatest problem in this respect is not in the state hospitals where the side reactions constitute, as a rule, nothing more than annoyances. It is in private practice that some of the concurrent reactions make it extremely difficult for the patient to function adequately in his usual setting."[37] Thus, side effects should be judged with reference to a patient's ability to function in a particular "setting." Since medicated patients function adequately in mental hospitals, side effects there constitute mere "annoyances."

Kline did not specify whether patients or psychiatrists endured the "annoyance"—recall how Denber ascribed patient attributes to psychiatrists—but another physician, Douglas Goldman, did. Goldman wrote that side effects "with the exception of agranulocytosis [a blood disorder] . . . are found not to be dangerous to the life or welfare of the patient if they are managed - [properly] . . . [T]he analogy to the expected discomforts of surgical convalescence is frequently pointed out. It is hoped, however . . . that new drugs can be developed which can achieve equally brilliant therapeutic results with less of the undesirable *and, to the clinician*, anxiety-provoking toxic side-effects."[38] Like Denber, Goldman located the relevant "anxiety" in psychiatrists rather than patients; unlike Denber, however, he treated the anxiety as a result of what medications actually did. Indeed, he almost made it appear that medication relieved patients' anxiety through transference: because of medication, patients lost anxiety, and psychiatrists acquired it. Kline's idea of functioning in a setting was less psychodynamic and more hardhearted, but Goldman agreed with Kline that side effects generally did not warrant discontinuing medication in a mental hospital.

One can easily imagine a physician being more troubled about side effects than Denber, Goldman, or Kline. Denber often appeared not to take side effects seriously. Goldman's analogy between the medication and surgical convalescence failed; convalescence lasted only a limited time, but one might take medication indefinitely.

If the appropriate benchmark was functioning in a setting, Kline was arguably right. Psychiatrists worried that distress could prompt patients to stop taking the pills—but a mental hospital could continue the treatment no matter what a patient felt. Beyond that, Jonathan O. Cole later explained how side effects might prove incapacitating outside of hospitals. He described a woman whose "stiffness in the arms and legs . . . made her unable to do her housework or care for herself or her family" and a man who "lost a job as a draftsman because his inking was too heavily done." Although Cole did not address the point, it appears obvious that in a mental hospital the woman would not have to "care for . . . her family" and the man would not have the "job as a draftsman." Thus, Kline's distinction was coherent. Yet what if one redefined the expectations for life in a mental hospital, or if the relevant ethical standard looked to the functioning of an organism—a person—apart from any particular setting? In either case, side effects became no less serious in mental hospitals than in the community.[39]

Lobotomists had used a test like Kline's. They counted it a success when patients could function in a setting, even if only as a passive worker or household member, despite surgically produced impairments. Criticizing lobotomy, Peter Sterling described one such "success": "[A] patient who had received three lobotomies, which ultimately resulted in a hemiparesis, hydrocephalus, and severe epilepsy, was considered to have been 'helped' by the treatment. The patient, not institutionalized before the surgery, and then considered 'bright,' now has an I.Q. of 61, no social life, no work, and *does* sit at home, passively, unresponsively."[40] The case moved Sterling to observe that the "[h]uman capacity for self-deception is almost boundless." Yet those applying the "function in a setting" benchmark are not necessarily deceived. If living at home constitutes a "function," this patient properly counts as a success. The problem arises from the "function" test, not self-deception. Yet Kline and others employed that test to judge the side effects of medication, and they continued to do so even after other legacies of lobotomy had fallen out of psychiatric favor.

The 1950s in Context

Some 1950s tenets now appear almost unthinkable. Trying to produce brain disease, aiming for "chemical lobotomy" or "chemical restraint," characterizing incapacitating side effects as "annoyances"—and annoyances to the physician, at that—appear brutal and crude. Someone who reiterated such views today would seem almost irrational about the use of medication.

Yet one should not judge too quickly. If medication does in fact tranquilize, or chemically restrain, or produce psychomotor indifference, then psychiatrists were merely being candid. A metaphor like "chemical lobotomy" is harder to judge, but we should not simply presume that it was inapt. Recent research suggests that medications have undesirable actions in the frontal lobes, the area targeted in lobotomy, and some medication effects were similar. In general, observations about side effects from the 1950s have held up fairly well—better than standard treatments of the same subject from the 1960s or early 1970s.

Less happily the practice of ignoring persistent side effects also began in the 1950s. The reception Hall's article received—and the lack of attention to early reports of tardive dyskinesia—portended later developments. Another enduring aspect of the period was the nature of the debate about side effects. Psychiatrists disagreed about how seriously to regard them: it was an ethical as much as a technical question. The dispute turned on whether patients *should* endure distress and other effects, not on whether those effects existed. Yet the debate took place almost entirely out of sight, leaving only slight traces in the printed record—much slighter than traces of ethical concern about lobotomy on the part of earlier psychiatrists.

Psychiatry put these ethical questions off for a decade and more, but they returned with a vengeance in the controversy over tardive dyskinesia.

Chapter 2

Public Health and Other Implications

W[HEN] CHLORPROMAZINE made its debut, the American public mental health system chiefly consisted of state mental hospitals. Enormous and expensive, these hospitals affected numerous interests. Governors and legislatures ran them. State treasuries paid the bills. Large numbers of people worked there, or lived there as patients. Because of the expense, the coercion of civil commitment, the occasional scandal, and the apparent allure of madness, the media and public often proved interested as well. So did academics, reformers and, particularly after 1960, lawyers and judges. The latter considered whether the hospitals operated outside the bounds of constitutional right.

Psychiatry's own interests included, but were not limited to, patients' well being. The repeated scandals over conditions, combined with the lobotomy debacle, had depressed the profession's own standing. Professional self-esteem and long-range prospects for research funding or insurance reimbursement both suffered.

Medications had obvious potential, but how they would, or should, affect the public health system remained a matter of debate during the 1950s. In the end, most of the concerned interests—psychiatrists, governors, legislators, reformers, academics, courts, and lawyers—had their say; to an extent rarely appreciated, they reached substantial agreement about what should be done. In this, they had the assistance of the federal government, which for the first time assumed a major role in matters of public mental health.

From the beginning, chlorpromazine had affected institutions at least as dramatically as it had individuals. Hospital wards became calmer and less chaotic. According to one physician, after the introduction of medication, his hospital had been able to add "television sets" on back wards, as well as "potted plants, glassware, and many other items we would never have dared put within reach of these patients before"; in addition, no patients remained in seclusion cells, all now wore clothes, and "our attendants are no longer complaining of torn shirts and bruises inflicted by combative patients." By 1956, according to Judith Swazey, little doubt existed that the effects of medication "on patients, on the atmosphere and operations of hospital wards, on hospital staffs, and on the hospital as a whole" had inaugurated "a new era in mental hospitals."[1] Still, it remained unclear how the changes should affect the hospitals' role or public mental health design.

In one view, the use of medications would make hospitals more effective, allowing them to fulfill their original mission. By reducing the real and figurative noise that interfered with treatment, medication might make old dreams come true. In this picture, revitalized mental hospitals continued to anchor the public mental health system; what Greenblatt had hoped to achieve by democratizing hospitals would be accomplished through medication. Thus, Fritz Freyhan observed in 1955 that "chlorpromazine therapy" had made possible "the social reconstruction of the mental hospital." That same year, the president of the pharmaceutical company that marketed chlorpromazine informed a psychiatric symposium that "[m]ore than half our hospital beds are occupied by the mentally ill, and we have no illusions that they will be emptied by chlorpromazine." As late as 1961 the Joint Commission on Mental Illness and Health—a congressionally sanctioned joint undertaking of the American Psychiatric Association, the American Medical Association, and other leading groups—observed that "tranquilizing drugs . . . might be described as moral treatment in pill form."[2]

Some psychiatrists had a more radical idea: medication would take the place of mental hospitals, with ex-patients receiving "maintenance" drug regimens in the community. One can hear echoes of this idea at the 1955 symposium; numerous participants spoke against it and emphasized the continuing importance of hospitals. Jay Hoffman described a "fantasy" or "dream" about chlorpromazine's possible impact: "The over-crowding of our state hospitals may be reduced and ultimately, new hospital buildings should be required chiefly for replacements only. More patients will be released after shorter periods of hospitalization and fewer patients will require re-hospitalization. More patients can be treated in the community, at clinics or in the psychiatrist's office without being hospitalized at all." He emphasized, however, that "administration of the drug alone" did not "provide . . . a firm basis for many—if any—discharges" and that patients on medication needed both "supportive therapy within the hospital" and postdischarge services in the community.[3]

Institutional Change

During the 1950s, governors and legislatures approved wide use of medication in state hospitals. Although costly, medication seemed likely to more than pay for itself by shortening hospital stays. Or so proponents argued.

Daniel Patrick Moynihan has described the effect of the financial argument on Governor Averill Harriman of New York. In 1955, Harriman made a pioneering decision to authorize major purchases of medications for the state hospitals. As Moynihan described it, Nathan S. Kline, then working at a New York state mental hospital, had introduced reserpine, "one of the first tranquilizers." It was, Moynihan remembered,

> a time when mental illness was seen as perhaps the most pressing problem New York State faced—bond issue followed bond issue to build institution after institution. On taking office . . . Harriman began to consider the implications of . . . [Kline's] discovery.
> . . . I was present at the meeting in the Governor's office in the spring of 1955 when it was decided to provide the tranquilizer to all patients system-wide. It was a $1.5 million bet. (Harriman would later explain that he was, after all, an investment banker.)[4]

Nonfinancial considerations surely influenced officials as well. The age venerated science and medicine, and a decision not to use medication would suggest opposition to progress. It would also make a politician more vulnerable in the inevitable next round of scandal over mental hospital conditions. "If Governor X had only agreed to buy more medication, this would not have happened," newspapers might write—regardless of the particular revelations rocking the hospitals. Thus, fiscal savings, medical progress, and political expediency all pointed toward a decision like Harriman's.

Many physicians saw opposite implications. They thought the purchase and use of medications would increase hospital expenditures. Besides the cost of drugs, they foresaw the need for more staff to serve patients newly amenable to psychotherapy and other measures. These physicians also envisioned increased research expenses.[5]

By the end of the decade, "major tranquilizers" were in wide use, inside and outside mental hospitals. According to one estimate, 60 percent of hospitalized patients received them. Many psychiatrists also considered maintenance medication necessary to prevent relapses after a patient had improved. Meanwhile, the hospitals' census slightly decreased. Although very modest, the decreases were historic; during the mid-1950s, for the first time in a century, the upward spiral in the state hospital census had reversed. Henry Brill and Robert Patton studied New York's hospital census with great care and attributed the decrease to the introduction of chlorpromazine.[6]

According to Moynihan, "the population of state mental institutions began to decline" almost as soon as Harriman decided to buy chlorpromazine.[7] He was hardly bragging; to the contrary, he lamented the disasters brought about by deinstitutionalization. Yet the systematic shift of patients from mental hospitals to the community—and the precipitous drop in the state hospital census—did not begin for another decade, until the mid- and late 1960s.

In 1955, the nation's public mental hospitals had housed 558,000 patients; in 1963, after nine years of increasing medication use, the figure had fallen to 504,600—a drop of about 54,000 or 10 percent. Over the next eight years, it fell by almost 200,000, or about 40 percent, to 309,000 in 1971. By 1974 it had fallen almost another 100,000, to 215,600. Medication became more widely used during this period, yet it remains obvious that medication alone could not produce the results that a conscious policy of deinstitutionalization *plus* medication did. So long as psychiatrists envisioned an important role for mental hospitals, as most did in the 1950s, deinstitutionalization would not achieve its later, explosive rate—a rate all the more remarkable because, with each passing year, the remaining chronic patients were sicker and more impaired than those released earlier.[8]

Brill and Patton did not think medications would supplant the hospitals to any significant degree. In 1962 Brill said, "I don't think we're seeing a general solution . . . that will wipe out mental illness and depopulate hospitals." Morton Birnbaum invented the legal "right to treatment" in 1960 because he believed that hospitals would remain the centerpieces of the mental health system, despite medication. Observing medicated patients, these and other commentators foresaw modest declines in the hospitals' census, dramatic improvements in hospital treatment, and the emergence of more effective outpatient facilities. They did not see the future that unfolded, one in which state hospitals existed only to reinstitute drug regimens for those who had relapsed and to house a small number of patients who, because of physical infirmity or demonstrated violence, seemed especially unsuited to community life.[9]

During this period, drug actions and public health did not seem so tightly related that only one future was imaginable. Just as psychiatrists disagreed about the effects of medication on individuals, they differed about the public health implications of the treatment. Not until the mid- or late 1960s would psychiatric, political, social, and legal visions converge on deinstitutionalization as the only model that comported with medical reality, social justice, and legal imperative.

The intellectual climate changed quickly, particularly in government and university circles. In 1962, a government panel recommended a system of community mental health clinics to President Kennedy, essentially ignoring the Joint Commission's call for improved hospital treatment. Kennedy responded with a speech that proposed federal funding for community mental health centers—a system made possible, he said, because of simultaneous advances in American morality and psychopharmacology. This liberal president's major domestic initiative encouraged states to dismantle their existing public mental health systems, once their major domestic programs. Federal incentives for deinstitutionalization were enacted, first in the form of the Community Mental Health Centers Act and later in the Medicaid program, which made most state mental hospital care ineligible for federal reimbursement.[10]

Academic thinking pointed in the identical direction. Influential sociologists and psychologists argued that social settings, rather than internal mental states, played a decisive role in supposed psychiatric problems. In a widely discussed book, the social scientist Erving Goffman depicted mental patients as people performing the social roles and degrading rituals assigned them by mental institutions.[11]

The psychologist David Rosenhan published a particularly influential study. Rosenhan designed an experiment with "pseudo-patients"—mentally healthy volunteers—who pretended to hear clanging sounds (a made-up auditory hallucination that had never been reported in the psychiatric literature). The pseudopatients then presented themselves to various in-patient psychiatric facilities, and all gained admission as inpatients. Once hospitalized, they feigned no other symptoms and honestly recounted their life experiences. Yet psychiatrists invariably failed to recognize them as mentally healthy, and failed to distinguish them from real patients upon discharge.[12]

Rosenhan concluded that the mental hospital *environment* was pathological, and he implied that mental illness—as the attribute of an individual rather than a relation between an individual and a social setting—did not really exist. If mental illness did exist, according to Rosenhan, it apparently "could not be known" in a mental hospital setting; the physicians, after all, had failed to distinguish normality from madness in his experiment. Rosenhan argued for less emphasis on global psychiatric diagnoses (for example, "schizophrenia") and for more targeted treatments (to deal with problems of living), but his conclusions implied that hospitals should be abolished. The problem with global diagnoses was that they tried to capture the whole person and failed; the problem with mental hospitals was that they literally captured a person but failed to help.

Rosenhan produced an elegant study, but the conclusions overshot his data in revealing ways. The idea that mental illness "could not be known" in mental hospital settings conflicted with his observation that "real" patients readily identified the pseudopatients as fakers. Some nurses suspected, too. Thus, mental illness, as a quality of a person, evidently could be detected in a mental hospital environment, at least by patients and nurses. A less profound interpretation than Rosenhan's required no excursions into epistemology or ontology and better fit his findings: psychiatrists simply worked carelessly, missing the obvious facts that patients and nurses saw.

The focus on environments and settings, as opposed to internal mental states, did not constitute a new development. A century earlier, the same focus had produced the idea of mental hospitals as morally restorative environments. After World War II, the attempts to revive moral therapy in mental hospitals rested on anthropological and sociological reflections about the social setting of the patients. Yet work like Goffman's and Rosenhan's turned earlier efforts upside-down. Once a supposed remedy for pathological social environments, the mental hospital now became the prime example of such an environment. Social science, a source of knowledge for improving mental hospitals in the early 1950s, demonstrated the hopeless and fatal flaws of hospitals in the early 1960s.

Rosenhan himself drew no conclusions about the use of medication, although he observed that patients frequently disliked drugs and often spit out the pills, while doctors seemingly prescribed the same medications and dosages no matter what the patient's condition. Yet his stance had broader implications. Obviously, if mental illness did not exist as an internal state of a person, medications could not cure it; no "specific pharmacological effect" was possible against a nonexistent disease. At the same time, if mental hospitals constituted inherently pathological environments, medication might represent good things because—for whatever reason—they speeded a person's release to the community. (Psychiatrists also thought that drugs improved the hospital environment.) Moreover, if one regarded medication as a method of changing specific, maladaptive behaviors—rather than as treatments for a global entity called "mental illness"—then medication could promote social adaptation and, in that way, too, conform to the sociological model.

Ideas of this kind were neither new nor confined to academic social science. Nathan Kline had used the concept of functioning in a social setting as a benchmark of tolerable side effects. Lobotomists used the same concept to measure therapeutic success.

These similarities were ironic. The new social science critiques of mental hospitals seemed forward looking and radical, yet they rested on the very premises and conceptual approaches that had made lobotomy appear successful. Thus, they looked backward more than forward. Nor were the critiques radical. In fact, they sanctioned what state governments already wanted to do. Merging the "functioning in a setting" concept of side effects with the similar concept of mental health, one obtained a mandate for rapid deinstitutionalization, aggressive use of medication in the community, and a high level of tolerance (by psychiatrists) for side effects in every setting—precisely the policies that took hold in the late 1960s.

Structures of Belief

The debates over public health paralleled the debates about the effects of medication on individuals. All turned on how profoundly drugs could change things. Did medication produce "specific effects" and fundamentally alter the course of disease, or merely calm patients? Should the public mental health system undergo a fundamental transformation, or would existing hospitals simply work better because of medications?

Related questions existed about psychiatric theory, with respect to individuals and institutions alike. Should psychiatrists produce far-reaching theories, like Deniker's, about the effects of medication on patients? Or should psychiatrists avoid high theory and focus on observed benefits and risks of treatment? Should psychiatrists think deeply about public health and the role of hospitals, or merely propose incremental adjustments in light of medications' institutional effects?

Besides these two areas—the direct effects of medication and the reach of theories, a third dimension of concern existed. Here, the issues involved the character and history of psychiatry, and similar questions arose. Just as psychiatrists pondered the effects of medication on individuals and institutions, they pondered the effects on their profession. They wondered whether drugs had exerted a kind of "specific effect" on psychiatry, one that eliminated its former vulnerabilities and transformed it into a modern and scientific medical discipline.

That concern implicated psychiatrists as individuals as well, for if medications had *not* transformed psychiatry, then medication-era clinicians resembled their counterparts from other eras. They still practiced in a field of questionable professional accomplishment, surrounded by unique ethical problems. That circumstance inevitably raised questions—warranted or not—about the competence and professional morality of individual physicians. Think of a lobotomist in the 1940s. Can one avoid a tendency to think badly of that physician, solely because he or she favored that procedure? Sensitive to such questions, psychiatrists feel a *personal* stake in the standing of a dominant psychiatric therapy such as medications.

This identification between therapist and therapy has an unfortunate consequence. It erases the distinction between criticizing a therapy and criticizing the physician. If a psychiatrist's professional self-worth depends on chlorpromazine having profound actions in the brain, for example, then anyone who questions the drug's mode of action is also attacking the physicians who use it. How, then, can one discuss basic questions about psychiatric treatments? It becomes natural to answer such criticisms in kind, by personally attacking the critic. This dynamic underlay Denber's charge of "hysteria" against those who viewed side effects more seriously than he did. It would also underlie later attacks on George Crane in connection with tardive dyskinesia.

In sum, questions about profoundness and medications arose in three dimensions—direct effects, theory, and the character of psychiatry. Each included individual and institutional aspects. And the resulting questions touched on the past, present, and future of patients, institutions, and the profession.

How the Dimensions of Belief are Related

The changes in thinking that occurred in the 1960s cannot be understood without appreciating how the three dimensions of psychiatric thought relate. One can suppose too easily that beliefs in one dimension—for example, regarding the direct effects of medication on patients—bound a psychiatrist, as a matter of logic or science, with respect to other dimensions. That mistake leads to impoverished history. Important historical changes fail to receive due attention because of the mistaken idea that they had to occur.

Standard versions of psychiatric history often make that mistake. They presume that discoveries about the effects of medication on individuals compelled—or at least strongly suggested—conclusions about public health, theory, and the psychiatric profession. As a result, matters that deserve an explanation—the changed beliefs about public health, theory, and psychiatry—fail to receive it. This same error impairs ethical judgments about developments as well. Too much that happened appears inevitable and beyond choice.

How do beliefs about the effects of medication on individuals relate to questions about public health, psychiatric theory, and the state of psychiatry? Clearly, some connections exist. If one believes medications produce *no* effects on individuals, then, barring a massive placebo phenomenon, one will not believe in a transformed public health system or profession either. Nor will psychiatrists theorize deeply about those nonexistent effects—although social scientists, like Rosenhan, might. Similarly, if one believes that medications *cure* mental illness, then one will also believe that drugs eliminate the need for mental hospitals, at least as we know them, and probably also believe that psychiatry has undergone a professional transformation. Moreover, such profound effects invite far-reaching theories to explain them.

These strong relationships exist at the extremes of belief, where medications appear either as cures or as worthless. Move away from the extremes—today, virtually no researcher accepts either one—and the situation changes. Given any plausible view of medications, ideas about how drugs affect individuals do not resolve the other questions, at least not alone. Rather, a wide variety of answers become possible.

Suppose, for example, that Dr. X believes that: medications produce specific effects on mental illness (although they fall short of a complete cure); psychiatric theory should offer far-reaching explanations of those effects; and because of medications, individual psychiatrists are no longer open to the old charges of incompetence or venality. Thus, X views drugs as a profound therapy with regard to the individual questions in all three dimensions—direct effects, theory, and professional character.

Given those views, X also might believe that drugs produce profound institutional effects, making possible a wholesale shift from hospitals to community care. That would produce a coherent set of positions, which many psychiatrists in fact accept. Yet X's premises do not lead inexorably to the conclusion that medications exert profound institutional effects, or mark a revolution in psychiatric history. Without self-contradiction, for instance, X instead might believe that: medications do not fundamentally affect hospitals (although the hospitals will function better); no fundamental rethinking of the public mental health system is in order; and medications represent only an incremental advance in psychiatry because they fail to completely cure schizophrenia and because older therapies produced good outcomes too.

Now consider the views of Dr. Y. Regarding individuals, Y believes that: medications merely tranquilize and lack specific effects on mental illness; deep explanations of the effects of medication on patients are unnecessary or unobtainable; and clinicians continue to face the old moral, professional and social dilemmas. About institutions, however, Y maintains that: the ability of medication to restrain or tranquilize patients makes possible a large-scale shift from hospitals to community care; it is imperative to rethink the public mental health system deeply, in order to take advantage of medication's potential; and the resulting system, based on community medication, will mark a revolution in the history of psychiatry.

X's and Y's positions are mirror images of each other. X sees medication as a profound individual therapy with modest institutional implications; Y sees medication as a modest individual therapy with profound meaning for institutions. Other possibilities also exist. A psychiatrists could see drugs as profound in some individual—or institutional—domains but not in others.

For example, a psychiatrist might recognize a powerful specific effect on mental illness but also believe that far-reaching theories to explain the effect remain out of reach. (Some held such views during the 1950s.) Or, if medications profoundly affect mental illness, the extent of the change in the psychiatric profession could remain modest—provided that one also believes older therapies produced profound effects. (Kalinowsky and Hoch, for example, believed that.) A psychiatrist might see profound changes within institutions yet refrain from deep theorizing about the future of public health.

Of course, some answers do affect others. And some combinations appear more natural. For instance, if Dr. A sees: profound drug effects on individuals and theorizes deeply about them, then A probably thinks medications transformed psychiatry. In part, that is because A's enthusiasm about other things seems likely to extend to questions about the character of psychiatry. Or consider Dr. B., who believes that: medication profoundly affects the functioning of institutions and that deep theorizing about the public health system is in order. Given those positions, B probably envisions large-scale deinstitutionalization of patients. If B also believes in: profound individual effects and deep theorizing about those effects, then B probably also believes that medication transformed psychiatry.

In each series, the first two beliefs are related to but do not strictly compel the third. Regarding institutions, for example, deep theorizing might lead B to conclude that large state hospitals should survive since they can perform better with medication and communities will never accommodate the patients—or because patients with schizophrenia relapse more when stressed and communities are stressful places. In that case, B's deep theorizing allowed a prediction of the future failures of deinstitutionalization. Similarly, B's belief in profound individual effects and deep theory might lead B to regard medications as "chemical lobotomies" and to see the medication era as a straightforward continuation of the 1930s. To reach those conclusions, B only needs to believe that lobotomy produced profound effects that resembled those of medication.

The first period of the medication era lasted through the early 1960s and harbored many viewpoints. Some psychiatrists regarded medications as tranquilizers but thought that treatment with medication might revolutionize public mental health. Some saw specific effects against illness but worried that side effects might impact the use of medication. Some engaged in deep theory but remained wedded to a hospital model of care. Some shunned deep theory but welcomed radical changes in public mental health. And so on. Psychiatric belief constituted a flexible structure, relatively loosely strung, with positions not too closely dependent on each other and without any single foundation belief undergirding the rest.

Things would change dramatically during the era's second period. In the early 1960s a single set of positions emerged. Medications appeared profound in every dimension, with regard to individuals and institutions alike. The structure of belief tightened, and unmovable foundational beliefs anchored it.

New discoveries did not produce these changes. The most surprising discovery of the time uncovered widespread, persistent neurological damage caused by medication—tardive dyskinesia—but that fact found no place in the new structure of belief. Nothing else that should have pushed psychiatric belief to the extremes—where structures inevitably tightened—came along. The 1960s revolution in psychiatric thought largely consisted of the appearance of a rigid structure, anchored by the belief that medication was, after all, a truly antipsychotic treatment.

Chapter 3

A New Vision of Medication

A RADICAL CHANGE in psychiatric thinking took hold during the early 1960s and inaugurated the second period of the era. The old diversity of viewpoint faded, and a vision that portrayed medication as profound in every dimension appeared. Psychiatrists saw profound effects on mental illness; researchers devised deep theories to explain how medication worked in the brain and how the public mental health system should work in society. Most supposed that medication had transformed psychiatry and eliminated the ethical dilemmas that had bedeviled psychiatrists in earlier eras.

This new vision took hold quickly, as if a major discovery had occurred. None had. Landmark research was published during the early 1960s, but its contribution was of a different kind. Two projects—one headed by Jesse F. Casey, the results of which appeared in 1960, the other a 1964 National Institute of Mental Health Collaborative Study led by Jonathan Cole—rigorously demonstrated the effectiveness of medication against many symptoms of schizophrenia, and the "clear superior[ity]" of medication to a placebo. Neither result surprised psychiatrists, since each confirmed widely held views. Thus, the findings should not have impelled a major change in thinking about medications. Yet they did.[1]

The two studies represented milestones because of their rigorous methodology. Each employed placebo controls, used a "double-blind" design (in which neither patients nor those evaluating their conditions were told which subjects were receiving placebo or active medications), and included a large number of patients. The failure to incorporate similar safeguards in earlier studies had led psychiatrists to overvalue lobotomy and to overlook the possibility that insulin coma therapy worked no better than a placebo.[2]

Casey and his collaborators published two reports in 1960. The first did not portray medication in any new way. Instead, it described the drugs as tranquilizers. Aside from the methodological innovations, the report read like a typical work of the 1950s. The 1964 Collaborative Study was different. Based on findings about the effectiveness of medication, it erected a new vision of "antischizophrenic" or antipsychotic medications.[3]

Standard versions of the history of psychiatry rest on the claim that the Collaborative Study—or some comparable research—made discoveries that produced the new picture of medications. Yet that picture did not emerge from Casey's investigation, despite its similar findings. In fact, the desire for a new vision explains the Study better than the Study can explain the new vision.

Effectiveness: The 1960 Casey Study

Casey's 1960 experiment included more than 800 patients at 37 different veterans' hospitals. Over a twelve-week period the subjects received one of four substances, including chlorpromazine or a placebo, in "double-blind" fashion. Most then participated in a twelve-week "blind crossover": some received the same treatment during this period—for a total of twenty-four weeks—while others were shifted from an active medication to placebo or vice versa. Throughout the experiment, psychiatrists rated subjects on a variety of symptoms, and subjects rated themselves.[4]

All subjects suffered from a "schizophrenic reaction," but their chronicity and levels of disturbance differed. Two-thirds were chronic and not disturbed. The others fell into the acute-disturbed, acute-undisturbed, and chronic-disturbed categories. Chlorpromazine proved "clearly superior" to the placebo and the other tested treatments in its capacity to relieve symptoms. It "produced striking improvement," Casey reported, particularly during the initial twelve-week period. That result, he observed, was "consonant with most clinical experience."[5]

Other findings were less expected. For one, patients who received a placebo after an initial twelve weeks of chlorpromazine "maintained much of the[ir] improvement." Casey surmised that "[s]ome carry-over effect may be obtained from treatment" with medications—a "surprising" result, he thought, given the prevailing clinical belief that patients relapsed quickly without medication. For another thing, placebo patients suffered significantly less "self-depreciation, a symptom of mental depression" than patients treated with active medication. That prompted Casey to speculate that medications may "aggravate" depression—a noteworthy possibility, but also one suggested by past "[c]linical evidence" and experience.[6]

The study's general side effect findings surprised Casey even more. Side effects were reported to be "minimal" overall, with none "severe." Only 7 out of

170 chlorpromazine patients had to leave the study because of side effects, most because of the "extrapyramidal syndrome." According to the participating hospitals, only 5 percent of chlorpromazine patients developed any "noticeable side-effects" at all.[7]

Casey discounted those results. The reports of a "comparatively small number" of side effects "could not be generalized beyond the present sample," he wrote. Presumably, he found the number too "small" based on "clinical experience," the same benchmark against which he judged other study results. Casey's explanation of the disparity—most study patients "had received tranquilizing drugs before," he wrote, and "[p]resumably . . . [had] become 'desensitized' to some of the side-effects"—seems unconvincing, however; his clinical experience had surely included many patients, like those in the study, who had received medication before and who still experienced side effects.[8]

Casey's language and thinking comported with views from the 1950s. He described medications as "tranquilizing agents," paid attention to subjective feelings, and doubted that medication really produced "minimal side effects" despite the findings of his own study. His use of older clinical impressions as a benchmark also bespoke continuity with the past.[9]

Moreover, unlike the authors of the Collaborative Study, Casey did not infer profound effects on schizophrenia or any profound mechanism of drug action from the findings about effectiveness. To the contrary, he implied that patients remained seriously ill despite the "symptomatic relief" that medication afforded. Thus, Casey observed that half of the subjects proved incapable of completing their own self-ratings, while those who did complete them produced "answers of doubtful reliability." One gets the impression not of patients making dramatic strides on medication but rather of people so impaired that they cannot describe their own mental condition in a meaningful way. In the same vein, Casey described the study's "average patient" as someone "severely ill" who "[i]n terms of the most realistic treatment goals . . . would require a minimal degree of nursing care and would participate, though not very much, in ward activities. If he were able to be released from the hospital, it would be in the care of his family, and the probability of his return would be high. He would be either unproductive economically or only partially self-supporting."[10] The use of medication apparently did not change these "realistic treatment goals."

Chronic patients had predominated in the study, but Casey did not claim that circumstance had significantly affected his results. Such patients "did not afford the most sensitive group for demonstrating therapeutic effects," he observed; presumably they had proved refractory to medications in the past (or else why would they be chronic?). Nonetheless, Casey found his "results . . . consonant with most clinical experience"—that is, about right. "Therapeutic effects" among less chronic, more disturbed patients would be "more easily demonstrable," Casey said, but he did not imply that the effects would differ in kind.[11]

Within the next few years, psychiatrists assiduously pursued lines of argument that amplified the benefits of medication' and obscured its side effects. Casey had not. To the contrary, he portrayed his results as understating side effects (supposedly because of the makeup of the study groups). He avoided arguing that the use of chronic subjects had produced an underestimate of the benefits of medication. Those things, as much as anything, mark Casey's article as a product of the era's first period.

Psychiatric viewpoints were already shifting, however. Some of these changes broke through in a second large-scale study that Casey published in the same year, 1960. This study rested on slightly later research and, except for Leo F. Hollister, different junior authors collaborated on it with Casey. Yet nothing in the work itself accounted for the departures from Casey's first 1960 article.

The second study compared chlorpromazine to four newer medications among recently hospitalized (as opposed to chronic) patients with schizophrenia. Physicians evaluated the subjects' readiness for discharge, among other things. Like Casey's first study, this one included hundreds of patients from various Veterans Administration hospitals, rated their symptoms and side effects, and proceeded in double-blind fashion.[12]

Casey again found chlorpromazine effective, as were three of the other four tested medications. Yet his write-up of the results differed in notable ways this time. The first study consistently referred to medications as "tranquilizing agents." The second avoided that term; it referred to medications instead as "phenothiazines" or "phenothiazine derivatives"—the name of their chemical family. Casey did not explain this change in terminology, and it had no connection to anything else in the report. The idea of medications as tranquilizers was simply falling into disfavor.[13]

Another difference involved side effects. The two studies reported a similar basic finding: very few patients suffered side effects serious enough to warrant dropping them from the experiment. Yet the second study did not reiterate Casey's earlier contention that clinical experience contradicted the finding of a low rate of side effects. Instead, it described "the comparative paucity of severe abnormalities, accounting for only a 3 % loss in the total sample" as its "most outstanding finding." The extent of less severe reactions did not even get reported; for that, the article referred readers to a forthcoming publication on the same experiment.[14]

The change in view and rhetoric was significant and pervasive. Blood disorders were chlorpromazine's most worrisome side effect, but none showed up in the study and "laboratory tests" failed to detect any. "These complications,"

Casey concluded, "may have been more feared in the past than was warranted." Moreover, some patients had received phenobarbital, a biologically active agent that, like chlorpromazine, induced drowsiness (but unlike chlorpromazine was not a tranquilizing drug); these patients experienced "abnormal symptoms" in numbers comparable to those on chlorpromazine—including some symptoms never before associated with phenobarbital. On that basis, Casey urged caution "in ascribing all that happens during drug therapy to the drugs being used." Yet the "surprisingly" high number of side effects reported with phenobarbital still did not explain the comparatively small number of such effects—and particularly extrapyramidal effects—reported with chlorpromazine. And, since the diagnosis of these effects rested on observation, not laboratory tests, this situation did not resemble the blood disorders. Here, psychiatrists—not tests—apparently had failed to detect problems.[15]

Evidently, Casey no longer tested the plausibility of research findings—including findings about side effects—against clinical experience. Clinical observation had a more subordinate relationship to research now. Casey envisioned a clinician taking the "considerable information" supplied by research about "clinical effectiveness, side effects and toxicity," adding "his personal experience," and then "select[ing] a specific drug for an individual patient." Thus, clinicians practiced in the interstices of research; the latter established everything important except the selection of a "specific" medication from among the many available.[16]

Regarding side effects in particular, Casey weighed the findings of a multicenter study more heavily than "clinical experience" or past psychiatric understandings. Leading psychiatrists had urged exactly that approach toward the benefits of medication. They had feared clinicians would exaggerate benefits and had believed rigorous studies would avoid bias. Yet it seems unlikely that clinicians would have the same tendency to overestimate side effects as they did benefits. Nor is it obvious that a large, double blind multicenter trial brings the same advantages to assessing side effects that it does to tests of efficacy.

The double-blind theoretically eliminates rater bias in favor of a treatment. Raters who do not know which patient is receiving which treatment cannot inflate the results of any treatment, unconsciously or otherwise. Nor does it make sense for them to inflate or deflate outcomes across the board. Doing so would make their favored, active treatment appear no better than a placebo.

The situation is different for side effects. Raters with an unconscious bias may underreport *all* side effects known to be associated with the active treatment. Doing so would make the active treatment appear safer. When evaluating therapeutic efficacy, treatments indistinguishable from a placebo fail; but when evaluating side effects, treatments indistinguishable from a placebo are ideal. Thus, bias can operate against finding side effects, despite the "double-blind"; quite possibly, such bias affected Casey's trials and, later, the Collaborative Study.

Whatever the explanation, Casey's change in thinking portended much larger shifts in psychiatry during the era's second period. The multicenter trial became a means of making past clinical—and even academic—understandings of medication appear irrelevant. Those observations lost weight because they apparently lacked the necessary methodological rigor. Yet older observations proved more accurate about side effects in the end.

Rigor had acquired an aura; it blinded psychiatrists to what had once been obvious. Or did psychiatrists want to forget the obvious?

The Collaborative Study

The Collaborative Study rigorously investigated one set of questions—and then offered revolutionary answers for a different set of questions entirely. It staked a claim to rigor on its very first page, noting that large multicenter trials had played a prominent role in other medical specialties, but not in psychiatry. Aside from Casey's recent investigations and a few older studies of premedication treatments, there was nothing, the Study's authors noted—and Casey had studied either chronic patients or newly admitted subjects who, for the most part, had a history of prior hospitalizations. Most patients in the Collaborative Study, by contrast, had no prior hospitalizations: half were enduring their first psychotic episode, and most of the rest were suffering only their second. Thus the Study represented the first research to rigorously examine the effects of medication on the patient group most likely to achieve "full rehabilitation" and to fully demonstrate the treatment's "potential public health impact."[17]

The claim to rigor—and the Study itself—had an interesting history, which Gerald Grob has described. In 1955, Mike Gorman, a lobbyist, and Nathan S. Kline helped persuade Congress to fund what eventually became the Collaborative Study. The National Institute of Mental Health was to perform the research, but the agency's leaders proceeded slowly. Robert Felix, the head of NIMH, feared that an insufficiently rigorous investigation of medication would yield overly generous and favorable conclusions, as had happened in earlier evaluations of lobotomy and shock therapy. Not wanting to repeat the same mistakes, Felix told a congressional committee in 1957 that the project required new methods of evaluation. Research did not actually begin until 1961.[18]

Published in 1964, the Collaborative Study became a classic. Swazey's history treated it as a defining moment of the medication era. Today, it remains an authoritative demonstration of the effectiveness of medication against schizophrenic symptoms.[19]

Like Casey, the Study's authors used rigorous methods to investigate the effects of medication on symptoms and to examine side effects. Yet the Study also drew conclusions about other issues, which lay at—or beyond—the limits of its research design. These issues included the nature, and not just the extent, of the benefits of medication; how those benefits came about; and the treatment's implications for public mental health. The Study's findings on effectiveness only confirmed what most psychiatrists already believed; the other conclusions ushered in a revolution in thinking about medications.

EFFECTIVENESS

The Study involved 463 newly admitted patients at 9 hospitals. In double-blind fashion, it evaluated four substances: chlorpromazine, fluphenazine (a newer phenothiazine that reputedly produced more side effects than chlorpromazine), thioridazine (a newer medication that reputedly produced fewer side effects), and a placebo. Patients received one of these agents for six weeks as researchers periodically rated their symptoms and side effects. The ratings also included a global score, reflecting the evaluator's impression of a patient's overall condition.

The three tested medications proved equally effective against symptoms. Over the six-week period, 95 percent of medicated patients improved. Seventy-five percent showed "much" or "very much" improvement. The placebo patients improved as a group too, but at a significantly lower rate. Twenty-three percent of placebo patients showed "much" or "very much improvement." Another 27 percent manifested minimal improvement, and the rest did not improve or became worse.

The advantage of medication over placebo was considerable. Only 5 percent of medicated patients—but 50 percent of placebo patients—did not improve. And only 25 percent of those on medications—compared with 77 percent on placebo—failed to show at least "much improvement."[20]

Despite this impressive advantage, the data did not necessarily suggest that everyone with schizophrenia should receive medications. Twenty-five percent of medicated patients failed to show "much" improvement, while 23 percent of placebo patients did. Thus, one might have concluded that almost half the patients in the sample were candidates for treatment without medication—particularly if some other reason to withhold medications, such as side effects, emerged.

Nor did the findings answer every important question about the effects of medication on symptoms. The Study did not determine how long improvement lasted. Since schizophrenia is a cyclical disease, this question had some significance. Nor did the Study determine how many additional placebo (or medicated) patients would have improved over a longer treatment period. If patients on placebo improved more slowly than those on medication—a plausible assumption—the six-week study period might have exaggerated the advantage of drugs. Finally, the Study did not examine how medication affected the course of schizophrenia over a patient's lifetime or, in the shorter term, how they affected someone's ability to work, relate to others, or derive satisfaction from life.[21]

In any case, the Study's findings on effectiveness did not resolve fundamental questions. Standing alone, the findings did not mean that medication worked profoundly, as opposed to affording only symptomatic relief. Moreover, an effective therapy could still produce terrible side effects. Nor did the findings unmistakably point toward a particular mental health system, or to a transformed profession. A psychiatrist could accept the Study's results regarding effectiveness and, without self-contradiction, still regard medications as tranquilizers, favor large state mental hospitals over community treatment, and judge psychiatry a profession essentially unchanged since the era of lobotomy. Indeed, many psychiatrists had subscribed to such positions in the 1950s, while believing medication effective against symptoms.

The unresolved questions did receive the Study's attention, however. Of these, only one—side effects—received any rigorous investigation. And in relation to side effects, the Study produced seriously mistaken results.

SIDE EFFECTS

The Study characterized side effects "as generally mild or infrequent" and as "more a matter of patient comfort than of medical safety."[22] "[S]ide effects do occur," it noted, but they "are for the most part trivial and more annoying and discomforting to the patient than potentially dangerous. They seldom necessitate discontinuance of treatment, at least in a hospital setting."[23] The low level of side effects "attest[ed] . . . to the general safety" of drugs.

To reach such conclusions, the Study used side effect checklists and rating scales. Evaluators examined patients and filled out the forms. The results were then compiled into a table listing side effects of "at Least Moderate Severity" and the percentage of affected patients. The checklists, however, omitted some significant side effects. The raters apparently underreported others. And the Study's general conclusions on the subject rested as much on rhetorical innovation as on data.

The most striking omission involved persistent effects. Being limited to six weeks, the Study could not determine whether, or how long, side effects lasted after medication stopped. Of course, a study of effectiveness need not address that issue. Without doing so, however, psychiatrists could hardly pronounce side effects "trivial" or medications "safe." Nor did the Study mention the possibility of persistent or permanent side effects.

Beyond that, Study checklists omitted dyskinesias: the very effects that some researchers had already found to persist. Other psychiatrists regarded dyskinesias as relatively common, reversible medication side effects, yet no dyskinesias, persistent or reversible, appeared on Study evaluation forms.[24] In connection with a later NIMH collaborative study, George Crane observed that: "[a] checklist of common side effects was prepared for the use of individual investigators, but since items describing disorders consistent with dyskinesia were not included in this list, data from the main project could not be utilized to assess the incidence of dyskinesia."[25] The same was true of the 1964 Collaborative Study.

It is true that the literature included relatively few reports of persistent or tardive dyskinesia; not until the late 1960s did it begin to receive much recognition in the United States. Few Collaborative Study subjects would have had tardive dyskinesia in any event; their exposure to medication was too brief. The disorder rarely develops within the first six weeks of treatment, except in elderly patients, and since a large majority of subjects were undergoing only their first or their second psychotic episode, they would have received little medication in the past. Yet even if the Collaborative Study could not investigate the persistence issue, why did it exclude a recognized side effect from its checklists? And why did it exclude the very effect that, based on the existing literature, seemed most likely to reflect permanent neurological harm from medication?

Although the tardive dyskinesia literature remained small, concern about permanent side effects permeated the air. Later, George Crane recalled that physicians had expected to discover permanent side effects from the very "beginning" of the medication era, although early suspicion had centered on Parkinson's disease–like symptoms, not dyskinesias.[26] For that matter, Jonathan Cole, the Study's principal author, had written in 1960:

> Another problem which might be associated with the clinical use of psychiatric drugs is the possible occurrence of irreversible brain changes. The only positive evidence on this point is derived from work with animals and is of questionable clinical significance. Both chlorpromazine . . . and reserpine . . . have been reported to produce fine neuropathological changes at the cellular level in monkeys. In both studies only a few monkeys were observed and essential controls were lacking. At the clinical level there is a complete lack of evidence that irreversible neurological changes occur in patients after prolonged drug administration. The absence of reported cases does not prove that such phenomena do not occur; on the other hand, if such phenomena were appearing frequently and were constituting a major problem, one would think that at least preliminary reports would have reached the literature by this time."[27]

Four years later, "preliminary reports" had "reached the literature," but the Collaborative Study ignored even the possibility of persistent side effects.

There were other reasons to suspect "irreversible brain changes." During the 1950s, Deniker had described dyskinesia as a characteristic brain response to a neuroleptic induced "disease." But if medication produced brain disease and dyskinesia, surely it might also produce a persistent dyskinesia. And only a decade earlier, the "chemical lobotomy" idea had invited comparisons between medication and a measure that produced permanent brain damage by design. Again, many 1950s psychiatrists believed that drug effectiveness depended on signs of brain malfunction, in the form of extrapyramidal symptoms; obviously, the possibility existed that the malfunctions would persist. In 1956, Hall reported that side effects could last months after drug discontinuation; thus, the malfunctions lasted at least that long.

The Study ignored these considerations, just as its protocols ignored dyskinesias. After the lobotomy debacle, a "safe" treatment could hardly induce permanent side effects. By fiat, the Study made the safety of medication a forgone conclusion.

In a different way, the Study abolished the "syndrome of psychomotor indifference" that had defined medications during 1950s. The component symptoms of the syndrome appeared on Study checklists; the syndrome itself did not. Thus, the Study reported facial or muscular rigidity and loss of movement—"motor indifference"—but each symptom appeared under a separate table entry. Among patients receiving chlorpromazine, for example, 12.5 percent showed "muscle rigidity," 3.5 percent had "loss of associated movements," and another 12.5 percent "facial rigidity"—all at the moderately severe level or higher. Since the Study did not indicate how many patients suffered multiple symptoms, or less severe symptoms, one cannot gauge the overall prevalence of motor indifference. It was clearly sizable, however.

If the Study unbundled the syndrome's physical components, it ignored the subjective ones. Lack of will or desire—mental "indifference"—did not appear on checklists. No subjective side effect did: no drug-induced distress or mental dysfunction of any kind. Like dyskinesia and persistence, those things were eliminated as a matter of definition and research design. And, as before, the Study's lead author had approached things differently in 1960. "[T]he parkinsonian syndrome," Cole wrote then, represented "a relatively clear-cut pharmacological action" of medications that, in extreme cases, produced a "pharmacological strait jacket"; "milder forms" of the syndrome, he continued, "may be an important form of behavioral toxicity which is not always readily apparent."[28]

Akathisia, another side effect, produces the opposite of psychomotor indifference. Patients move restlessly, sometimes displaying distinctive movements of their feet or knees. They often feel a distressing desire to move as well. Hating the endless jumpiness, irritability, and distress, many patients find akathisia the least endurable side effect.[29]

Study tables ignored the subjective symptoms of akathisia and reported low rates for the physical ones. Under "Akathisia—restlessness of feet," the tables reported a prevalence of 6, 12, and 5 percent for the three tested medications, and 4 percent for placebo. A second table entry, "restlessness," reported higher figures: 39 to 47 percent in the medicated groups, 38 percent among those receiving placebo. It is not clear whether the "restlessness" figures included only— or any—cases of akathisia, but in any event drug-placebo differences were remarkably small. Today psychiatrists recognize akathisia as "common" and cite prevalence estimates as high as 70 percent.[30]

The Study's slighting of subjective response and behavioral change appear remarkable, especially since Cole had emphasized them in his earlier writing. In his 1960 essay, Cole also wrote:

> [A]ny broad consideration of behavioral toxicity in man must take into account both the subjective mood changes and the objective performance changes induced by drugs. . . .
>
> Many unpleasant side effects of a drug may appear when the drug is given in usual therapeutic dosages. . . . Such unpleasant drug actions . . . are often closely related to the desirable pharmacological properties of the drug, and can be produced in almost any patient if moderately large doses of the drug are used, although there may be considerable individual difference in this regard.
>
> The most impressive characteristic of the psychiatric drug literature is the absence of serious concern about adverse effects these drugs may be having upon behavior.[31]

These strictures, like the possibility of permanent neurological changes, were forgotten in the Study.

Even accepting its data at face value, the characterization of side effects as "trivial" or "generally mild or infrequent" reflected more art than accuracy. The Study's own tables indicated that a number of side effects occurred fairly frequently, at the moderately severe level or worse. Almost half the patients suffered drowsiness that qualified; 15 percent to 20 percent developed nausea; almost 1 percent became faint or passed out. As noted earlier, the Study also reported considerable drug-induced parkinsonism.

Apparently, the phrase "*generally* mild or infrequent" meant that more side effects occurred at mild than at severe levels, and that more were infrequent than common. On that reading, even if 49 percent of patients developed tardive dyskinesia, side effects would remain "generally" mild and infrequent: the mild side effects still would outnumber the severe ones. The word "generally" had acquired a remarkably literal meaning.

The Study also labeled side effects "more a matter of patient comfort than of medical safety." Yet another therapy that induced "at least moderate" parkinson's disease symptoms in perhaps a quarter of patients would not likely be described as a measure that affected only "patient comfort." Parkinson's disease, after all, represents a serious brain impairment. During the 1950s, the same syndrome led psychiatrists to hypothesize a medication-induced brain disease. And earlier reports often used more descriptive terms than "discomfort"—describing patient anguish, for example. In any case, since "comfort"—like other subjective states—did not get registered or measured in the Study tables, "discomfort" could mean almost anything, including "anguish."

In large part, the Study arrived at its conclusions about side effects by redefining older terms, such as "safety" and "seriousness." It then found that medications fared well under the new definitions. The redefinitions advanced no scientific purpose; they merely allowed the Study to minimize the significance of side effects.

ANTISCHIZOPHRENIC EFFECTS

The Study minimized side effects by excluding known phenomena from its categories, drawing inferences from the resulting absence of negative data, and applying new meanings to terms such as "safety." It pursued a similar strategy in relation to the benefits of medication, except that now it aimed to enhance, rather than minimize, the changes associated with drugs. The Study assiduously collected data about benefits and then rhetorically magnified what it found by applying new meanings to old terms. In this way, it produced questionable general conclusions about the quality of patients' improvement and the workings of medications against disease.

The data showed that medication lessened many schizophrenic symptoms, such as incoherence or hallucinations. That led the authors to conclude that medications exerted a "diverse and generalized effect . . . on the schizophrenic process." Moreover, since "[a]lmost all symptoms and manifestations characteristic of schizophrenic psychoses improved with drug therapy," the authors also concluded that "phenothiazines should be regarded as 'antischizophrenic' in the broad sense." In short, because medication affected many symptoms of schizophrenia, it qualified as an "antischizophrenic" agent. On the same basis—the number of affected symptoms—the Study announced a judgment about the "quality of drug-induced changes." "The effects of . . . [medications] are not only quantitative, in that a large percentage of patients improved," the authors wrote, "they are also qualitative, in that a wide range of schizophrenic symptoms and behavior are favorably altered."[32]

All this prompted a challenge to prevailing nomenclature and views. Psychiatrists still thought of medications as "tranquilizers," according to the Study, and still considered the drugs' primary effects as "alleviation of anxiety, diminution of overactivity, and reduction of disturbed behavior." Yet subjects who "were not overactive, excited, belligerent, or deluded" nonetheless showed improvement of such symptoms as incoherence of speech, slowness in speech, indifference, disorientation, and hallucinations. For that reason, the authors considered it "questionable whether the term 'tranquilizer' should be retained."

What emerged from the Study's inferences, judgments, and conclusions was an entirely new picture of medications. Medications did not constitute tranquilizers, as many psychiatrists had thought. Rather, psychiatry now possessed a true "antischizophrenic" agent that counteracted "the disease process" and thereby produced "impressive" qualitative change, while causing only "trivial" side effects.

This new picture, or vision, of medication defines the second period of the drug era. Yet it did not rest upon any new or unexpected factual discovery. To the contrary, psychiatrists had long recognized that medications ameliorated numerous symptoms of schizophrenia—the fact from which almost everything else supposedly followed.

The Study allowed as much. Its findings "*confirm* . . . [medications'] diverse and generalized effect" the Study said, obviously referring to an existing understanding among psychiatrists. A year later, Jonathan Cole wrote that the Study had "presented evidence to confirm what was generally believed—that phenothiazines . . . have a wide variety of clinical effects beyond tranquilization." Why, then, did psychiatrists suddenly change their minds—or at least their nomenclature—reject tranquilizer theory, and proclaim "antischizophrenic" effects against the "disease process?"[33]

The older views of medication had rested on different, richer, definitions of "qualitative," "antischizophrenic," and "tranquilizer." A "qualitative" change or "antischizophrenic" effect occurred when a patient seemed free of schizophrenic illness, not merely when symptoms—even a lot of them—appeared less florid. Thus, an article almost contemporaneous with the Study noted that medicated patients "changed dramatically" in behavior but concluded that the "observed changes did not suggest that the patients were any less schizophrenic." Rather, they were merely "exhibit[ing] . . . less florid symptomatology." For example, a patient who no longer did "cartwheels" in response to imaginary voices might "appear . . . more 'normal,' " but the voices—and so the disease—remained nonetheless. Such changes did not qualify as "qualitative" improvement: "The drug enables some patients to function independently of the hospital, while for others bizarre behavior is not sufficiently reduced and they must remain hospitalized. A third group of patients improve enough while on drugs to function part-time on their own. Nevertheless, all of these patients are still schizophrenic, and there is no evidence that any enduring and fundamental change has been achieved by medication."[34] That view of medications dominated during the first period of the medication era, but the same picture—and the same usage—emerged whenever a psychiatrist avoided the Study's equation of "qualitative" or "antischizophrenic" with "large number of symptoms." For example, in 1975 Columbia University psychiatrists provided the following account of their medicated subjects: "Although all patients were in remission from all psychotic signs, this left room for considerable psychopathology, as well as vocational and interpersonal difficulties. Our patients ran the gamut from those with a complete lack of psychopathology and with no functional impairment to others with chronical dysphoria [unhappiness] and marked vocational and social ineptitude, viz., chronic psychiatric invalids supported by public assistance who led dismal, empty, withdrawn lives. But none had delusions, hallucinations, disorganized speech, or bizarre behavior."[35] These observations did not contradict those of the Study or implicate any question of fact: the differences between the accounts resulted from the Study's definitions.[36]

Definitions cannot be mistaken, but they can confuse or appear arbitrary. The definitions used in the Study had those failings. They turned "chronic psychiatric invalids" with "dismal, empty, withdrawn" lives into beneficiaries of "antischizophrenic" effects and "qualitative change." As a result, once well-recognized distinctions between quantitative and qualitative, between treatments that ameliorate symptoms and those that cure a disease, disappeared. The Study did not call attention to its new definitions, either. Thus, readers could, and did, conclude that "antischizophrenic effects" and "qualitative change" represented discoveries about medication rather than proposals about what to say.

Viewed one way, this resort to new definitions appeared unnecessary. For in addition to rating particular symptoms, the Study also produced "global ratings" regarding the overall condition of patients. By themselves, these ratings suggested positive conclusions about medication. After six weeks of treatment, 54 percent of medicated patients received a global rating of "moderately mentally ill" or worse; 30 percent were "border-line mentally ill"; and 16 percent were "normal, not ill at all." Putting the findings in their best light, the authors of the Study observed that "almost half of . . . [medicated] patients do not show enough residual symptoms to be judged even 'mildly ill' after this short period of treatment."[37]

Why did the Study rely on the number of affected symptoms, not the global ratings, to justify claims about impressive qualitative change and antischizophrenic effects? In fact, the global ratings produced a less than stunning result. If 16 percent of medicated subjects received a "normal" score, so did 5 percent to 10 percent of the placebo patients. While hardly insignificant, the difference fell short of the miraculous. The apparent advantage of medication over a placebo increased in the category of "borderline mentally ill": 30 percent of medicated and about 10 percent of placebo subjects received that designation. Yet "borderline" represented a more subjective, less revealing category than "normal." For example, the patient described earlier, who no longer performed cartwheels in response to his auditory hallucinations, might well earn this rating because he could work a few hours a week.[38]

Moreover, even including borderline cases, the medication results did not dramatically differ from those claimed for other therapies in psychiatry. In 1955, Vernon Kinross-Wright provided estimates of the outcomes produced by various schizophrenia treatments, including medication:

Significant clinical improvement or better:

Custodial and supportive treatment only	29%
Convulsive shock therapy	49%
Insulin coma therapy	61%
Chlorpromazine	88%

Remission & much improved/social recovery or better:

Custodial and supportive treatment only	19%
Convulsive shock therapy	29%
Insulin coma therapy	48%
Chlorpromazine	76%

Complete recovery:

Custodial and supportive treatment only	5%
Convulsive shock therapy	6%
Insulin coma therapy	21%
Chlorpromazine	37%[39]

He concluded that chlorpromazine "appears to be superior" in effectiveness. Indeed, his estimates put medication in a better light than the Study did. For example, he thought medications produced "complete recovery" in 37 percent of cases, about twice as often as insulin coma; the Study found only 16 percent of patients free of symptoms, about double the placebo outcome. Yet these larger differences had not prompted Kinross-Wright to conclude that medication worked in a different way from older treatments. Rather, like many psychiatrists of the 1950s, he considered chlorpromazine a powerful tranquilizer that blocked patients' capacity to react to the world.[40]

Thus, the Study's global ratings did not radically distinguish medication from other schizophrenia treatments. The ratings did not make medication appear revolutionary. Medication did not seem "antischizophrenic" in the large number of cases in which patients failed to earn a rating of cured or even borderline. The Study's equation of "number of affected symptoms affected" with "antischizophrenic effects" suggested, however, that medications generally worked profoundly in every case. Judging by the global ratings, many patients seemingly derived little or no benefit from medications, judging from the existence of antischizophrenic effects, it appeared that everyone with schizophrenia benefited profoundly.

Before the medication era, psychiatrists' global judgments had notoriously overestimated biological therapies. Officials at NIMH strove to avoid precisely that mistake in the Study, so they focused on discrete disease elements and symptoms. Yet the Study did not avoid the old problems. Evaluations of lobotomy had failed, for example, because they did not capture the entire person; upon seeing someone who had undergone the procedure, a lay person was often struck by aspects of the person that the surgeon had ignored or minimized. The lists of discrete symptoms in the Study could produce the same discrepancies, and in fact did so when the authors equated number of symptoms affected with "antischizophrenic" effects and "qualitative" changes. The Study did not measure patients' capacity to relate to others, precisely the kind of thing lobotomists had ignored. Studied in the same way, lobotomy probably would have affected a large number of disease symptoms, too; one of the problems with the procedure was that it affected so many aspects of personality. Thus, the definitions in the Study would have made lobotomy an "antischizophrenic" therapy that produced "impressive qualitative changes" in patients. Innovations in definition and rhetoric had merely reintroduced the old problems.

FUNDAMENTAL SYMPTOMS AND TRANQUILIZATION

The authors of the Study seemed to appreciate these difficulties, and they fashioned two arguments to enhance the case for antischizophrenic effects. The first argument appeared in a reanalysis of Study data that Cole and other NIMH researchers published in 1965. This new analysis portrayed three symptoms of schizophrenia—facial grimacing, slowed speech, and indifference to environment —as "fundamental" to the disease, observing that each had improved with the use of medication but not with a placebo. Although a fourth "fundamental symptom," incoherent speech, responded better to placebo than to medication, the authors cautiously concluded that medication affected "the fundamental [schizophrenic] disease process" in ways that a placebo did not.[41]

This analysis employed a meaningful definition of "antischizophrenic," but it also involved problems that went unnoticed by the authors. The Study had not demonstrated that medication produces patterns of symptomatic change different from those of other biological therapies, such as coma or lo-botomy. Those other treatments simply had not been tested in the Study, so one could draw no inferences about the superiority of medication. Moreover, if facial grimacing and indifference constituted "fundamental" aspects of the disease, what to make of the capacity of medication to *cause* those symptoms in the form of side effects? Orofacial dyskinesia resembled grimacing; psy-chomotor indifference was a trademark of major tranquilizers in the 1950s. If ameliorating those symptoms reflected a "fundamental" improvement in schiz-ophrenia, by the same logic producing the symptoms indicated a "fundamen-tal" worsening—or, as Deniker had thought, the infliction of a brain disease.

This possibility received no attention, however. Side effects that mimicked "fundamental" aspects of the disease remained "trivial" or, in the case of dysk-inesia, wholly ignored. Yet a "fundamental symptoms" approach actually en-hanced the significance of tardive dyskinesia. If dyskinetic grimaces became permanent, that suggested a permanent exacerbation of the disease as well. By the late 1960s, the argument about "fundamental" symptoms attracted little at-tention, and the increasing number of reports about tardive dyskinesia may ex-plain why.

Another argument used to buttress "antischizophrenic" effects was im-plied in the Study itself. It rested on the supposed weaknesses of the idea that medications worked as tranquilizers. The reasons for regarding medications as "antischizophrenic"—their "diverse and generalized" effects and the benefits re-alized by nonhyperactive patients—also supposedly undercut the tranquiliza-tion concept. Although the evidence for "antischizophrenic," and against "tranquilizing," overlapped, the demise of the principal competing theory made the former view more plausible.

The Study's side effect findings enhanced the argument. For several reasons —the high reporting threshold, the splintering of "psychomotor indifference" into smaller discrete elements, the likely underreporting—it found less "tran-quilization" than many 1950s psychiatrists did. And if medications did not "tranquilize," how could they constitute "tranquilizers?" Yet the Study never as-serted that mild levels of indifference were rare. The authors may have found their own "indifference" ratings less than credible. According to the Study, the "tranquilizer" view was "oversimplified." Yet it should have qualified as "false" if medication actually reduced patient apathy and produced little "indifference," as the Study claimed.

A more obvious flaw lay in the failure of the Study to describe tranquil-ization theory in the form that psychiatrists had actually held it. The theory did not mean that drugs tranquilized patients and nothing else happened. Rather, it supposed that people with schizophrenia hallucinated less, manifested less pressure of speech, and so on, *because* they were tranquilized. That did not preclude diverse effects on symptoms; it merely posited a less specific method of pharmacological action. The Study found tranquilization inadequate by ignoring the actual content of the theory.

Remarkably, when Cole and other NIMH researchers revisited the data in 1965, they went so far as to suggest tranquilization as an *explanation* for the diverse effects of medication:

> What possible meaning can be ascribed to the wide variety of clinical effects of the phenothiazines? One popular notion . . . is that the varied psychopathology of schizophrenia is produced by a common core of anxiety to be found in every schizophrenic patient, and since the drugs relieve anxiety there is only an apparent varied effect. To some extent our results are consistent with this interpretation since more than 95 per cent of our patients manifest Agitation and Tension, the symptom measure which most closely approximates anxiety. . . . If the phenothiazines serve to dampen physiological arousal, the exaggerated behavior known to us as symptoms will not be produced. For this hypothesis to be valid, it is not necessary for "arousal" to be correlated with the symptoms it is the basis of, since arousal lead to an exaggeration of personality characteristics, which differ among patients.[42]

In short, tranquilizer theory represented a promising explanation of the "apparent varied effect" of medication.

The popular current name, "antipsychotics," followed from the Study: its idea of abandoning the word "tranquilizer" prevailed. Younger researchers and clinicians simply stopped referring to medications as "major tranquilizers." Medications became "antipsychotics"—rather than "antischizophrenics"— because psychiatrists used them to treat conditions other than schizophrenia, a practice itself in tension with the idea that the treatment targeted fundamental schizophrenic processes.

The Collaborative Study Vision

Psychiatrists proceeded as if the Study had uncovered new facts about medication—as if "qualitative change," "antischizophrenic in the broad sense," and "trivial side effects" represented true discoveries. That created the appearance of a major research and treatment breakthrough, and matters did not rest there. Much of the profession went on to further inflate Study conclusions, beyond what its own authors had claimed. The "Collaborative Study vision" of medication had a reach and a force that surpassed the Study's own.

Judith Swazey's history of chlorpromazine appeared in 1974, and it reflected the new vision. According to Swazey, the results of the Study "still stand as the most definitive demonstration of a fact gradually perceived by psychiatrists during the 1950s: that CPZ [chlorpromazine] is not just a 'glorified sedative,' a drug uniquely effective in controlling psychotic excitation, but a true 'antischizophrenia' drug, with highly specific actions against the range of symptoms characterizing the schizophrenic illness."[43] The Study had equated the wide range of affected symptoms with "antischizophrenic" actions "in the broad sense." In Swazey's view that "demonstrat[ed]" that medications constituted "true" antischizophrenia agents with "highly specific" actions against the disease. The Study's "broad sense" fell far short of that, however. Swazey was depicting medication as something closer to a "magic bullet" against schizophrenia than the Study had.[44]

The new vision of medication took hold with such force that inconsistent data could not penetrate it. Thus, a few reports suggested that high doses of conventional tranquilizers produced "rapid and substantial" improvement in schizophrenia—improvement that rivaled, or even exceeded, what antipsychotics produced. Surprised, the authors of a 1992 American Psychiatric Association task force report wrote:

> Although conventional wisdom suggests that benzodiazepines
> [tranquilizers, such as Valium] would not be useful in schizophrenia,
> except perhaps to reduce akathisia, there are now several studies,
> some controlled, that suggest that benzodiazepines sometimes are
> surprisingly effective, particularly in higher doses. These studies have
> generally been only of a few weeks duration.
>   In a 24-hour controlled study, Lerner . . . found that . . . [tranquil
> izers and antipsychotics] were essentially identical in efficacy and . . .
> all patients improved substantially . . . Maculam . . . found that
> improvement during 3 weeks on . . . [tranquilizers] was essentially the
> same (59.2%) as after 3 weeks on . . . chlorpromazine. . . .
>   Hass described remarkable decreases in psychopathology on a high-
> dose . . . [tranquilizer] regimen.[45]

The studies cited in the report appeared between 1964 and 1983, but psychiatrists largely ignored them, and they became mere curiosities. Their fate, and the task force's surprise, reflected the triumph of the Study vision. Conventional wisdom held that tranquilizers could not perform like antipsychotics only because the Study made it so. When antipsychotics were known as "major tranquilizers," psychiatrists would have expected high doses of ordinary tranquilizers to yield such results.

As the "antipsychotic" label took hold, it became associated with a theory of how medication worked in brain—a subject the Study had not explored. The theory identified schizophrenia with an imbalance of a brain neurotransmitter called dopamine. Medication supposedly redressed the imbalance and so reversed the disease.

Many psychiatrists—particularly those who testified in courts or spoke to the media, and clinicians more than researchers—perceived a profound, almost tautological relationship between "antipsychotic" effects and the dopamine theory. Since medications are "antischizophrenic," they have antischizophrenic actions in the brain. Since medications reduce dopamine activity, an excess of that dopamine activity must cause schizophrenia. And since medications act on the neurochemical cause of schizophrenia, they must affect symptoms profoundly. Each tenet followed from and reinforced the others.

In this way, the dopamine hypothesis inflated and tightened the Study picture of medication. Medication did not just produce "antischizophrenic effects in the broad sense," as the Study said; rather, it reversed the causes of schizophrenia in the brain. That made it a "truer" antischizophrenic agent. The result was a tightly wound system of psychiatric belief, but one based on specious connections between ideas. From our adoption of the word "antischizophrenic," we cannot infer that a dopamine imbalance causes schizophrenia. From our observations about dopamine activity alone, we cannot infer that medication acts on the causes of mental illness, or that it produces better results than other therapies that work in entirely different ways. Nothing makes those inferences necessarily false, either: necessity simply has no place in the analysis. Yet large numbers of psychiatrists seemed to feel that the dopamine research and the Study conclusions about "antischizophrenic" effects had settled the fundamental questions of how—and of how well—medications worked.

The logical and factual errors of simple imbalance theory—and also the power of the Study vision that produced it—emerge from a 1991 overview by Kenneth Davis. According to Davis, the theory began with observation that drugs that "increase dopamine activity generally worsen the symptoms of schizophrenia." After 1980, however, data emerged that challenged the theory. For one thing, "a substantial proportion of schizophrenic patients are resistant to treatment with neuroleptics." For another, "schizophrenic-like symptoms are rarely, if ever, induced in nonschizophrenic individuals when they are administered drugs that augment dopaminergic activity." Moreover, medications "only partially . . . alleviat[e] . . . negative, or deficit, symptoms" of schizophrenia—an indication, Davis wrote, that these "symptoms may be unrelated to excessive dopamine activity." Finally, recent research had revealed that "excessive dopamine activity" does not occur "in all brain regions" of people who have schizophrenia.[46]

Although Davis did not distinguish them, these challenges to dopamine theory fell into two categories. Those in the first arose from research that postdated the formulation of dopamine hypothesis, and so from facts unknown to the psychiatrists who developed it. For example, only later experiments demonstrated that otherwise healthy people rarely develop schizophrenic symptoms because of increased dopamine activity and that some people with schizophrenia show too little dopamine activity—rather than too much—in some regions of their brain. These results clashed with the dopamine imbalance idea, but by themselves did not suggest that any systematic vision of medications lay behind it.

The second category suggests exactly that. Here the challenges arose from facts that had been apparent in the first period of the medication era. Psychiatrists knew then that "a substantial proportion of schizophrenic patients are resistant to treatment with neuroleptics," and also that "neuroleptics are only partially effective in alleviating . . . negative, or deficit symptoms." No experiment was required to elicit such facts. Rather, the Study vision was required to obscure them.

Positing antischizophrenic effects and reductions in dopamine activity, imbalance theory concluded that excess dopamine activity caused schizophrenia. Davis argued from the opposite direction. Since medication often fails to produce antischizophrenic effects, he reasoned, a simple excess of dopamine activity cannot cause the disease. Davis's point appears obvious, but many psychiatrists under the sway of the Study missed it. Since they inferred antischizophrenic effects from the dopamine hypothesis itself, the hypothesis became irrefutable—and Davis's later point became impossible to grasp. After the vision dissolved, it became obvious once again.

Davis's analysis illustrated not just the force of the vision and the consequences of its collapse, but also how standard views of the medication era ignore the vision's rise and fall—indeed, its very existence. Thus, Davis did not distinguish between the two types of flaw in the theory; he wrote as though recent discoveries underlay all of them. Why did psychiatrists forget what they had known in the first period of the era—that patients often respond to medications partially, or not at all? By Davis's account—standard among psychiatrists today—no rollback of prior understandings ever occurred, and so no explanation for the gap is required. A vision is transparent and undetectable to those who accept it; and the Study vision lives on in modern approaches to psychiatric history.

As a part of that vision, the dopamine hypothesis had far-reaching consequences. By raising the concept of a "true antischizophrenic treatment" to the neurochemical level, it appeared to suggest that other types of explanation were fundamentally flawed. Tranquilization theory was no longer just misleading, as the Study portrayed it; now it offered an entirely wrong kind of explanation. It posited vague mental states, such as anxiety, when medication lent itself to explanations in terms of the brain. If "antischizophrenic" sounded more rigorous than "tranquilization," neurochemical processes sounded more rigorous still. Thus, dopamine theory helped to make psychiatrists' lack of attention to patient psychology appear like a clear scientific advance, and to make older psychological approaches seem quaint and misguided.

It also reinforced the idea that virtually everyone who suffered from schizophrenia responded well to medication, if the right dose were found. Since medication reversed the disease process in the brain, everyone with the disease ought to benefit. And if medication produced a good response in almost everyone, whatever response medications produced was good by definition.

The theory also allowed psychiatrists to trivialize side effects even more. The Study had made side effects unimportant; but dopamine theory made them profoundly so. It put to rest any idea of medication inducing a brain disease, as Deniker had thought, or of side effects as necessary. The theory depicted medication impelling the brain in the direction of normality, not disease. That remained so even as pharmaceutical companies continued to screen for "antipsychotic" compounds by identifying substances that produced psychomotor disorders in animals.

More generally, the dopamine hypothesis seemed to validate an unbalanced approach to benefits and side effects, like that of the Study. The Study's authors discerned profound meaning in the benefits of medication ("antischizophrenic in the broad sense") but virtually none in the side effects ("trivial"). They treated benefits and side effects differently in the tables, reporting all benefits but only "moderately severe" (or worse) side effects. Yet one could just as easily reverse that focus and find significance in the pattern and nature of side effects, as Deniker had.

The Study gave no reason for amplifying benefits; imbalance theory did. It placed benefits in a rarefied scientific domain—brain neurochemistry—and thereby made side effects pale in comparison. To be sure, side effects had a neurochemical basis, but they did not reflect neurochemical processes as important as the dopamine balance that underlay schizophrenia. By emphasizing some brain processes and not others, the dopamine hypothesis shifted attention from the neurological dysfunction associated with medication.

Dopamine theory also diverted attention from medication-induced distress and other "subjective" patient feelings. Just as psychological conceptions of disease paled beside neurochemical ideas, so did patients' psychological reactions pale beside their neurochemical processes. The dopamine hypothesis made patients' feelings and psychology appear less important than their biochemistry. Biological psychiatrists need not have thought this way; the fact is that many did.

Patient psychology retained one role in the new vision: it accounted for patients' well-known dislike of medications. The most neurochemically oriented psychiatrists thought that "feelings" or disordered thinking led patients to invent or overreact to side effects and to stop taking medications for that reason. Similar views had appeared in the 1950s, but imbalance theory made it even easier to dismiss patients' reactions: after all, the patients could not fully appreciate the biochemical improvements that medications produced. And after dopamine theory, attributing something to "feelings" was often tantamount to dismissing it as unimportant.

The effects and mechanism of medication were only two of the issues facing psychiatrists. What implications did medication hold for public mental health and mental hospitals? What role should clinical judgment play? Finally, had medication transformed psychiatry? The Study devised far-reaching answers to these questions—and psychiatrists extended and inflated those answers. Just as psychiatrists posited more profound effects and produced a deeper theory than the Study, so they discerned more profound implications for institutions and for psychiatry. As that happened, psychiatric thinking became more monolithic.

Psychiatric Transformation

By the late 1960s, psychiatrists regarded medication and "antischizophrenic" effects as the engines of a medical revolution that had transformed their profession. Swazey's history both described and reflected that view. Yet the Study itself had posited a basic continuity between medication and older somatic treatments:

> Although it has been clear for many decades that acute schizophrenic
> patients had reasonable chances of improving with available treatments,
> there generally has been a cautious and skeptical, if not nihilistic,
> attitude toward the prognosis of schizophrenia. However, in the past two
> decades, the situation has greatly improved, and considerable optimism
> now attends the treatment of acute schizophrenia.[47]

Since the "reasonable chances" for patient improvement dated back "many decades," the Study was crediting premedication treatments, presumably those of the 1930s "biological revolution." The reference to the "past two decades" when the "situation" "greatly improved" is vague, but a reasonable interpretation is that although psychiatry had performed well since the 1930s, psychiatrists came to appreciate that fact only after World War II—and perhaps only after chlorpromazine.

According to this view, the use of medication did not mark a radical break with the recent therapeutic past. Instead, one of its most important effects was to alter psychiatrists' attitudes. Just as Greenblatt thought that insulin coma therapy benefited patients by raising hospital-staff morale, the Study depicted medication as increasing the optimism of all psychiatry. And in some passages, that appeared to represent the major accomplishment of medication: "The findings . . . lend strong support to the rising optimism about and confidence in the treatment of acute schizophrenic psychoses. Even among the placebo-treated group, almost half the patients were rated as having improved to some extent."[48] This passage portrayed the placebo results as further reason for optimism; it was a far cry from Swazey's medication-produced "revolution in psychiatry."

Swazey's view was limited in a different way. Although she portrayed psychiatry as transformed by the use of medication, she seemed to recognize that Study data fell short of establishing "antischizophrenic" effects. She described its results on that point as "the most definitive demonstration of a fact gradually perceived by psychiatrists." That suggested, however, that the Study fell short of constituting a "definitive demonstration" in the scientific sense. Perhaps it qualified as a "demonstration" only because psychiatrists had "perceived" its truth ahead of time. Yet if Swazey doubted the Study's case for "antischizophrenic effects," how could she go on and make the even stronger claims about "highly specific actions" against schizophrenia?

The answer lies in two differences between Swazey and the Study. The first concerned the state of psychiatric thinking in the early 1960s. The Study depicted psychiatrists who still regarded medications as "tranquilizers"; Swazey described psychiatrists who "perceive[d]" that medications represented not tranquilizers but a "true" antischizophrenia treatment. From the perspective of the Study, only a real "demonstration" could change psychiatrists' minds; from Swazey's perspective, no such demonstration was required, since psychiatrists already recognized the point. A minor historical revision effectively changed the burden of scientific proof.

So did an almost literal shift in vision. The Study did not presume that "antischizophrenic effects" were something psychiatrists could virtually "see," if they only looked. Swazey suggested exactly that, however. If psychiatrists actually "perceived" antischizophrenic effects, little further demonstration would be required by way of proof from the Study.

This is not the only example of a change in thinking about medications that depended upon revising one's account of what now seemed or had once seemed evident. In Casey's first multicenter study, he doubted data indicating a low level of side effects because of what he had seen in other patients; in his second study, however, Casey accepted similar findings and did not comment on what had seemed evident before. Similarly, Davis rejected the dopamine hypothesis partly because many patients respond badly to medication—but he apparently thought nothing of the fact that earlier dopamine theorists had failed to notice what now seemed evident.

PUBLIC HEALTH IMPLICATIONS

The Study urged a revolutionary change in public mental health: deinstitu-tionalization. It did not directly rest this argument on the supposed antischiz-ophrenic effects of medication, but soon psychiatrists did precisely that. They linked the supposedly profound effects of medication on patients with profound changes in the public mental health system.

The Study's own public health conclusions represented something of a reach. Its principal finding—that medication proved significantly more effec-tive than a placebo against schizophrenic symptoms—did not carry any un-mistakable implications for the pressing issues of public mental health. The finding did not directly relate to the merits of state hospitals versus general hos-pitals, or large state hospitals versus small ones, or even hospitalization versus community care. The Study's design had not even distinguished between gen-eral and state hospital patients. And the authors of the Study themselves ob-served that the Study's results did not bear directly on community medication programs.[49]

Other research results did relate to that issue, and the Study briefly de-scribed them. Some research, it said, indicated that intensive community use of medication would "obviate the necessity for hospitalization in a significant proportion of acutely ill . . . patients." Other work demonstrated that "a sig-nificant percentage of patients experience relapse" if medications are with-drawn. Still other findings suggested that medications helped "prevent . . . chronicity." Yet taken together, this work demonstrated only that some hospi-talizations would become unnecessary with intensive community use of med-ication. It did not show how many patients would be better off, or worse off, under such a system. Nor could one confidently say that results medication achieved in a hospital—the only treatment setting investigated in the Study—would also be achieved in the "community." Psychiatrists had sharply distin-guished between side effects in hospitals and the same effects in the community; why should the benefits of medication be any different? Someone taking Study results at face value might well conclude that patients should continue to re-ceive medication in hospitals, at least until equally rigorous research—a "com-munity" collaborative study—was completed.[50]

Notwithstanding the doubtful relevance of its findings, the Study urged major public health reforms. Looking with disfavor upon "custodial care in pub-lic mental hospitals," it called for a "fully public health approach" that employed "psychiatric services in general hospitals" and also delivered medication to pa-tients "on an ambulatory basis or in day-care centers." This wording straddled the divide between reformers who envisioned a modest role for redesigned state hospitals and those who urged a still more pronounced shift away from state institutions—for that matter, away from hospitals of any kind. The Study did not spell out details, but it approvingly cited both the report of the Joint Commission on Mental Illness and the "recent special message of the President"—documents that embodied the competing positions.[51]

The Study based its recommendations not so much on how medication worked inside patients as on how psychiatrists worked with medication. For the first time, it observed, psychiatry possessed a treatment "effective in a large number of patients" that was also "inexpensive and relatively safe" and "capable of being administered in a wide variety of treatment facilities" without "highly specialized equipment or staff." The last feature distinguished medication from coma and convulsive treatments; those measures "required highly trained personnel and special anesthesia facilities" and did not lend themselves to a "wide variety" of settings. For the same reason, they failed the expense test. Whether they qualified as "safe" the Study did not say; it was a moot point, since they did not lend themselves to community use. Nor did the Study mention lobotomy, in this, or any other, connection.[52]

What the Study did not suggest was that older therapies lacked the required effectiveness—or even that medication was markedly more effective. The idea of medication as a revolutionary advance, which pervades later accounts, simply did not appear in the Study at this point. What about medication being "antischizophrenic in the broad sense"? The Study did not consider whether older somatic treatments qualified as "antischizophrenic" in the same sense; it claimed only that placebos did not. The omission would have made it difficult to distinguish medication from older therapies, even if the authors had wanted to do that. But they apparently did not; this is as close as they came:

> As long as the available treatments required specialized settings and highly trained personnel, a fully public health approach to acute schizophrenia could never be developed. However, with the introduction of the drugs, it is now more feasible to treat acute psychoses in a variety of clinical settings. The results of this and other studies suggest that the wide range of acute schizophrenic psychoses, with its [sic] diverse symptoms and manifestations, can be treated in many settings, including psychiatric services in general hospitals, and by extrapolation, probably also on an ambulatory basis or in day-care centers.[53]

The passage suggested a parallel between "diverse symptoms and manifestations" of schizophrenia and the "variety of . . . settings" in which physicians could treat the symptoms with medication. The Study never said explicitly that only treatments "antischizophrenic in the broad sense" would work in diverse settings. Yet one might draw that conclusion. How else did "[t]he results of this . . . stud[y] . . . suggest that . . . schizophrenic psychoses, with its diverse symptoms and manifestations, can be treated in many settings"?

Thus, medication may have qualified as "antischizophrenic" in a second "broad sense," because of the broad range of settings where psychiatrists could administer them. The Study did not develop this idea; other psychiatrists did so later. Yet there is nothing profound, or even necessarily desirable, about a procedure's capacity to work in a variety of settings. Transorbital lobotomy—the eye socket operation—was highly portable too, requiring neither an operating room nor a general anesthetic. Walter Freeman, who developed the procedure, sometimes performed it in motel rooms. No one would claim that transorbital lobotomy qualified as "antischizophrenic" on that account.[54]

Nor was it true that only "antischizophrenic" therapies could sustain patients in a variety of community settings. Suppose, for example, that medications constituted powerful tranquilizers, and nothing more. Psychiatrists still might find a level of "tranquilization" that calmed patients sufficiently to permit a life in the community but did not produce enough stupor to prevent patients from tending to basic needs. Such a treatment would be as portable as an antischizophrenic drug, despite a distinctly unprofound method of action.

The equation of "antischizophrenic" with "usable in diverse settings" might seem fanciful, but some figures soon embraced a conception very much like it. Reformers—mostly policy analysts and lawyers—came to treat any intervention as desirable if it got patients out of mental hospitals. That effectively collapsed the distinction between "antischizophrenic" and "community setting," although the reformers often had little interest in how medication worked and even may have doubted the existence of "mental illness." Less radically, some psychiatrists used "functioning in a setting" as a benchmark of therapeutic success. Yet that approach, like the approach of the reformers, collapsed the distinction between antischizophrenic treatments and treatments that allowed patients with schizophrenia to function in community settings. Housing arrangements, community counseling, and social work might enjoy the same status as medication because they too assisted patients to live in community settings.

From the point of view of most psychiatrists, that had unfortunate consequences. It blurred the distinction between psychiatry, on the one hand, and public policy, psychology, and social work on the other—a result that many practitioners of those other disciplines, but not most psychiatrists, favored. It also deprived the "antischizophrenic" concept of any significance in public debates. If "antischizophrenic" meant "conducive to community life," it no longer afforded a reason for deinstitutionalization; rather, it simply described the role of medication.

Thus, a gap opened between the Study and visions of public mental health to its left and its right. The Study cited medication's cost, ease of administration, and safety as the keys to deinstitutionalization. The soon-to-be prevailing vision in psychiatry—the right—would attribute deinstitutionalization to the "antischizophrenic" effects of medication that produced revolutionary improvements in patients' conditions. Meanwhile, on the Study's left, radical critics argued that either mental illness did not exist or that public policy and law should act as if it did not. In either case, the supposed "antischizophrenic" effects (in psychiatrists' sense) of medication were irrelevant—but its capacity for maintaining patients in the community apparently was not.

During the late 1960s and early 1970s, it appeared that pivotal battles about psychiatry and public mental health might rage along this fault line. As patients poured out of state hospitals, some academics and state officials declaimed against the "medical model." Lawyers and courts declared that psychiatry had to yield to patients' right of "liberty." Psychiatrists felt besieged. It seemed they might lose a supposed "war" between psychiatry and law—a war in which a host of disciplines and figures allied themselves against their profession, and in which "antischizophrenic" effects and science might prove irrelevant.

For the most part, it was a phony war. Whatever the critics intended, or really thought, neither policymakers nor courts ever seriously challenged the use of medication to achieve deinstitutionalization. The apparent conflict between ideas about medication as "antischizophrenic" and denials that mental illness existed never seriously threatened either position; the notion that medication profoundly affected disease worked in tandem with claims that no disease existed. Psychiatrists wanted to use medication because of its "antischizophrenic" properties; many state officials and academics favored medication because anything seemed better than hospitals; lawyers tolerated medication—indeed, hardly noticed the treatment until the late 1970s—because other things seemed more important. Each stance aimed toward deinstitutionalization, slighted medication side effects, and downplayed the serious impairments of many former patients.

The Collaborative Study Vision

The Collaborative Study vision entailed a highly integrated network of beliefs. Medication had profound benefits against schizophrenia and reversed a neurochemical disease process in patients' brains. Side effects were trivial. The combination of benefits and side effects made possible a new public mental health system, based on community administration of medication. Taken together, these developments transformed psychiatry. In short, psychiatrists had profound theories about medication, which had profound effects on patients, and carried profound implications for public mental health and the character of psychiatry and its history.

These beliefs seemed inextricably linked. The extent of the public health change would confirm the extent of the medication-induced changes in patients

—and the extent of the changes in patients would confirm the desirability of public health reforms. Those changes underscored the historic uniqueness of medication, which in turn suggested the uniqueness of modern psychiatry. Or one could argue backward, from the evident transformation in the character of psychiatry to the uniqueness of psychiatric medication to the desirability of public health changes. Everything confirmed everything else.

Research did not compel these large conclusions, just as data did not underlie those of the Study. Instead, it appears that hoped-for conclusions skewed the both the Study and the vision. Data did not lead to the new conception of medication so much as desired changes in public health and psychiatry did. Once created, the same desires sustained it. Nothing inconsistent with the new vision could receive recognition; everything had to confirm everything else.

The Study took on the aspect of a scientific miracle. Like other miracles, it became an event that confirmed the most profound beliefs of its adherents. Or it may have appeared miraculous because it aligned psychiatrists' professional hopes and aspirations with the facts about medication in ways that had seemed impossible before—and that later events showed impossible in fact.

Viewed today, after the miracle has faded, the Study appears quite different from the way it looked to Swazey in 1974. Far from being the foundation for psychiatry's future advance, or the culmination of a past process through which psychiatrists "gradually perceived" the truth about medication, the Study appears discontinuous with future and past alike. The syndrome of psychomotor indifference loomed large in the 1950s, but disappeared in the pages of the Study. Tardive dyskinesia loomed large in the future, but the Study ignored persistent side effects and dyskinesias. Antischizophrenic effects seem ever more evanescent. The Study and the vision held together for only a moment.

The past has not yet caught up with the Study vision. In 1967, the future did. At a medical conference in Paris, George Crane reported that a quarter of the patients in a second NIMH collaborative study had the symptoms of tardive dyskinesia. Eminent psychiatrists attacked this finding over the next decade; with the vision's components so interdependent, the entire structure might collapse if it got this point wrong. By 1980, Jonathan Cole—the lead author of the Study—accepted Crane's conclusions, and the vision indeed disintegrated.

Chapter 4

Tardive Dyskinesia and George Crane

1967

THE COLLABORATIVE STUDY vision of medication was vulnerable at many points, ranging from "antischizophrenic effects" to the slighting of the distress experienced by medicated patients. Yet the principal challenge came from tardive dyskinesia, the side effect whose existence had been ruled out by the very design of the Study. Since tardive dyskinesia was usually irreversible, it conflicted with Study claims about the safety of medication. Since it reflected probable neurological damage, psychiatrists could not plausibly dismiss it as a result of patients' "feelings" or psychology; some psychiatrists tried nonetheless. The dopamine hypothesis magnified the benefits of medication by moving them from the realm of psychology to those of neurochemistry; tardive dyskinesia would magnify the potential harms of medication in the same way. Tardive dyskinesia seemed quite capable of provoking public and government scrutiny of the near universal use of medication and the associated blueprint for public health reform.

The earliest reports of tardive dyskinesia appeared in Europe in the late 1950s. They described small numbers of cases in which dyskinesias appeared after patients had received medication for an extended period of time. These dyskinesias persisted when medication was discontinued, and they appeared to become permanent.[1]

Although tardive dyskinesia probably involves neurological damage, it initially received little notice from American psychiatric journals, or from American psychiatrists. As late as 1972, a psychiatrist could comment that "[m]ost of the literature supporting . . . [tardive dyskinesia's] existence comes from European studies."[2]

Although not a psychiatric journal, the *Journal of the American Medical Association* (JAMA), a prestigious general medical publication, did take notice in 1965. A JAMA editorial cautioned physicians who employed "high and prolonged dosages of phenothiazine drugs" to "be aware of the possibility of permanent sequelae following use of these agents." The editorial cited a 1964 British study of dyskinesia and a JAMA article about persistent changes in skin pigmentation apparently caused by the drugs' effects on melanin. "[P]roof of presumed structural damage due to a neurotoxic effect of the phenothiazines must await neuropathological study," the editorial observed, but it noted that animal studies had detected such damage already.[3]

The JAMA editorial appeared only ten months after the Collaborative Study, yet it offered a marked contrast with the lack of concern shown in the Study—and by most of American psychiatry—about persistent side effects. No similar warning would appear in a leading psychiatric journal until 1973, eight years later. Yet even the JAMA editorial understated the apparent problem. Describing persistent effects as "rare," it cautioned that they "should not detract from the general usefulness of the phenothiazines in the management of the schizophrenic illness." The claim of "rarity," however, ignored Hall's article, "Neurotoxic Reactions," which had appeared nine years before in JAMA and described large numbers of persistent medication side effects. If the persistence of an effect indicated brain damage, as the editorial suggested, the problem was more serious than it acknowledged.[4]

George Crane, a research psychiatrist at NIMH, did take the problem seriously. In January 1966 he organized a workshop on tardive dyskinesia and the brain. There, he reported on two surveys that he had conducted. In one group of patients, 18 percent had dyskinesias, according to Crane; in the other group, 25 percent did. These figures equaled the highest yet reported. In September of the same year, Crane coauthored an article with George Paulson. Examining 182 chronic, medicated patients at Paulson's North Carolina hospital, they found 15 percent with symptoms of tardive dyskinesia. The mere presence of dyskinesias did not establish medication as the cause, but Crane and Paulson concluded that "strong evidence" implicated drugs in "the great majority" of cases. They also speculated on the likelihood of drug-induced brain damage, and labeled the concluding section of their article "Epicrisis."[5]

Reviewing the published literature in February 1968, Crane reported that twenty-six papers (almost all of them foreign) had dealt with tardive dyskinesia between 1957 and mid-1966. Crane noted that "three groups of investigators" had detected signs of the disorder in significant numbers of medicated patients. A German team reported "approximately 100 cases in a population of 443"; French psychiatrists found it in "103 out of 417 chronic patients"; and British researchers, focusing on "severe irreversible symptoms," reported "13 of 250 women . . . afflicted by this disorder." (This was the report noted in the 1965 JAMA editorial.) Taken together, published studies described five hundred patients—"a number . . . far from being impressive considering the many millions . . . being treated with neuroleptics," Crane observed. Yet he found both the occasional reports about large numbers of afflicted patients and the increasing number of reports "disconcerting."[6]

Crane argued cautiously. He observed that the "cause-and-effect relationship between neuroleptics and tardive dyskinesia is difficult to establish with certainty and is based only on indirect evidence." He did not offer his own estimates of prevalence. And even his terminology was moderate. Other psychiatrists had labeled the disorder "terminal extrapyramidal insufficiency syndrome," which suggested that very common extrapyramidal side effects like rigidity or akathisia represented early stages of a possibly permanent neurological disorder. "Tardive dyskinesia" was a less threatening term. Moreover, others reported that akathisia persisted along with the dyskinesias, but Crane made no such claim. Nor did he cite Deniker's theory that drug-induced "encephalopithies" (dyskinesias and other diseaselike neurological changes) produced the clinical benefits of drugs—a theory that would have made tardive dyskinesia a fundamental aspect of drug actions.[7]

Yet Crane concluded that medication probably caused tardive dyskinesia. The "more detailed clinical histories," he argued, showed that "dyskinesias were not present in patients prior to their treatment with neuroleptics." Moreover, the characteristic tongue and jaw movements of tardive dyskinesia were "easily recognized," but "rare" before the drug era. "To my knowledge," he wrote, "this syndrome has not been described in any other condition except as a sequela of von Economo's encephalitis [sleeping sickness]."[8]

Despite its caution, Crane's article clashed with the Study vision of medications. It took seriously the possibility of persistent side effects and brain damage—possibilities the Study ignored. Beyond that, Crane's writing style departed from the Study norm. The Study had employed conclusory, colorless language: "mild and unimportant" side effects, "impressive" benefits, and bland-sounding lists of systems. In contrast, Crane described tardive dyskinesia in graphic, unflinching language:

> The tongue permanently projected forward and backward following a rapid rhythm; at times the projection is to the side, sometimes to the right, sometimes to the left; a torsion motion, or rotation on its axis complicates its incessant coming and going motion. The mouth is half open and lip movements accompany this continuous dyskinesia.[9]

And:

> Movements of the lips and tongue are grotesque, often socially objectionable, and thus are a source of considerable embarrassment to the patient and his family. As a rule, however, patients do not complain of these symptoms, particularity if they are demented. The neurological

syndrome may cause a number of complications, such as hypertrophy of the tongue and ulcerations of the mouth. The speech may become dysarthric to the point of being incomprehensible. In extreme cases, swallowing may become difficult and this may cause a considerable loss of weight. Severe dystonia involving muscles controlling the balance of the body and of the head may be painful and thus greatly reduce the patient's activity.[10]

Crane provided a verbal picture of people with tardive dyskinesia; the Study had supplied abstractions and visions of public health. Such clashes of style and substance would continue over the next decade.

By the time Crane's review of the literature appeared in print, he had already announced his own findings about tardive dyskinesia in another forum. At a Paris conference in October 1967, Crane reported that over a quarter of the patients on an NIMH research ward showed symptoms of tardive dyskinesia. He now described the case for cause and effect as "persuasive"; reported that 4 percent of medicated patients developed new dyskinesias over a six month period; observed that the condition sometimes improved over the course of a year, despite continued medications; suggested an association between dyskinesias and drug-induced tremors or stiffness; and reported an uncertain relationship between tardive dyskinesia and past medication dosage, except that very high doses "seemed to produce more dyskinesia."[11]

Crane also included revealing data about the persistence of tardive dyskinesia. His research population consisted of the patients in a second NIMH collaborative study, and the researchers conducting that experiment, not Crane, controlled the administration of medication. For their own reasons, however, they had withdrawn medication from thirty-four patients whom Crane later found with dyskinesia. After "a three month drug-free period," Crane reported, twenty-nine of those thirty-four "still manifested dyskinesia . . . [although] the severity of symptoms seemed to have decreased in half the sample." Thus, Crane had confirmed that the disorder persisted after medication was withdrawn.[12]

Finally, Crane examined how tardive dyskinesia affected patients' lives— an un-Study-like issue that he approached in un-Study-like terms:

> Due to the difficulty of communicating with patients of this type it was not easy to determine whether they were distressed by their abnormal movements, or even aware of them. No individual of [sic] this sample of 400 patients was severely impaired [by tardive dyskinesia]; however subjects showing moderately severe or sustained dyskinesia were made conspicuous by such movements in the environment of the chronic hospital ward where one takes for granted peculiarities of behavior, bizarre patterns of movement and odd manifestations in appearance and apparel.[13]

When Crane had finished presenting this paper, the conference moderator announced "a request for an emergency discussion." Nathan S. Kline and Herman Denber, eminent American psychiatrists, rose to challenge Crane's findings. In relatively brief remarks, they aired what would become the dominant themes of psychiatric debate for the next fifteen years.[14]

Kline began. He observed that the published literature included a report of dyskinesia affecting 40 percent of patients, so that "no one would quarrel as to the occurrence [of dyskinesias] while on medication." The "quarrel" instead concerned reversibility: whether "there is a danger . . . that some damage will be done that persists beyond the use of the drug." And "almost without exception," Kline insisted, such damage did *not* occur. The sole exception involved patients "brain-damaged in one form or another, either arteriosclerotic, having prior lobotomies, etc." Based on existing literature, Kline declared that "out of a total of 100 million patients . . . treated with phenothiazines throughout the world, a total of 83 are reported with tardive oral dyskinesia, of whom 50 were brain damaged." In an article elaborating on his remarks, Kline asserted that "there are less than two dozen reported cases [of tardive dyskinesia] in non-brain damaged patients among 100 million estimated [medication] users" and, therefore, the finding of tardive dyskinesia is "not of great clinical significance."[15]

Kline offered other, not entirely consistent criticisms in Paris. If Crane had seen anything, he said, it was only "stereotypic movements" typical of schizophrenia or patients "moistening . . . [their] lips." Mouths dry out when people become agitated, Kline observed; dry mouths also occur as a transient side effect of some drugs. Moreover, people with schizophrenia "are notorious lovers" of stereotypic movements, which represent "a kind of conditioning." Kline himself had been "quite successful in deconditioning . . . [one such] patient" in his practice.[16] In any event, tardive dyskinesia did not constitute a major challenge—for patients or psychiatrists: "The fact is that some patients shuffle their feet and others have minor dyskinetic movements. So do non-patient populations, not on phenothiazine drugs."[17]

How had Crane committed such grievous errors? Kline implied that desire had distorted Crane's judgment: "I feel that we already have enough epidemics—and even the best diseases are not enough. Let us not produce another epidemic of side-effects and papers, unless there is real evidence for it, either clinically or scientifically."[18] The word "epidemic" perhaps appealed to Kline because tardive dyskinesia resembled the aftermath von Economo's encephalitis, the so-called sleeping sickness that reached epidemic proportions after World War I. In any event, his meaning seemed clear: *Crane* bore responsibility for the only real epidemic threatening psychiatry, the "epidemic of . . . papers." What patients had to fear was not medication, and not tardive dyskinesia, but George Crane—and presumably any other physician who reported widespread, persistent side effects from medication.

Denber spoke more explicitly and more harshly than Kline during the "emergency discussion." He asserted—wrongly—that Crane considered his own data unreliable; accordingly, Denber could not understand why Crane reported them. (Crane stood by his data, replying, "Dr. Denber does not know the patients of [sic] this presentation, so he is in no position to judge the correctness of my evaluations.") Continuing, Denber said, "To make such sweeping conclusions and to imply that phenothiazines are extremely dangerous . . . would really require some further explanation. This has not been given."[19] Further, Denber and his team had "examined the same patients that Dr. Crane has examined at Manhattan State Hospital" and "were unable to confirm his observations."

Echoing Kline, Denber thought Crane "in many instances" had mistaken "schizophrenic stereotypies for dyskinetic movements." Denber allowed that "it is incontestable that some patients develop dyskinesias after . . . [drug] treatment," but he did not say how many did, or concede that the dyskinesias became permanent. Instead, he insisted upon "sober, unemotional, objective and unbiased observations"—something Crane evidently had failed to produce.[20]

More explicitly than Kline, Denber portrayed Crane as the salient threat to public health. "[S]weeping, generalized conclusions" like Crane's would "undo the past 15 years of work" in psychiatry, Denber said. (Chlorpromazine had appeared fifteen years earlier.) And Denber urged "each psychiatrist who treats patients to speak for and defend them"; presumably, they needed defense against Crane.

Crane answered briefly. In response to Kline, he said, "The disease is rare because it is not reported. For instance, no patient included in my presentation was reported in the literature." Nor had he confused dyskinesia with schizophrenia: "The difference between schizophrenic stereotypies and this neurological syndrome is very marked; as one becomes familiar with this syndrome there is no difficulty in distinguishing the two types of clinical manifestations."[21]

In fact, the criticisms were inconsistent as well as vehement. According to Kline and Denber: as many as 40 percent of patients had reversible dyskinesias, yet Crane had seen nothing; Crane had seen only schizophrenic mannerisms; Crane had seen dry patient mouths; and any side effect of medication was reversible, despite Crane's observation that it persisted. Apparently, the only impossible alternative was the existence of widespread tardive dyskinesia; every other explanation or combination of explanations—including Crane's supposed personal and professional flaws—trumped the possibility that medication produced a common, persistent side effect.[22]

Although widely anticipated a decade earlier—and being reported now by Crane—widespread, persistent side effects from medication had become inconceivable to Kline and Denber. The phenomena fell outside the prevailing vision in psychiatry: it could not exist. Hence, Crane must have been seeing things. The pre-Study view of medication as disease-inducing agents, the early comparisons between drug effects and brain encephalitis, the 1950s report of persistent side effects—all had passed from psychiatric memory, for no apparent scientific reason.

Other aspects of the Paris exchange reflected the ascendancy of the Study vision in psychiatry. Kline maintained that the rarity of reports about tardive dyskinesia meant that the condition was rare. Yet if Crane had reported a previously undiscovered benefit of medication, Kline surely would not have dismissed it because of an absence of previous reports. Doing so would rule out all new discoveries favorable to medication. Clearly, Kline's presumption applied only to findings that clashed with the prevailing vision.

Or consider Kline's argument that tardive dyskinesia resulted from prior brain damage. Three years earlier, the 1964 British report by Hunter had noted that all the dyskinetic patients had suffered brain damage before receiving medications. Based on such reports, Kline presumed that preexisting brain damage somehow destroyed the causal and ethical links between medication and tardive dyskinesia.[23] Yet Hunter had drawn the opposite conclusion:

> It is not surprising that a brain already damaged either by physical treatments, in particular ECT and leucotomy [lobotomy], by cerebrovascular disease, or by the changes of senescence is more sensitive and either shows drug damage earlier or in more obvious form. . . .
>
> Once this syndrome is generally recognized we suspect a spate of cases will come to light, especially since ten years have now elapsed since phenothiazines were introduced into psychiatry.[24]

Other researchers agreed with Hunter's conclusion that "the damaged brain is more vulnerable to phenothiazine poisoning," but phenothiazines themselves "may cause permanent neurological damage." For example, in 1966 Schmidt and Jarcho wrote that "[i]t might be expected . . . that persistent movement disorders [caused by medication] would signal permanent brain damage." Crane and Paulson made a similar suggestion, attributing tardive dyskinesia to a likely "structural defect, presumabl[y] . . . in the basal ganglia areas" that "could be biochemical or anatomical, or both."[25] The 1964 JAMA editorial, noting reports about an association between dementia and dyskinesia, presumed that both conditions resulted from brain damage induced by medication. But Kline would have blamed the dementia for the dyskinesia. In his view, medication did not damage brains; rather, already damaged brains—abetted by psychiatrists like Crane—harmed medication and its good reputation. Cause and effect ran backward in his account.

Psychiatric history ran backward too. Kline managed to blame lobotomy for tardive dyskinesia by attributing some of the preexisting brain damage to that procedure. In that way, he ascribed medication-caused harm to an earlier psychiatric era, faulting the old therapeutic regime for the flaws of the new one. Thus, he omitted Hunter's reference to ECT—an older somatic therapy still in use—as another predisposing influence for tardive dyskinesia; if ECT produced the disorder, some psychiatric responsibility would exist in the present.

The past played another exculpatory role in Kline's critique. He asserted that patients did not appear very different in 1967 than they had during the premedication era. Apparently, medication caused little dyskinesia, or the dyskinesia was not noteworthy, or both. Here, Kline was following a line of argument offered in 1964 by Leo Hollister, a coauthor of Casey's multicenter studies. Responding to the early reports about tardive dyskinesia, Hollister wrote:

> [E]xtrapyramidal syndromes . . . appear . . . to be reversible most of the time. A few instances of prolonged dyskinesias have been reported in elderly patients treated with phenothiazines, reserpine, or electroconvulsive therapy. It must be remembered that bizarre tics and mannerisms are part of the symptoms of psychosis. Masticatory movements in edentulous [toothless] patients have been called to my attention; however, I have observed toothless old crones in trolley cars making similar motions long before any of the present drugs were known.[26]

Like Kline, Hollister implied that the commonness of the symptoms in premedication-era settings—Hollister's "toothless old crones in trolley cars" and Kline's shuffling, slightly dyskinetic patients—made it unlikely that medication caused the symptoms in the first place and also made the symptoms less important even if medication did cause them.

In 1957, Hollister had produced a similar argument (and anecdote) about another supposed drug complication: " 'brainwashing' or 'will control.' " Dismissing concerns, he wrote, "For a long while, the classic story of a fallen woman has begun with an alcoholic episode. If the story is now changed to include a tranquilizing drug instead of gin, there is still no more reason than before to believe that either is the primary cause of the behavior."[27] Like his account of tardive dyskinesia, this one concerned the most seriously regarded side effect of the time. Both advanced an argument with an anecdote about the conduct of women; and both exuded a Raymond Chandler–like air, with trolley cars and a "fallen woman." Moreover, both minimized medication-caused harm by invoking a familiar image from the past. Medication may have constituted a revolutionary therapy, but it had not changed these visions of Hollister's.

Denber's resort to history was starker and less literary. Psychiatrists had to defend the past fifteen years of psychiatric progress, he declared. Evidently, "progress" consisted of the developments that had produced the Study vision; since Crane's discovery undermined that vision, it could not possibly constitute "progress" itself. Rather, Crane's findings by definition constituted an attack on "progress."

Denber's remarks suggested a hardening of his views about side effects—and about dissent within psychiatry. In 1956, he had criticized the "rather curious, anxiety-ridden, almost hysterical tone [that] has permeated case reports of . . . [side] effects in this country."[28] In 1967, condemning Crane, he called for "sober, unemotional, objective, and unbiased observations." Separated by a decade, the two statements both presumed that psychiatrists overreact to side effects because of their own anxiety or overemotionality. Yet the 1967 remarks included additional elements: bias, lack of objectivity, even malevolence. Earlier psychiatrists needed to calm down; Crane needed to be "defended" against. Crane considered patients' sweeping tongue movements to be pathological; Denber thought the same about Crane's "sweeping . . . conclusions."

Kline's remarks also reflected a change in his attitude, and a hardening of his psychiatric position. In 1956, he had dismissed side effects as "nothing more than annoyances" in mental hospitals but acknowledged that the same effects could make "it extremely difficult for the patient to function adequately in his usual setting." By 1967, Kline refused to acknowledge that anything attributable to medication was even "annoying" patients, in or out of mental hospitals.[29]

Crane was right, but even if he had been mistaken, the response would remain remarkable. Why should mere error suggest incompetence and bad faith? To be sure, tardive dyskinesia conflicted with the Study vision, but other researchers—including Crane himself—had described tardive dyskinesia before. By and large, psychiatry simply had ignored it. Why did Crane's 1967 paper produce so strong a reaction?

Part of the answer lies in the growing number of articles about tardive dyskinesia. By 1966, Schmidt and Jarcho thought that the occurrence of "dyskinetic reactions . . . in response to phenothiazines" was "well established in the world literature"; they expressed surprise that a contrary "consensus" had "survive[d] . . . despite many observations which contradict it." Yet they also thought the consensus would shortly change, since the evidence was such that "one can no longer deny the occasional persistence of drug-induced dyskinesias."[30]

Schmidt and Jarcho were right about the evidence but mistaken about the consensus changing. Perhaps psychiatrists would have become strident about denying tardive dyskinesia at about this time in any case, yet George Crane and his presentation clearly hit a nerve. The reasons lay in Crane's position, and in his substantive approach. Crane was an American psychiatrist, at a time when most tardive dyskinesia reports came from overseas. His position at NIMH— the agency that had conducted the Collaborative Study—placed him at the center of American psychiatric research. Indeed, Crane had used the subjects in a second NIMH collaborative study as his research population. And he organized tardive dyskinesia conferences and workshops, under NIMH auspices, that lent legitimacy, and even urgency, to tardive dyskinesia as a research problem. No other American psychiatrist interested in the disorder held a comparable position.

Crane's 1967 paper was also substantively unique, for it simultaneously attacked four assumptions that had allowed psychiatrists to dismiss tardive dyskinesia or downplay its importance. These assumptions were: tardive dyskinesia occurred rarely; drug-induced dyskinesias almost never persisted; preexisting brain damage accounted for most of the few persistent dyskinesias; and when tardive dyskinesia occurred, it did not present a major problem for patients. When one assumption failed, psychiatrists typically fell back on another—a technique well illustrated in Kline's remarks.

Crane's paper challenged all four assumptions at once, and so it left no escape. Crane rebutted the assumptions about rarity and reversibility with data. He challenged the assumption about preexisting brain damage by studying "a rather typical institutionalized population of chronic schizophrenic patients." Nothing suggested these patients had unusual brain damage; NIMH had presumably chosen to study them because they seemed typical. Finally, Crane rebutted the claim that tardive dyskinesia made little difference to patients by describing the almost grotesque symptoms in detail, and by noting that patients afflicted with the disorder stood out "even in . . . [an] environment where one takes for granted peculiarities of behavior, bizarre patterns of movement and odd manifestations in appearance and apparel."[31]

In the process, Crane undercut the claims of the 1964 Collaborative Study about impressive clinical improvement and "antischizophrenic" drug effects. Although his 1967 paper did not address those points explicitly, it depicted wards where patients remained so impaired, despite medication, that one could not tell whether they were conscious of their dyskinetic movements—movements more bizarre than the symptoms of their mental illness itself. Crane also asked whether "reported cases of dyskinesia" would "affect the future use of neuroleptic agents"—a question that might well not arise if drugs truly produced immense benefits.[32]

Other psychiatrists had posed the same question. The 1964 article that prompted the *JAMA* editorial described permanent side effects as "an urgent matter" and lamented the "unfortunate tendency to give drugs freely and, once prescribed, to continue them indefinitely." Others, such as Schmidt and Jarcho, expressed bewilderment at psychiatry's lack of attention to persistent side effects. In their own way, Denber and Kline echoed such concerns: they feared that tardive dyskinesia, if it existed, *would* prompt a fundamental rethinking of medication practice.[33]

Degkwitz, who had authored a very early report about tardive dyskinesia, addressed the subject poignantly—"as a clinician because we clinicians are the ones who produce tardive dyskinesias"—at the close of the 1968 NIMH workshop that Crane had organized. Workshop participants saw films depicting "fairly severe cases of dyskinesia," he noted, "but many such cases can be seen if one takes the trouble of walking through the wards of mental hospitals." Estimating that 20 to 25 percent of medicated patients were afflicted, Degkwitz lamented the fact that "[d]uring the last 15 years drugs have been given to a large portion of psychiatric patients with little thought of what the risks are." "I feel," he concluded, "that we should revise our therapeutic approach with drugs as the risk seems to be considerable."[34]

As these remarks demonstrate, Crane's views alone did not make him unique. Yet, after all was said and done, Kline and Denber were probably correct to call attention to Crane's own personal and professional qualities. He acted with such commitment and determination that psychiatrists at the time readily recognized—or stigmatized—him as the force behind efforts to obtain recognition for tardive dyskinesia. Writing in 1974, Henry L. Lennard and Arnold Bernstein of the University of California at San Francisco's department of psychiatry described Crane as the "foremost" investigator among those "placing themselves in the unpopular position of calling . . . [tardive dyskinesia] to the attention of the medical profession, the drug industry, and . . . government agencies." Reviewing developments in 1986, Phil Brown and Steven C. Funk agreed.[35]

Two circles of psychiatry seemed to exist in the mid-1960s. One—centered in Europe, but with American representation—had discovered persistent side effects of medication and considered them profoundly significant. The other, centered in the United States, had a comprehensive vision of medication, adhered to the idea of "mild and unimportant" side effects, and treated reports of tardive dyskinesia either as of marginal importance or as profoundly mistaken. George Crane moved within the second circle, but he stood with the first. Nor did he believe that the two could simply ignore their differences and coexist. Not surprisingly, then, Crane came to be viewed as a traitor to his profession, or as a medical hero, depending on one's viewpoint. Combined with the remarkable nature of the developments, the large role played by this one individual lends a dramatic air, even a fateful one, to the era.

Chapter 5   Tardive Dyskinesia

                             1967–1976

Except to a few researchers, tardive dyskinesia remained invisible until the early 1970s. It was as if the disorder simply did not exist. Drug package inserts ignored it; so did clinicians and mental hospitals. Nor did tardive dyskinesia influence public mental health policy: deinstitutionalization accelerated. Afterward, Crane recalled "strong opposition on the part of the medical profession, industry and . . . government agencies [to] . . . accept[ing] tardive dyskinesia as a serious medical problem" during this period.[1]

Opposition also existed within research circles. According to Crane, "prominent" academic psychiatrists "denied the existence [of tardive dyskinesia] or felt . . . [it] was unimportant." Yet work by Crane and other interested researchers continued to appear in journals. Increasingly, these researchers included psychiatrists from the United States. Exactly as Kline had feared, an "epidemic of papers" about tardive dyskinesia began breaking out.[2]

The Epidemic of Papers

Between 1967 and 1972, six articles by investigators other than Crane reported rates of tardive dyskinesia above 25 percent. Five found a rate higher than 30 percent, including a 1972 study by psychiatrists at Duke and Vanderbilt universities; they determined that 32 percent of patients at one institution and 38 percent at another manifested symptoms. These results, they concluded, "confirm[ed]" Crane's reports about the "alarmingly high prevalence" of "this disfiguring condition."[3]

By now, Crane considered the basic facts well established. In 1970, he cited "more than 50 papers" that demonstrated "neuroleptic drugs can cause dyskinesias." In 1973, he declared that "compelling evidence" linked medications to the condition; in addition, new studies confirmed that drug-caused dyski-nesias remained "unchanged after months or years following discontinuation of all neuroleptics" in "a large percentage of cases."[4]

Beyond the basics, Crane painted an even more dire picture than before. He now described tardive dyskinesia as "a terminal state of an extrapyramidal disturbance with pseudoparkinsonism being an intermediate stage"—in short, he had concluded that common, supposedly reversible side effects *did* ripen into persistent neurological dysfunctions. Crane observed that patients with drug-induced Parkinson's symptoms developed tardive dyskinesia more often, and their Parkinson's symptoms tended to disappear as dyskinesias emerged; more-over, there was at least one case of "permanent dystonia attributable to . . . [med-ications, with] a progression from parkinsonism to dystonia." Not just the onset of tardive dyskinesia, but also its treatment, seemed more troubling. Thus, Crane criticized suggestions for suppressing symptoms with higher doses of medications; such measures often produce temporary improvement, he ob-served, but "[c]ommon sense suggests . . . extreme caution" because "the risk of causing further damage to the brain is a very real one." Since no effective ther-apy existed, "the primary concern of the physician should be . . . prevention," he concluded.[5]

The researchers and academics who disagreed with Crane held their fire, at least in public. Kline restated his rejectionism in a 1968 article for the *Amer-ican Journal of Psychiatry*—and Kline's remained the last such article by a promi-nent individual psychiatrist for almost a decade. Beginning in 1973, mainstream psychiatry chose to speak collaboratively on issues raised by Crane; "task forces" of distinguished psychiatrists were assembled and reported in that year, and again in 1980. (The 1973 task force even included Crane.) For the rest, some researchers reported low rates of dyskinesia, just as some reported higher rates. Yet only a few junior figures published criticisms of Crane's results in these years. Leading psychiatrists did not dispute Crane's views; they just ignored them.[6]

The Question of Spontaneous Dyskinesias

One issue did receive considerable attention: the rate of so-called "spontaneous dyskinesia," or dyskinesia *not* caused by medication. The clearest case was a dys-kinetic patient who had never received medication. And the number of these cases had an important bearing on Crane's claims. To determine the true rate of medication-induced dyskinesia, one had to first subtract the spontaneous cases. For example, if 27 percent of medicated patients and 20 percent of never-medicated patients developed dyskinesia, the rate of medication caused dysk-inesia would equal 7 percent.[7]

Kline had sketched an argument along this line in 1967, claiming that premedication-era patients had "minor dyskinetic movements." Leo Hollister had done the same with his observation about "toothless old crones in trolley cars making similar motions long before any of the present drugs were known." Crane's increasing certainty that medication caused tardive dyskinesia rested partly on reports that compared high dyskinesia rates among medicated patients with very low rates among the unmedicated. For example, a study of nursing home patients reported that "two out of 100 untreated residents exhibited dyskinesia whereas 20 out of 52 individuals receiving neuroleptic drugs were afflicted."[8]

Reviewing these studies in 1968, Crane observed that eleven out of fourteen reported significantly higher dyskinesia rates among medicated patients. Most found a spontaneous dyskinesia rate of 1 to 3 percent. The remaining three studies found comparable rates of dyskinesia among medicated and unmedicated patients, and Crane suggested two possible reasons why. Either the medicated patients had too little exposure to drugs, or else the researchers counted very mild movements almost indistinguishable from normal behavior. Either factor diminished the differences between medicated and never-medicated groups.[9]

Crane conducted his own rather elegant investigation of the issue. He went to Turkey, where some long-term hospitalized patients had only "minimal" exposure to medication. Such groups no longer existed in the United States: drugs were prescribed too widely. Examining ninety-seven of these Turkish patients, Crane found none with dyskinesia. By contrast, three out of forty Turkish patients with "moderate" drug exposure manifested dyskinesias. Crane concluded that dyskinesias did not result from "progressive chronic psychosis" or from "prolonged institutionalization," as some had charged; rather, they were "related to drugs."[10] Crane reported these results at the 1968 tardive dyskinesia workshop, where Degkwitz announced similar findings. Surveying two thousand geriatric patients in German mental hospitals and homes for the aged, Degkwitz found a dyskinesia rate of about 1 percent among those with no significant exposure to medication. Among medicated patients, the rate equaled 20 or 25 percent.[11]

In light of later controversies about the premedication era—and also in light of Kline's and Hollister's assertions—perhaps the most important workshop contribution came from a British psychiatrist, Muriel Jones, who described investigations that she and Richard Hunter performed on a chronic British mental hospital ward. The ward housed 127 patients, all admitted before 1946. About one-third had never received medication; the remainder had, either in the past or at the time of the study. Over a two-year period, Jones and Hunter performed repeated neurological examinations and reviewed patient charts. Today, populations of chronic, never-medicated patients with schizophrenia no longer exist in the industrialized world, and psychiatrists can only speculate about the movements that Jones and Hunter saw for themselves and carefully investigated.[12]

At the outset, Jones and Hunter "were struck by the number" of never-med-icated patients "reported [on charts] to have had abnormal movements." Ex-amining the patients, Jones and Hunter observed abnormal movements of various kinds. Among the patients who had never received medication, how-ever, none had the mouth movements typical of tardive dyskinesia and only one of forty-five—approximately 2 percent—showed dyskinetic movement in another area of the body. By contrast, 22 percent of women patients who had received medications in the past and 26 percent of those currently receiving them manifested dyskinesias.[13]

Jones and Hunter distinguished four types of abnormal movement: tremor; choreo-athetosis, or purposeless movements, including those of the tongue and jaw—the movements that represented tardive dyskinesia; tics, or short, sudden, and repetitive muscle contractions; and stereotypical movement, or "move-ment . . . not in itself abnormal but . . . [made] so by repetition" such as "rock-ing . . . [or] hand movements . . . [or] lip smacking and munching." They also noted the appearance of "extreme restlessness," or akathisia, which was "not uncommon in the early stages of mental illness . . . apparently independent of [drug] treatment." Except for tardive dyskinesia, each type of abnormal move-ment had appeared more frequently than they had expected, in untreated and treated patients alike.[14]

Jones and Hunter drew three conclusions. First, medication caused almost all tardive dyskinesia–like movements. Second, movements other than tardive dyskinesia resulted from "the disease process" as well as from medication. Third, medicated patients showed more abnormal movements *of all kinds*, including stereotypies and tics.[15]

The "significance" of this last finding was "not clear" to Jones and Hunter, but some of the data behind it appeared striking. Tremor had appeared in 24 per-cent of never-treated women, 26 percent of women currently receiving med-ication, and 33 percent of women who had received medication in the past. The comparable figures for tics were 10 percent (never treated), 20 percent (current treatment), and 26 percent (past treatment); and, for stereotypical movements, 24 percent, 60 percent ,and 52 percent. It seems particularly remarkable that medicated women developed stereotypies—symptoms of schizophrenia—more than twice as frequently as those never medicated. Jones and Hunter concluded that the problem of distinguishing drug-caused movements from spontaneous movements, or from symptoms of mental disease, remained unsolved—*except for* tardive dyskinesia, which medication clearly caused.[16]

Thus, Jones and Hunter produced powerful evidence *against* the theory that schizophrenia caused dyskinesias. They also provided data suggesting that med-ication possibly caused the same abnormal movements—stereotypies and tics—that characterized schizophrenia. In short, the possibility that medication enhanced schizophrenia was better supported than the possibility that schizophrenia produced dyskinesias. Yet the former received no attention in psychiatry, while the latter has survived despite all the evidence against it.

Another workshop participant, A. B. Baker (a University of Minnesota neurologist) echoed many of Jones and Hunter's conclusions. In response to a question from Crane, Baker described the "bucco-lingual" symptoms manifested in "patients treated with neuroleptic agents" as "a new syndrome" that was not "seen at the bedside in any of the extrapyramidal disease," except possibly as a result of "epidemic encephalitis." In the latter case, Baker speculated, "just the right combination of lesions occurred in certain individuals to produce the same picture as resulting [sic] from our drugs." "That is exactly what I wanted to hear from you Dr. Baker," Crane replied. The exchange suggests that Crane already had received unpublished criticism that charged he had mistaken symptoms of schizophrenia or other diseases for a new drug side effect.[17]

Animal Data

The 1968 workshop produced other data, based on animal research, that enhanced the case for medication as the cause of tardive dyskinesia. In one report, Samuel L. Liles and George D. Davis described an experiment in which they damaged the brains of cats and produced symptoms that resembled tardive dyskinesia. Hearing the presentation, Crane was especially impressed by the fact that "the cats shifted their weight from one foot to the other"—"a common manifestation . . . in drug-induced dyskinesias of humans."[18]

Like Jones and Hunter's work, some of the animal research also suggested a possibility that medication produced mental pathology, along with abnormal movements. Thus, Gerald A. Deneau and Crane described monkeys who received high doses of chlorpromazine. While on medication, the animals "demonstrated moderate slowing of motor activity, decreased vocalization, and virtual cessation of the lively social interaction of monkeys housed together." Some of the animals also "developed acute neurological effects, specifically restlessness . . . [and] dystonic postures." One monkey manifested "[a]bnormal tongue movements"; another "showed dramatic postural disorders followed by prostration"; a third "developed a tendency to bite various parts of his body . . . inflicting on himself severe injuries"—injuries that, combined with "other complications" required that the "animal . . . be sacrificed."[19]

Ruthmary K. Deuel, a neurologist, examined the monkeys at Crane's invitation and found "a broad spectrum of motor abnormalities," including "tongue dyskinesia." In one case

> [The] monkey . . . characteristically displayed tongue movements
> about two hours after chlorpromazine. . . . [P]laced alone in an

observation cage . . . [h]e huddled in one corner . . . in slowly
changing bizarre postures. . . . [H]is head nearly touched the floor
while his rump was up. . . . He appeared to gnaw at his right wrist at
times. His feet were inverted one at a time, so that his weight
sometimes rested on the lateral aspect of a foot. . . . In this state the
monkey ignored proffered food, and responded to threat with only a
brief glance and backward movement of the ears.

When the cage door was opened the monkey did not change his
posture or movements, despite the very close approach of several
humans. After three minutes had elapsed . . . he suddenly jumped out
of the cage, agilely and quickly ran around the animal room, and
eluded capture as handily as a normal monkey. When returned to the
cage he resumed the head down posture and dystonic movements.
(The sudden burst of normal activity was reminiscent of such episodes
in humans with Parkinson's disease.)[20]

Deuel and Crane offered different interpretations of these observations.
Deuel thought the monkeys' disorder "appears closest to the dyskinesias seen
in humans after administration of phenothiazines," although the two were not
"directly equivalent." Crane registered surprise that the monkeys' movements
abated within twenty-four hours of discontinuing drugs. "[W]e thought we
would find the chronic types of dyskinesias," Crane said, "but we didn't"; rather,
the symptoms were "more consistent with those of Parkinsonism and acute
dystonias."[21]

Yet Crane, like Deuel, noted enduring behavioral changes. "[S]everal hours
after the dose was delivered the monkeys were decidedly tranquilized," Crane reported, while twenty-four hours later "the colony appeared to have normal motor
activity, but to be 'very well behaved.' " "[T]wenty months after the study began,"
Crane continued, "it was apparent that all the animals were less playful and bois-
terous than non treated controls" even in the absence of medication.[22]

Work like this was a world apart from visions of targeted antischizophrenic
effects and mild side effects. It suggested the 1950s paradigm of tranquilizing
and disease-inducing agents, not the Study's picture of medication. On the other
hand, the workshop included little explicit debate, or even discussion, of the
issues that divided psychiatrists. "[M]ost participants took it "for granted" that
medications caused tardive dyskinesia. Yet reading the transcripts, one finds few
signs that psychiatric "progress" hung in the balance, as Denber had claimed a
few months earlier. Kline, who attended the workshop, only asked a few questions, and nothing resembling the Paris "emergency discussion" occurred. At
the close of workshop, George Paulson expressed his "personal . . . delight . . .
that . . . we did not get too involved with [the] cause and classification of tardive dyskinesia and thus we were not slowed down"—even though Paulson also

noted that the workshop had been convened "mainly because of the problem with tardive dyskinesia."[23]

On a few occasions, a hint of the high stakes did emerge. I noted two examples earlier: Degkwitz's poignant closing statement about the responsibility of clinicians and Crane's reply to A. B. Baker, "That is exactly what I wanted to hear from you." A third was Muriel Jones's closing statement: "Apart from saying how privileged I felt to be here hearing all these new ideas, I would like to emphasize that what we have been studying basically are syndromes resulting from therapy and it may be that the cost of relief of symptoms, particularly in psychiatric patients chronically medicated[,] may be too high in terms of the risk of persistent dyskinesias."[24]

The Case of Frank J. Ayd

Most psychiatrists—along with the institutions connected to public mental health, such as professional organizations, public agencies, and pharmaceutical manufacturers—followed the course Paulson described at the workshop. They did "not get too involved with [the] cause and classification of tardive dyskinesia"; hence, they "were not slowed down." The same was true of most researchers.

One researcher who did take an early interest was Frank J. Ayd. Ayd is an instructive figure, because mainstream psychiatry more or less adopted his position later, during the early 1970s, and he left an unusually full record showing how his views had evolved.

Ayd achieved prominence before the Collaborative Study, and he never fully accepted the new vision of medication. For one thing, he continued to regard medications as "tranquilizers" which "provid[e] . . . amelioration of symptoms" without affecting the "persistence of the basic affliction." He also wrote in a style that resembled Crane's more than it did that of the Collaborative Study. Most important, he remained open to possible truths that psychiatrists under the sway of the Study vision did not. Moreover, since he published a newsletter about medication, Ayd could not simply stand on the sidelines, silent about the issues, in the way other leading psychiatrists did after 1967.[25]

In a 1963 article, Ayd had pronounced side effects "totally reversible." In 1966, however, he took note of the "steady increase of published reports" about tardive dyskinesia. Writing in his *International Drug Therapy Newsletter*, Ayd described the disorder as "evolv[ing] . . . as imperceptibly as the unfolding of a flower."[26]

The "true incidence" of the disorder was "difficult to determine," Ayd observed in 1966, and he noted estimates ranging from 0 percent to over 20 percent. Yet he suspected that "the incidence . . . may be higher than available data suggest." For one thing, "the symptoms may be suppressed by high doses of a neuroleptic and may not appear until the dose is reduced or the drug withdrawn." Moreover, Ayd guessed that psychiatrists usually failed to notice the symptoms. "[C]hronic patients in understaffed, overcrowded hospitals may have undetected mild to moderate abnormal movements," he wrote, "because . . . only gross disturbances are looked for and more subtle manifestations of drug toxicity escape notice or are dismissed as inconsequential." By 1967 Ayd pronounced himself "quite certain" that "the true incidence of this most disabling syndrome is higher than the available data suggest." Although he did not say so, Ayd had probably canvassed patients on his own—the obvious way of settling the question.[27]

While Ayd was becoming more "certain" that medication produced high rates of tardive dyskinesia, he was also becoming more defensive about existing medication practice. In June 1966, he declared "prevention" of tardive dyskinesia "imperative" because the condition was "so resistant to treatment." If signs of it began to appear, Ayd urged that psychiatrists "change the phenothiazine, interrupt the course of therapy, reduce the dose, or, if at all possible, eliminate the offender in order to reverse the dyskinesia early in its course." In patients still free of dyskinesia, he urged consideration of "drug holidays" or "intermittent neuroleptic therapy" in order "reduce the risks" of a patient ever developing it. On the other hand, Ayd wanted tardive dyskinesia "considered in proper perspective"—over "50 million patients" had received medications already and "no adequate substitute for these drugs in the treatment of schizophrenia" existed. Thus, "this and other side effects must be accepted as an unfortunate but, at present, inevitable price for the benefits of this therapy."[28]

The passage demonstrated Ayd's ambivalence. Discussing clinical approaches, he urged the prevention of tardive dyskinesia and "if at all possible" discontinuation of medication at the first sign of the disorder. From a larger "perspective," however, he regarded tardive dyskinesia as an unavoidable "price" of using medications. Thus, Ayd had managed to anticipate many of Kline's *and* Crane's positions at the Paris conference—not an easy thing to do. Still, Ayd's view was coherent: it meant that psychiatrists should avoid and reverse *many*, even though not all, cases of tardive dyskinesia, and that under those conditions medication should not be abandoned as a psychiatric therapy.

In July 1966, Ayd suggested one element of a coherent prevention strategy. After describing some of Crane's findings, Ayd extrapolated a principle: "[H]igh doses of neuroleptics are most likely to produce this disorder in susceptible individuals." He concluded, "The benefits of high doses, particularly in chronically ill patients over 40 years of age, in most instances, are so dubious that instead of prescribing high doses, treatment of another sort should be employed."[29]

Thus, Ayd urged that prevention efforts be targeted at a particular group of patients. Yet what precisely was Ayd proposing for these patients? On a casual reading, "treatment of a different sort" suggested a dramatic change. But that was not the case. Since the targeted group was receiving "high doses," "treatment of a different sort" included standard doses of medication—the doses that had probably produced the high dyskinesia rates Ayd had already acknowledged. Here, his ambivalence had produced vagueness—what would "treatment of another sort" mean to clinicians?—and that vagueness made his proposals seem more far-reaching that they were. "Treatment of another sort" represented more a rhetorical option than a clinical one.

Ayd's ambivalence soon produced not just vagueness but self-contradiction. In 1966, he first called for a "proper perspective" on tardive dyskinesia; in 1968, he reiterated his plea, but added some new language to it: "Persistent dyskinesia must be considered in proper perspective. *Fortunately, in view of the millions of patients treated with neuroleptics in the past 14 years, only a small minority have developed this affliction.*"[30] To support the "small minority" assertion, Ayd cited his own 1963 article, which had reported a dyskinesia rate of "less than 1 percent" and declared side effects "totally reversible." Given Ayd's current views, the citation made no sense, for by 1966 he was "quite certain" that "the true incidence of this most disabling syndrome is higher than the available data suggest"—and the available data already included prevalence estimates above 20 percent. That represented far more than a "small minority."

Although torn, Ayd was moving toward the idea that medication practices should change relatively little, despite tardive dyskinesia. He had become concerned that a widespread persistent side effect might result in the "use of neuroleptics" being "stopped." Evidently, he did not believe that psychiatrists could, or would, prevent a large enough number of cases to forestall public and regulatory pressure to "stop" the use of medication. Thus, he ended up by devising a vague formula that sounded dramatic—"treatment of a different sort"— and then by ignoring or denying what he already knew about the prevalence of tardive dyskinesia. He was retreating from his former prevalence estimates because of what he perceived as their inconsistency with his ideas about prescribing medication. Ayd concluded: "No one wants to revert to the conditions that prevailed . . . [in the era before medications]. Yet this could happen if the use of neuroleptics was stopped. What is necessary is constant vigilance to insure early detection of this neurologic syndrome and when it is discovered to promptly resort whenever possible to treatment of another sort."[31]

Lobbying and the Threat of Lawsuits

In 1973, a Food and Drug Administration and American College of Neuropsychopharmacology Joint Task Force addressed the issue of tardive dyskinesia in a Special Report. Task Force members included Ayd, Crane, and Cole, along with other psychiatrists from public, academic, and research settings. The Task Force's charge was to help revise medication package inserts and to educate physicians about the risks of tardive dyskinesia. In a larger sense, however, its obvious mission was to provide a definitive statement about the disorder.[32]

Until this point, drug companies and most psychiatrists had, as a result of what appeared almost a conscious strategy, ignored tardive dyskinesia. Why the change in 1973? Two significant influences were the "epidemic" of papers and Crane's continuing efforts at NIMH. There was another factor too: the prospect of lawsuits by tardive dyskinesia victims demanding compensation. In 1974, Henry L. Lennard and Arnold Bernstein linked a "major drug manufacturer['s]" new-found willingness to acknowledge tardive dyskinesia in package inserts to its "having settled a lawsuit for damages brought by a patient with tardive dyskinesia." Lennard and Bernstein wrote as if that settlement had become common knowledge in psychiatric circles. And litigation constituted a growing threat precisely because of the growing research literature on tardive dyskinesia.[33]

The appearance of such lawsuits had been inevitable, and—if nothing changed—so was their success. Most of psychiatry might be following the Collaborative Study protocol and ignoring tardive dyskinesia, but lawyers and tardive dyskinesia victims had no reason to do likewise. And it took only one victim and one lawyer to create a major legal precedent, after which other lawyers and victims would immediately follow. In this respect, the dynamics of litigation differed from those in psychiatry: a single George Crane–type figure in litigation would produce a raging "epidemic" of lawsuits in very short order.

As long as drug companies and physicians ignored tardive dyskinesia and refused to warn patients about the risks, plaintiffs seemed likely to prevail. Thus, drug companies now had to acknowledge tardive dyskinesia in their literature. To avoid public incredulity—and a possible repeat of the lobotomy debacle—psychiatry at large had to do the same. Thus, the interest in not being "slowed down" by tardive dyskinesia now required paying some attention to the disorder. At the same time, nothing suggested that the public was ready to accept widespread brain damage among patients as the price of public health or psychiatric reform. Acknowledging tardive dyskinesia or not acknowledging it—both raised serious potential problems.

The Special Report seemed calculated to avoid each horn of the dilemma by adopting a solution like Ayd's. It produced vague phrasing, like his, that sounded far-reaching but allowed for narrow interpretations, accompanied by an estimate of the prevalence of tardive dyskinesia that was at once vague and too low. As a new, corporate entity, the Task Force did not have prior positions of its own to contend with; nor did it take account of its members' prior—and still sharply conflicting—views. Thus, no question of self-contraction or of consistency with past statements arose, as it had for Ayd.

The Task Force described tardive dyskinesia as "*presumably* a result of treatment with antipsychotic drugs." This phrasing bridged the gap between Crane and Ayd, who regarded medication as the cause of tardive dyskinesia, and Cole, who maintained a rejectionist stand until 1976. The Special Report was no less vague about the prevalence of tardive dyskinesia. It asserted "the near impossib[ility]" of assessing prevalence "with any assurance" since "clear criteria" did not "exist" for distinguishing "minimal tardive dyskinesia" from normal movements, and since "most" investigations had failed to adequately define the population being studied. According to the Statement, tardive dyskinesia was "rarely seen in acute psychiatric units," although "prevalences on the order of 20 percent have been reported in very chronic, older institutionalized patient groups." Without further discussion, or evidence, it announced a conclusion: "Perhaps 3 percent to 6 percent of patients in a mixed psychiatric population receiving neuroleptics would exhibit some aspects of this syndrome at one time or another. Patients with symptoms overt enough to be recognized by a casual observer are not uncommon. Patients with severe and incapacitating conditions are quite rare, fortunately."[34]

These figures were remarkably low, particularly considering the membership of the Task Force. Crane had reported a prevalence rate of 27 percent in a mixed psychiatric population; Ayd thought the disorder underrecognized. Yet the task force estimated that "3 percent to 6 percent" of patients would show symptoms "at one time or another." Since some cases abated, this translated into a figure of about 2 to 4 percent of patients with symptoms at any single moment—a figure about one-tenth of Crane's and far below Ayd's earlier suggestions. Crane, for one, did not agree that the disorder was "rarely seen" in acute patients.

Moreover, the Special Report exaggerated the supposed methodological difficulties. Standard studies, including Crane's, never counted "minimal" movements and did include precise descriptions of the research population. Yet this work had still produced prevalence figures that were orders of magnitude higher than those reported by the Task Force. And the Special Report ignored methodological difficulties that yielded *under*estimates of prevalence. For example, the Task Force noted that medication temporarily "masked" dyskinesias but did not point out that this effect resulted in psychiatrists missing patients with the disorder.

In some ways, the Task Force followed in Denber and Kline's footsteps. Like them, it elevated mistaken clinical impressions—the "3 percent to 6 percent" figure—over documented research findings. It also produced a strikingly low prevalence estimate, given the state of the research, although not as low as

Kline's one in a million figure. And its sharp distinction between chronic and acute patients comported with Kline's view of dyskinesias as schizophrenic mannerisms (sicker patients would have them) and damaged brains as the causes of the disorder. Why else suppose that acute patients would fail to develop tardive dyskinesia at the rate seen among chronic patients? If chronic patients developed more dyskinesias because of their longer exposure to medication, acute patients would do the same as they continued to receive drugs. Yet the Task Force wrote as if acute and chronic patients differed in some fundamental though unspecified way.

Denber and Kline had made no clinical concessions to tardive dyskinesia, but the Task Force's clinical recommendations paralleled Ayd's, sometimes in almost the same language. "Tardive dyskinesia," it said, "has been accepted as an undesirable but occasionally unavoidable price to be paid for the benefits of prolonged neuroleptic therapy." Yet the disorder should be prevented whenever possible—"[i]f possible neuroleptics should be discontinued at the first sign of tardive dyskinesia." In the event symptoms worsened, "a clinical choice between two evils must be made. The use of the lowest possible dose . . . adequate to control psychopathology would appear to be the best thing to do." Chronic patients represented a special case. "Complete withdrawal" was indicated as a preventive measure—before tardive dyskinesia appeared—provided that the "clinical state remains stable without antipsychotic drugs." In the opinion of the Task Force, "[m]any chronic patients" could in fact "be satisfactorily maintained for long periods without antipsychotic drugs." Generally, it called for "[m]inimizing the unnecessary use" of "high doses" in chronic cases.[35]

Further reassurance—along with alarm about a different sort of risk—appeared in an editorial that the *Archives of General Psychiatry* published alongside the Task Force's work. Written by Daniel X. Friedman, the editorial adopted the tone of a psychiatrist reassuring a needlessly anxious patient. Friedman gave no sense of the opposing positions on the Task Force, or of the concerns that had preceded its formation. Instead, he concluded that medications could still "be used with confidence" and that "the overwhelming clinical and objective evidence"—Denber used the same idea of "objective evidence" to exclude Crane's work—"indicates that . . . a majority of . . . schizophrenic patients" should receive medication. Since Friedman agreed that dosages should be reduced and medication withdrawn among chronic patients, it appeared that a great majority of those not chronic should continue to receive medications.

Friedman saw real dangers, but they did not arise from medication. Rather, he read the *Report* as a "remind[er] . . . that pharmacotherapy should never be trivialized into a mindless routine—either by physicians or the public." Thus, the acknowledgment of tardive dyskinesia became not a watershed event but the occasion for repeating truisms and somewhat mysteriously implicating the "public" in the problem. Friedman added, "Communications such as these [the *Report*] may be viewed by uninformed alarmists as an opportunity to trivialize the suffering of the mentally ill, while offering their personal agendas or brand of salvation to replace soundly conceived treatments." However, he noted, the Special Report really "demonstrates a fact systematically overlooked by extremists among the consumer advocates, Federal planners, and the Jovian gamblers with medical education. . . . That fact is that there indeed are resources in American psychiatry exercising medical accountability and equipped to exert scientific scrutiny over issues which affect the welfare of the mentally ill."[36]

Thus, Friedman managed to fault the "public" as much psychiatrists for "trivializ[ing]" pharmacotherapy. He treated tardive dyskinesia as a threat only because some might use it to "trivialize the suffering of the mentally ill" and to advance their own "personal agendas." That perfectly captured Denber and Kline's view of Crane and tardive dyskinesia in 1967. Meanwhile, Friedman regarded the history of tardive dyskinesia as a reassuring saga of "medical accountability" and "scientific scrutiny"—an exercise in historical revisionism of the highest order on his part.

Without intending to do it, Friedman had shed light on why Task Force members, like much of psychiatry, systematically underestimated the extent and significance of tardive dyskinesia. They feared how the "public" and the government would react to the existence of a widespread, permanent side effect. So, according to the Task Force, no such effect existed. The minimum that had to be acknowledged was acknowledged—nothing else.

The Task Force members had produced a single statement, without any apparent dissent, but their profound disagreements soon erupted, and their evident compromise collapsed. Within two years, Cole would minimize the extent and implications of tardive dyskinesia, in some ways going even beyond Kline and Denber. Crane, on the other hand, reported higher estimates of the prevalence of tardive dyskinesia and lower estimates of the benefits of medication. Nor did Crane allow historical revisionism like Friedman's to go unanswered. In its place, he offered a scathing account of psychiatry's response to tardive dyskinesia.

A Compromise Collapses

Crane reopened these matters before they ever really closed. In 1973, at about the same time the Special Report appeared, Crane published an article entitled "Clinical Psychopharmacology in Its 20th Year" in *Science* magazine. The article adhered to Task Force prevalence estimates when it cited specific numerical figures; in every other way, it ignored the Special Report. Compare Crane's numerical estimates—"The number of [affected] patients . . . cannot be ascertained. In mental hospitals, 2 or 3 percent of all patients exhibit some motor disorder consistent with tardive dyskinesia, but the percentage may rise to over 50 among patients over age 60 who have been exposed to neuroleptics for 3 years or longer"—with his commentary—"Permanent neurological disorders have become very common among patients treated with neuroleptics. . . . [T]ardive dyskinesia has become a common sight in all wards of hospitals where drugs are administered routinely for long periods of time" and "The frequency with which . . . [tardive dyskinesia] occurs in patients receiving neuroleptics in clinics and private offices is less well known. Neurologists claim that it is not uncommon."[37]

Crane did not explain the tension between the overall numerical estimate of 2 to 3 percent, and his figure of 50 percent for the elderly—about twenty times higher. By common consensus, older patients suffered at significantly higher rates, but this discrepancy seemed inordinate. Nor did Crane explain how "permanent neurological disorders" could become "a common sight" when the general prevalence figures remained so low. And he did not inform his *Science* readers of the far higher findings from his own research.

Similarly, Crane failed to explain why the "number of patients . . . afflicted cannot be ascertained" when he, and others, had "ascertained" the percentage of afflicted patients, at least in hospitals. Crane may have had in mind technical issues, such as the lack of surveys of outpatients, or the general difficulties of extrapolating from any single surveyed population—with a certain mean age, history of drug exposure, and so forth—to the entire population of those who had received medication. Such issues made it harder to arrive at a precise, all-encompassing prevalence figure, yet they meant only that a precise figure "*had not* yet been ascertained," not that a it was impossible to do so. Moreover, psychiatrists could extrapolate from particular populations—say, young patients on medication for more than three years—to an approximate overall figure. And no technical issue accounted for Crane's 1967 results, which were ten times higher than his 1972 figure. Consciously or otherwise, when Crane wrote "cannot be ascertained" he may have meant "is not supposed to be ascertained."

Crane often argued cautiously, but no other work of his bears marks of self-censorship like these. He probably adopted low Task Force prevalence figures because of some prior understanding or agreement. Nothing suggests that *Science* insisted upon it. Nor does it seem likely that Crane used low figures to makes his pleas for a reconsideration of prescribing practices more palatable. Throughout his career Crane took the opposite tack, and his articles in psychiatric journals continued to cite the higher figures.

In any event, the remainder of the article belies any possibility that Crane was trying to make himself, or his arguments, more palatable to psychiatrists. "Clinical Psychopharmacology in Its 20th Year" is the most forceful criticism

ever written of the medication era. And without mentioning the Collaborative Study by name, Crane rebutted it at almost every point.

Where the Study posited profound drug benefits and mild side effects,
Crane described the reverse. Where the Study evoked the image of a future
mental health system, Crane portrayed the present results of past system reforms.
Where the Study praised optimistic, forward-looking psychiatrists, Crane
looked backward and castigated psychiatrists for ignoring brain damage.

Crane began with the present, observing that almost all seriously mentally
ill persons received medication even though "fewer than 50 percent of patients
hospitalized for several years improve in response to neuroleptics" and even
though the capacity of medication to forestall relapse, while significant, was not
overwhelming. Summarizing the literature, Crane asserted that "60 to 70 percent of acute schizophrenics on no drugs are readmitted [to hospitals] within
one year, while only 20 to 30 percent receiving some form of drug therapy require rehospitalization within 1 year." Thus, 30 to 40 percent did not relapse
within a year, despite being medication-free, while 20 percent to 30 percent
relapsed despite medication.[38]

Turning to side effects, Crane noted that medication produces a variety of
well-known, if sometimes "poorly understood" reactions, such as akinesia and
parkinsonism. Clinicians seemed "willing to take a certain amount of risk in
prescribing drugs for a serious disease such as schizophrenia," and therefore tolerated these effects. That was understandable, if perhaps questionable in some
instances. Yet the "attitude of the physicians, drug companies, and government
agencies toward tardive dyskinesia" was "more difficult to explain in terms of
contemporary community standards."[39]

Crane traced existing prescribing practices to imperatives of the new public mental health system. Mental hospitals had closed or dramatically reduced
their number of beds, he observed. Yet chronic patients still needed hospitalization, and many discharged patients relapsed and required readmission. In response, hospitals retained readmitted patients "for only a short time" and
"provided only substandard psychiatric and nursing care." "This situation," he
continued, "has generated the feeling that drug therapy is indispensable," with
psychiatrists and nurses "firmly convinced that most patients would become
unmanageable if the use of drugs were discontinued." As a result, physicians
prescribed medication to virtually everyone. Meanwhile, "the main function
of . . . [community treatment] is to dispense drugs"; and "physicians, nurses,
guardians, and family members" respond to any unwelcome development with
medication: "[D]rugs are prescribed to solve all types of management problems,
and failure to achieve the desired results causes an escalation of dosage. . . . [T]he
prescribing of drugs has in many cases become a ritual in which patients, family members, and physicians participate."[40]

In Crane's view, prescribing medication for virtually all patients had always been unwarranted, but the practice had become utterly indefensible because of tardive dyskinesia. Yet, despite considerable evidence of the existence of the disorder, "many physicians are still unaware of this problem or seem to be completely unconcerned about it, although tardive dyskinesia has become a common sight." Drug companies and federal agencies "[o]nly recently have . . . shown some interest." Until 1972, drug package inserts "devoted one sentence to the description of permanent neuroleptic effects." These inserts "did not describe the manifestation of tardive dyskinesia, but emphasized, incorrectly, its rarity and likelihood to occur [*sic*] only in elderly or neurologically predisposed individuals." By 1973, many companies had yet to change their package inserts. And researchers still used side effect checklists that omitted tardive dyskinesia.[41]

Crane called for additional research and more physician education. Yet those things were not enough. Imperatives of the new public health system had made caregivers "dependent . . . on chemical agents." Adjustments in that system were a sina qua non of reform.

Crane did not favor eliminating medication, nor did he want a wholesale return to older practices. Many thought that acknowledging tardive dyskinesia would result in the demise of community-care programs, he observed, but such "apprehensions" were unjustified; "it was never suggested that the use of neuroleptics should be abandoned." Instead, the issue was the medical soundness of current prescribing practices. Crane's view point was clear: the "indiscriminate and excessive use" of medication for all schizophrenic patients (and for nonpsychotic subjects) . . . [is] certainly not justified medically."

Medically sound prescribing practices would require institutional changes, but not the end of the new public health system. "[M]ore selective prescribing," Crane wrote, "will put new demands on hospitals, outpatient facilities, and private practitioners" and also "create conflicts with families and administrators." For some patients, "rehospitalization" might prove "necessary." And, "since the use of chemotherapy is accepted procedure," some psychiatrists would "fear . . . lawsuits." In Crane's mind, however, such institutional consequences paled beside the medical need for "discriminate" use of medications.[42]

Crane evidently hoped that the Special Report would provoke change in psychiatry. Other Task Force members regarded it as an endorsement of current practice, by and large. In 1975, Crane and Cole aired the competing positions in a remarkable exchange at the New York Academy of Science.

More starkly than ever, Crane criticized psychiatric developments, including almost every aspect of the Study vision. Cole adhered to the Task Force compromise only in terms of prevalence figures—exactly as Crane had done two years before. Otherwise, Cole echoed Denber and Kline's pre-1973 rejectionism.[43]

Crane went first, delivering a paper entitled "Two Decades of Psychopharmacology and Community Mental Health: Old and New Problems of the Schizophrenic Patient." In this paper he raised his prevalence estimate for tardive dyskinesia to "30 to 50 percent of patients who have been treated with drugs for several years" and mentioned no difficulties in assessment. Furthermore, he asserted that drug-induced parkinsonism and changes in heart function became persistent; cited evidence that medications harmed fetuses; and explicitly compared drug-induced neurological damage to the aftermath of encephalitis.[44]

Crane also saw fewer, and more modest, benefits from medication. "Major drug studies," he wrote, "have shown that, at most, 50 percent of schizophrenics derive some benefit from neuroleptics." Moreover, "those who improve do not show anything approaching a recovery from the disease." According to Crane, it even remained unclear whether patients had better long-term outcomes than they did in the premedication era.[45]

He also portrayed the performance of psychiatrists in an unflattering light. Clinicians held unfounded views about medication, deriving much of their information from drug company "promotional material." For example, they increased dosage needlessly, and by the time they noticed a patient improving, the dosage far exceeded that which had produced the improvement in the first place. In general, Crane thought little of clinicians' ability to weigh benefits against side effects. "This issue," he wrote, "will be beyond the reach of clinical assessment as long as [each patient's supposed need for drugs] . . . is an article of faith to be accepted without question."

Psychiatric research suffered from similar maladies, in Crane's view. Researchers ignored important issues in order to carry out medication trials for drug manufacturers and for public agencies that supported their work. Consequently, they failed to study serious drug complications, such as potentially fatal changes in the heart. At the same time, researchers overestimated the value of large-scale studies and statistical techniques that demonstrated medications' effectiveness. (Cole's Collaborative Study constituted the most famous example, though Crane did not identify it in so many words.) Crane sounded one hopeful note: far lower dosages might prevent neurological damage, without significant loss of benefit—a fact that made continued use of standard regimens even more deplorable.[46]

Crane considered the new public mental health system a disgrace. "At this point," he wrote, "it is difficult to determine how much the therapeutic effectiveness of drugs and how much a change in policy of mental health care contributed" to the "exodus" of patients from state hospitals. Whatever lay behind it, the shift produced sad consequences for many former patients, and only debatable benefits for others. Discharged chronic patients often lived in inner cities "left to their own devices . . . exploited and abused . . . in the most dilapidated areas." The more fortunate lived with their families, but often under circumstances of great strain. Those who "try to be readmitted [to a mental hospital] are turned down." More and more end up in jails. The very old and the very deteriorated still require hospital-level care, and "[a]ny attempt to treat them elsewhere only replicates, often at greater cost, what is now provided by the traditional state institution."[47]

While studies showed it "not only feasible but also advantageous" to maintain many former mental hospital patients in community treatment, Crane cautioned that the results of these studies had been overgeneralized:

> The greatest error of contemporary psychiatry is the large-scale application of methods and technologies that may be successful only when applied to selected samples of patients under the most favorable conditions. Consequently, many of the early gains made in the field of psychiatry have been offset by an unrealistic estimate of what new therapeutic approaches can do for mentally ill and socially handicapped persons. [In addition, a] . . . health program largely dependent on drugs and community resources ignores the fact that less than half of schizophrenic patients benefits [from] drug therapy and that the community no longer provides a therapeutic environment for individuals who are unable to cope with the ordinary stresses of life.[48]

Finally, Crane attributed the clinical, research, and public health failings to a new set of causes. "The neglect of a serious health problem for so many years," he had written in the 1973 *Science* magazine article, "has deeper roots than mere ignorance of facts." He explained it as a shortfall of technical vision, an "example of large-scale and inefficient application of a potentially useful technical discovery without consideration for its long-term effects on the individual and his environment."[49] Now, two years later, Crane attributed the problems to systematic political imperatives and compromised patients' medical interests:

> Psychopharmacology and community psychiatry have become part of a system serving the interests of many groups, while the need[s] of the mentally ill often play a subordinate role. As long as this system has the power to decide what is good for the patient and for society, the emphasis will be on short-term gains, at the expense of the long-term effects that untested programs may have on the individual and his environment.[50]

Neither clinicians, researchers, nor the government had lived up to their medical obligations, in Crane's view, because they were no longer responding to medical imperatives. Full-blown controversy about tardive dyskinesia had begun with Denber and Kline's charges that Crane lacked professionalism. Now, Crane had turned those charges against the profession.

Cole responded. He began by discussing progress in psychiatry, the postures consistent with such progress, and Crane's contrarian stance:

> Psychiatry these days seems to be under attack. I have even attacked it myself on occasion. Despite the pleasure one may get from vigorous assaults, most of these attacks seem unwarranted, ill-considered, and much more detrimental than helpful to progress in the field. Much as I sympathize with occasional points made by Dr. Crane in his paper, I am opposed strongly to his overall approach and to a majority of his specific criticisms. He obviously has undertaken the role of Cassandra within psychiatry, foreseeing doom in many aspects of our current scientific and clinical operations. Being an optimist, I see problems where he sees catastrophes and tend to see no problem whatever in many areas where he sees significant problems. It may be a matter of the optimism-pessimism balance in some instances; in other instances, it is a matter of evaluating the available evidence.[51]

Cole's images—psychiatric progress, attacks on progress, Crane's personal attributes—re-created Denber and Kline's 1967 rhetoric. Cole moderated their severest themes, but only to a degree. Cole had sometimes criticized psychiatry himself; Crane's likely problem lay in his "optimism-pessimism balance"— a problem seemingly less severe than the near professional derangement Denber had diagnosed in 1967. To use an exaggerated analogy, Denber had viewed Crane as a virtual psychotic, engaged in destructive behavior for no apparent reason. Cole saw him more as the victim of a character disorder—a man who fell at the far extreme of the "optimism-pessimism balance." On the other hand, since that "balance" vaguely suggested the chemical imbalance theory of schizophrenia, Crane's problem might be more serious than it sounded to a lay ear. Moreover, Cole's Collaborative Study had described therapeutic optimism as a signal development, perhaps even more important to modern psychiatry than the advent of medications. And Crane lacked it.

From his more optimistic stance, Cole challenged Crane. To begin with, "schizophrenic patients, even under the borderline treatment procedures currently often in vogue, such as inadequate dosages . . . and mediocre arrangements for aftercare in the community, nevertheless often do quite well, . . . far better than . . . in the old days, when they were chronically warehoused in sterile and depressing institutions."[52]

In relation to tardive dyskinesia, Cole reported his own observation that only about 5 percent of "chronically treated schizophrenic patients" had "evident tardive dyskinesia." Nor did he regard the disorder as related to dosage or length of drug exposure. Tardive dyskinesia, he said, was "probably attributable to idiosyncratic factors and preexisting organic brain problems, diagnosable or nondiagnosable."[53]

That 5 percent figure seemingly coincided with that of the Task Force. Yet Cole's was actually lower. The Task Force's estimate covered a "mixed population" of acute and chronic patients; Cole's, only those "chronically treated" with medications—a group the Task Force had implied might have a 20 percent prevalence.

The rest of Cole's statement carried rejectionism farther than Denber or Kline ever did. Cole's suggestion that "nondiagnosable" brain abnormalities caused tardive dyskinesia was irrefutable; no possible discovery could undermine it. His implicit claim was that undamaged brains respond well to medication; thus, if tardive dyskinesia appeared, it necessarily followed that the brain had been damaged to begin with. (The force of Cole's claim would diminish, however, as more patients developed tardive dyskinesia; his argument would become absurd, although still irrefutable, as the number of afflicted patients approached 100 percent.)[54]

Cole took a rejectionist stance toward prevention efforts as well. Dosage and duration of treatment were unrelated to tardive dyskinesia, he thought. Thus, clinicians could do little to prevent the disorder in an individual case. Unless psychiatrists medicated *no one* because of a slight, general risk of tardive dyskinesia—a risk really attributable to preexisting brain damage—it appeared that they should go on medicating everyone, as before, despite the disorder. Crane had seen some hope in much lower doses; Cole thought current dosages "inadequate."

Regarding other side effects that Crane cited—cardiac complications and harm to fetuses—Cole found the literature too scanty to warrant a judgment. He also considered the implications murky:

> The position we would be in if we had the data Dr. Crane proposes is interesting to consider in passing. For example, supposing you knew that all schizophrenics given neuroleptic drugs stood 1 chance in 10,000 of sudden death due to . . . [changes in the heart] and supposing you also knew for a fact that schizophrenic patients in the absence of neuroleptic drug treatment stood only 1 chance in 30,000 of having such an occurrence—what would you do? I submit that the truth about the incidence of the various unpleasant things Dr. Crane mentions will probably complicate decision making rather than simplify it unless the drugs turn out to be completely blameless, which is not unlikely.[55]

Cole did not directly respond to Crane's other observations about side effects, such as the claim that parkinsonism became persistent. Nor did he address Crane's comparison of side effects to the aftermath of encephalitis, or the suggestion that clinicians used medication without regard to risks and benefits, or the assertion that half of patients derived no benefit from medication. Cole did say that "neuroleptic drugs are substantially better than placebo (75 percent improvement rate versus 25 percent)"—a finding derived from the Collaborative Study, but one not inconsistent with Crane's argument. If 25 percent improved without medication, and another 25 percent failed to improve with medication, then 50 percent would not benefit—assuming the degree of improvement remained constant.[56]

At times, Cole seemed to miss the point. Crane did not think that cardiac complications or other side effects would "simplify" clinical decision making. On the contrary, Crane believed that clinicians used drugs as an article of "faith" and that side effects *should* complicate decisions. And Crane had not failed to note the lack of definitive research about various side effects. He objected precisely to that lack of research, and tried to explain why side effects had been ignored.

Conceivably, additional research might illuminate deinstitutionalization issues as well. Yet direct comparison of the old and new mental health systems had become all but impossible: the old system no longer existed. One's view of history—to use Cole's phrase, one's position on the "optimism-pessimism balance" in relation to the old mental health regime—probably contributed as much as anything did toward one's evaluation of deinstitutionalization.

Nothing in Cole's remarks had suggested any doubt. Yet within a year, Cole would reverse his stand and adopt positions about the benefits and side effects of medication that duplicated Crane's. And mainstream psychiatry would follow in Cole's footsteps, just as it had done in 1964.

Chapter 6   The Vision Unravels

Dᴜʀɪɴɢ ᴛʜᴇ mid- and late 1970s, the Study vision lost its hold over leading researchers. Cole endorsed much of Crane's account of tardive dyskinesia and adopted many of Crane's views about the benefits of medication as well. Other investigators rediscovered the psychomotor indifference syndrome. Some turned their attention to medication-induced distress, reopening the inquiry into patient psychology. In other areas, however, no change occurred. Public mental health policy continued on the same course: indeed, the pace of deinstitutionalization accelerated. Clinicians prescribed medications and overlooked side effects, as they had before; they remained faithful to the Study vision even as its principal author, Cole, abandoned it.

Tardive Dyskinesia

Jonathan Cole performed an about-face in 1976, a year after the exchange with Crane. Then, he had embraced rejectionism; now, he adopted a Crane-like view of tardive dyskinesia. In the process, Cole abandoned much of the Study vision.

Cole advanced his new views in an article, "Maintenance Antipsychotic Therapy: Is the Cure Worse than the Disease?" which he coauthored with George Gardos. This article described tardive dyskinesia as "a major therapeutic challenge." Vestiges of Cole's old positions remained—the article said that tardive dyskinesia "*seems* to be associated" with medications and it reported prevalence estimates "between 0.5% and 40%"—but most of the discussion and Gardos and Cole's urgent clinical recommendations made little sense unless they considered the link between medications and tardive dyskinesia firmly established.[1]

In 1975, Cole had thought medication dosages and the length of treatment unrelated to tardive dyskinesia. Now Gardos and Cole urged a dramatic change "because of the seriousness of the long-term complications . . . primarily tardive dyskinesia." "[E]very chronic schizophrenic outpatient maintained on antipsychotic medication should have the benefit of an adequate trial without drugs," they wrote. Even in nonchronic cases, "an attempt should be made to determine the feasibility of drug discontinuance in every patient." Thus, "the dangers of tardive dyskinesia" appeared to be serious, and Cole proceeded as if the risk increased with additional exposure to medication.[2]

Gardos and Cole's recommendations reflected a more Crane-like assessment of benefits as well. Reviewing relapse rates among medicated and placebo outpatients, they concluded that "perhaps as many as 50% . . . might not be worse off if their medications were withdrawn." Cole had trumpeted impressive qualitative changes and antischizophrenic effects in the Study; here, by contrast, the beneficial effects of medication seemed limited to preventing relapse.[3]

Evidently, Cole had changed his thinking about fundamental issues. Yet he did not explain why, or even note that a change had occurred. The article mentioned "recent publications" about tardive dyskinesia, but it cited research that dated back almost ten years. And no significant new findings about the benefits of medication had appeared since Cole's exchange with Crane.

In a 1977 article, Gardos and Cole offered reasons for concluding that medication caused tardive dyskinesia, but almost all these reasons—the disorder was not described before medications; reported rates were increasing dramatically with increased medication use; unmedicated patients had "significantly" lower rates; symptoms often emerged upon withdrawing medication or reducing the dosage—had been advanced years earlier without convincing Cole. The 1977 article offered one new reason—experimental manipulations of dopamine levels produced dyskinesia-like symptoms, suggesting a plausible mechanism by which medications might cause the disorder—but that hardly seemed decisive. The new experiments were not more suggestive than Crane's discussion, a decade earlier, of dyskinesia-like symptoms in rats and cats on medication. Moreover, it was always conceded that medication could produce dyskinesia; even Kline admitted that the questions concerned rate and persistence. Thus, it seems unlikely that data produced Cole's sudden and unexplained change of mind.[4]

Nathan Kline also reversed his stance in 1976—in a book chapter coauthored with George Simpson, who had been a member of the 1973 Task Force. Noting that Kline had "at first questioned the existence of the syndrome," the chapter revisited virtually all Kline's 1967 arguments. Instead of Kline's 1967 prevalence estimate (1 in a 1,000,000) or the Task Force figure (3 percent to 6 percent) Simpson and Kline wrote, "One can say confidently that the numbers are substantial enough to make . . . [tardive dyskinesia] a matter of extreme importance even if we assume conservatively that only 10% of patients on long-term or maintenance therapy develop this disorder."[5] In place of Kline's earlier reliance on preexisting brain damage, they cited "organicity" as a "debatable" contributing factor. Kline had charged Crane with confusing schizophrenic mannerisms and dyskinesias; Simpson and Kline now counted "psychiatric and neurological mannerisms" among the confounding factors that made "[p]revalence figures vary from practically 0 to 40%." In 1967, Kline had implied that dyskinetic movements occurred commonly before the medication era; Simpson and Kline now noted the "lack of sufficient information concerning the extent of movement disorders in chronic hospitalized patients in the preneuroleptic era." Kline had claimed that he cured a patient's symptoms using deconditioning techniques; Simpson and Kline now described two cases of "agitated patients suffering from depression whose lives were a total misery at least partially because of their dyskinesias." Even Kline's 1967 "epidemic of papers" warning—a figure of speech that evoked tardive dyskinesia's resemblance to encephalitis—produced echoes in 1976: Simpson and Kline described a tardive dyskinesia victim who had also suffered encephalitis.[6]

Thus, the principal author of 1967 revisionism joined the principal author of the Collaborative Study in acknowledging tardive dyskinesia. Kline's about-face was not nearly as stark, however. Almost a decade had passed—not a year, as in Cole's case—and Kline, unlike Cole, acknowledged his earlier position. At the same time, Kline did not acknowledge his most important shift: he had abandoned the cascading factual suppositions and tiers of fall-back positions of 1967.

What lay behind Cole's and Kline's new positions? One likely factor was a 1975 class action lawsuit asserting the right of patients to refuse medication. As medical director of the patients' hospital, Cole found himself involved in the case. This was not the first time that litigation spurred a rethinking of tardive dyskinesia; an earlier lawsuit had preceded the formation of the 1973 task force. Yet, if Cole and Kline had not felt scientifically vulnerable, no lawsuit could have changed their minds.

What Kline had feared in 1967, the "epidemic of papers," had come to pass. Psychiatric journals were always open to tardive dyskinesia research, but the number of articles and interested researchers were increasing rapidly. So were reported prevalence estimates—a development that especially troubled Gardos and Cole. In 1977 they expressed alarm because one group of investigators had "found that 2.2% of drug-treated, hospitalized patients showed tardive dyskinesia," but eight years later a different group "using the same rating scale in a similar population obtained a prevalence rate of 56%." Gardos and Cole concluded that although "other factors may have played a role in this astonishing increase," clearly "a significant increase in the number of tardive dyskinesia cases during the last ten years" had occurred. Yet Gardos and Cole suggested no mechanism that could produce such an increase; nor did they allude to earlier reports of high rates by Crane and others. Probably more significant than the actual prevalence increase was the increase in researchers reporting high figures.[7]

Forces within psychiatry—which no lawsuit had created—were undermining the Study vision. Evidence of that process also emerges from research involving psychomotor indifference and medication-induced distress. These effects had faded from awareness because of the Study, but they began to reemerge in the mid-1970s, as Cole and Kline were changing their minds about tardive dyskinesia. This did not result from the spur of litigation or other outside pressure: courts and regulators continued to ignore such problems. Instead, it was as if the Study vision could maintain its grip only for so long until medical investigation finally broke free of it. Ten years after the Collaborative Study, and probably spurred by the tardive dyskinesia controversy, that was happening.

Psychomotor Indifference

The syndrome of medication induced "psychomotor indifference," or diminished physical and mental activity, seemed obvious to psychiatrists of the 1950s: it prompted them to call medications "major tranquilizers." Nor did patients overlook it, of course. Complaints about "one's head . . . [being] fuzzy," feeling like a "zombie," "emptied out, devoid of ideas," "as though I am walking with lead in my shoes" been a constant refrain from patients during the medication era. One of the most remarkable legacies of the Study was psychiatrists' reduced awareness of these phenomena.[8]

The Study vision focused on brain processes. As it did that, patient feelings and states of mind faded in significance. Psychiatry became an applied brain science, combined with the social science of community mental health. In the process, it relegated realms of human feeling and action to a nether world of inquiry, lost somewhere between the brain and the community. In 1978, Theodore Van Putten and Philip R. May observed that "schizophrenics have been asked every question except, 'How does the medication make you feel?' "[9]

A brief communication in the 1970 *British Journal of Psychiatry* sheds light on why psychiatrists did not to ask that question. Two research psychiatrists injected themselves with a single dose of medication and described the effect as

> marked and very similar in both of us: within ten minutes a marked
> slowing of thinking and movement developed, along with a profound
> inner restlessness. Neither subject could continue work, and each left
> work for over 36 hours. Each subject complained of a paralysis of
> volition, a lack of physical and psychic energy. The subjects felt
> unable to read, telephone or perform household tasks of their own

will, but could perform these tasks if demanded to do so. There was no sleepiness or sedation; on the contrary, both subjects complained of severe anxiety.[10]

Medicated patients commonly experience the same feelings. "Paralysis of volition" and lack of "energy" result from the syndrome of psychomotor indifference. "Profound inner restlessness" and "severe anxiety" represent akathisia. Yet the Study vision precluded significant patient distress from medications. And so, consistent with that vision, the authors simply presumed that patients did not experience what they just had. Instead, they speculated on the differences between "normal" and sick brains—differences that might explain why "normals," but supposedly not mentally ill persons, felt distress. What psychiatrists had once considered a typical patient response to medication could longer exist, not even after researchers experienced it themselves; it had become unknowable because of the prevailing vision. Here at least, theorizing about the brain served as a simple escape from unwelcome clinical reality.

When a psychiatrist not under the sway of the Study experiences medication, he or she assumes patients and psychiatrists feel the same things. The psychiatrist Samuel Gershon later wrote: "Anyone who takes a drug such as chlorpromazine or haloperidol gets a neuroleptic-induced deficit syndrome: that is, one's head is fuzzy, it feels as if it is packed with cotton, one cannot think straight, and one cannot do one's work. I have tried taking these drugs, and it is extremely difficult to get your thoughts straight. They should be tried by many doctors who prescribe these agents!"[11] Gershon erred only in thinking that the experience of medication would necessarily enlighten psychiatrists; it had not enlightened the authors of the 1970 communication to the *British Journal of Psychiatry*.

In 1975, three Columbia University psychiatrists—Arthur Rifkin, Frederic Quitkin, and Donald F. Klein—rediscovered the psychomotor indifference syndrome in patients and called it "akinesia." Akinetic patients, they explained, manifest "a lessening of spontaneity, paucity of gestures, diminished conversation and apathy." The condition could resemble depression, demoralization, or schizophrenic withdrawal, and the authors commented that psychiatrists rarely recognized it as a medication side effect. They called their article "Akinesia: A Poorly Recognized Drug-Induced Extrapyramidal Behavioral Disorder."[12]

As if proving the point, the authors soon published another paper, this one reporting that 35 percent of patients on a long-acting medication developed severe akinesia and could not continue with an experiment because of the condition. Yet the same patients had been judged as having "no more than minor side effects" on this medication during an earlier part of the same experiment. The authors did not say so, but it seemed obvious that the raters had "poorly recognized" akinesia during the earlier stage of the experiment and had judged the afflicted patients as therapeutic successes.[13]

Subjective Distress

Rifkin, Quitkin, and Klein noted that akinesia often resembled unhappiness and depression, but they regarded the condition as a "behavioral disorder" rather than a matter of a patient's subjective distress. At about the same time, however, other researchers were examining "neuroleptic dysphoria"—medication-induced distress or unhappiness—in its own right.

According to one psychiatrist, "the subjectively experienced and objective signs of neuroleptic-induced mental side effects have been well known since the discovery of chlorpromazine." Yet the Study vision ignored such phenomena, particularly patients' distress. Distress detracted from Study claims about "qualitatively impressive" drug effects—distress is not impressive—and it revealed aspects of medication that did not fit the antischizophrenic model. It also compromised the ideal of nearly universal use of medication—could psychiatrists medicate people who became tormented or depressed as a result?— and so threatened public health objectives. Moreover, widespread distress suggested a harshness and tolerance for suffering on the part of psychiatrists reminiscent of the lobotomy era. Like tardive dyskinesia, then, distress simply could not exist.[14]

During the 1950s, psychiatrists had paid somewhat more attention to patient distress, though many considered it relevant only because affected patients might stop taking medication. Pockets of interest survived the Study vision. Just as some researchers continued investigating tardive dyskinesia, a few—again, mainly European—described depressive, or worse, reactions to medication.[15]

Leo Hollister, an interesting transition figure, played a role here comparable to that of Frank Ayd in the tardive dyskinesia controversy. A coauthor of Casey's multicenter studies, Hollister had written leading articles about medications during the 1950s and early 1960s. As an established authority, he held a position similar to Frank J. Ayd's when the Collaborative Study appeared. And, like Ayd, he acknowledged facts that the Study—and then many younger researchers—did not. Indeed, Hollister had noted the early reports about tardive dyskinesia; he was the psychiatrist who depicted "toothless old crones in trolley cars" with dyskinesias prior to the drug era.

Hollister saw much more important implications in medication-induced distress. He repeatedly urged clinicians to consider not only patients' "objective response" but also their "subjective response" to medication. In part, the usual reason lay behind his advice: "Unless a patient tolerates a drug well, he is not likely to maintain treatment faithfully." And, since patients varied in their distaste for particular side effects—one patient "may prefer restlessness rather than impairment of . . . sexual capacity"; another might prefer the opposite—psychiatrists should select a medication with care.[16]

This was standard advice from a psychiatrist who recognized patients' "subjective response" to medication. Hollister went further, however. "Some patients," he argued, "may tolerate antipsychotic drugs so poorly that no drug treatment should be given." The idea of a common drug effect severe enough to warrant discontinuing treatment was provocative; at the time leading psychiatrists were resisting precisely the same notion in Crane's work on tardive dyskinesia.[17]

Hollister hedged his point, however. His use of the word "may" suggested that poorly responding patients might not exist at all, or if they did, that their response might not qualify as poor enough to discontinue medication. Hollister reduced the sting from his recommendation in a more inventive way as well; tentatively, he suggested that patients whose medication was withdrawn for this reason did not, after all, suffer from true schizophrenia:

> As these patients tend to be less psychotic than most schizophrenics, with retention of insight and marked somatization, it may be that they represent a "schizopreniform" [only apparently schizophrenic] group rather than true schizophrenia [*sic*]. One should bear in mind that to take antipsychotic drugs, one must be crazy, either literally or figuratively. The ability to tolerate these drugs seems to be directly correlated with the severity of the psychosis.[18]

Hollister did not cite studies or any fact-gathering at this point. Just as trolley rides had convinced him that dyskinesia predated medication, clinical observation apparently persuaded him that some patients (how many? after how long a period on medications? chronic or acute?) tolerated drugs so badly that medication should be withheld. Combined with reports about "normals" experiencing distress after taking medication, these observations led him to conclude that poorly responding patients might not suffer true schizophrenia at all. In this way, Hollister reconciled patient distress with a key tenet of the Study vision: the idea that almost everyone with schizophrenia responded to medications well.[19]

Nonetheless, Hollister had offered a rare suggestion, comparable to Ayd's vague calls for "treatment of another sort." Neither man forgot what psychiatrists had known during the 1950s, yet both adapted themselves to prevailing Study notions. Hollister, in particular, excelled at reconciling inconvenient phenomena (dyskinetic movements, patient distress) with the prevailing vision; he did that partly by making the vision a little blurred.

During the mid-1970s a few researchers began to approach medication-induced distress in a different way, applying standard investigative techniques to the problem. They described patients' distress, estimated its prevalence, and treated it as a matter of clinical significance. Moreover, they did not attempt to reconcile their findings with prevailing ideas about antischizophrenic actions or near-universal drug effectiveness. Like the late 1960s and early 1970s articles about tardive dyskinesia, this literature examined phenomena that should have been obvious but that the Study obscured. Both bodies of work stand out because of their literary style and evocative descriptions of patients; they ignored Collaborative Study–like conventions of thought, approach, and analysis.

Theodore Van Putten, a UCLA psychiatrist, performed a role analogous to Crane's, authoring or coauthoring the leading studies about patients' subjective reactions. In a 1974 article, Van Putten examined how distress affected patients' willingness to take medication—the usual subject. Yet Van Putten approached it as a serious research question, not anecdotally, and concluded that the "reluctance" to take medication and a "dysphoric" (i.e., unhappy or depressive) drug response were both "usually related" to the extrapyramidal side effects of medication.[20]

When other psychiatrists noticed patient distress, they often attributed it to mental pathology or character flaws. In this view, patients only *thought* they reacted badly to medication, and they thought so because of their mental illness, or because they liked feeling ill. Or else they were lying and exaggerating. In the same way, psychiatrists had supposed that tardive dyskinesia resulted from a preexisting condition (brain damage), constituted a manifestation of schizophrenia, or, as Kline had argued, reflected patients' "love" of dyskinetic movements.

Van Putten ignored such rationalizations. Instead, he described patient unhappiness as a natural outgrowth of side effects such as akinesia and akathisia. In addition, like Crane, he portrayed affected patients in graphic language, noting that they "complained bitterly" about medications, "craved" anything that might diminish their distress, and found life "unbearable" because of the side effects. In one passage, Van Putten noted that "gross" side effects "can be tolerated for a short interim within the supportive confines of the hospital," but "even mild" effects, if prolonged, "are difficult to tolerate for an outpatient." These effects might "not be compatible with a useful life in the community," as, for example, if muscular stiffness prevented a "clerk typist" from doing "her job" or a tremor "socially incapacitat[ed] . . . a self-conscious woman."[21]

This constituted the same distinction between hospital and community that Kline had drawn the 1950s. Van Putten was reviving pre–Collaborative Study knowledge (along with some of the old phrasing and the apparent preference for examples involving women, and doing so in the era of deinstitutionalization, when the problem of side effects outside hospitals could no longer be dismissed in passing. Van Putten also implied that side effects remained serious within hospitals, where Kline deemed them mere "annoyances."

The article never quite said that drug-induced distress warranted medical and moral concern in its own right. Nor did Van Putten say that akinesia might qualify as intolerable in the community, even if one had a job as a clerk or typist. Yet he portrayed the problem of distress as real, attributed it to medication, and treated it as a matter of significance—all departures from prevailing practice.

In early 1975 Van Putten published another article, "The Many Faces of Akathisia," that developed his earlier themes. Here, Van Putten described patients distressed, even tormented, by akathisia; quoted Kalinowsky's 1958 observation that akathisia "can be more difficult to endure than any of the symptoms for which [the patient] was originally treated;" estimated the condition's prevalence at 45 percent, and noted that the "subtler akathisias often go unrecognized by the physician—but not by the patient." Van Putten also observed that akathisia often ended with patients refusing medication or, on occasion, in "dramatic exacerbations of psychosis." The article also stands out for its stark descriptions of patients' feelings on medication: "fright, terror, anger or rage, anxiety, and . . . sexual torment." Even its graphic title marked a departure from the dry, technical style of the day.[22]

Van Putten and a coauthor, Philip R. A. May, reconsidered subjective reactions in a 1978 article, "Subjective Response as a Predictor of Outcome in Pharmacotherapy: The Consumer Has a Point." As the title suggests, it examined whether patients suffering from medication-related distress had worse clinical outcomes. In 1974, Van Putten had effectively expanded the Study definition of side effects to include distress and subjective reactions; in this article Van Putten and May expanded the inquiry into clinical outcomes to include the same factors.[23]

At the outset, they recorded patients' response to a test dose of medication —and the results were not what the Collaborative Study would have led one to expect. Van Putten and May reported that "patients varied widely in their subjective response"—a finding at odds with the idea that people with schizophrenia respond to medication uniformly and well—and that 40 percent "had a dysphoric response." Four of these patients "refused further treatment." Moreover, the distress was not transient or short-lived:

> Can we assure a patient with an early dysphoric response that he will "get used to" the medication? Apparently not: 88% of the dysphoric responders eventually refused to continue taking chlorpromazine because of a persisting dysphoria, against only 23% of the euphoric responders. . . . [M]ost [dysphoric responders] . . . complained throughout their treatment with chlorpromazine of feeling "drugged," of having "no drive or ambition," of being "drowsy," "tired," and "slowed up."[24]

Van Putten and May also reported that the patients with dysphoric reactions to the test dose had worse clinical outcomes, at least in the short term. "An early dysphoric response," they wrote, "augurs a poor prognosis for further treatment with the drug." Such results would hardly surprise a lay person, but in light of the Study vision the conclusions were extraordinary.[25]

In 1980, Van Putten and May, along with a third coauthor, Coralee Yale, set out to identify patients who should *not* receive drugs. "Although most schizophrenic patients improve if given medication," they wrote, "a substantial number do just as well without it and some get worse or develop adverse effects. Regrettably, controlled research on prediction of response has been meager, and our current of state of knowledge is not impressive." Examining the predictive effects of patients' early response to medication, the authors reported a "consistent correlation" between changes in a patient's condition after the first two days of medication and the same patient's condition after a month of treatment. Thus, "when patients get worse early on in drug treatment . . . something may need to be changed." One such "something" was the dose, but the authors judged the likelihood of "eventual benefit" from increasing the dose as "slight." Another "something" was changing the drug, but no data existed on that point. "It is possible," the 1980 article concluded, "that the patient might do just as well, or even better, without drug treatment."[26]

Thus, prominent researchers—May had conducted a famous study of the effectiveness of medication—argued that the challenge facing psychiatrists was to identify the "substantial number" of patients who should not receive medication. In contrast to the almost universally effective treatment described in the Collaborative Study, Van Putten and May portrayed medication as generally useful, but also as highly distressing, unnecessary, and perhaps clinically harmful in a substantial minority of cases. Their assessment differed little from Crane's in 1973, and they had not even mentioned tardive dyskinesia.

Thus, psychomotor indifference and subjective distress followed a trajectory that paralleled that of tardive dyskinesia. In each case, recognition faded from awareness after the Collaborative Study, though psychiatrists who had achieved prominence in the 1950s, such as Ayd and Hollister, continued to pay some attention. Next, psychiatrists like Crane and Van Putten approached the problem independently of the vision. Their articles portrayed the effects of medication graphically. In the akinesia articles by Rifkin, Quitkin, and Klein, one can almost sense the moment when the blinders fell, and they saw what had been before them all along. All these authors implied that many patients should not receive medication; Crane and Van Putten and May said so explicitly. Their conclusions—indeed, the very subjects they investigated—clashed with the Study vision.

Clear evidence that the Study vision had unraveled appears in a letter by

Brian G. Anderson and others, published in the 10 September 1981 issue of the *New England Journal of Medicine*. Anderson described how three "normal" subjects and also a young psychiatrist responded to a single dose of medication. Thus, the letter dealt with the same subject as the brief communication in the 1970 *British Journal of Psychiatry* that had detailed the experiences of Belmaker and Ward after they took medication.[27]

The "effects were of unexpected severity and duration," Anderson reported. As in the 1970 experiment, all the 1981 subjects experienced "pronounced akathisia" and "dysphoria." Some also developed panic attacks, an inability to concentrate, severe anxiety, fatigue, impairment of fine motor coordination, sedation, or decreased libido. Moreover, the effects persisted in a number of instances, although the subjects had received only one dose. Akathisia lasted for "36 hours to five days," for example, while the dysphoria persisted for periods that ranged from three days to more than a month. To explain this persistence, Anderson theorized that medication had altered neurotransmitter "receptor sensitivity." And he speculated that "[a]kathisia and dysphoria after the use of neuroleptic drugs in psychiatric patients may be more common than is generally realized."

Anderson's approach differed vastly from that of Belmaker and Ward, despite the overlap in their findings. Under the sway of the Study vision, the earlier psychiatrists presumed that people with schizophrenia did not suffer widespread distress on medication. The presumption overrode their own experience of the drugs, as well as the notorious fact that patients frequently complained about distress. Finally, Belmaker and Ward's speculations about normal and schizophrenic "brains"—which grew out of their presumption about patient nondistress—lent the prestige of brain science to their enterprise. The resulting circle of presumptions and reasons was as implausible as it was inescapable—much like the similar system of presumptions that Denber and Kline had deployed against tardive dyskinesia.

Anderson did not rebut the old presumptions: he ignored them. He did not ask whether "normal" persons' experience of medication shed light on patients' experiences; he just proceeded as if they did and as if it mattered. And as if one would naturally look to the brain for an explanation of the deleterious effects of medications, as well as their benefits.

What had been inconceivable to Belmaker and Ward appeared obvious to Anderson: the Study vision exerted no hold over him. Indeed, once free of its constraints, Anderson immediately saw what Hall, Swain, and Jackson first reported in 1956: side effects, other than tardive dyskinesia, commonly persist after medication is withdrawn.

Like Crane and Van Putten, Anderson described phenomena that psychiatrists had acknowledged during the first period of the medication era, but that the Study ruled out. The work of these psychiatrists suggested that the Study vision could last only so long—it had been a decade and a half—before ordinary observation, the openness of medical journals to dissenting views, and the sheer number and diversity of medical researchers discredited it.

By about 1980, then, the Study vision seemingly had run its course. How could old views survive the new research? At this point, one might have predicted that psychiatrists would withdraw many patients from medication and that research into psychomotor indifference, subjective distress, and tardive dyskinesia would intensify in the future, along with work on persistent side effects other than tardive dyskinesia. Indeed, it seemed possible that the shift of research attention and rhetoric to the brain might end up demonstrating not antischizophrenic effects but a large number of persistent brain impairments associated with medication.

None of those things happened. Clinical psychiatry virtually ignored the new findings. And the paths of tardive dyskinesia and other side effects soon diverged. Tardive dyskinesia became a focal point of research, public discussion, and litigation, while medication-induced psychological distress, psychomotor indifference, and persistence in general would receive only sporadic attention from a few interested researchers.

In fact, two aspects of Anderson's letter suggested reasons for caution about the future. First, although Anderson made the point circumspectly, his letter suggested that psychiatrists had grossly underestimated the extent and persistence of medication-caused distress. Yet Anderson did not ask how that could have happened. Tens of millions of patients had received medication over a period of three decades and, as Anderson made plain, the effects on subjects were unmistakable. A profession that had erred in such way could presumably make comparable mistakes in the future.

The second reason for caution lay in psychiatrists' lack of awareness of medication-era history and of their changes in thinking about medication. Reading Anderson's letter, one would never guess that more than a decade had passed since the prevailing vision had virtually ruled out observations such as his. Nor would one guess that he had rediscovered something described twenty-five years before in the *Journal of the American Medical Association*. The Study vision had swept away what preceded it, and now *it* was being swept away—but psychiatrists seemed unaware both of what had occurred in the first instance, when the Study appeared, and that it was happening again.

Chapter 7   Medication and Litigation

During the late 1960s, with the Study vision ascendant in psychiatry, a new kind of litigation appeared: cases with the avowed goal of transforming public psychiatry through law. "Right-to-treatment" cases sought massive reforms in state mental hospitals. Other lawsuits challenged hospital commitment schemes, demanding more restrictive legal standards and more robust procedural protections for patients. These cases, often class actions and typically the work of legal aid, civil liberties, or other public interest lawyers, captured the imagination of lawyers, legal scholars, and the public.[1]

Ample injustices warranted legal action. Commitment standards were lax; meaningful commitment hearings almost nonexistent. Within hospitals, patients generally led bleak and empty lives, punctuated by violence, incompetent treatment, and abuse of almost every description.

In principle, lawsuits challenging such conditions need have had no connection to the Study vision. Yet the lawsuits meshed with that vision almost perfectly. Reform litigation advanced the cause of deinstitutionalization and near-universal treatment with medication. And it downplayed—indeed, virtually ignored—side effects until the late 1970s.

Right-to-treatment cases typically produced a rapid reduction in hospital populations. Commitment reforms, if they accomplished anything, tended to do the same. And except in some anomalous early lawsuits, the use of medication received virtually no attention. Through the mid-1970s, reform attorneys asked for nothing that might impede widespread use of medication.

The Collaborative Study had ignored side effects, but the reform lawsuits virtually ignored medication altogether, its side effects and benefits alike. In the eyes of lawyers and courts, constitutional "liberty," not medication, drove developments; thus, in the heyday of reform litigation, medication became all but invisible.

Psychiatrists took a different view, of course. Some treated constitutional "liberty" the way lawyers treated medications—that is, they ignored it. More often, psychiatric accounts attempted to explain why forced psychiatric treatment was consistent with patients' rights to liberty or exceeded the right to liberty in importance. Some accounts depicted reform litigation itself as a consequence of the use of medication: only because of drugs, the argument went, could hospital conditions improve and patients get discharged in connection with court orders.[2]

These last claims were debatable. State hospitals occasionally had worked well before medication. On the eve of the medication era, psychiatrists like Greenblatt thought hospitals could work well again. Moreover, as the current plight of homeless mentally ill persons demonstrates, deinstitutionalization required nothing more than a willingness to tolerate its consequences. On the other hand, it may well be true that hospitals in fact would not have improved—and that the public would not have tolerated deinstitutionalization—without medication.

Whether or not medication supplied the necessary precondition for reform lawsuits, an earlier revolution in the law was absolutely indispensable. In 1954, as chlorpromazine debuted in American mental hospitals, the Supreme Court decided *Brown v. Board of Education*. A momentous decision, *Brown* did more than prohibit racial segregation in public schools. It eventually changed the role of courts in numerous areas of national life that had nothing to do with race—including, eventually, the lives of the mentally ill.

Over the following years, the Court extended *Brown* in three ways, and in the process made the Constitution an instrument for transforming society. First, it applied the antisegregation principle to state activities across the board, including public transportation, parks, and courts. By the early 1960s, it was clear that the justices meant to uproot racial segregation as a state-sanctioned way of life, and not merely to end official segregation. Schools not only had to rescind rules that racially discriminated, for example; they also had to produce truly integrated classrooms. Thus, the justices found in the Constitution principles capable of overturning social practices, no matter how old or entrenched, and affecting people's lives in ways that only legislation had before.[3]

Second, in order to implement the principle of nonsegregation, the justices sanctioned what became a virtual court takeover of public school systems. By the 1970s, lower federal courts were exercising vast powers over public education. Judges were making the kind of decisions about public institutions that only executive officials and legislatures had made previously.

Third, the Court deployed the Constitution as an instrument of social transformation in relation to issues other than race. For example, in the 1960s the Court declared that the word "liberty" in the Fourteenth Amendment prevented states from regulating contraception and extramarital sexual activities in traditional ways. During the 1970s, decisions about abortion and other rights contributed to a revolution in the status of women.[4]

It required little imagination to extrapolate from these developments to state psychiatry. If courts could direct the operation of public schools in the name of constitutional values, could they not do the same for public mental hospitals? If a state could not consign people to a second-class life because of the color of their skin, could it consign people to horrid institutions because of the supposed condition of their mind? If "liberty" precluded states from restricting sexual freedoms, did it not also preclude states from constructing definitions of "mental illness" that deprived people of their physical freedom? As litigation over public psychiatry unfolded, advocates and opponents alike regarded it as a crucial test of the Supreme Court's willingness to carry out *Brown*-type transformations in other areas of social life.[5]

Historically, courts had played a minimal role in public mental health matters. Involuntary patients might enjoy a nominal right to request a court hearing, but few hearings ever took place. Typically, psychiatrists filled out forms and determined matters for themselves, applying statutory standards that, as late as the 1950s, spoke largely to a person's medical need for treatment. Even if judges had heard such cases, they likely would have deferred to the judgments of psychiatrists, the experts on "insanity." Nor did courts generally interfere in the internal operation of state hospitals, despite the often scandalously bad conditions within the institutions.

The Right to Treatment

The concept of the constitutional "right to treatment," like the Study vision in psychiatry, first appeared in the early 1960s. It marked a radical departure, but it quickly achieved wide acceptance—again, like the Study vision. And to an even greater extent than the Study vision, it emerged from a single document: a 1960 article, "The Right to Treatment," that appeared in the *American Bar Association Journal*.[6]

Morton Birnbaum, a lawyer and a physician, authored "The Right to Treatment." For legal authority, Birnbaum could cite only expanding ideas about "liberty" and the example of *Brown v. Board of Education*. Yet his article offered an appealing, intuitive idea. Persons involuntarily confined for psychiatric treatment, he argued, must have that treatment. Without it, hospital confinement served no valid purpose. Thus, a court should recognize a right to treatment and, when the right was violated, order the patient's release.

Appearing four years before the Collaborative Study, Birnbaum's article rested on a vision of medications and public mental health that would be diametrically opposed to that of the Study. He proposed the right because he thought state hospitals should remain the centerpieces of public mental health, notwithstanding the increasing use of medication and the lure of community care. He did not consider medication a revolutionary treatment, and he deplored the emerging tendency to discharge medicated patients rapidly, even though many "continue to relapse and return to hospitals as before" and others "remain in their communities but are unable to adapt adequately even though their more disturbing symptoms are no longer present."[7] Quoting another physician, Birnbaum urged,

> Until we know a lot more about so-called mental disease and until we can treat the total person more successfully, let us continue to improve upon what we are able to do and not measure success by chemically induced tranquillity and the rate at which we discharge patients from our hospitals.

He added his own observation:

> Although it is hoped that new methods of treatment will be discovered that will allow a valid [ethical?] rapid increase in the discharge rate of the institutionalized mentally ill, at present, it appears that no such methods are on the horizon; therefore, it should be assumed that the need for more personnel and physical facilities will continue to exist.[8]

Clearly, Birnbaum did not regard medication as the necessary "new method . . . of treatment."

One aspect of the proposed right troubled Birnbaum. It was "[a]dmittedly . . . radical," he acknowledged, "to release a mentally ill person who requires further institutionalization, solely because he is not being given proper care and treatment." Under that circumstance, release jeopardized the "health and welfare" of both the patient and "members of the community." Yet Birnbaum's proposal mandated release as the remedy for violations, and it would come into play if states continued to neglect the hospitals.[9]

The problem led Birnbaum to formulate a political and social argument. The dangers that arose from discharging patients because of right to treatment violations "can be removed simply by our society treating these sick people properly. This is an important reason why the right . . . is being advocated. For if repeated court decisions constantly remind the public that medical care in public mental institutions is inadequate, not only will the mentally ill be released from their mental prisons, but, it is believed that public opinion will react to force the legislatures to increase appropriations sufficiently to make it possible to provide adequate care and treatment."[10] In short, Birnbaum saw the threat of court-ordered discharges as a means of persuading political figures and the public to increase support for the state hospitals.

In 1966, the District of Columbia Circuit Court of Appeals—a court second in prestige and influence only to the Supreme Court—adopted Birnbaum's right to treatment theory. The court implausibly derived the right from vague language in a local statute and therefore did not reach the question of whether the Constitution required it. Yet the decision was widely considered a milestone on the way toward general recognition of the right to treatment. And it endorsed Birnbaum's remedy. "Unconditional or conditional release may be in order," wrote Judge David Bazelon, "if it appears that the opportunity for treatment has been exhausted or treatment is otherwise inappropriate."[11]

Bazelon's opinion stirred an outpouring of legal comment and support. Yet no patient anywhere appears to have received a discharge because a court found treatment inadequate. Within a few years, the right to treatment assumed an entirely different form and became associated with a different remedy.

A single lawsuit, *Wyatt* v. *Stickney*, transformed the right. *Wyatt* began in 1970 as legal challenge to funding cuts affecting Alabama state hospitals. The original plaintiffs were state hospital employees, whose jobs were at risk. Among other things, the workers alleged that firing them would compromise patient treatment. At that point, the federal trial judge, who had presided over large-scale desegregation lawsuits, recast the case. The employees dropped out, law reform and public interest attorneys took over, and all the institution's patients became the nominal plaintiffs.[12]

Wyatt had become a class action and in doing so transformed the remedy for the right to treatment. No longer would courts threaten to order a patient discharged for lack of treatment. Nor would they threaten discharges for all patients. Instead, the remedy became an injunction directing the institution to transform itself in order to enhance treatment. The focus had shifted from individuals to the entire institution, and from treatment actually rendered to a hospital's capacity to afford treatment in the future.

The *Wyatt* defendants challenged the existence of a constitutional right to treatment but reached a detailed agreement with plaintiffs' lawyers about what the right would require, if it did exist. Reduced to writing, the agreement resembled a hospital operational manual and capital plan. It stipulated such things as staff-patient ratios, employee qualifications and training programs, the format of patient treatment plans and charts, physical spacing and building standards, the construction of bathrooms and laundry operations, and the temperature of shower water. When the trial judge found the right to treatment in the Constitution, as expected, the agreement became a comprehensive court injunction.

On paper, the *Wyatt* decree appeared a reasonable means of accomplishing Birnbaum's objectives. In fact, the reform lawyers had very different goals in mind. In 1974, Alexander D. Brooks, a leading scholar, described "what is perceived as the basic strategy" of *Wyatt*-type right to treatment cases, namely "requir[ing] . . . a standard of care that would be so difficult [expensive] for most states to meet that it would be necessary to release large number of patients from state hospitals in order that the patients remaining would receive adequate treatment." Some attorneys hoped that *Wyatt*-type decrees would prompt states to close their mental hospitals entirely.[13]

Across the United States, *Wyatt* spawned numerous similar actions and class action consent decrees. Whatever the actual intention of the attorneys involved, the litigation typically resulted in significantly smaller hospitals and more patient discharges. For example, the Alabama hospital in *Wyatt* lost 60 percent of its patient census between 1970 and 1975, while an Ohio state institution lost almost 30 percent in less than two years of its census during a right to treatment lawsuit; the number of new admissions per year dropped 60 percent. In general, lawyers for the patients and the mental health department shared the goal of downsizing hospitals and deinstitutionalizing patients; the only real opposition often came from hospital employees, as in *Wyatt* itself.[14]

Even when patients' lawyers started with different objectives—or with no objective beyond the vague one of subjecting hospitals to the law—acquiescence in deinstitutionalization assured a "victory" in the eyes of newspapers and funding agencies. Such victories always lay within reach, since they accorded with the wishes of the defendant mental health department. Thus, lawyers claimed credit for what the states wanted to do all along.

Despite the basic agreement, details of the decrees sometimes provoked bitter controversy. Lawyers typically sought improvements in the hospitals' physical plant, staffing levels, interior furnishings, and programs, even as the hospital census was falling. Those things required funding, when states generally wished to spend less, not more, on the hospitals. Real differences also arose over timing—the lawyers wanted change faster—and especially about the degree of subsequent judicial supervision of the agreement. Yet none of these disagreements altered the decrees' fundamental alignment with deinstitutionalization, and the concomitant widespread use of medication. Court decrees required improved staff-patient ratios; discharging patients brought that about.[15]

Although the phrase "right to treatment" remained, the class actions confounded Birnbaum's original aspirations. The right became a means of achieving deinstitutionalization and hospital downsizing, the very things Birnbaum had wanted to prevent. He based his construct on the inadequacy of medication and the need for mental hospitals; the right became an instrument for replacing hospitals with a system of community medication.

The class actions also inverted Birnbaum's idea of the role of the courts. He hoped the prospect of judges releasing untreated patients would trigger public outrage, which would translate into hospital improvements. The cases actually accomplished the opposite. *Wyatt*-type decrees turned the downsizing of state hospitals into a mark of constitutional progress, comparable to the demise of racially segregated schools. They put the courts' imprimatur on massive deinstitutionalization. Could hospital discharges resulting from court scrutiny, constitutional right, and the patients' own lawyers possibly represent a bad thing? By dampening public concern over deinstitutionalization, the lawsuits turned Birnbaum's dream into his nightmare—and then turned it into reality. And no one noticed the difference.

Without the right to treatment, mental hospitals would have continued as legitimate objects of litigation. The institutions' physical environment, safety levels, and nonpsychiatric services would have remained issues. Prison inmates enjoyed constitutional protection in those respects, and they possessed no right to treatment. What the right sanctioned were demands for additional treatment staff, new programs, and "therapeutic" environments—the very things that lent *Wyatt*-type suits a revolutionary aspect.

These "treatment" demands made deinstitutionalization appear progressive both constitutionally and medically. It was one thing to release large numbers of patents as part of improving "treatment"; it would have been quite another to discharge some patients in order to make state hospitals safer for others—as would have been true if the lawsuits had sought safety, but not treatment. In the latter case, obvious questions arise about the ex-patients' well-being and the interests of the public. With "treatment" as the driving force, such concerns fade. "Treatment"–related deinstitutionalization meant progress; "safety"-related deinstitutionalization would have involved "dumping" or, at best, triage. Birnbaum thought that court-ordered discharges resulting from the failure to treat would arouse public ire; he did not foresee that discharges related to the legal right to treatment would calm public concern instead.[16]

Not least of all, the class actions departed from Birnbaum's original conception of medication. Unlike Birnbaum, reform attorneys showed no concern about the use of medication to achieve large-scale deinstitutionalization. In fact, they paid no significant attention to the treatment, even in the heyday of the Study vision.

Though supposedly comprehensive, *Wyatt*-type decrees said little about medications and incorporated no meaningful restrictions on their use. A typical decree prohibited lobotomy (although the hospital probably had not performed one in a decade) and also included a right to refuse electroconvulsive therapy (which state hospitals rarely employed by this time either). Yet when it came to medication, which almost all patients received, the decrees included only a vague right against "excessive" or "unnecessary" treatment. Such provisions could hardly produce results, since it was not clear what hospitals were supposed to do differently. No physician had ever characterized a medication prescription as "excessive" or "unnecessary," and the decrees did not define those terms. Even if the words possessed a clearer meaning, the decrees lacked any mechanism for review or enforcement.

The language about medication was boilerplate and did not relate to any actual problems. No decree purported to judge "excess" or "necessity" by considering side effects, for example. For that matter, the phrasing implicitly presumed that medication was generally "necessary"—just as a ban on "unnecessary lobotomy" would have presumed that lobotomies were usually necessary too. Later in the decade, some decrees included hospital pharmacy reforms or standards that discouraged the prescription of more than one medication at a time—measures that, however useful, did not prevent hospitals from administering medication to almost all patients, regardless of the effects.

Remarkably, lawyers and courts simply ignored the ferment in psychiatry over medication during the first half of the 1970s. Thus, tardive dyskinesia played no role in the cases or the decrees. Neither did recommendations of leading psychiatrists that medication be withdrawn from chronic, hospitalized patients—the very group that predominated in the hospitals and whose interests the reform lawyers supposedly represented. The patients' own complaints about side effects seemingly did not register with the attorneys either.

A half-decade after *Wyatt* created the right to be free of "excessive or unnecessary medication," George Crane inspected the Alabama hospitals involved in the case as an expert witness. He found medication practice miserable, even in comparison with state hospitals elsewhere. Similarly, a New Jersey state hospital that had operated under a *Wyatt*-type decree was later shown never to have diagnosed a case of tardive dyskinesia; despite the decree, staff members acted as if they had never heard of the condition. These outcomes were all but preordained: the class actions focused on every aspect of the hospitals except medication.[17]

Legal theory, as it unfolded in *Wyatt*-type cases, went even further. It proceeded as if medication lacked constitutionally significant benefits *and* side effects—in short, as if the treatment did not exist. During this period, courts understood the right to treatment as requiring either "minimally adequate" treatment or, in a more generous formulation, "such individual treatment as will give . . . [patients] a reasonable opportunity to be cured or to improve . . . [their] mental condition." To establish a violation, then, attorneys had to prove that hospitals had failed to provide minimal or reasonable treatment. Yet nearly all patients received medication, which, according to leading researchers, constituted a revolutionary, "antischizophrenic" therapy. Even cautious psychiatrists regarded medication as the best available therapy for most patients.[18]

Given that, medication should have qualified easily as a treatment that afforded patients "a reasonable opportunity to . . . improve." And since almost every patient received medication, right-to-treatment claims should have failed. They did not, because this obvious implication of psychiatric thinking received no legal attention. Right-to-treatment theory developed as if the medication revolution in psychiatry had never occurred.

Lawyers and courts did not exclude medication from the constitutional calculus because they considered the treatment ineffective. They never articulated that view; in any event, it was clearly wrong. Rather, medication had become like the air: something ever present, in fact indispensable, but worthy of only passing comment. Indeed, the air in mental hospitals probably received more attention from courts, because of the need for ventilation and the risks of tuberculosis.

The right to treatment inhabited a theme park–like world, not the world of medication-era psychiatry. Here, relics like lobotomy and indiscriminate electroconvulsive therapy lived on as dragons that lawyers and courts could slay using *Wyatt*-type decrees. For the less adventurous, right-to-treatment theory recreated the world of nineteenth-century moral therapy, where staff and social environment and good order (now meaning a constitutional order) mattered above all. As in any good theme park, the most salient aspect of reality—in this case, the medication that pervaded the hospitals—was nowhere to be seen. Meanwhile, outside the park gates, decrees legitimated developments in the real world.

Commitment Reform

The other widely litigated issue in this period concerned standards and procedures for mental hospital commitment. Beginning in the late 1960s, courts struck down existing rules and practices as unconstitutional. In their place, courts required formal commitment hearings and, in most instances, the benefit of attorneys for persons facing involuntary hospitalization. Purely medical standards for commitment—that the person be "in need of [psychiatric] treatment," for instance—also fell. Findings of "dangerousness" to self or others, together with serious mental illness—not mere need for treatment—became minimum constitutional requirements for commitment.

Obviously, these changes had the potential to reduce the mental hospital census by making it impossible to commit—or retain—patients who would satisfy older criteria. A scholarly controversy exists about whether the newly heightened standards and procedures actually reduced the amount of hospitalization. Many studies indicate that they did not do so—not unless a hospital wanted, for its own reasons, to reduce its population. Under the new commitment standards, hospitals still could have committed many more people than they did, and could have kept them hospitalized for longer periods. Moreover, suggestive evidence exists that actual commitment proceedings often remained perfunctory and did not change nearly to the extent that one would have expected from reading appellate court decisions—much clinical medication practices typically continued unchanged, despite the advice of researchers.[19]

If commitment reforms meant less than commonly supposed, they still dovetailed with new public mental health imperatives. For example, courts allowed commitment hearings to be delayed for a period of twenty days or more from the time a patient arrived at the hospital. Most patients were stabilized on medication and then discharged within that period. It followed that if someone responded to medication as expected, no hearing took place. In eras when hospital confinement anchored the public mental health system, states avoided holding hearings about deprivations of physical liberty. Now medication anchored the system, and states usually avoided hearings on *that* subject; court hearings occurred only if medication failed to produce the usual results and the older expedient of extended hospitalization loomed. Even when hearings occurred, they ostensibly concerned questions of discharge, not medication—although state practices varied on this point. During the late 1960s, one federal court even allowed patients to remain medication-free before the hearing, a right that later cases abandoned.[20]

Thus, lawyers and courts accommodated the medication revolution while ostensibly paying no attention to it. Psychiatrists hailed the use of medication as an antischizophrenic breakthrough; lawyers virtually ignored the treatment. Yet both arrived at the same policy conclusions and took measures with the same practical effects. The Study vision in psychiatry, the thinking of "antipsychiatrists," and the varieties of reform litigation all converged on a program of nearly universal use of medication. The much talked about "war" between law and psychiatry was a phony war—or perhaps was really just a series of maneuvers by two battalions on the same side.

The Right to Refuse Medication

There are also suggestive historical parallels between legal and psychiatric developments. The 1960s in law resembled the 1950s in psychiatry; it was a kind of delayed "first period" of the era. Medication issues received legal attention then in ways they no longer did afterward: the imperatives of universal medication and deinstitutionalization did not completely drive legal developments yet. *Wyatt* put an end this first period, playing a role in law comparable to that of the Collaborative Study in psychiatry.

Morton Birnbaum's 1960 right-to-treatment article belonged to the law's first period. So did the decision allowing patients to refuse medication until their commitment hearings. Moreover, there was a moment in the late 1960s when the right to refuse medication seemed about to become a principal objective of legal reform efforts—only two or three years before medication virtually disappeared as a subject of legal concern.

The "right to refuse" rested on a conventional legal ground: the prerogative of competent persons to choose their own medical treatment. Although committed to hospitals, involuntary patients were rarely subjected to incompetency proceedings; thus, they remained legally competent. Even if a patient was adjudicated incompetent, common principles pointed to the selection of someone other than a hospital physician as the guardian—if only to avoid a potential conflict of interest. Finally, little legal precedent allowed states to assume control over the biological functioning of even an incompetent person.[21]

Historical precedents for overriding a patient's refusal to take medication did exist, but they were not the kind likely to attract support in the late 1960s. State hospitals had forced therapies such as lobotomy and insulin coma therapy—and, before that, procedures that removed teeth and ovaries—with few, if any, legal formalities. Yet few would cite this history to support the idea of forcing psychiatry's prevailing therapy on patients. In terms of general Supreme Court precedents, only a notorious 1927 decision upholding compulsory eugenic sterilization suggested that states could directly and seriously alter an individual's biological functioning in order to advance public objectives—and that decision, although never overruled, had been placed in doubt by a 1942 Supreme Court case.[22]

Because of the substantial legal arguments, and because courts and legislators had recognized a right to refuse other somatic treatments in psychiatry, many supposed that courts would also recognize a right to refuse medication. Among these commentators was Alan Stone, professor of law and medicine at Harvard. Indeed, some state attorneys general supposed that the right already existed in the early 1970s, though the state hospitals typically acted as though it did not.[23]

With medication so ubiquitous in hospitals and so disliked by many patients, litigation asserting the right to refuse appeared "inevitable." The question arose frequently, although informally, in commitment hearings, but since these cases did not produce published court opinions—and, according to the prevailing view, medication issues fell outside the scope of the hearing—no legal precedent resulted. As of 1974, the leading law and psychiatry text could find only four published decisions on the right to refuse. In two cases, individual prisoners had objected to a federal penitentiary's practice of forcing them to take medication; both lost their cases in 1968, with the trial court treating their arguments in a perfunctory way. At about the same time, a Michigan woman recovered monetary damages because a physician had forcibly medicated her while she was "temporarily" committed to a private psychiatric hospital. (Her commitment qualified as "temporary" because she was awaiting a formal commitment hearing.) In this case, the plaintiff's estranged husband had arranged for her hospitalization under questionable circumstances, and the Michigan Supreme Court held both that a "husband can[not] force medical care upon his wife" and that private psychiatric hospitals lacked the power that public institutions had to force treatment on temporarily committed patients. None of these lawsuits was a class action, or concerned a state hospital; and none involved the kind of nonprofit, law reform organizations that would soon bring right-to-treatment suits.[24]

The fourth case, *Winters v. Miller*, was different. Filed in the late 1960s, it pitted a state hospital against a reformist legal organization, the New York Civil Liberties Union. Bruce Ennis, the civil liberties union attorney, would go on to play the leading role in *Wyatt* and eventually became the country's best-known mental-hospital-reform lawyer. Based on *Winters*, one might have foreseen medication refusal rather than the right to treatment becoming the focal point of reform litigation.[25]

In the *Winters* case, a public mental hospital forcibly medicated a temporarily committed woman who had not yet had her commitment hearing. She asserted religious reasons for refusing all hospital treatment, and sued for damages. In 1969 a federal trial court dismissed her complaint, concluding that mental hospitals had the legal power to force treatments. The Second Circuit Court of Appeals overturned that decision in 1971 and remanded the case for trial. The Second Circuit's reasons were not entirely clear, but at a minimum it appeared that a nondangerous, temporarily committed person should have a judicial commitment hearing before being forced to receive medication, at least when the patient's objection rested on religious grounds.[26]

Despite this success, *Winters* did not spawn other legal challenges to forcible medication. Ennis himself soon described the case as primarily about the rights of religious believers in mental hospitals—not as a challenge to the prevailing biological therapy in psychiatry. Ennis wrote a book about his litigation experiences, and it said nothing about the benefits or risks of medication, or about the nonreligious reasons why someone might refuse the treatment. Nor did the court's opinion in *Winters* address those matters; it cited legal abstractions, not the nature and attributes of medications. Indeed, the opinion treated "medications" as an indiscriminate category with a fungible membership, noting only that "for the most part" the drugs Ms. Winters had received consisted of "rather heavy doses of tranquilizers." Had the hospital forced Ms. Winters to take aspirin or an allergy pill, the analysis would have remained the same: the issue was "medications" in general, not the particular drugs that states and psychiatrists now favored.[27]

This approach to medication was remarkable. Psychiatry was already in ferment over Crane's report of widespread tardive dyskinesia, and the *Journal of the American Medical Association* had already editorialized about the dangers of permanent side effects. Yet none of that concern had managed to penetrate the world of lawyers and courts, or the legal analysis of rights.

Wyatt would make the medical attributes of medications irrelevant to the legal right to treatment. *Winters* managed to make the same attributes irrelevant to questions of patients' refusing the treatment. The case represents a high point in legal awareness of medication before *Wyatt* and, at the same time, a harbinger of *Wyatt's* achievement in making medication legally invisible.

Law and Psychiatry

Obvious parallels existed between the pre–Collaborative Study period in psychiatry and the pre-*Wyatt* period in law. Both involved relatively more serious attention to medication, although in law that period was briefer. Both professions escaped rather obvious ethical issues by retreating to abstractions. Psychiatrists shifted their gaze from patients' manifest side effects to a hypothesized "schizophrenic disease process" and then to the brain. Lawyers looked first to classic legal rights, such as Ms. Winters's religious freedoms, and then, in *Wyatt*, to a constitutional (and psychiatric) invention, the "right to treatment."

After *Wyatt*, professional judgments and processes in the law produced anomalous results, just as they did in psychiatry after the Collaborative Study. The way attorneys handle medication issues resists explanation in terms of classic lawyer-client relationships. Lawyers supposedly voice their clients' concerns, and patients vehemently complain about medications. Many patients experienced distress; some hated the side effects; significant numbers incurred neurological damage. For good or ill, the treatment dominated their feelings and experiences in hospitals. Yet reforming lawyers paid virtually no attention.

Some attorneys recognize an obligation to safeguard a client's real interests, particularly when someone suffers from a serious mental illness. That paternalistic obligation does not help explain the lack of attention to medication, however. Many patients had ample reason to complain about the treatment, whether they actually did so or not. And issues receiving attention from psychiatric researchers—such as tardive dyskinesia or distressed and nonbenefiting patients—played no apparent role in lawyers' thinking.

Medication raised serious legal and moral questions, and leading psychiatrists recognized them. Denber and Kline well understood the legal and moral implications of tardive dyskinesia; that was precisely why they criticized Crane. The overly optimistic vision of medication in the Collaborative Study implicitly responded to the same problems. Psychiatry attempted to sidestep ethical and legal issues with the concepts of "safe" and "antischizophrenic" medications; lawyers and courts simply ignored them.

Like the Study vision, reform litigation arbitrarily ruled out the serious problems connected to medication and thereby promoted public support for policies that depended upon near universal use of the drugs. Faced with public objections, states now could attribute deinstitutionalization and hospital downsizing to courts and legal reforms. Those programs suddenly resulted from constitutional compulsion, not public health policymaking. And since the Constitution compelled such policies, debating their wisdom was pointless. What the states wanted to do had been transformed, through the alchemy of litigation, into an inexorable requirement of constitutional justice.

The Study vision had posited such enormous benefit and such minimal side effects from medication that questions about public mental health policy seemingly answered themselves. The law's approach was both cruder and more blatant than that. Right-to-treatment litigation eliminated problems by rendering medication invisible; with drugs out of the picture, all that remained for the public to see in state hospitals were bleak surroundings and people deprived of liberty. Commitment cases had a similar tendency: they defined liberty as freedom from hospitalization, and then made liberty, so defined, the overriding political and moral value. Court decisions allocated every living arrangement—except for mental hospitals—to the realms of constitutional "liberty"; it followed that an ex-patient confined to a room in a boarding home and under the complete control of the home's owner enjoyed liberty, but the same person in a public mental hospital did not. Who could deny that more liberty is preferable to less? Finally, in the context of a "right to refuse," *Winters* obliterated any recognizable legal distinction between psychiatric medication and aspirin.

Thus, lawsuits converged with the prevailing vision in psychiatry. During the early and mid-1970s, those who considered medication a near cure for mental illness agreed on the same program of public health transformation as those who took no notice of medication, or even of mental illness. If the Collaborative Study was right, a new public mental health system was called for. If the Study erred in its most basic premises—because mental illness did not exist—"antipsychiatrists" found the same reforms in order. So did reform lawyers. The psychiatrists' logic of "antipsychotic" treatment and the lawyers' logic of "liberty" had nothing to do with one another, but they arrived at the precisely the same conclusion.

Class Actions and the Right to Refuse Medication

Like researchers, lawyers and courts could ignore the side effects of medication —and medication itself—only for so long. In psychiatry, investigations into tardive dyskinesia, psychomotor indifference, and medication-induced distress finally compelled attention. In the law, it was class action, right-to-refuse-medication litigation—and a few cases involving monetary damages because of tardive dyskinesia—that brought medication issues to the foreground.

In the late 1970s, two class actions, *Rogers* v. *Okin* and *Rennie* v. *Klein*, asserted a constitutional right to refuse medication. Each was the work of a law reform agency—a legal aid office in *Rogers*, a state-funded mental-patient-advocacy agency in *Rennie*—and each named state mental hospitals as defendants. These cases attracted enormous attention from lawyers and psychiatrists, produced front-page stories in leading newspapers, and became the prototypes for other litigation.[28]

Rogers began in 1975 as a legal challenge to patient seclusion and forced medication practices at Boston State Hospital. *Rennie* started in 1977 as a lawsuit by a single medication-refusing patient; by the next year, it had turned into a class action against five New Jersey state hospitals. In neither case did the medical ferment over tardive dyskinesia play a significant role during the early stages of litigation. No named plaintiff in *Rogers* had the disorder or developed it during the lawsuit. The original plaintiff in *Rennie* became a victim of tardive dyskinesia only after his case had begun.[29]

Rogers and *Rennie* produced trial court decisions in 1979. The *Rogers* opinion, like the *Winters* decision, focused on legal abstractions. Yet the *Rogers* court considered tardive dyskinesia a noteworthy factor. "Recent studies," the judge wrote, "suggest that tardive dyskinesia is more widespread . . . than previously [thought]." These studies estimated that over 50 percent of chronic patients and 40 percent of outpatients developed the condition. Nonetheless, the trial did not explore the actual prevalence of tardive dyskinesia at Boston State. The court merely observed that "several" defendants conceded that some unidentified patients at the hospital (though not the named plaintiffs) had the disorder.

Rennie also dealt in legal abstractions. Yet to a far greater extent than *Rogers*, the trial explored tardive dyskinesia and other side effects. The trial record showed that as of 1978—ten years after Crane's landmark paper, five years after the task force—no New Jersey hospital physician had acknowledged a case of tardive dyskinesia. Except in rare cases, the charts of afflicted patients failed to note even the existence of abnormal movements, no matter how severe. When the charts did mention bizarre movements—either because a patient's relatives had noticed, or, as was true in one instance, because the grotesque symptoms precluded a life outside the hospital for the patient, and nothing else was wrong with him—physicians never attributed the symptoms to tardive dyskinesia. Instead, they diagnosed abnormal movements as "nerves" or said that mental illness caused them. Occasionally, physicians dismissed the symptoms as "faking," even though the movements are extraordinarily difficult to feign: one would have to perform odd movements every few seconds during every single moment of wakefulness. Nor did faking make any sense, since hospitals would not discontinue medication in the face of symptoms anyway.[30]

The responses of physician to other side effects varied. If another drug could ameliorate side effects, physicians would often give it—assuming they noticed the side effect in the first place. If the side effect did not respond to a second drug, doctors regarded it as they did tardive dyskinesia—denying its existence, attributing it to nerves, or pronouncing it "faking." There was no evidence that doctors recognized the possibility of a patient responding to medication with distress, or by becoming depressed, or that doctors thought a patient could respond so badly that drugs should not be given at all.

The American Psychiatric Association later argued that New Jersey mental hospitals were exceptional and aberrant. In fact, they were typical. George Crane inspected the New Jersey institutions and testified that their medication practices—and their handling of side effects, including tardive dyskinesia—did not differ from that of other state hospitals. Indeed, the Joint Commission on Accreditation of Hospitals accredited these institutions, evidently finding nothing remarkable in the claim—reported on accreditation forms—that no patient out of thousands had ever developed tardive dyskinesia in New Jersey.[31]

Some New Jersey psychiatrists were surely inept, but their lack of knowledge or medical art cannot explain what happened. It required no medical training to see the bizarre, sometimes grotesque movements that physicians refused to acknowledge. Their recourse to "faking" and "nerves" as explanations approached absurdity. And hospital medical directors, who presumably knew that their institutions were reporting zero dyskinesia rates to accrediting authorities, conceded midway through the trial that 25 percent to 50 percent of their patients actually had tardive dyskinesia. Even so, the absence of any diagnosed cases before the trial had caused them no concern whatever.[32]

Remarkably, New Jersey mental hospital psychiatrists had spontaneously created a clinical version of 1967-style rejectionism. Denber and Kline denied the existence of abnormal movements, attributed movements to the patients' disease, and remarked that patients "loved" stereotypical gestures. The refusal of New Jersey psychiatrists to acknowledge the movements and their ideas about "nerves" and "faking" substantially duplicated those rationalizations, albeit less artfully. Their reasons were similar as well. Denber and Kline had worried that tardive dyskinesia would preclude widespread use of medication in psychiatry. The New Jersey doctors worried that tardive dyskinesia would preclude widespread use of medication at their institutions. Faced with the same problems, they deployed the same rationalizations and arrived at the same solutions.

The *Rennie* record included less about subjective distress from medication. Yet the case of John Rennie himself shed light on the problem. Rennie testified about his anguish and depression on medication. Severe akathisia tormented him. And considerable evidence supported his belief that Prolixin, the medication his physicians favored, made him suicidal. All that, and not tardive dyskinesia, had led to Rennie's lawsuit.

Rennie's physicians never acknowledged his distress, though it was often obvious, any more than they later acknowledged his tardive dyskinesia. During cross-examination, one physician shed light on how physicians rationalized the matter. A board-certified psychiatrist, she acknowledged Hollister as a leading authority in psychiatry. When asked about Hollister's suggestion that patients with a poor drug response might not have true schizophrenia or benefit from medication—and the possibility that those characterizations fit Rennie himself—she hesitated. Finally, she reasoned that since physicians already had determined that Rennie suffered from schizophrenia and that he was seriously ill, Rennie did not—according to Hollister's theory—also have a poor drug response. Thus, Hollister's idea that poor responders might be less ill became the idea that patients could not respond poorly if doctors wanted to administer medication.

Rationalizations and arbitrary presumptions again ruled out contraindication to medication. The evidence of one's senses, or the complaints of patients, did not register. Here too New Jersey's clinicians were retracing researchers' footsteps: their analysis of Rennie's distress resembled that of the Collaborative Study's authors, who completely excluded psychological reactions and effects.

The *Rennie* and *Rogers* rulings produced little change, even in the hospitals that had been sued. Both decisions allowed psychiatrists to override a patient's refusal in "emergencies." *Rennie* also allowed forced medication if an "independent psychiatrist" approved—and the "independents," who viewed themselves as consultants to the hospital rather than adjudicators or arbitrators, almost always did approve. *Rogers* imposed more stringent requirements, including a court adjudication of incompetency, before a hospital could override patient refusals in nonemergent circumstances. Yet the hospitals recognized relatively few acts of drug refusal—nothing like the quarter to half of patients that, based on Van Putten's research, one might have expected. In any event, the defendants appealed both cases and the ultimate outcome remained in doubt.

Rennie and *Rogers* had an immediate effect on the thinking of leading psychiatrists, if not on clinical practice in state hospitals. The strategy of ignoring tardive dyskinesia, or downplaying its seriousness, had proved impossible to sustain in litigation. *Rogers* took the disorder seriously, citing prevalence estimates that exceeded those of the 1973 task force by a factor of ten. The *Rennie* trial judge, a moderate Republican, castigated hospital psychiatrists for ignoring tardive dyskinesia and other side effects. Notions that had thrived in the culture of mental hospitals—and in the larger culture—because of the prevailing Study vision utterly collapsed when exposed to court scrutiny.

Just as repeated scandals over mental hospital conditions once rocked psychiatry, it now seemed that a similar cycle of scandals might involve medication. According to George Crane, a portrait like the one painted of New Jersey would emerge from any state hospital under comparable scrutiny. Reporting on *Rennie* and *Rogers*, the national press carried some of the most critical articles about a prevailing psychiatric therapy since the era of lobotomy. Nor could anyone predict public reaction to a widespread neurological impairment caused by a biological therapy in psychiatry: the profession's "lobotomy problem" might have survived the medication revolution after all. Psychiatry's achievements in the medication era—public acceptance, medical respect, patient trust, research funding—all seemed at risk.[33]

Virtually every public actor, aside from the courts, had benefited from the new public mental health system, if only because of funds saved for other government programs. Now *Rennie* and *Rogers* suggested a skeptical judicial attitude. Psychiatric issues had become questions of civil rights during the 1970s, and a judiciary that distrusted the judgments of psychiatrists could act in countless ways to the profession's detriment. And any substantial right to refuse medication threatened the foundations of the modern public mental health system.

The right to refuse was not the only problem, either. Might courts prohibit the use of medication outright when patients had tardive dyskinesia? Given the prevalence estimates described in *Rogers*, that would prove cataclysmic. Some psychiatrists' reactions to *Rennie* and *Rogers* suggested that the roof had fallen in.

Making matters worse, some private lawyers were suing for monetary damages for tardive dyskinesia. In 1979, two such cases produced judgments of liability—and eventual damages awards against the offending psychiatrists of more than $760,000 in one case and $1,500,000 in the other. Other lawsuits produced out-of-court settlements. Reporting these developments, C. Thomas Gualtieri and Robert L. Sprague predicted "a sharp upswing in the number of [damage] cases filed, and probably in the number of cases won in court as well."[34]

As early as 1974, Lennard and Bernstein had explained that damages actions would prove difficult to defend when psychiatrists failed to acknowledge tardive dyskinesia. That course was "unethical" for the obvious reasons, but Lennard and Bernstein pointed out that it also "unwise." The psychiatrist's "resistance to recognizing the condition and . . . procrastination in acting responsibly" would likely "cast doubt both on his competence and his concern for his patient" in the eyes of judges and jurors. Conversely, if a psychiatrist acknowledged tardive dyskinesia, "treatment can be rationalized [in court] on the basis of accepted medical practice undertaken in the best interest of the patient and with good intent, weighing risk and benefit." Put differently, a psychiatrist who behaved like the *Rennie* physicians—the norm—might have to pay substantial damages. Gualtieri and Sprague arrived at similar conclusions, arguing that the "only way" to prepare for burgeoning litigation was "to improve standards of medication practice with respect to neuroleptic drugs" and pay "serious attention" to the use of medications.[35]

These analyses were astute, but they failed to consider a troubling further possibility. If psychiatrists conceded that their patients had tardive dyskinesia, might not the law impose liability for that very reason—or at least require a real, and not just "rationalized," weighing of benefit and risk that would require withdrawing medication from significant numbers of patients? Just as no one could predict the scope of future court injunctions, the content of new legal liability rules remained uncertain.

One thing seemed clear, however. Chaos loomed if courts intervened in any serious way, either through injunctions or by awarding substantial damages that discouraged the use of medication. Existing programs, staffing levels, and patient placements all presumed unfettered use of medication within hospitals and in the "community." Even if psychiatrists somehow preserved order, they still faced the prospects of judicial second-guessing and public scorn. Psychiatric practice could become a nightmarish blend of high malpractice exposure (as in obstetrics and gynecology), intrusive judicial oversight (comparable to that in a school desegregation decree), and public disdain (like psychiatry during the lobotomy era).

Whatever the future held, the litigation had one immediate effect. It concentrated public, medical, and legal attention on tardive dyskinesia. Within psychiatry, the disorder had epitomized the problems with the Study vision and had eclipsed other difficulties, such as distress, Parkinson's syndrome, and the limitations on the benefits of medication. The right-to-refuse-treatment cases strengthened that tendency, and extended it to the public arena. There, as well as within psychiatry, the idea took hold that tardive dyskinesia represented the make-or-break issue for prevailing medication practice. Other weaknesses in the vision failed to engage the courts, and apparently the public, in the same way.

In both its literal and extended sense, "tardive dyskinesia" constituted the only remaining threat to the revolution in public mental health. By the late 1970s, the shift from large state hospitals to a system of short hospitalizations (if any), community living, and long-term medication was largely complete. Few envisioned any counterrevolution, or desired one. States did not want to reinstitutionalize the former patients, and neither the remaining hospitals nor community facilities wanted to withhold medication. Reformers generally urged more rapid deinstitutionalization and more funding for community programs.

Some critics thought that deinstitutionalization had gone too far, too fast; a few—including some prominent psychiatrists—suggested that more patients belonged in hospitals. Yet such criticisms rarely implicated basic medication policies. On the contrary, critics suggested that too few patients received medication in the community, and they urged "outreach" in order to convince (or compel) the recalcitrant to take their medicine.

After *Rennie* and *Rogers*, however, the tandem of tardive dyskinesia and litigation seemed capable of producing a major upheaval. In 1980, Gardos and Cole observed that "the response of the [psychiatric] profession" to tardive dyskinesia "has shifted from curiosity and mild concern to panic," and a task force of the American Psychiatric Association described tardive dyskinesia as "a cause of increasing concern to the medical profession and the general public." Something had to give.[36]

Chapter 8

Jonathan Cole and Another Task Force

By 1980, THE Study vision, which had produced the revolution in public health, threatened that revolution. Psychiatric research belied Study claims about a safe and antischizophrenic treatment. As a result of *Rennie*, *Rogers*, and the threat of malpractice cases, this research could no longer be ignored. In *Rennie*, for example, New Jersey physicians adhered to the Study vision, and the result verged on disaster.

Leading psychiatrists abandoned the Study vision in 1980 in order to save the public health and medication revolutions. As in 1973, a prestigious task force on tardive dyskinesia was formed, and it issued a single statement. As in 1973, that statement concealed serious internal disagreements. This time, the disagreements reflected a dispute about how best to defend the revolution in psychiatry' after the collapse of the Study vision.

The 1980 Task Force

Participating in the *Rennie* appeals, the American Psychiatric Association (APA) announced that it had created a new task force on tardive dyskinesia. Footnote 23 of the APA appellate brief depicted tardive dyskinesia as the only side effect warranting extended discussion; reprised aspects of 1967 rejectionism, such as the existence of "abnormal involuntary movements" before the medication era; implied that the tardive dyskinesia issue had arisen only recently; and notified the judges of its new "task force" to "study" the issues. The APA had managed to omit almost every relevant development between 1956, when Hall first reported persistent side effects, and 1979, when its brief was submitted.[1]

The 1980 Task Force included four members: Jonathan Cole; George

Simpson, who had served on the 1973 Task Force and coauthored Kline's acknowledgment of tardive dyskinesia; Ross J. Baldessarini, the chairperson and a Harvard Medical School professor; and John M. Davis, an authority on schizophrenia and medication. The Task Force also employed Cole's junior coauthor, George Gardos, as a consultant. Conspicuously absent from its membership was George Crane, who had recently testified in *Rennie*.

In 1980 the Task Force published its Report and a separate, official Summary. Although titled "Tardive Dyskinesia," the Report comprehensively surveyed the actions, benefits, and side effects of medication. That same year, Gardos and Cole published their own article, "Overview: Public Health Issues in Tardive Dyskinesia," which departed from the Task Force's account in important ways. By putting their views in a separate article and not presenting them in a dissent from the Report, they followed Crane's 1973 example.[2]

Before being appointed, all the Task Force's members had recognized tardive dyskinesia as a side effect of medication. The Task Force did so as well, without dissent. What remained were the matters of gauging tardive dyskinesia's frequency and seriousness, formulating clinical recommendations, and offering a new rationale for the public mental health system and existing clinical practice. Gardos and Cole differed from their colleagues about each of these points, especially about the rationale.

The Task Force produced a series of conservative and inconsistent estimates about the frequency of tardive dyskinesia. According to a key passage of its Report,

> The reported prevalence of tardive dyskinesia . . . has varied between
> .5 and 65 percent; a mean value of about 20 percent can be estimated
> from surveys including tens of thousands of psychiatric inpatients.
> Differences in definition of the syndrome, patient populations,
> methods of case ascertainment, and neurological assessment make an
> accurate statement concerning prevalence virtually impossible. As a
> very rough estimate, currently at least ten to 20 percent of patients in
> mental hospitals and at least 40 percent of elderly, chronically
> institutionalized or outpatients [sic] exhibit more than minimal signs
> of probable tardive dyskinesia attributable to or associated with
> neuroleptic drug treatment. Of these cases, perhaps 25 to 50 percent
> are potentially reversible.[3]

This passage left it unclear whether the 10 to 20 percent figure included elderly patients. The Report's summary section suggested that it did not do so. There, the Task Force said that tardive dyskinesia affected "perhaps ten to 20 percent of patients exposed to neuroleptic drugs for more than few months. These rates *may more than double* in the elderly."[4]

Still another formulation appeared in the "Summary" published in the

American Journal of Psychiatry: "It is nearly impossible to specify the precise prevalence rates of tardive dyskinesia since there is no currently accepted standard for diagnosis. . . . Certainly, clinically appreciable cases occur in at least 10%-20% of the patients exposed to neuroleptic drugs for more than a year, and the rate is probably higher among the elderly."[5]

These different phrasings approached inconsistency. Aside from a casual approach toward the period of time during which patients had been exposed to medication ("a few months," "more than a year," or no period specified) and the population being described ("patients in mental hospitals" or "patients exposed to neuroleptic drugs"), the three versions differed in their views of elderly patients ("at least 40 percent of elderly"; "rates *may more than double* in the elderly"; "the rate *is probably higher* among the elderly") and nonelderly patients ("as a very rough estimate . . . *at least* ten to 20 percent"; "*perhaps* ten to 20 percent"; "nearly impossible to specify . . . certainly, clinically appreciable cases . . . in at least 10%-20%") alike. Constant was the idea of uncertainty, the absence of an overall estimate that included the elderly, and an apparent reluctance to cite *any* figure higher than 20 percent.

Compared with other recent estimates, the figures seemed low. In 1979, for example, two Cornell University professors reviewed the literature and produced an overall estimate of between 24 and 56 percent. The year after the Report was issued, two NIMH researchers found that the reported prevalence rate had risen from a mean of 13.6 percent in studies published before 1970 to 25.7 percent in studies published between 1976 and 1980.[6]

Task Force members had themselves produced significantly higher estimates. Davis coauthored the 1972 study reporting prevalences rates above 30 percent in mental hospitals. For their part, Gardos and Cole left little doubt that the correct figure exceeded 20 percent. Their "Overview" noted that Baldessarini, the Task Force chairperson, had arrived at a 15 percent mean prevalence for studies published through 1972, but that "[m]ore recent reports . . . have placed the prevalence of tardive dyskinesia close to 50% in both in- and out-patient populations." And the "Overview" suggested no reason to doubt the higher figures. Instead, it reported early results from Cole's own, ongoing incidence study: Cole was finding that 4 to 5 percent of medicated patients develop tardive dyskinesia during each year of drug treatment. If "the risk remains the same during a second, third, and subsequent year," Gardos and Cole wrote, "the risk . . . of developing tardive dyskinesia might be 20–25% over a 5-year period." Obviously, based on the same assumptions, the figure would continue to rise in succeeding years.[7]

The Task Force also ignored its own figures, which appeared elsewhere in the Report. Discussing the "Range of severity of TD," it cited and seemingly endorsed "two recent surveys of American patients" which found that "about

two-thirds had . . . mild dyskinesias; another one-fourth to one-third had moderately severe, clinically significant dyskinesia . . . [and] fewer than 15 percent
had widespread, severe, disabling, or disfiguring" conditions. The Report also
cited with apparent approval a "very recent" survey of hospital patients which
"revealed that prevalence rates of minimal [dyskinetic] abnormalities exceeded
60 percent, while the prevalence of moderate abnormalities was close to 30 percent and of severe impairment less than ten percent." Yet such findings undercut
the Task Force's own estimate. If between one-quarter and one-third of patients
suffered "moderately severe" dyskinesias, and over 10 percent had "relatively
severe" symptoms, how could the overall prevalence rate fall between 10 and
20 percent, as the Report claimed?[8]

The Task Force cited these studies to demonstrate that "greater sensitivity to minor . . . abnormal movements" increased reported rates of tardive dyskinesia and supposedly made it difficult to "to arrive at a fair estimate of the
clinical significance of the problem." Yet the correct conclusion seemed to be
the opposite one. The studies basically agreed on a prevalence rate for various
levels of severity: about 10 percent, severe dyskinesia; 30 percent, moderately
severe dyskinesia or worse; over 50 percent, mild or borderline symptoms or
worse. Thus, one *could* estimate the number of tardive dyskinesia cases reliably;
and the Report's conclusion to the contrary seemed mistaken. For that matter,
all the figures dovetailed with Crane's 1967 finding that 27 percent of hospitalized patients had at least moderate dyskinesia. Despite the ensuing controversy and supposed assessment difficulties, the best recent work had largely
reproduced Crane's original finding.[9]

There was a related anomaly in the Report. When the Task Force discussed
factors that confounded or confused prevalence estimates—such as varying
severity levels or supposedly high spontaneous dyskinesia rates among the elderly—it assumed that only overestimates could result. Yet these factors cut
both ways, and they often produced underestimates—a point Simpson had
made in 1976. Thus, researchers could define the disorder too narrowly, as well
as too broadly: mild or questionable movements could represent early, real tardive dyskinesia. Most studies indicated that spontaneous dyskinesias occur
rarely; elderly patients simply develop tardive dyskinesia faster than others. And
many researchers, including Crane, had excluded "mild or questionable cases"
and still arrived at prevalence estimates far higher than those of the Task Force.
Contrary to the Task Force's claims, the real problem lay in psychiatrists overlooking symptoms of tardive dyskinesia, not in overdiagnosing them.[10]

In sum, the Task Force's prevalence estimates excluded the elderly for no
apparent reason, except that elderly patients develop tardive dyskinesia at high
rates; contradicted data that the Task Force itself deemed reliable; and rested
on the mistaken premise that confounding factors could operate only to exag-

gerate the real prevalence of the disorder. These features made the 1980 Report seem like a milder version of the 1973 Special Report, which in turn was a milder-sounding variant of 1967 rejectionism. The 1980 Task Force published a prevalence estimate two or three times higher than that of its 1973 predecessor, but it still strained to produce the lowest figure that was not completely incredible. In 1967, that figure had been one in a million; in 1973 it had been about 3 percent; in 1980, it was about 15 percent.

Regarding issues other than tardive dyskinesia, the Report took a different approach and announced less enthusiastic conclusions about medication than one might have expected. For example, the Task Force approached the issue of relapse by aggregating the results of various studies, some of which covered periods of only a few months. These studies found a mean relapse rate of 58 percent for patients on placebo, and 16 percent for those on medication. In experiments that followed patients for two years, however, the difference narrowed: about 80 percent of placebo patients and 40 percent of medicated patients relapsed. After thirty months, about 90 percent of placebo patients and 50 percent of medicated patients did so.[11]

Although the results demonstrated a highly significant advantage for medicated patients, the Task Force interpreted this data cautiously. Medication "seem[ed] to prevent later exacerbations of psychotic symptoms," it wrote, but the benefits were "not always obvious" in chronic schizophrenia. Moreover, although medication "improved" the "level of function" of patients with schizophrenia "at least over periods . . . of a year or so," it was "less certain" that "the availability of antipsychotic drugs has truly modified the life-long pattern of adaptation in schizophrenia in comparison with the best treatments available before their introduction in 1952." (The relapse studies did not extend past thirty months.) The Report also expressed doubt about the "improved level of function" of medicated patients. "[M]ost of the outcome assessments," according to the Task Force, "have been frankly crude, with an emphasis on the most easily measured changes, such as grossly psychotic behavior or the need for increased medication or hospital care," while paying little attention to the "finer levels of cognitive, psychological, and social function." That comment applied, of course, to the Collaborative Study itself.

The Report concluded that drug treatment "is typically only *partially* successful," and that some patients "appear to respond [to medication] undramatically, or not at all." Moreover, since about half of placebo subjects did not relapse within a year, it appeared that "not all psychotic patients require prolonged neuroleptic treatment." Finally, "maintenance treatment with neuroleptics . . . [was] supported by scientifically sound data *only for schizophrenia.*"[12]

The Task Force also took a cautious view of how medication worked in the brain. It described drugs as more than mere tranquilizers, but "rarely, if ever, *curative.*" Although research had demonstrated that "antipsychotic agents interfere with actions of dopamine" that alone did "not prove that antidopamine effects are either necessary or sufficient for antipsychotic efficacy." In short, the dopamine theory of schizophrenia and "antipsychotic" action was unconfirmed. The Report used the terms "antipsychotic" and "neuroleptic" interchangeably.[13]

Finally, the Task Force adopted a cautious stance on possible medication-induced persistent neurological changes other than tardive dyskinesia. Noting some concerns, the Task Force found "no evidence to suggest that generalized toxic or degenerative changes occur in CNS [central nervous system] function" as a result of medication, and no convincing evidence of any drug-induced persistent dementia. At the same time, however, it noted that akathisia "may persist or reoccur indefinitely," and that a "rabbit syndrome" of mouth tremors might be a "variant of parkinsonism"; a chart noted that the period of "maximum risk" for this last disorder was "mos.–yrs.," like tardive dyskinesia's. In any event, the Task Force defined tardive dyskinesia so broadly—it included abnormal movements of any extremity, abnormalities in posture or breathing, speech difficulties, and an akathisia-like restlessness as well as the commonly observed movements of the tongue, mouth, and jaw—that one might wonder whether the disorder itself represented "generalized toxic or degenerative changes."[14]

The recommendations of the Task Force accorded with its cautious analysis. It urged clinicians to weigh the benefits and risks of medication, consider an individual patient's response, and exercise clinical judgment. Uncertainties about the benefits of medication and the supposed uncertainties about tardive dyskinesia broadened the range of this clinical judgment; the less that medical knowledge constrained clinicians, the greater the role of "clinical judgment alone." Implicitly, the Task Force urged society to allow clinicians to proceed in this way as well. It presumed that medically, socially, and ethically acceptable decisions would follow.[15]

The particular recommendations of the Task Force fell into four overlapping categories, each with a different relationship to the overarching framework of individualized clinical judgment. The first category consisted of cases that called for especially sensitive, careful clinical weighing. Here, the Task Force placed cases of tardive dyskinesia. Tracking the recommendation of the 1973 Task Force, the Report considered "the theoretical treatment of choice" for tardive dyskinesia to be "discontinuation of neuroleptics," since "available data suggest that tardive dyskinesia is often reversible if neuroleptics are withdrawn, especially early in its course." Yet the Task Force did not strongly endorse this "theoretical treatment." Instead, it noted that some patients would suffer exacerbation of symptoms and relapses as a result of discontinuing medication. The "dilemma" that resulted demanded especially careful clinical judgment: "[T]he clinician, with the patient and family, must weigh the risk of psychiatric worsening, which may be seriously life-disrupting or even life-threatening, against the risk of tardive dyskinesia. Since tardive dyskinesia seems not to be a relentlessly progressive neurologic disorder, it may be prudent to continue neuroleptic therapy temporarily if the psychiatric indications are sufficiently compelling."[16] It seems clear how clinicians would decide: they regarded virtually every patient as better off on medication. Moreover, "temporary" continuation of treatment might last indefinitely; the Task Force suggested no time limit.

Treatment of nonschizophrenic conditions with medication also required sensitive clinical weighing. Physicians often prescribed long-term drug regimens for manic depressive illness, mental retardation, and organic brain syndrome. No "scientifically sound data" had yet validated such practices, however. Thus, "the possible benefits must be *carefully weighed* against the potential complications," the Task Force wrote. Yet it was far from clear how clinicians could carefully weigh an unknown, as the Task Force suggested, or make up for ignorance with added care in deliberation.[17]

An overlapping category urged clinicians to consider a particular factor as they weighed the benefits and risks of medication. Among these considerations were: the absence of studies demonstrating drug benefits in nonschizophrenic disorders (something that also called for "careful consideration"); the fact that tardive dyskinesia often did not worsen over time; and the existence of non-drug-responsive patients. Viewed broadly, most of the Report fell into this category since it described facts relevant to clinical judgments.

A third category included recommended procedures for developing significant clinical facts or implementing clinical judgments. Here the Task Force's recommendations ranged from general and obvious to precise and pointed. It urged clinicians to make a "deliberate and sustained effort . . . to maintain patients on the lowest effective amount of the drug;" review the effectiveness of drug regimens "at least every 6 months;" and conduct "regular" examinations to detect tardive dyskinesia. More striking was its recommendation to periodically withdraw medication from chronically hospitalized patients with schizophrenia—or at least to dramatically reduce the dosage. Since medication temporarily masks tardive dyskinesia's symptoms, especially at higher doses, discontinuing drugs or reducing the dosage would aid diagnosis by uncovering "masked" dyskinesias. It would also allowed an informed reassessment of the continuing need for medication.[18]

This recommendation fell short of Gardos and Cole's 1976 call for drug-free trials, since it applied only to the chronically hospitalized. Yet it went much further than the Task Force's general advice about dosage and periodic assessment. The Task Force was requiring concrete steps to discover the lowest effective dose and to determine whether patients still benefited at all. Clinical judgment would prevail, but it did not appear that clinicians should have discretion to bypass the dosage-reduction and discontinuation procedures entirely. "Even if such a trial with less medication has been unsuccessful within the past year," the Report noted, it "should be reconsidered at regular intervals and seriously attempted for most [chronically hospitalized] patients."[19]

This recommendation continued the tradition of singling out chronic, hospitalized patients for special preventive measures. Ayd had done so in the late 1960s, as did Friedman in 1973. The reason was that chronic patients obviously fared badly on medication: good responders usually did not remain chronically hospitalized. Thus, the benefits of drugs carried less weight in these cases.

The Task Force emphasized another consideration, as well. It observed that many patients in the community were also faring badly on medication. Yet dose reduction or elimination was rarely possible for outpatients, it wrote, because of the "the ubiquitous and critical shortage of adequate aftercare systems." Because of that "shortage," clinicians would probably fail to detect relapse during a drug-free or dose-reduced period until the relapse became pronounced. In contrast, psychiatrists constantly observed hospitalized patients and could quickly reinstitute medication or raise dosages when necessary.[20]

These observations by the Task Force confirmed Crane's claim that existing systems of community care produced inflexible medication regimens. Crane had urged changes in the system, but the Task Force drew an opposite conclusion. It supposed that drug prescription within the community had to remain inflexible—and the risks of medication tolerated—because of the shortcomings of public mental health.

The fourth category of recommendation did not involve the discretion of clinicians at all. Rather, the Task Force weighed benefits and risks for itself. Based on the results, it announced a course of action that clinicians should follow. One example involved patients who had recovered from an initial episode of apparent schizophrenia. Left untreated, some of these patients never suffered a second episode. Others turned out to have manic depressive illness or some other nonschizophrenic disorder. The Task Force concluded, "Commitment of a patient to prolonged [maintenance] treatment with neuroleptics requires more than one acute psychotic episode without full return to optimal prepsychotic status, objective evidence of continuing psychosis, or good recovery but frequent recurrences that suggest the likelihood of further recurrences."[21]

Less explicitly, the Task Force weighed benefits and risks when it marked the acceptable bounds of clinical discretion. It obviously determined that the benefits of medication presumptively outweighed the risks in the largest category of cases: patients with schizophrenia, who responded at least partially to drugs, who had not demonstrated a capacity to do well drug-free, and who appeared free of tardive dyskinesia. Despite the future risk of tardive dyskinesia, clinicians could justifiably prescribe medication in these cases. Indeed, the

Report said little about when clinicians could justifiably withhold drugs from such patients.

Taken as a whole, the Task Force's recommendations aimed for modest changes in clinical practice generally, and more substantial changes in the treatment of those chronically hospitalized. Yet there was little reason to suppose that anything would actually change. The Task Force did not illustrate any general recommendations by providing examples of individual cases where a clinician should withhold drugs. And why should the Task Force exert more influence over clinicians than Gardos and Cole, whose earlier advice about withdrawing medication from large numbers of outpatients had been ignored?

The Task Force recommendations lacked enforcement or monitoring mechanisms. For example, one could easily identify hospitals and psychiatrists administering medication to virtually everyone with schizophrenia or manic depressive illness, and therefore running afoul of the recommendations. By contrast, a long-term drug regimen for a single patient who suffered from manic depressive illness would not necessarily indicate that the prescribing physician was ignoring the Task Force; conceivably, the physician had carefully considered the lack of studies demonstrating drug effectiveness in manic depressive illness before deciding to prescribe—exactly as the Task Force recommended. Yet if the same physician prescribed such regimens in *all* cases of manic depression—or for all patients with tardive dyskinesia—the recommendations would have failed.

The Task Force, however, focused only on individual decisions. It did not say that hospitals and clinicians should monitor general practices, or take steps to bring to bring those practices into compliance. Nor did it urge accrediting authorities or public agencies to police hospitals or physicians engaging in the disapproved practices. As the *Rennie* case demonstrated, the Joint Commission on Accreditation of Hospitals was capable of accrediting mental hospitals that reported no tardive dyskinesia cases among their patients.

The focus on individual decisions had a related consequence: the uncritical acceptance of the new public mental health system. Since individual clinicians did not control that system, they could not consider possible changes to it as they weighed benefit and risk. And since the Task Force was primarily concerned with the contours of clinical judgment, it did not consider systematic changes in public health either.

Thus, the Task Force had exempted outpatients from its drug-free trial recommendation because of the inadequacies of community care. And it might easily have extended the point. Since relapse presents more danger in the community, should not outpatient status itself weigh in favor of long-term medication in all cases? That had been Crane's observation in 1975, and the Task Force seemingly adopted it. It cited inadequacies in community treatment but did not recommend periodic drug-free trials for outpatients in *adequate* programs. Instead, it simply presumed all community programs inadequate—or, what amounted to the same thing, presumed that community programs inevitably required long-term medication regimens.

In the end, the Task Force had acknowledged the importance of tardive dyskinesia and offered prevalence figures two to three times higher than those of the 1973 task force, but it had nonetheless endorsed most long-term use of medication. Prevalence figures like those of the Task Force had once seemed to threaten the wide use of medication and the reliance on community care. Now, according to the Task Force, the high prevalence figures made little difference in practice.

The idea of individualized clinical judgment underlay that conclusion. There were serious risks associated with the use of medication, according to the Task Force, but the risks should be addressed by psychiatrists exercising judgment about particular patients—not by courts or legislatures or the public. The Task Force did not claim that as a matter of principle courts, legislatures, and the public should always lack a say in medication matters. That argument would be unlikely to succeed, because the civil rights revolution had constitutionalized so many other aspects of American life; and it would be hypocritical, because the public mental health revolution had itself relied on courts, public offices, and public opinion to achieve its objectives.

The Task Force case for clinical judgment rested instead on four arguments. First, tardive dyskinesia represented the principal risk of medication. Second, the risk did not exceed manageable dimensions. Third, general measures—such as periodically withdrawing medications from chronic, hospitalized patients—would diminish the risk further, and also demonstrate a psychiatric commitment to minimizing the amount of harm. Fourth, psychiatrists would follow the advice of the Task Force and balance benefits and risks carefully. These arguments remained implicit rather than being overtly stated, but the Report made little sense without them.

All four were highly questionable, or simply wrong. In fact, medication carried other substantial risks, such as subjective distress, which patients feared more than tardive dyskinesia. The Task Force's prevalence estimates were too low. Psychiatrists seemed likely to ignore the Task Force's principles in relation to chronically hospitalized and community patients alike.

Much was at stake. Adherence to the recommendations would demonstrate psychiatry's bona fides, but a failure to comply would suggest the opposite: that medication-era psychiatrists, like those in earlier eras, could not seriously address the obvious ethical issues associated with a prevailing therapy. In this way, the Task Force had offered a highly vulnerable defense of psychiatry, and a defense that could boomerang. Gardos and Cole tried to offer a better one.

Gardos and Cole's Overview

Just as Crane had not labeled his 1973 article a dissent from the first task force, Gardos and Cole did not style their 1980 article a dissent from the second. Yet it was exactly that. To begin with, they separated themselves from the Task Force's vulnerable factual assertions. Their "Overview" offered significantly higher prevalence estimates than did the Task Force. Moreover, Cole's incidence study avoided most of the methodological problems that, according to the Task Force, confounded such estimates. Since Cole was examining "incidence"—the number of new cases that appeared in a given population in a given time—preexisting movements did not confound his investigation. Nor did investigators' varying degrees of sensitivity to abnormal movements present a large problem.[22]

Beyond that, Gardos and Cole did not consider tardive dyskinesia to be medication's only serious risk. Here, they relied on "a scholarly review" by none other than George Crane:

> Crane described three types of "neuroleptic induced encepha-
> lopathies": 1) reversible, 2) irreversible or slowly reversible, and 3)
> juvenile reversible symptoms. The irreversible category includes
> hyptonia, dystonias, and Parkinson-like syndromes in addition to the
> well-recognized manifestations of tardive dyskinesia. To underscore
> Crane's view, a number of surveys that have focused primarily on
> tardive dyskinesia have also shown an even higher prevalence of
> parkinsonism, often despite usual anti-Parkinson drug treatment. Not
> only are there apparently treatment-resistant cases of drug-induced
> Parkinson-like syndromes in numbers comparable to those of tardive
> dyskinesia, the functional impairment resulting from akinesia, rigidity
> and tremor may well equal if not exceed the usually minimal
> functional disturbance of tardive dyskinesia. The need for a more
> comprehensive approach to the problem of the long-term side effects
> of antipsychotics in place of a narrow focus on tardive dyskinesia
> alone cannot be overemphasized.[23]

Gardos and Cole did not estimate the number of patients who suffered from a long-term side effect, but—given their already high estimate for tardive dyskinesia and the existence of "comparable" number of parkinsonism cases—the figure probably exceeded 50 percent, perhaps by a lot. Unlike the Task Force, then, they did not depict moderate risks easily managed by clinical judgment.

Gardos and Cole seemed to argue against giving undue attention to any side effect, including tardive dyskinesia, because medication produced so many. This represented the opposite of the Task Force's claims about manageable side effects. In any case, Gardos and Cole offered no suggestions for managing the other long-term effects. Having explained that parkinsonism and akinesia constituted threats at least equal to that of tardive dyskinesia, they ignored those effects—and their own admonitions—in the remainder of the article. In effect Gardos and Cole played one side effect off against the other, arguing that none should receive undue attention because so many existed.

About tardive dyskinesia, however, the "Overview" offered significantly milder recommendations than had the Task Force. Like the Task Force, Gardos and Cole urged psychiatrists to examine patients for tardive dyskinesia, periodically review the need for continued medication, and "attempt . . . to find the minimal effective dose level." In other instances, however, they weakened the Task Force's specific conclusions and recommendations, making them vaguer. Where the Task Force had determined issues for itself, Gardos and Cole returned those issues to the realm of clinical judgment.

According to the Task Force, for example, a single psychotic episode did not warrant long-term drug treatment. Clinicians who prescribed long-term regimens after a single psychotic episode would be ignoring a Task Force recommendation. Gardos and Cole, on the other hand, merely observed that "patients who have had one or two psychotic episodes are not necessarily candidates for indefinite drug therapy"—an observation too vague to have an effect on clinical practice. Similarly, the Task Force had urged careful consideration before prescribing medication for nonschizophrenic conditions, since no research supported the use of medication in those cases. Gardos and Cole merely called for "[a]voidance of antipsychotics whenever suitable alternatives are available (e.g. lithium or antidepressants for patients with affective illness, antianxiety agents for neurotic anxiety)." Their advice treated medication as a default treatment: if something else worked, use it; if not, administer medication. Cole had come a long way from the Collaborative Study's picture of a close fit between the condition being treated (schizophrenia) and the treatment ("antischizophrenic" medication).[24]

Remarkably, Gardos and Cole also diverged from the Task Force's recommendation to periodically withdraw medication, or at least reduce the dosage, in the case of a chronically hospitalized patient. That recommendation had not gone as far as Gardos and Cole's own advice to clinicians in 1976. Yet in their "Overview," they suggested that a recommendation like that of the Task Force went too far, and they withdrew their own earlier advice. Gardos and Cole wrote, "In patients who have never received an adequate trial without antipsychotic drugs withdrawal could be considered [here, a footnote cites Gardos and Cole's 1976 article], but *this recommendation is not generally accepted* because of the substantial risk of psychotic relapse."[25] This statement lacked directive force; if drug withdrawal "could be considered," it did not *have* to be. Gardos and Cole now favored a less far-reaching measure: periodic drug-free intervals of three or four weeks, a period "usually too short to precipitate psychotic relapse but long enough to uncover dyskinesia." That would aid in diagnosing the disorder but, unlike the Task Force recommendation—and their own 1976 advice—it would not help determine whether the patient could do as well drug-free.[26] With that, Gardos and Cole abandoned their own principal recommendation for dealing with tardive dyskinesia. In 1976, they had estimated that as many as 50 percent of patients would do as well off medication, and they had urged clinicians to identify these patients. Now, the benefit estimate and the insistence on individualized determinations were both gone.

Clinicians had ignored their 1976 recommendation, but rather than decry that fact, Gardos and Cole tried to explain and defend it. A "substantial risk of psychotic relapse," according to the "Overview," had led clinicians to reject the option of withdrawing medications. Yet Gardos and Cole had known in 1976, when they formulated the recommendation, that a "substantial" risk of relapse existed; their point was that a "substantial" chance of nonrelapse—or at least, of no additional relapse—also existed, and exploiting that chance represented the best way of minimizing the number of tardive dyskinesia victims. In 1980, that goal virtually receded from sight.

The relevant research conclusions had not changed since 1976, however. To document the "substantial risk," Gardos and Cole cited a single source, a 1975 review of the literature on relapse by Task Force member John M. Davis. Yet Davis's article had appeared *before* Gardos and Cole recommended medication withdrawal in 1976, and Davis's review examined still earlier studies. Moreover, Davis's 1975 article generally agreed with Gardos and Cole's 1976 recommendation about medication withdrawal. In the studies Davis reviewed, 65 percent of placebo patients relapsed, compared with 30 percent of patients on maintenance medication. Davis concluded that "[b]ecause not all of the patients . . . relapsed with the discontinuance of medication, it logically follows that not all patients should necessarily be maintained on maintenance medication, particularly those in whom relapse would not be expected." Indeed, Davis described the claim that "all schizophrenic patients benefit from maintenance neuroleptics" as a "straw man" because "no physician believes [it]." Five years later, however, the "Overview" portrayed clinicians as generally accepting that "straw man" argument—and Gardos and Cole acquiesced to that argument, rather than objecting to it, citing Davis for support.[27]

The "Overview" noted that clinicians "generally" would not withdraw medication from patients who already had tardive dyskinesia—even though withdrawal constituted the best, and perhaps the only, treatment for the disorder. Surely, if the presence of tardive dyskinesia did not prompt clinicians to withdraw drugs, the mere risk of it would not do so either. Thus, Gardos and Cole effectively conceded that tardive dyskinesia would not significantly affect clinical decision making about long-term drug regimens.

If clinicians would not withhold drugs, would they change their prescribing practices in other ways that did not increase the risk of relapse? Gardos and Cole had their doubts. "[M]any chronic schizophrenic patients receive antipsychotic doses greatly in excess of what is needed," they observed—a turnabout from Cole's 1975 insistence during the debate with Crane that doses were "inadequate." More generally, Gardos and Cole cited Crane for the "disquieting fact" that "presentation of relevant facts in lecture form may lead to no measurable changes in drug prescribing habits, a finding in accord with the experience of most teachers of psychopharmacology." In short, clinicians probably would ignore obvious measures for reducing the risk of tardive dyskinesia and would continue to prescribe medication as if serious side effects did not exist—as if, one might say, the Collaborative Study had been correct.[28]

Thus, Gardos and Cole diagnosed side effects more harshly than the Task Force and offered a more discouraging picture of clinicians. The Task Force portrayed manageable risks and clinicians willing to manage them; Gardos and Cole disagreed on both counts. How, then, did Gardos and Cole also arrive at milder recommendations than Task Force had?

The difference lay in their fundamental justification for existing medication practice. Gardos and Cole did not rely on individualized clinical judgment. "Because antipsychotic compounds remain the cornerstone of the treatment of acute and chronic schizophrenia," they wrote, "these drugs cannot be replaced." That was a circular statement, if the question was *why* drugs constituted the cornerstone of treatment, or whether they should remain so. Gardos and Cole seemed to mean that the existing system of treatment *itself* compelled clinicians to prescribe medication.[29]

This represented a historic shift. Since 1964, psychiatrists had approached the relationship between the public health system and individual clinical decision making from almost every conceivable direction. The Collaborative Study had supposed that the ease of administering medication made possible a new system of public health whose desirability seemed self-evident. Later, many psychiatrists imagined a simpler relationship: they thought the aggregate of clinical decisions—which, because of medication's benefits and safety invariably prescribed the treatment—produced a new public mental health system almost automatically. Crane imagined a simple model too, but one that went in the opposite direction. He argued that the imperatives of the new public mental health system dictated clinical decisions to use medication—decisions that, in his eyes, were often medically indefensible. Frank Ayd straddled this divide; he wanted clinicians making medication decisions on medical grounds, but he also insisted that tardive dyskinesia be kept "in proper perspective" in order not to undermine the new system of public mental health. The 1980 Task Force ostensibly relied on pure clinical decision making, but in fact it arrived at a position not unlike Ayd's: it recommended withdrawing medication from many "chronically hospitalized" patients, but not from patients in the "community." Thus, chronic patients, the relics of the old public mental health system, could live under the old system's rules; in the "community," the new rules applied.

Gardos and Cole's justification for current medication practice began with the public mental health system: they adopted not just Crane's view of side effects but also Crane's idea that the public health system dictated clinical decisions and practically compelled universal prescribing of medication. Where Crane had objected, however, Gardos and Cole accepted the inevitable; they turned it into the "cornerstone" of medication-era psychiatry.

In this light, one may understand how Gardos and Cole could criticize clinicians for ignoring the advice of psychiatric researchers and, at the same time, withdraw a pivotal recommendation of their own because clinicians were ignoring it. The contradiction fades in light of the new role of the public mental health system. Some medication practices—for example, prescribing medication even though a particular patient might receive little benefit—are inherent in the system. Short of altering the system, they cannot be changed. Since Gardos and Cole took the system's survival to be a matter of first principle, they accepted such practices. Thus, they abandoned their 1976 suggestion about withdrawing medication; clinicians simply would not do it within the confines of the system. Other reforms, such as dose reduction, seemed less likely to disrupt the system, and Gardos and Cole thought dosages should change. Yet they recognized that clinical inertia might carry over to these practices as well.

The "Overview" and Task Force Report offered utterly different rationales. The Report's arguments would have collapsed if the Task Force had acknowledged what Gardos and Cole did: that clinicians hardly ever withdraw medication because of tardive dyskinesia; that clinicians ignore measures, such as dose reduction, that reduce the risk of tardive dyskinesia without increasing the chances of relapse; that the risk of developing tardive dyskinesia is high, and the risk of developing *some* long-lasting side effect extraordinarily high. The Task Force rested everything on individualized clinical decision making; Gardos and Cole presumed that clinicians do not really individualize their decisions and that clinical judgments typically expose patients to unnecessary risk.

Gardos and Cole had taken Frank Ayd's "proper perspective" on long-term side effects and made it the only perspective; even clinical judgment paled in comparison.

The Third Period of the Medication Era

The "Overview" and the Task Force Report marked the demise of the Study vision among researchers, and so the end of the second period of the medication era. The Study had been theoretical and visionary. It had explained how drugs worked (antischizophrenically), characterized their benefits and risks in global terms ("impressive" and "qualitative"; "mild and unimportant") and discerned their public health implications. The 1980 Task Force eschewed both theory and vision. It never took seriously the possibility that tardive dyskinesia revealed something important—biologically, morally, or socially—about medication. Nor did Gardos and Cole, who declined to look seriously at anything except existing public health arrangements.

Study-era psychiatrists had made research findings the driving force behind the public mental health system. Now many of those findings turned out to be fundamentally mistaken. Yet the public health system and related system of clinical prescribing would remain intact. The Task Force accomplished that feat partly by ignoring the public mental health system, but also by accommodating the system in its recommendations on withdrawing medication. It looked at public health largely as a clinician would—and a clinician would be powerless to change the system.

The "Overview" proceeded in a more radical way: it turned the old arguments on their head. The Study vision had presumed that the public mental health system should change in light of medications' properties and research discoveries. The "Overview" presumed that maintaining the existing public mental health system was the first imperative of all, and that it limited the significance of side effects and of research findings. Prescribing patterns could not change if the public health system depended upon them, no matter what research showed. From 1967 onward, leading psychiatrists had tried to save the Study's premise by refusing to acknowledge inconvenient research findings; that stratagem having failed, Gardos and Cole now counseled abandonment of the premise and acknowledgment of the inconvenient facts.

Cole was senior author of both the Study and the "Overview." In the 1964 Study, he had viewed the existing public mental health system through a lens made out of the properties of medication. In the 1980 "Overview," he used the existing public mental health system as the lens. Had Cole followed his 1980 approach in 1964, he would have insisted on exploiting the properties of medication in ways that preserved the then existing system of public mental health—the network of large state mental hospitals.

Why did Cole change his mind? For that matter, why did he write the "Overview"? He and Gardos shared wide areas of agreement with their Task Force colleagues; they hardly would have disapproved if clinicians had followed the Task Force's recommendations. Gardos and Cole believed clinicians *would* ignore the recommendations—not that they *should*. Nor did the recommendations pose any threat to the existing system of public mental health.

Gardos and Cole hinted at an answer: it was something they called the "public health viewpoint." "Viewpoint" could not explain their factual disagreements with the Task Force: their high prevalence figures, for example, or their portrait of clinicians' performance. They reported Cole's findings about tardive dyskinesia as correct, and described clinicians' inflexibility as something obvious to every teacher of psychopharmacology. On those matters, Gardos and Cole thought they were right—not that they had a different "viewpoint" from the Task Force. Indeed, it was the Task Force—not they—who depicted uncertainties about medication that warranted different clinical viewpoints.

A clue about the meaning of "viewpoint" appears in Cole's 1975 exchange with Crane. There, Cole distinguished two kinds of disagreement among psychiatrists. The first reflected varying "evaluat[ions of] . . . the available evidence." The second resulted from the differing positions of psychiatrists along the "optimism-pessimism balance." Cole took the optimistic side, while Crane was a Cassandra, with positions "much more detrimental than helpful to progress in the field." "Viewpoint" in 1980 served somewhat the same function that "optimism-pessimism balance" had in 1975. It involved matters crucial to "progress in the field" that did not turn on the "available evidence."

In 1980, preserving progress required a different response from 1975. Indeed, the "Overview" was anything but optimistic. In fact, the Task Force's relative optimism had provoked Gardos and Cole's dissent.

Ultimately, Gardos and Cole's disagreement with the Task Force turned on the perceived demands of "progress in the field." By 1980, the principal task consisted of defending "progress" against threats posed by litigation and possible adverse public reactions. The Task Force Report cited "medico-legal" issues and "public" concern over tardive dyskinesia; the "Overview" described "panic" among psychiatrists over "the likelihood of increasing litigation" involving the disorder.

The "Overview" and the Report differed in "viewpoint" because each followed different strategies for these problems. By minimizing the prevalence of tardive dyskinesia, the Report followed the path taken by Denber and Kline, the first task force, and Cole himself in 1975. This strategy had an obvious rationale: all other things being equal, public and judicial concern about medication would rise and fall with the tardive dyskinesia rate. The less tardive dyskinesia, the less concern.

Within the Task Force's clinical balancing framework, high prevalence figures actually mattered very little—apart from the medico-legal concerns. True, higher figures entailed an increased probability of a patient developing tardive dyskinesia. Yet the Task Force concluded that patients already suffering from tardive dyskinesia could continue to receive medication. Following the same approach, it could have endorsed nearly universal medication and also cited a prevalence rate like Gardos and Cole's. Supposing that every medicated person developed tardive dyskinesia, the benefits of medication might still outweigh the risks. Thus, if the Task Force produced artificially low prevalence figures, something other than the imperatives of its clinical judgment model must explain why.

Imagine an American Psychiatric Association lawyer devising a defense of medication practice in 1980. By then, denying the existence of persistent side effects no longer constituted an option. Given the state of the psychiatric literature, it would be unbelievable, and *Rennie* demonstrated that it would not work. One could, however, minimize the number and severity of tardive dyskinesia cases while ignoring other persistent or significant side effects. Tardive dyskinesia represents an important concern, one could argue, but the disorder is not widespread or serious enough to require a wholesale rethinking of existing practice—and, in any event, the judgment of individual clinicians constitutes the best approach to the issue. That was the Task Force's position.

Such a strategy carried significant risks, however. The lowest defensible prevalence estimate had increased, for one thing. Twenty percent, the Task Force's upper figure, represented a far cry from 0 percent, or 6 percent, the high estimates from 1967 and 1973. Moreover, many researchers subscribed to far higher figures than those of the Task Force and, according to Gardos and Cole, the figures would continue rising. If the Task Force reconciled judges and the public to a 15 percent rate, a new defense might be required when 25 percent or 50 percent of medicated patients developed tardive dyskinesia.

The problem was generic. As long as psychiatrists defended existing practice on the ground that tardive dyskinesia's prevalence stood at (only) X percent, the defense might collapse when the figure rose. The "only X percent" defense also lost plausibility as X rose in absolute terms. "Only X" verged on incoherence as X neared 50 percent; it became absurd as X approached 100 percent. Beyond that, the process of upward revision cast doubt on psychiatrists' competence and integrity. If anyone remembered the earlier estimates and revisions—admittedly, a big "if"—psychiatrists might appear venal.

The Task Force Report had yet another vulnerability. Its argument for existing practice rested on the legitimacy of clinical judgment. Yet Gardos and Cole surmised that clinicians would pay little attention to Task Force recommendations. And *Rennie* again suggested the likely result. During the litigation, the state promulgated new procedures and guidelines for dealing with tardive dyskinesia. The hospitals ignored them. In the trial judge's eyes, that made the hospitals appear incompetent, even duplicitous. And one might reasonably fear that a similar judgment awaited psychiatry at large, should it ignore its own prescriptions—as Gardos and Cole believed it would.

Gardos and Cole avoided the Task Force's problems by conceding virtually everything that made its Report vulnerable. The "Overview" posited a large, not small, number of tardive dyskinesia cases. It predicted future increases. It acknowledged other persistent side effects, with consequences for patients comparable to tardive dyskinesia's, or worse. It presumed clinicians would remain inflexible about medication prescribing.

No foreseeable future development threatened this analysis. If Gardos and Cole's argument was cogent to begin with, it would remain so almost no matter what happened. The "Overview" had acknowledged everything in order to change nothing. It secured the medication era against future research findings and gave it immunity from a future George Crane.

Gardos and Cole also insulated psychiatry and the public health system from past controversies. Neither the history of the tardive dyskinesia nor the original reasons for deinstitutionalization now mattered. The "Overview" produced a public mental health system with no beginning and no end. The Task Force Report also divorced the public mental health system from questions about side effects, benefits, and drug actions that appeared crucial only a few years before, but Gardos and Cole achieved a more radical and lasting separation.

A Parallel Development: Subjective Distress

Compared with tardive dyskinesia, subjective distress from medication played a small role in the upheavals of the 1970s. Distress hardly figured as a factor in the *Rogers* and *Rennie* trials, though patients suffering from it often wished to refuse medication. When Task Force members reconceptualized the case for medication in 1980, they did not treat distress as a significant problem.

Despite that, distress followed a research trajectory like that of tardive dyskinesia. Both fell outside the Study vision; by the mid 1970s, each side effect nonetheless resulted in recommendations for withdrawing medication from a significant number of patients. There was a general unraveling of the Study vision, something that went beyond accumulating findings about tardive dyskinesia.

The parallels continued through 1980, reflecting the same broad intellectual currents at work. Just as Gardos and Cole abandoned a recommendation for withdrawing medication because of tardive dyskinesia in 1980, Van Putten and May abandoned a similar recommendation regarding subjective distress in 1981. Van Putten and May produced no overarching framework, as the Task Force and Gardos and Cole did, but then subjective distress had always seemed less portentous than tardive dyskinesia. In its own way, their shift in approach toward distress signaled the same sea change: psychiatry was closing ranks around existing medication practice during these years—and doing so largely because of threats from outside.

In 1981 Van Putten and May published "Subjective Response to Antipsychotic Drugs," an article about the relationship between medication-induced distress and a patient's willingness to take medication. They reported that 49 percent of subjects in an experiment experienced no distress from medication; 22 percent experienced at least some distress; and the remainder were either "noncommittal" (about 20 percent) or "inaccessible" (about 10 percent). Few patients who experienced distress after a single dose agreed to try medication again, and these refusing patients did poorly overall. Van Putten and May observed that reactions to side effects could depend on an individual's psychology and that, while the "dysphoric responders had somewhat less symptomatology before treatment," these pretreatment differences in condition were "useful for prediction" only in extreme cases.[30]

Van Putten and May's figures resembled their earlier findings, although they were reporting fewer distress cases and their noncommittal/inaccessible category seemed large. But this 1981 article ignored the possibility that Van Putten and May had highlighted just the previous year—"that the patient might do just as well, or even better, without drug treatment." Van Putten and May also ignored the possibility that staff were reacting with hostility to the refusing patients, thereby worsening their condition. Instead, Van Putten and May wrote as if all patients should receive medication as a matter of course:

> It seems to us that, particularly at the very beginning, dysphoric responses must be minimized, since an early clear-cut dysphoric response was a nearly foolproof predictor not only of noncompliance but of refusal to try any other antipsychotic drug. Further, these dysphoric responders felt wronged by the drug and by the doctor or institution that prescribed it. It is, we think, persons like this who develop adversary relationships with staff, and even become spokespersons in the various consumer movements that equate antipsychotic drugs with "psychiatric assault" and "chemical straightjacketing."
> . . . At a practical level, schizophrenic patients with a history of dysphoric response . . . are at risk for another dysphoric response, certainly at conventional dosage levels. Such patients should be started on a very low dose and, in our opinion, should receive a prophylactic antiparkinson drug.[31]

This discussion marked a departure from Van Putten and May's other recent work in emphasis, approach, and style. Van Putten's 1974 article, for example, had observed that "[e]ven mild extrapyramidal involvement can be unbearable and lead to outright drug reluctance or self-prescribed reduction of dosage." In the 1981 article, the "unbearable" nature of side effects emerges only inferentially, as we learn that some patients will not bear them. Again, the 1981 article suggested that "much may depend on the emotional meaning a side effect has for the individual patient"—a point also implied by Van Putten earlier. In the earlier articles, however, Van Putten's point was that medication produced emotional distress; in 1981, it was more that distress represented an idiosyncratic emotional response—just as some psychiatrists had portrayed tardive dyskinesia as the idiosyncratic response of a previously damaged brain.

Van Putten and May now attached a different kind of significance to the patient voice in medication matters. They subtitled their 1978 article "The Consumer Has a Point" and concluded: "[S]chizophrenics have been asked every question except, 'How does the medication agree with you?' Their response is worth listening to." The 1981 article, in contrast, observed that "dysphoric responses must be minimized" partly because the affected patients "become spokespersons in the various consumer movements that equate antipsychotic drugs with 'psychiatric assault' and 'chemical straightjacketing.' "[32] In short, these consumers did *not* have a point, and their collective responses were *not* worth listening to. The imagery of the two articles clashed head-on.

Clearly, concerns about outside interference into psychiatry—concerns that had reached a fever pitch because of tardive dyskinesia and federal lawsuits—colored Van Putten and May's substantive approach. The Task Force had described such concerns as "medico-legal," and they had underlain Gardos and Cole's "public health viewpoint." Here, they produced a similar result.

Like Gardos and Cole, Van Putten and May backtracked, without acknowledging the change, from an earlier recommendation about withdrawing medication. Their shift differed from Cole's in significant ways: Cole had denied tardive dyskinesia's importance; Van Putten and May had pioneered explorations of patient distress. Cole had also offered a stronger, more precise withdrawal recommendation that should have proved harder to abandon. Cole backtracked after cryptically noting that psychiatrists had failed to heed his earlier advice; Van Putten and May accomplished their shift more elegantly, by setting themselves a different research task. They turned from the problem of identifying distressed patients who should not receive medication to the problem of minimizing distressed patients' acts of drug refusal and protest. Without self-contradiction, they could return one day to the former problem. Still, it seemed remarkable for Van Putten and May to argue that patient distress— which they once described as "fright, terror, anger or rage, anxiety, and . . . sexual torment"—mattered because distressed patients joined consumer movements. Like the Report and the "Overview," they found less medical significance in a side effect than had previously been supposed.

Psychiatry's visionary time of seeing large implications and drawing large conclusions—about the benefits of medication, the causes of schizophrenia, the proper configuration of the public health system, the brain, and even about errors in the prevailing vision—had ended. An absence of vision, and of professional emotion, replaced it. From 1980 to the mid-1990s, the third period of the medication era, research results accumulated but mattered less. Neither clinical practice nor public mental health nor any large view of medication depended on them any longer. Whether psychiatrists subscribed to the Task Force's picture of clinical judgment that ineffably produced acceptable outcomes, or Gardos and Cole's "viewpoint" that refused to countenance anything that threatened the existing public health system, or Van Putten and May's example of asking less challenging questions and thereby getting less provocative answers—and most psychiatrists probably subscribed to all three, together—the result was the same.

The Collaborative Study had justified a new public mental health system by supplying wrong, misleading, or inflated answers to research questions. Now psychiatrists presumed that those answers did not fundamentally matter: indeed, that no answers did. It was if the Study's findings had been unnecessary, as if little had been at stake in the battles with Crane, as if psychiatrists had been mistaken about the implications of serious side effects.

The older presumptions did not fall before new technical discoveries or ethical arguments. They simply disappeared—much as the side effects of medication had disappeared in the Study. Both events reflected fundamental changes in thought or, as Gardos and Cole would say, in "viewpoint." Neither signaled any scientific advance.

Psychiatrists had never paid real attention to their past, and the new absence of vision precluded attention to possible futures. Only the present remained. Gardos and Cole's own "viewpoint," which sought to ensure that nothing of significance changed, had prevailed.

Chapter 9   Absence of Vision

Clinical Psychiatry, Public Health, and Law

Dᴜʀɪɴɢ ᴛʜᴇ ᴛʜɪʀᴅ period of the medication era—from 1980 to the early 1990s—the patterns established by the Task Force's work and the "Overview" held firm. Neither tardive dyskinesia, nor subjective distress, nor poor drug response significantly affected prescribing practice or public health developments. Psychiatrists invoked both Task Force–style balancing and Gardos and Cole's concept of medication as the system's "cornerstone"; there no longer seemed to be any need to choose between the rationales. That was because the threat from courts and the right to refuse treatment, which provoked the disparate justifications, had quickly evaporated.

What remained after the collapse of the old vision was simply the absence of any vision. In the heyday of the Study, the effect of medication on brains, the disease, institutions, and the profession had seemed tightly connected—a single structure, with interlocked parts, built upon Study tenets. That edifice was now gone, at least in the eyes of researchers. With it went the idea of a scientific vision capable of animating research, clinical practice, public health, and law. Everything seemed less portentous as a result.

The clinical balancing model did not attempt to connect the public health system to the effect of medication on the brain or disease. The system did not follow from antischizophrenic effects or fundamental discoveries about the brain; it simply existed, constraining clinical judgment but outside the bounds of clinical influence or vision. In effect, the Task Force effectively urged everyone—including the general public and the courts—to defer to a process of clinical judgment that simply did not look beyond individual patients.

Unlike the Task Force, Gardos and Cole posited a structure that linked medication and public health. Yet they did not discern any scientific or rational design to the structure—nothing comparable to the Study vision.

Instead, the components were merely frozen into place, resulting in a rigid, yet fragile, edifice. Medication represented the "cornerstone," but only in the sense that changes in medication practice would bring the edifice down. Gardos and Cole avoided any perspective outside the system and noticed little except its rigidity.

Psychiatrists remained concerned about public policy and public perception, of course. Threats to psychiatry from those quarters remained alive, at least in memory. Nothing guaranteed that the public would adopt views as conservative and narrow as those of psychiatrists. Beyond that, public perceptions and policies affected research funding and health insurance coverage for psychiatric services, and the threat of malpractice lawsuits because of tardive dyskinesia had not disappeared. Yet in the end, it seemed obvious that the medication revolution would remain unscathed.

Clinical Practice

Clinical practice did not change after the Task Force's recommendations or because of the general acknowledgment of tardive dyskinesia's importance. Task Force guidelines were "honored more in the breach than the keeping," according to Gualtieri and Sprague, while researchers' recommendations "seem to have had little, if any effect on actual physician behavior." Mental hospitals simply did not withhold medications. In 1991, for example, researchers reported that every chronic patient at a California state institution—including the 18 percent with tardive dyskinesia—"had received neuroleptic drugs continuously during hospitalization." Yet chronic, institutionalized patients supposedly represented the leading candidates for medication withdrawal.[1]

Nor did the average dose decrease because of supposed concern about tardive dyskinesia or other side effects. On the contrary, dosages appear to have risen significantly. In 1988, Gerard T. Reardon published a study of medication prescriptions at a community mental health center, a state hospital, and a general hospital psychiatric ward; he found that "the overall mean dose doubled at each center between 1973 [when the first task force recognized tardive dyskinesia] and 1982." These results, according to Reardon and his coauthors, "confirm[ed] . . . the impression of many clinicians and investigators that higher doses of antipsychotics are routinely being used."[2]

A study by Julie Magno Zito and others reached similar conclusions. In 1987, Zito reported that 95 percent of patients with schizophrenia admitted to a New York psychiatric hospital had received neuroleptic medications—a higher percentage than researchers at the same institution had found in 1968—and that it appeared patients were receiving doses "clearly in excess of current guidelines" that "may contribute to . . . unrecognized behavioral toxicity." (Zito tempered the last conclusion only because of uncertainties about equivalent dosages of different antipsychotic medications.)[3]

Thus, clinicians had responded to signal research developments of the 1970s—the recognition of widespread tardive dyskinesia and other side effects; the realization that medication usually conferred limited benefit—by administering medication to virtually every hospital patient and by significantly increasing the dose. Zito's research suggested something else as well. Over the years, she observed, psychiatrists had increased their use of higher-potency medications. High- and low-potency agents produce the same therapeutic effects, but the higher potency drugs yield those effects—and produce side effects—at lower absolute or numerical dosages. The side-effect profiles also differ. At therapeutically equivalent (rather than numerically equal) doses, higher-potency agents produce relatively more akinesia and akathisia, while lower-potency drugs produce more sedation. And some high-potency medications are available in relatively long-acting biweekly or monthly injections.

According to Zito, 35 percent of patients received high-potency drugs in 1970 and 52 percent received them in 1984. Similarly, the lowest-potency medications made up 30 percent of prescriptions in 1970, but only 12 percent in 1984. Since patients receiving the different classes of medication appeared equally ill, and had about the same number of previous hospitalizations, Zito theorized that neither the severity of illness nor any possible need for long-acting agents explained the shift to high-potency agents. A "more compelling argument," she wrote, arose from "the difference in side effect profiles of the two drug groups, which may allow a greater tolerance for high doses of high-potency agents. Low-potency agents produce more sedation and hyptotension, which are debilitating and readily observable effects, whereas the extrapyramidal effects [for example, akinesia and akathisia] of the high-potency agents until recently were often difficult to distinguish from new symptoms of illness."[4]

In short, since the side effects of high-potency medications were less inconvenient or annoying to clinicians, the clinicians favored those drugs and administered them at higher doses. In light of the past two decades of research, that development was perverse. The higher doses produced more tardive dyskinesia, and the higher-potency medications produced subjective distress. If Zito's hypothesis was correct, clinicians had not merely ignored researchers' recommendations: they had selected medications in order to do the exact opposite.

Zito's suggested explanation reflected badly on clinical practice in other ways as well. Since akinesia and akathisia "were often difficult to distinguish from new symptoms of illness," she thought clinicians possibly overlooked those side effects. Yet that would mean clinicians missed apparent "new symptoms of illness," and favored medication that seemed to make patients sicker. During the 1950s and 1960s, psychiatrists had used figures of speech suggesting that it was physicians' tolerance of side effects, rather than patients', that really mattered; during the 1980s and 1990s, clinicians seemed to prescribe that way.

These developments had a parallel in the realm of ideas because clinical psychiatry still adhered to the Study vision of medication. Psychiatrists prescribed as though Study claims about antischizophrenic effects and trivial side effects had proved accurate. Moreover, to judge from journalistic accounts and courtroom testimony, many clinicians still described schizophrenia as a disease caused by "chemical imbalances" of dopamine in the brain; regarded medications as agents that corrected those imbalances; considered side effects generally mild; and thought of medication refusal as an act explainable only in terms of the patient's mental illness or incapacity. Clinicians acknowledged tardive dyskinesia but almost invariably concluded that drug benefits outweighed the harm.[5]

The resulting gap between research and clinical views resembled something found in some systems of religious belief. Theologians may hold sophisticated views of existence and nothingness, while ordinary believers picture humanlike, personal gods. In the same way, clinicians pictured brain imbalances, antipsychotic effects and a near-universal favorable response to medication—the vision that researchers had invented and then abandoned. Researchers, meanwhile, saw almost nothing. The Study vision evidently afforded a better justification for clinical practice than the Task Force or Gardos and Cole; thus, clinicians used it to justify medication practice to patients, relatives, and the public—exactly as researchers had used it two decades before to justify public mental health reforms.

The Public Mental Health System

Like clinical practice, the public mental health system behaved during the 1980s and early 1990s as if the Study vision had been proved correct. Average length of hospital stay decreased; state hospitals became smaller, if they existed at all; medication anchored the public health system more than ever. The number of in-patient beds in public institutions declined from 558,922 at the start of the medication era (1955), to 475,202 shortly after the Study appeared (1965), to 137,810 at the end of the second period (1980), to about 110,000 near the end of the third (1993). Plotting these figures, one would not guess that tardive dyskinesia, subjective distress, or less-than-Study levels of effectiveness even existed.[6]

Problems inherent in the public health system—the tendency to medicate virtually everyone with schizophrenia, high doses, proliferating side effects—

received little attention. The general question of a connection between questionable patterns of prescribing medication and public health imperatives faded from awareness. Meanwhile, other public health problems, not obviously related to medication, achieved notoriety. Homelessness among the mentally ill and occasional acts of violence by severely ill persons released from—or refused admission to—mental hospitals were prime examples. Proposals for modest reform sometimes appeared, but rarely calls for fundamental change. For instance, to deal with homelessness among the mentally ill in New York City—a condition affecting tens of thousands of people—the city opened a special hospital unit with a handful of beds and announced its intention to transfer some of the homeless to the shrinking state hospital system.[7]

Some researchers documented the public health problems in depth and urged serious reforms, including significantly more community tracking of patients, dramatic increases in community housing, enhanced services and—possibly—real increases in the number of inpatient beds. This research generally met the same fate as investigations into side effects like subjective distress; it went largely uncontradicted, but made little difference in practice.[8]

The remedy that commanded the most attention involved outreach to bring more mentally ill people into community treatment programs. These proposals typically assumed that all mentally ill homeless people who refuse medication should receive the treatment. What should be done about patients who responded poorly or persistently refused to take medication? No one had good answers, since virtually no place would accommodate such people, outside of a very few research settings. Thus, what Crane had regarded as the fundamental problem of clinical psychopharmacology and public health—the insistence on medicating everyone with schizophrenia—became the self-evident solution to every problem that arose.[9]

Both within psychiatry and outside it, commentators blamed a variety of agencies for the problems of the public mental health system. The lawyers who brought suits and the courts that decided them; the legislatures that supplied inadequate funding for community programs; the politicians with other priorities; the bureaucrats; even the public, whose interest seemed limited, and whose members often opposed neighborhood housing for those with serious mental illness—all came in for criticism from one quarter or another. Only the psychiatrists who created the Study vision—and the medication practices that supposedly had made the new system possible—escaped blame.[10]

Law and the Courts

The possibility of serious judicial intervention into mental hospital medication practice was suggested by the 1978 trial court decisions in *Rennie* and *Rogers*. Both recognized a right to refuse medications. Two years later, the appellate courts issued their opinions, and the possibilities for dramatic change disappeared.

The *Rogers* appeal nominally affirmed the right to refuse medication, but it diluted that right almost to the vanishing point. Under the trial court decision, hospitals could force patients to take medication in nonemergency circumstances only if a court first found the patient incompetent and then determined that the patient, if competent, would have consented to the treatment. Depending on the definition of "competent," the numbers of such patients would vary widely. Yet as long as hospitals acknowledged the fact that some patients refused medication, this remedy seemed likely to make many patients drug-free. The decision's numerous critics certainly thought that was so.

The appeals decision in *Rogers* retained an "incompetency" standard but overturned the general requirement of a court competency hearing. Instead, it returned the case to the trial court "for consideration of alternative means for making incompetency determinations in situations where delay could result in significant deterioration of the patient's mental health." Those "alternative means" would allow hospital psychiatrists to make the incompetency determination, because psychiatrists generally supposed that all "delays" in administering medication could produce "significant deterioration." Nor would a guardian or a court have to decide whether a patient deemed incompetent should receive medication. Instead, the court of appeals required only "some mechanism for periodic review by nontreating physicians of the full treatment history of patients to ensure that the treatment physicians are in fact attempting to make treatment decisions as the patients would were they competent." In other words, mental hospital doctors would review their colleagues' decisions and uphold forced medication of patients as long as it appeared that the patient was incompetent and that, if competent, the patient would have consented to medications. More precisely, the reviewing physician had only to conclude that another hospital physician had "attempt[ed]" to make those determinations.[11]

Such requirements were satisfied so easily that they were virtually meaningless. Hospital psychiatrists typically presumed that every patient, if competent, would consent to the treatment. In any event, physicians seemed highly unlikely to find that a colleague had made no "attempt" to satisfy the applicable standards. *Rennie* had demonstrated that state hospital psychiatrists would subscribe to outlandish beliefs—a tardive dyskinesia rate of zero, for example—if that is what it took to medicate patients. Surely, it would prove even simpler to ascribe incompetence to a patient, and good faith to a medical colleague, which was all that *Rogers* required.

The court of appeals used a similar approach to the question of medicating patients in emergencies. The trial court had defined "emergency" as a situation in which patients were "more likely than not" to cause harm if left un-medicated. The appellate court rejected that standard. Instead, it required only that a hospital psychiatrist "determin[e] . . . that the need to prevent violence in a particular situation outweighs the possibility of harm to the medicated in-dividual." Whatever that new test meant, it warranted "emergency" medica-tion whenever a psychiatrist perceived little harm to a patient from a few doses of medication and also a "need" to prevent violence. Psychiatrists would almost invariably perceive both.[12]

Unsurprisingly, Alan Stone—professor of law and medicine at Harvard, president of the American Psychiatric Association, and a severe critic of the *Rogers* trial court decision—pronounced himself largely satisfied with the ap-pellate court's work. Indeed, Stone noted that the court had largely followed his own analysis and "adopted . . . remedies" that he had proposed. Stone's one re-gret was the failure to rule out all possibility of patients in mental hospitals re-fusing medication; Stone thought that only patients who were legally subject to involuntary medication should remain in hospitals. This position represented a logical extension of Gardos and Cole's "Overview": patients who did not com-port with the existing psychiatric structure—of which the use of medication con-stituted the "cornerstone"—should be simply expelled. Patients would conform to the system, rather than vice versa, and a perfect harmony would result.[13]

The *Rennie* appeal yielded somewhat different legal language, but essen-tially the same result. The Third Circuit recognized a right to refuse medica-tion, but overturned key aspects of the trial court's remedy, including the requirement that "independent psychiatrists" review forced-medication deci-sions. Instead, the appellate court upheld a system of in-hospital, physician peer review, the very system that had produced most of the abuses described in the record. At the same time, the Third Circuit held that the right to refuse med-ication warranted a high degree of constitutional protection in the form of a legal standard known as the "least restrictive alternative." Under that test, a state could force medication only when "necessary" and only when no alter-natives could achieve the state's constitutionally valid objectives.[14]

In other legal contexts, such as freedom of speech, the least restrictive al-ternative test usually resulted in a court declaring government action uncon-stitutional. In *Rennie*, the court had something different in mind. It declared forced medication a "medical" matter and described the least restrictive alter-native standard as "merely" a means "to advise the psychiatric community that a conscious weighing [by psychiatrists] of the constitutional liberty interest in any determination of proper treatment alternatives is necessary." Thus, what constituted a stringent, court-applied standard in every other constitutional set-ting here served to only "advise" psychiatrists, who supposedly would consider that obscure legal concept in their future medical decision making. The possi-

bility that psychiatrists would decide forced-medication issues differently because of the court's constitutional "advice" seemed nil.

In only one other federal case had a court used the least restrictive alternative standard in such a feckless way. That case was *Rogers*. Addressing the
issue of "emergency" medication, the First Circuit admonished the trial judge
to allow state psychiatrists to perform the "difficult" and "necessarily ad hoc balancing" of competing individual and state interests and to "limit its own role
to designing procedures for ensuring that the patients' interests . . . are taken
into consideration and that antipsychotics are not forcibly administered absent
a finding by a qualified physician that those interests are outweighed in a particular situation and less restrictive alternatives are unavailable."[15]

Why had these courts deployed a technical, mandatory legal standard as a
mere admonition to psychiatrists—a group that lacked legal training and probably would not understand it? The courts could have said, simply, that medical
procedures and standards for forced medication generally satisfied the Constitution. Whether right or wrong as a matter of law, that formulation would have
described the holdings accurately.

The explanation lies in the unusual dilemma that medication presented
the courts. Constitutionalizing medication practice ran the risk of undermining the "cornerstone" of modern public mental health. Courts would bear responsibility for the resulting chaos and perhaps find themselves helpless to
create a viable, working substitute for what they had destroyed. That counseled
restraint and deference to psychiatric practice. On the other hand, allowing
state physicians to inflict permanent neurological damage and other serious side
effects, on a scale historically unprecedented for any other state intervention,
and to do so over patients' protests, seemed unthinkable. Faced with a seemingly impossible dilemma, the *Rennie* and *Rogers* appellate courts decided to
have it both ways: they gave psychiatrists latitude to proceed without interference, and they gave patients and constitutional precedent some reassuring
(though, in practice, largely empty) legal formulas.

In doing so, the judges acted much as psychiatrists had when faced with a
similar dilemma. Frank Ayd, like the 1973 and 1980 task forces, crafted verbal
formulas that seemed to constrain clinicians on first glance, but actually meant
much less than they seemed to say—and that proved utterly unenforceable in
practice. The *Rennie* and *Rogers* appellate decisions did the same.

From a different vantage point, these legal decisions represented a rhetorically happier variant of Gardos and Cole's approach. The courts deferred
to existing practice, just as the "Overview" did. Yet the courts also suggested
that existing practice was somehow consistent with the highest and most stringent (constitutional) standards. Gardos and Cole had more honestly described
a gap between clinical practice and researchers' conclusions.

The Supreme Court remained to be heard from. In 1979, while the *Rennie* and *Rogers* cases were pending in the courts of appeal, the Supreme Court ruled that purely medical investigation and hospital procedures constituted "due process" for children whose parents had signed them into state mental institutions. The Court resolved the issue in an unusual way, by treating the medical procedures as a review of the *parental* judgment to hospitalize the child more than of the state doctors' decisions to admit the patient. And the court did not decide whether, or when, the Constitution required a formal hearing *after* a child's admission to the institution. Nonetheless, the Supreme Court, after a decade of studiously avoiding decisions on "law and psychiatry" issues, had upheld a scheme of pure medical review and, at least in relation to one issue, overturned a system of formal, legal procedures and standards mandated by a lower court.[16]

This ruling seemed full of portent. It bore on the large problem of whether courts should transform the operations of state hospitals and psychiatry in the name of constitutional "liberty," as they had recently transformed public schools in the name of Fourteenth Amendment racial equality. Some writers had urged that course, as noted earlier. By the late 1970s, however, school busing had proved unpopular. Other court-mandated measures for public schools had not produced overwhelming educational successes. Particularly with changes in the Court's membership, it appeared that the Justices might decide to become less activist and less interventionist in a variety of areas.

Subsequent decisions demonstrated that a majority indeed had adopted that posture in the area of law and psychiatry. In 1981 the Court overturned a wide-ranging lower court decision that had applied the "least restrictive alternative" test to the operation of a Pennsylvania state school for persons with developmental disabilities. Without addressing the constitutional questions, the Supreme Court overturned a lower court order for wholesale deinstitutionalization of the school's residents.[17]

In a 1982 case, *Youngberg v. Romeo*, the Supreme Court did address constitutional questions. *Romeo* involved the same Pennsylvania state school as the earlier case, and the court of appeals again had used the least restrictive alternative test as a measure of the school's constitutional obligations. The Supreme Court overturned that result. It rejected the application of the least restrictive test to the internal operations of the school; refused to recognize any rights that would seriously interfere with the institution's functioning; and decreed that state officials would not be liable for deprivations of liberty within the school, or for harm to its residents, unless a decision by school professionals constituted "such a substantial departure from accepted professional judgment, practice, or standards as to demonstrate that the person responsible actually did not base the decision on such a judgment." Under that formulation, no liability existed for purely mistaken or even negligent decisions; rather, the offending official had to act in a way that was not recognizably professional at all. In case any doubt remained, the Court declared that "courts must show deference" to professional judgment and accord institutional officials "a presumption of correctness"—a presumption required, the Court wrote, "to enable institutions of this type— often, unfortunately, overcrowded and understaffed—to continue to function."[18]

That phrasing put to rest the fear—or, depending on one's view, the hope— that federal courts would mandate significant changes in state psychiatry. The lower courts in *Romeo* had found the school's basic operations inherently in con- flict with the Constitution. The Supreme Court decreed that no conflicts of that kind could exist. It adopted, as a canon of constitutional interpretation, the principle that the Constitution "enable[d] institutions of this type . . . to function" despite their flaws.

Romeo did recognize minimal rights to safety in the institution and to free- dom from restraints, but these rights were subject to the professional judgment test. The Court also recognized a constitutional right to treatment, but one so limited that it probably added nothing to the other rights. This treatment right did not guarantee an effort to improve patients' conditions; rather, it was an ad- junct to the previously recognized rights to institutional safety and freedom from restraint. If treatment would reduce the need for physical restraint or enhance a patient's safety—for example, by lessening the patient's aggressive tendencies and thereby minimizing the chance that other patients would retaliate—then it was subjected to the same professional judgment test as other decisions affecting safety or freedom of movement. Beyond that, the Court declined to say whether any further right to treatment existed—for example, to treatment that would im- prove one's mental condition, as Birnbaum had proposed two decades earlier. A minority opinion written by three justices would have recognized a right to treat- ment in order to prevent a patient's *deterioration* in the institution.

Technically, *Romeo* left important issues unresolved. Would the Court rec- ognize a more robust right to treatment in the future? Would the professional judgment test apply to actions for injunctions, as well as lawsuits for damages? Would the Justices apply the professional judgment test to the issues sur- rounding medication? Since *Romeo* did not decide those issues, lawyers still could offer arguments. Yet the case powerfully discouraged further mental hos- pital reform litigation. In some instances, defendants successfully reopened pre-*Romeo* right-to-treatment decrees in the lower courts and obtained relief from onerous requirements. The overriding issue always had been the Supreme Court's willingness to transform public mental health institutions in the name of the Constitution. The Court had dodged and hedged for years, but *Romeo* signaled unmistakably that it would not do so.[19]

On the same day it decided *Romeo*, the Court addressed *Rogers* and *Ren-*

nie. Without deciding the issue of a right to refuse medication, the Court returned both cases to the lower courts for reconsideration: *Rogers*, in light of the possibility that Massachusetts state law might recognize a more substantial right to refuse than the Constitution did (even though the Court never said what kind of refusal right the Constitution included) and *Rennie* because of the possibility that the legal principles in *Romeo* would govern the question.[20]

The remand in *Rogers* produced two decisions. One, by the highest court of Massachusetts, rested on state law rather than the federal Constitution. This decision gave hospitalized patients who wished to refuse medication the right to a court hearing on their competency and the right to a judicial determination of the question whether they would have consented to medication if competent. Thus, it returned to the principles of the trial court's decree. The decision also allowed forced medication, without court approval, to prevent the "immediate, substantial, and irreversible deterioration of a serious mental illness" or to deal with a patient who "poses an imminent threat of harm to himself or others . . . if there is no less intrusive alternative." The second *Rogers* decision came from the federal court of appeals, which found that the right to refuse medication under state law, as recognized by Massachusetts's highest court, exceeded any conceivable federal constitutional right to refuse. In reaching this conclusion, the court cited intimations that the Supreme Court would allow state hospital doctors, rather than judges, to make the determinations necessary for forcing patients to take medication.

The *Rennie* remand produced a decision by the Third Circuit reiterating its conclusion that medical procedures for overcoming patient refusals satisfied the Constitution. A majority of the judges also concluded that the professional judgment test governed medication refusal, and that the court's earlier reliance on the least restrictive alternative test could not survive the Supreme Court's *Romeo* decision. This made no practical difference, of course, since the earlier decision had upheld the system of medical procedures. Judge Adams, who originally voted for the least restrictive alternative test, now cast the decisive vote in favor of professional judgment; he explained that the earlier decision constituted nothing more than a judicial admonition to psychiatrists.[21]

Throughout the 1980s, these variations of the right to refuse medications received recognition in different cases. Yet the differences did not matter very much in the end. Neither version of the right, nor any in between, significantly affected the prescribing of drugs or—as far as anyone can tell—the incidence of tardive dyskinesia and other side effects.

Decrees like *Rennie*, which allowed hospital officials to override a patient's refusal, could at most guarantee that individual physicians would conform to prevailing prescribing standards in the hospital. But the prevailing practice entailed medicating virtually all patients, whatever the actual benefits or side effects in a particular case. That circumstance, rather than an occasional deviation by an individual physician, produced the high incidence of tardive dyskinesia and other problems. Moreover, as the trial record in *Rennie* demonstrated, hospitals found ways to consider medication "voluntary," even if that meant threatening to hold the patient down for an injection.[22]

Despite their substantial court procedures, rights like those specified in *Rogers* seemingly have little more effect. As the psychiatrist Paul Appelbaum observed, very few patients are reported to refuse medication for any substantial time in the first place. Moreover, if the hospital does recognize a patient's act of refusal, judges almost invariably uphold forced medication. A review in Massachusetts, for example, found that courts allowed it 98.6 percent of the time. A number of state courts have allowed hospitals to force medication on patients who are acknowledged to have tardive dyskinesia. Beyond that, most seriously mentally ill persons receive medication outside hospitals—and nothing guarantees any attention whatever to their objections.[23]

Surveying the actual results of a right to refuse, Appelbaum found important benefits. The right, he thought, engendered negotiations between refusing patients and their psychiatrists. Noting that about 25 percent of patients react to medication with distress and about 30 percent cite side effects as a reason for refusing, Appelbaum supposed that "it should be possible to end many refusals by negotiating . . . about the dose and type of medication," since those things will alleviate the problems.[24]

Although negotiation undoubtedly occurred, some of Appelbaum's conclusions verged on being fanciful. For instance, obviously aware of suggestions for withdrawing chronic, hospitalized patients from medication, Appelbaum thought it "possible" that "chronic patients with intractable symptoms" may "be able to persuade their psychiatrists to respect their desires to decline medication." No evidence was cited for such "possibilities." Nor did Appelbaum note that clinicians had ignored researchers' advice about withdrawing medication from chronic patients for over a quarter of a century. How deteriorated, chronic patients would acquire the wherewithal to persuade clinicians—on a point where leading researchers had utterly failed—remained a mystery.[25]

Again, Appelbaum's assumption that a comfortable dose exists for everyone arose from his views about law and about what should be done, not from research. And while 30 percent of patients may cite side effects as a reason for refusing, as Appelbaum wrote, many more patients suffer from them. If the Yale Tardive Dyskinesia Study estimates are correct, a majority of Appelbaum's nonrefusing and "negotiating" patients will develop tardive dyskinesia, not to mention other treatment complications.[26]

The fact that few patients remain medication-free for any length of time because of a right to refuse medication gave Appelbaum satisfaction, since he believed that "it makes no sense to create a system that allows us to hospitalize people against their will and then decline to treat them with medication." Once again, that reflected his undefended assumption that all seriously ill patients (with the possible exception of chronic patients who are negotiating with their physicians) should receive medication, whether they want to or not. In fact, researchers estimate that 10 to 40 percent of patients do not measurably benefit from medication, and refusal litigation simply did not help this group.[27]

For a decade, the Supreme Court had appeared unlikely to uphold a substantial right to refuse, yet the Court had not decided the question. In a 1990 case, *Washington v. Harper*, it finally did so. *Harper* proved surprising, but only because the justices upheld forced medication with so few reservations.

Although *Harper* involved a prison, courts consistently apply its constitutional holding to mental hospitals, albeit with occasional differences in phrasing. A majority of the justices in *Harper* held that prisons could forcibly medicate inmates if institutional doctors and officials concluded that: the inmate has a serious mental illness; administering medication would enhance the institution's security; and medication is in the patient's "medical interest." That test is easily satisfied, since psychiatrists believe medication is in the interest of everyone for whom they prescribe the treatment, and the use of medication obviously enhances institutional security. Three justices dissented, likening the use of medication to electroconvulsive therapy or lobotomy.[28]

Harper was a notable ruling. Apart from the death penalty and the military draft, the Supreme Court had never sustained the compulsory use of so dangerous a measure as forced medication, or one that could alter a person's physical functioning as dramatically. *Buck v. Bell*, a 1927 decision, represented the previous high-water mark; there, the Court upheld forced eugenic sterilization of an institutionalized "feeble-minded" woman. Yet *Buck* did not go as far as *Harper*. *Buck* emphasized that the surgery threatened no harm, beyond the intended effect of sterilizing the patient. Nothing suggests that the Court would have allowed sterilization if the surgery produced purposeless movements of Ms. Buck's extremities, or other medication-like side effects.[29]

The *Harper* majority did not avoid the issue of side effects, exaggerate the benefits of medication, or resort to the idea that medication restored brains to a normal state. "The purpose of drugs," the majority wrote, "is to alter the chemical balance in a patient's brain, leading to changes, intended to be beneficial, in his or her cognitive process." Leaving out the "chemical balance" phrasing, exactly the same thing could have been said about lobotomy.[30]

The appellate opinions in *Rennie* and *Rogers* had invoked spurious legal tests, such as the "least restrictive alternative" and had obscured the role of security considerations in forced-medication decisions. The Supreme Court did none of that in *Harper*. Under the thin cover of a person's "medical interest"—

a concept that they had invented—the justices accepted neurological changes and damage as part of prison security programs.

Harper marked an end to judicial ambivalence. The *Rennie* and *Rogers* decisions had resembled the contemporaneous Task Force Report in their ambiguity and reluctance to acknowledge sad realities. Indeed, those decisions essentially adopted the Task Force clinical model, by implausibly adding technical legal standards like "the least restrictive alternative," to the scope of clinical judgment. By contrast, *Harper* followed the rationale of Gardos and Cole's "Overview": it presumed that medication had to be used, and it rather unflinchingly accepted the consequences.

Harper confirmed the existing understanding: federal courts would have no discernible impact on the operation of psychiatric institutions, the design of public mental health, or the use of medication. Psychiatrists like Appelbaum appreciated that fact and noted it with satisfaction. State malpractice lawsuits based on tardive dyskinesia represented the only possible threat to current practice, and nothing suggested that it was great enough to make a discernible difference.

In terms of its overall effect, litigation over the right to refuse medication legitimated questionable medication practice and obscured once-obvious medical and ethical issues. Lawsuits enhanced public and professional awareness of tardive dyskinesia, but they also contributed broad acceptance of permanent neurological damage as an acceptable price of using medication. Before *Rennie* and *Rogers*, it appeared far from clear that the public would accept a tardive dyskinesia rate as high as 10 percent; that was why psychiatrists underreported the disorder. After the right-to-refuse cases, a 50 percent tardive dyskinesia rate seemed well within reason—regrettable, certainly, but hardly cause for any radical changes.[31]

Without right-to-refuse litigation, the public would have faced a choice: accept widespread permanent side effects or demand significant alterations in psychiatric practice. With courts ostensibly taking care of the problem, the necessity for that choice seemingly evaporated. Patients' rights were being respected; courts were scrutinizing psychiatry. What more could one ask?

By speeding acceptance of questionable practice and quieting moral and medical doubts, the right to refuse medication followed in the footsteps of the right to treatment. Treatments lawsuits had legitimated wholesale deinstitutionalization; the right-to-refuse cases legitimated the techniques (near universal medication) and consequences (for example, tardive dyskinesia) that deinstitutionalization entailed.

To appreciate what happened, it is helpful to consider what did not. No reform case portrayed the high level of side effects or the permanent neurological damage associated with medication as legal wrongs in themselves. No case sought a remedy that would have made a significant difference—for example, an injunction protecting someone against tardive dyskinesia or requiring that some patients remain medication-free. *Rennie* paid the most attention, but it still treated side effects as a reason for recognizing a right to refuse—not as an independent problem or constitutional wrong. And no court required hospitals to regain the capacity of managing mentally ill patients without medication—a capacity lost because of the pervasive use of the drugs.

Without such measures, the most robust right to refuse medication left judges facing a stark reality. Since virtually no institution—community or otherwise—was willing or equipped to deal with psychotic episodes without medication, the judges who heard cases would a consign patient to a hopeless limbo if they upheld his or her refusal. Unsurprisingly, judges preferred not do that. The fact that courts upheld virtually all applications to force medication reflected this failure of the public health system, not any success of medication.

And so it happened that the main developments in twentieth-century public mental health—deinstitutionalization, near universal medication, side effects, and neurological impairment on a scale previously unknown—remained largely outside the circle of legal attention and concern. The fact that this happened was remarkable. No less remarkable was the widespread feeling that lawyers and courts held psychiatry under siege and threatened to intrude into the very core of psychiatric institutions and practice. In fact, the principal effect of litigation was to shore up the Study revolution in public mental health.[32]

Psychiatrists like Paul Appelbaum complained that litigators and courts failed to appreciate the science of psychiatry. That got things backward, though. Psychiatry would have faced more stringent legal scrutiny if lawyers had taken the science more seriously. Withdrawal of medication—an option recommended by distinguished psychiatrists since the late 1960s—never became a legal demand; tardive dyskinesia seemed more portentous to Crane and Kline and Cole than it ever did to attorneys; side effects such as subjective distress, which attracted the concern of some leading psychiatrists, hardly interested lawyers or courts. Contrary to the usual claims, it was precisely lawyers' insufficient appreciation of psychiatry that allowed the profession and the public health system to stay the course.

During the third period of the medication era, psychiatry possessed no compelling vision of medication to offer the courts. Such a vision had existed in the 1960s and 1970s, but judges seemed poised to intervene dramatically into psychiatry nonetheless. Now, with the vision gone, law and psychiatry moved in perfect step with one another—like separated dance partners, occasionally gesturing forcefully in each other's direction as part of their performance.

Chapter 10   Absence of Vision

Research

THROUGH THE 1980s and early 1990s, research into medications evidenced the same absence of vision as clinical practice, public health, and law. Researchers studiously avoided any comprehensive picture; nothing comparable in scope to the Study vision emerged. Instead, researchers interested in larger themes generally followed the example of the Task Force, summarizing results from disparate research areas.

This absence of vision manifested itself in a number of ways. For one, researchers often failed to see some obvious implications in their findings, particularly those that cast medication in a negative light. For another, researchers failed to connect findings about the safety or effectiveness of medication with issues in public mental health. Until 1980, psychiatrists as diverse in viewpoint as Crane and Cole had seen the public health connections; after 1980, they disappeared from view—as the "Overview" (and, by example, the Task Force Report) had said they should.

Yet another failure of vision involved the overall effects of medication. With some notable exceptions, researchers generally did not ask how medication affected patients' lives. That issue typically got lost in a maze of narrow research results. A comprehensive picture of medication risks did not emerge, either. One investigation might examine tardive dyskinesia; a second, subjective distress; a third, the rare "neuroleptic malignant syndrome" that could prove fatal. Yet evaluations of risks in the aggregate did not appear. Once, the Study vision had obscured overall patient outcomes; after 1980, an absence of vision did the same.

Along with loss of vision, some prominent researchers also lost their sense of optimism about the future. Jonathan Cole was a case in point. In his 1975 exchange with Crane, Cole retained the optimism that he had voiced in the

1964 Study. By 1986, it was gone. In that year, Gardos and Cole reported that "enthusiasm" about medication had faded since the 1960s because of "the recognition of tardive dyskinesia . . . and the realization that the drugs are far from curative and often fall short of producing satisfactory symptom relief."[1]

Gardos and Cole's observation reflected yet another absence of vision related to psychiatry's past. They dated the changed outlook about medication to the 1960s. Yet few researchers had recognized tardive dyskinesia as a serious problem then, and most—led by Cole himself—considered medications a truly "antischizophrenic" therapy. In effect, Gardos and Cole were attributing Crane's outlook during the 1960s to psychiatry at large—a remarkable historical reversal. They had excised the period of upheaval that followed the Study, and Cole's own rejectionist views, as if those things had never happened.

Gardos and Cole's failure of historical vision was complete. They did not portray psychiatric progress, or indeed any coherent historical pattern; history itself had all but disappeared. This represented a significant departure for Cole. In the Study, he depicted psychiatrists' optimism as both the result of past progress and as the engine of future advance. In 1975, he treated optimism as something like a choice that psychiatrists should make in the interest of progress, and he faulted Crane for not doing so. Now, with optimism having become lack of enthusiasm, Cole ignored the currents of psychiatric history. In Cole's new version, no significant history existed; the absence of historical vision was nearly total. That posture comported well with his 1980 account of timeless public mental health systems and medication practices that seemingly had no connection to research findings or, for that matter, to anything else.

Interesting research did occur, however, despite the prevailing ethos in psychiatry. In fact, much interesting work appeared because of it. The absence of vision meant that neither persistent side effects nor doubts about the action of medication carried significant consequences for public health or clinical practice. That being so, reports about such matters rarely provoked strong reactions—from psychiatrists or anyone else. Not enough was at stake, with clinical, public health, and legal developments so disconnected from medication's effects. In this respect, the third period of the medication era was the opposite of the second, when a tightly knit vision had filled every finding with significance, making it a potential subject of psychiatric politics.

On occasion, psychiatrists still criticized a finding because of its possible policy implications. For example, the conclusion that patients with schizophrenia in an investigation had deteriorated over a six-year period despite standard care and medication treatment received criticism because the results "could be employed to shape policy regarding allocations of . . . public resources for the treatment of schizophrenia." Yet such responses were rare, and in any event paled beside the old attacks on George Crane. Findings about medication no longer mattered all that much.[2]

How Medication Works in the Brain

Throughout the third period of the medication era, researchers continued to investigate links between medication, dopamine, and schizophrenia. No clear picture emerged, but the results belied any simple picture of dopamine causing schizophrenia. Researchers noted, for example, that the "atypical" drug clozapine produced the same kind of clinical benefits as other neuroleptics, yet affected different neurochemical receptors in the brain. That mitigated against any particular kind of receptor—including any particular kind of dopamine—"causing" schizophrenia. The discovery that people with schizophrenia may suffer from excess and depressed dopamine activity in different regions of their brains also undermined any simple equation of "antischizophrenic" with "dopamine inhibiting."

A 1993 article by Caligiuri, Lohr, and Jeste illustrated the approaches—and the absence of vision—in this area. Caligiuri and his coauthors found mild Parkinson's disease–like symptoms in 30 percent of never-medicated people with schizophrenia. Typically, such symptoms are associated with decreased dopamine activity in a particular brain system. Yet the dopamine hypothesis linked schizophrenia to *increased* dopamine activity. Attempting to reconcile the finding and the dopamine hypothesis, Caligiuri advanced a "highly speculative" idea: perhaps reduced dopamine activity in one brain system, and therefore the Parkinson's symptoms, constituted a "compensatory mechanism" for coping with excess dopamine activity associated with schizophrenia elsewhere in the brain.[3]

In the 1950s, a psychiatrist like Deniker would have offered a different interpretation—in fact, the opposite one. Deniker thought medications induced an artificial brain disease associated with the Parkinson's-like syndrome of psychomotor indifference. He could have hailed Caligiuri's finding because it demonstrated that medications further reduce pathologically low levels of dopamine—that is, that they worsen a disease-like state. Such a theory would be vague and speculative, possibly even useless, but no more so than Caligiuri's.

Caligiuri's article reflected an "absence of vision" in some of the ways described earlier. It undermined the strong dopamine hypothesis—a mainstay of the Study vision—by producing contrary findings. It endorsed no new comprehensive picture of its own and suggested its "compensatory mechanism" with great tentativeness. Yet it also ignored implications that reflected badly on medication: here, the possibility that medication exacerbated a pathological condition in the brains of many people with schizophrenia.

Caligiuri's analysis demonstrates how the absence of vision could leave old—and no longer justified—implications of the Study portrait intact. His compensatory mechanism supposed that medication affected brains in benign ways. That idea had been encapsulated in the dopamine hypothesis, which Caligiuri's results did not support. Yet he ended up hypothesizing a compatible result. More generally, researchers could demonstrate that the Study vision had misrendered this and that detail, but still draw few negative conclusions about medication.

Gardos and Cole had done something similar with the public health system. After the Study underpinnings of that system collapsed, they concluded that nothing had really changed. In research as in public health, the absence of vision meant that nothing replaced the old Study structure; it lived on as a kind of afterimage and still guided psychiatrists' action and thinking. Researchers had more in common with clinicians than at first appeared.

Side Effects

The third period produced broad consensus about the existence of side effects, including tardive dyskinesia. The agreement did not extend to prevalence figures, however; researchers continued to offer a wide range of estimates for various effects. Researchers also disagreed about the seriousness of side effects, although few would describe them as "trivial" or "mild."

Tardive dyskinesia still epitomized the risks of medication. Psychiatrists continued to regard it as the profession's most important test—if not its only test—medically, ethically, and legally. The rationales of the 1980 Task Force Report and the "Overview" both survived; indeed, they became largely interchangeable. Psychiatrists invoked Report-style clinical balancing and "Overview"-style public mental health considerations as if they represented two sides of the same coin. After the threat from courts evaporated, it no longer really mattered which rationale was selected. Thus, the Task Force's Chairperson, Baldessarini, invoked the "Overview's" rationale in 1988: despite "some unwanted effects," he wrote, medication "remain[s] the cornerstone of treatment."[4]

Although prevalence figures varied, they also exceeded earlier estimates —as Gardos and Cole had predicted. A 1993 literature review reported a mean estimate of 24 percent. In 1994, eight authors, including Gardos and Cole, found a prevalence greater than 30 percent among outpatients. And although a 1992 Task Force raised the earlier estimate only slightly—declaring that it "would probably be safe to say that between 15% and 20% of patients receiving chronic neuroleptic treatment will have some evidence of tardive dyskinesia"—it continued Task Force tradition by relying on studies demonstrating a much higher rate: here, incidence studies reporting that 5 percent of young adults, and 30 percent of older patients, develop tardive dyskinesia during *each year* they were exposed to medication.[5]

The risk for older patients indeed appeared higher. In 1993, two psychiatrists reported that 49 percent of elderly patients developed tardive dyskinesia within forty weeks of starting treatment, a *weekly* incidence that exceeded 1 percent. A 1995 study by Dilip V. Jeste, a leading authority, examined tardive dyskinesia's incidence among elderly and middle-aged outpatients receiving "relatively low doses." After one year, 26 percent of these patients developed tardive dyskinesia; 52 percent developed it after two years, and 60 percent after three. Jeste pronounced his findings "distressing" and expressed impatience because basic questions remained unresolved despite numerous investigations.[6]

Estimates for longer periods and for all age groups came from the Yale Tardive Dyskinesia Study. "The results are disconcerting," William M. Glazer observed in 1993, because "[a]bout two of every three patients maintained on neuroleptic treatment can be expected to develop persistent TD within 25 years of continued exposure." After fifteen years, an estimated 50 percent of medicated patients would develop the disorder, according to Glazer.[7]

Those incidence figures did not necessarily contradict lower prevalence estimates, since some dyskinesias disappear over time. Estimates of the remission rate varied widely, however, ranging from 2 percent to 60 percent. Glazer suggested other reasons why "prevalences of 50% or more are seldom observed in cross-sectional studies." Such studies "often classify mild cases as noncases," he observed, and "TD cases may be less likely than noncases to be selected for prevalence studies" in the first place. Besides, "the proportion of patients in most cross-sectional studies with more than 10 years of exposure [to medications] is small, possibly because . . . [such patients] are less likely than patients with less exposure to be selected for these studies." Glazer concluded that reported "prevalence findings may indicate very little about the occurrence (risk) of TD in specific populations at risk"—a rather devastating indictment of a large body of work.[8]

Researchers also recognized a variety of persistent side effects that might, or might not, count as tardive dyskinesia. In 1985, Stephen M. Stahl wrote:

> [T]oday we are faced with so many variants of neuroleptic-linked "tardive dyskinesia" that the term may be nearly obsolete, or at least may require more careful definition. Thus, at least seven variants of tardive dyskinesia have blossomed in the literature. These include: (1) classic tardive oral-buccal-lingual-masticatory dyskinesia; 2) tardive limb dyskinesia; (3) tardive dystonia; (4) tardive psychosis (supersensitivity); (5) tardive Tourette's syndrome [a syndrome of facial tics]; (6) tardive dysmentia [mental retardation]; and now, perhaps, tardive akathisia.[9]

No generally accepted estimates existed for the prevalence of these other effects.

Still another possible complication of tardive dyskinesia involved cognitive functioning. Jeste and a coauthor (a psychologist) reviewed the literature in 1994 and reported that twenty-seven out of thirty-one studies had found "that TD [tardive dyskinesia] patients performed worse on cognitive tests than similar patients without TD." Despite this showing, Jeste continued, "numerous methodological limitations" allowed "challenge[s]" to the apparent "strong association" between cognitive impairment and tardive dyskinesia. Jeste again expressed frustration at the lack of firm conclusions on the subject: "[I]n spite of 31 publications and 27 years of investigation, the association between movement abnormalities and cognitive functions . . . remains unclear." On the other hand, Jeste's own research found that the severity of dyskinesia consistently correlated with the severity of neurological impairment. He concluded that "[i]t is likely that TD involves an alteration of brain function that affects both motor and cognitive control," although it "remain[ed] . . . unclear" how much schizophrenia itself contributed to the association.[10]

Despite the uncertainties, work like Jeste's suggested that persistent medication-induced "alteration[s] in brain function" extended to more functions, and affected more patients, than psychiatrists generally believed. A still more alarming picture might have emerged if psychiatrists considered the persistence of effects such as distress or akathisia, as described in Anderson's 1981 report and Hall's 1956 article.

Even apart from the persistence issue, side effects like akinesia, akathisia, and distress remained in the shadows. Each continued to receive attention from some researchers. Yet only tardive dyskinesia and neuroleptic malignant syndrome, a rare but potentially fatal complication, were considered "serious" by most psychiatrists.[11]

Still, the research into these other effects produced alarming findings. Those who investigated akathasia, akinesia, and distress—many from outside the United States—typically expressed surprise at its previous neglect in research and clinical practice. Yet little happened. Alarming findings were not refuted; rather, the entire matter was largely ignored. These effects became the professional hobbyhorse of a few, and of little interest to almost everyone else; they suffered the fate that probably would have awaited tardive dyskinesia, had it not been for George Crane. Tardive dyskinesia "broke through" to serious mainstream attention; these effects did not.

Akathisia is an example. Many patients find this syndrome of restlessness and distress the most intolerable effect of medication. Writing in 1991, the Australian researchers Perminder Sachdev and Celia Loneragan noted that akathisia was "common but little studied," despite the fact that Ayd and Van Putten had identified it years earlier as "one of the commonest and most distressing side effects." Reviewing the literature, Sachdev and Loneragan painted a disturbing picture.

According to a 1959 estimate, 14.4 percent of medicated patients had akathisia; a 1961 study put the figure at over 21 percent; and a 1983 investigation, at 25 percent. They noted Van Putten's 1975 estimate of 45 percent, and his later finding that 75 percent of patients on one medication, and 46 percent on another, suffered from the disorder. Moreover, by the mid-1980s, researchers recognized persistent and chronic akathisia; in these forms, the disorder either appeared with an increase in dosage and then slowly diminished or, like tardive dyskinesia, emerged later in treatment and persisted after withdrawal of medication. Sachdev and Loneragan also noted a high degree of overlap between tardive dyskinesia and chronic akathisia: in some studies, all or nearly all of the chronic akathisia victims also suffered from tardive dyskinesia.[12]

The authors recommended "prevention, with the optimal use of antipsychotic drugs" as "the best strategy." Yet that did not always alleviate the problem. Like tardive dyskinesia, chronic akathisia resisted treatment. The acute form "usually" but not always "respond[ed] to a cession or reduction in the dose." Yet that was "often not possible because of the clinical status of the patient"; accordingly, "alternative strategies have to be used, most of which are only partially successful." In short, psychiatrists could not alleviate chronic akathisia because they did not know how, and often did not alleviate acute akathisia because of concerns about lowering the dosage.

Sachdev and Loneragan did not question the reluctance to lower dosages. Instead, they invoked a rationale for existing practice that resembled Gardos and Cole's "cornerstone" of treatment, coupled with guarded optimism about future *research*:

In the absence of any suitable alternatives, it is quite obvious that neuroleptic drugs will be used in psychiatry for a long time. It is, therefore, appropriate that such a common and distressing side effect of these drugs as akathisia is now receiving the attention from researchers that it deserves. The last decade has highlighted some of the complexities of the problem. The next phase of research should include further delineation of the syndrome, attempts at understanding its pathophysiology, and adequate efforts to establish its treatment.[13]

Overoptimistically, Sachdev and Loneragan thought that the recent attention the disorder had received from a few investigators, including Van Putten, indicated that improvement was at hand.

Researchers in the area of medication-induced distress did not view the "next phase of research" with as much hope. Many did not much look to research for the solution at all, although, like Sachdev and Loneragan, they found it "surprising" that an obvious problem connected to medication had received little attention. Abandoning the "cornerstone" rationale, some investigators urged clinicians to modify prescribing practices in light of patients' medication-caused distress.[14]

One such investigator was the psychiatrist Samuel Gershon. Writing in the *Acta Psychiatrica Scandinavica*, Gershon described his own subjective experience on medication and urged psychiatrists to take test doses in order to understand how patients felt. His plea for clinical empathy did not strictly conflict with Sachdev and Loneragan's call for future research, but the emphasis clearly differed. Gershon's laments about the condition of patients and clinical neglect recalled remarks by anguished tardive dyskinesia researchers like Degkwitz during the late 1960s.[15]

The parallels extended to questions of remedy. Some investigators urged dosage reduction (even to the point of zero) in order to minimize patients' subjective distress and akathisia—just as Crane and others had once urged such measures for tardive dyskinesia. Thus, a 1984 study by Van Putten, May, and others reported that patients generally did well on one-fifth the usual dose of long-acting medication. Standard and low doses produced comparable relapse rates in the experiment, although other research had found somewhat higher relapse rates in patients given very low doses. Van Putten and May did not rule that out that possibility; they even identified some of their own low-dose patents who seemed undermedicated. Yet they also noted that "even if more protection is provided by the higher dose, it is at a price." Patients given higher doses suffered more dysphoria and, apparently, more side effects of all kinds. Only at the article's conclusion did the authors suggest that these things mattered because comfortable patients "may show better compliance with drug treatment"; until then, it had appeared that the "price" in suffering might be too high, period.[16]

Some historical perspective on the problem came from Leo Hollister. From 1957 through about 1970, Hollister had advanced the idea that patients who experienced distress on medication were not as ill—or as much in need of drugs—as other patients who responded better. In a 1992 letter, Hollister recalled his thinking from those years and offered some contemporary conclusions. He began by noting the recent claims that "neuroleptics produce dysphoria in humans" and that "this revelation should lead to a reevaluation of the clinical use of these agents." Hollister agreed about the dysphoria but rejected the suggestions for changes in prescribing. The facts about dysphoria had been known many years before, Hollister remembered. Clinicians had used medication despite the dysphoria for the "simple" reason that "[n]othing better was available." "To some extent," he observed, "the same situation applies today."[17]

Hollister suggested that his own views had not changed. In fact, however, his rationale in 1992 was completely different from the one he had advanced in 1970 and before. Then, he argued that patients who could not tolerate medication might not be "crazy"—or, at least not truly schizophrenic—and that "[s]ome patients may tolerate antipsychotic drugs so poorly that no drug treatment should be given." By 1992, he was claiming that medication should be given despite patient distress because "nothing better was available." The old rationale posited a Study-like fit between medication's effects and the medical needs of mentally ill persons; Hollister had presumed that people who responded with distress probably did not need medication, and that people who needed medication probably did not respond with distress. The 1992 letter, on the other hand, invoked standard post-1980 justifications: the idea of medication as the cornerstone of treatment and of prescribing as the outcome of clinical balancing since "nothing better" was available.

In 1992, Hollister found it "discouraging" that contemporary "concern about the unpleasantness of these drugs" had developed "without any awareness of the extensive evidence available earlier." His letter ended with the unfinished phrase, "Those who ignore history. . . . " Yet Hollister had done exactly that. His letter projected rationales from the third period of the medication era back onto the second. Hollister neither remembered nor apparently could imagine that psychiatrists had once subscribed to the Study vision, and that acknowledging patient distress had carried implications for medication practice. Instead, he assumed that the third period's absence of vision had existed in the second period as well.[18]

In 1992 Hollister wrote as if his former views had never existed. He seemingly failed to recognize that the past could differ from the present. Thus, he imported into thinking about psychiatry's history the same absence of vision that marked medication research and public health analysis.

Benefits of Medication

Researchers continued to report that medication ameliorated schizophrenic symptoms and reduced the number of relapses. Yet fundamental issues remained. Few studies investigated the question of whether patients fare better over their lifetimes because of medication; those few studies suggested opposite conclusions. Similarly, the questions of whether medication interfered with the capacity to relate to others or to hold a job attracted relatively little attention, although an occasional study suggested a potential for serious impairment. George Awad noted in 1992 that the question of patients' "quality of life" on medication remained a neglected subject. Indeed, literature about it seemed no better developed than the comparable literature on lobotomy had forty years before; in this area, Hollister's dictum about "ignoring the past" might actually have applied.[19]

During the mid-1990s one basic question did receive attention: the extent to which medication protected against future relapse. Since psychiatrists lacked firm knowledge about the long-term effects of medication, or its effects on interpersonal functioning and quality of life, preventing relapses assumed that much more importance on the "benefit" side of the clinical equation. Analyzing a similar question in 1976, Gardos and Cole had recommended withdrawing medications from large numbers of patients. In a 1995 issue of the *Archives of General Psychiatry*, a new generation of researchers revisited the matter.

The lead article, "Neuroleptic Withdrawal in Schizophrenic Patients: A Review of the Literature," was coauthored by four researchers, including Patricia L. Gilbert and Dilip V. Jeste. Gilbert and Jeste reviewed published studies in which the experimental subjects received medication initially, and then some had the medication withdrawn. Gilbert and Jeste reported the by now familiar, almost staggering variations in result: the reported relapse rates in sixty-six studies "ranged from 0% to 100%." Overall, they found a mean relapse rate of 53 percent among the subjects withdrawn from medication, and 16 percent among the subjects who continued receiving the treatment. The mean length of the experiments was 9.7 months.[20]

Discussing the findings, Gilbert and Jeste returned to familiar themes: medication as the "mainstay" of treatment; tardive dyskinesia as the epitome of treatment risk; the need for individualized risk assessment and balancing. Yet they gave familiar phrases more than the usual formulaic meaning. Gilbert and Jeste took the withdrawal option seriously and highlighted the existence of patients who apparently derived no benefit from maintenance medication—much as Gardos and Cole did in 1976.

Although the withdrawn patients "had a relapse rate more than three times higher" than those who remained on medication, Gilbert and Jeste pointed out that "approximately half of all the patients withdrawn from neuroleptic therapy remained stable without relapse over average follow-up periods of 6.3 to 9.7 months, while, despite neuroleptic maintenance, 15.6 percent patients [sic] relapsed over an average follow-up period of 7.9 months." Moreover, they suggested that the failure to reduce dosages slowly before withdrawing medication might have significantly increased the relapse rate. In a study that followed patients for six months, 8 percent of patients slowly withdrawn from medication relapsed, compared with 50 percent of those withdrawn more quickly. Finally, Gilbert and Jeste reported that withdrawing medication usually caused little harm, since patients who relapsed usually returned quickly to their pre-withdrawal condition after resuming the medication.[21]

The way Gilbert and Jeste framed the issue suggested their seriousness about withdrawal. The literature made possible "divergent clinical recommendations," they wrote.

On the one hand, it could be argued that neuroleptic withdrawal is extremely risky, with the chances of relapse more than three times greater. . . . Psychotic relapse is associated with a possibility of patients harming themselves and/or others; it is certainly likely to disrupt the patient's and family's lives and may result in hospitalization, with the attendant psychosocial and financial costs. On the other hand . . . nearly half the patients do not relapse when kept off neuroleptic therapy over a 10-month period. Maintaining medication would seem unnecessary, especially considering the risk of persistent TD [tardive dyskinesia]. This is a clinical as well as a medicolegal dilemma. . . . The optimal solution in a substantial proportion of cases would probably be to slowly taper the neuroleptic therapy to the lowest dose that would control the symptoms of schizophrenia to a satisfactory degree. In some patients, the lowest dose may be zero—stopping neuroleptic therapy.[22]

Gilbert and Jeste seemingly rejected Gardos and Cole's "cornerstone" viewpoint and went well beyond Task Force–style clinical balancing. They asserted that medication "would seem unnecessary" for patients who can avoid relapse without it, and that many such patients existed. What remained for clinicians to "balance" in these cases? The very idea of "divergent . . . recommendations" from researchers implied a competition of ideas and necessity for choice at a research level—not merely an ineffable process of balancing at the level of clinicians.

Gilbert and Jeste also put clinicians in an unusual light. The "patient, caregiver, or treating clinician," they observed pointedly, may refuse to "comply with the proposed medication withdrawal." Thus, they avoided the usual picture of clinicians judiciously balancing alternatives; instead, they grouped clinicians with patients and caregivers since each group resists proposals to withdraw medication.

This article appeared in the wake of a public controversy about experiments that withheld medications from people with schizophrenia. Probably because of that, the *Archives* invited distinguished psychiatrists to comment on Gilbert and Jeste's paper. The resulting contributions represented a wide range of thinking—and a rare public airing of sharp differences of view among leading psychiatrists.[23]

A point of general agreement was the uncertainty about relapse issues. Gilbert and Jeste pointed out that many studies either supplied no definition for relapse, counted very slight symptoms, or treated patients as relapsed whenever a clinician decided to reinstitute medication. The results might well overstate the real risk of relapse. Gilbert and Jeste also noted that "not all the work undertaken has been published" and that "there may be a bias" because "studies with negative results may not see print." Presuming that "negative results" mean those that depict medication in a less favorable light, their point echoed Glazer's observation about published studies about tardive dyskinesia.[24]

Ross J. Baldessarini, the chairperson of the 1980 Task Force, coauthored the first commentary with Adele C. Viguera. They cited the uncertainties about relapse noted by Gilbert and Jeste and added others as well. Some studies included subjects who did not suffer from schizophrenia; some used high doses or multiple medications; some failed to specify the duration of treatment; and some did not say how recently patients had experienced an acute psychotic episode before medication was withdrawn. "Such uncertainties," Baldessarini and Viguera concluded, "severely limit the conclusions" that could be drawn from the existing literature.

Nonetheless, Baldessarini and Viguera did suggest some conclusions of their own. Reanalyzing the Gilbert-Jeste data, they found that slowly tapering the dosage to zero over a period of two weeks or more was associated with a much lower rate of relapse, as compared with dropping the dosage to zero in less time (usually one day). "The proportion of patients relapsing per month was threefold greater after abrupt discontinuation," they reported.[25]

Their reanalysis produced an even more striking result. Baldessarini and Viguera found

> [a]n extraordinarily large (13-fold) excess of relapse risk arose within the first 3 months after discontinuing neuroleptic treatment (50 percent vs 3.8 percent). The cumulative relapse risk rose moderately for those continued on maintenance medications to an average of 28.5 percent by 2 years. In contrast, there was little additional gain of risk after the first 3 months after drug discontinuation, with a maximal risk of 54 percent to 62 percent by 12 months. The relative risk fell over time to less than twofold.[26]

Citing similar results in studies of lithium withdrawal and manic depressive illness, Baldessarini and Viguera posited an "iatrogenic-pharmacologic stress effect" that produced extraordinary relapse rates or a dramatic worsening of condition during the three months following abrupt withdrawal of treatment. This effect could "inflate drug vs no -drug comparisons"; indeed, the authors thought it possible that abrupt withdrawal produced "clinical risks for morbidity or even mortality . . . [that] sometimes exceed those associated with the natural history of the untreated illness." In short, patients withdrawn from medication might relapse more quickly and fare worse than similar patients who had never received drugs.[27]

"[T]he full clinical and research implications [of this phenomenon] . . . remain to be clarified," Baldessarini and Viguera wrote. They urged further research but did not themselves explore its "clinical implications." If the effect existed, however, it meant that medication produced somewhat less protection against relapse than clinicians or researchers had believed. It also suggested previously unsuspected "clinical risks for morbidity or even mortality" for the many patients who, on their own, regularly stopped taking medication.[28]

The commentary by William T. Carpenter and Carol A. Tamminga developed the arguments for medication withdrawal or dose reduction. They depicted the problem against a stark background:

> Years of a narrow treatment focus on psychosis and rehospitalization (rather than broad psychopathologic and quality-of-life assessment), apprehension regarding litigation, and the false hope that increasing drug dose will increase efficacy have led to excessive medication for most patients despite adverse effects, high rates of non-compliance, and patient dissatisfaction.[29]

This description resembled Crane's in 1973.

Carpenter and Tamminga described clinical and research situations where medication withdrawal might be appropriate. These included the cases of stable patients who refused medication; older, stable patients at high risk for tardive dyskinesia; pregnant women; stable patients who had suffered only one psychotic episode; and research that required placebo comparisons or a current medication being "washed out" of a patient. Finally, Carpenter and Tamminga also described a "targeted medication" strategy that employed medication only when a patient's symptoms appeared or became worse. This approach produced obvious benefits, but patients relapsed somewhat more often than they did on continuous maintenance medication. Under experimental circumstances, targeted medication plus enhanced care in other respects had produced relapse results on a par with standard maintenance treatment.

The next commentary, by John F. Greden and Rajiv Tandon, was the opposite of Carpenter and Tamminga's in almost every way. Carpenter and Tamminga cited an enduring pattern of overprescribing; Greden and Tandon described "traditions of stopping treatment, administering it intermittently, or seeking the lowest effective dose." They found each "risky," and challenged all. "Treatment [i.e., medication] probably should never be stopped," Greden and Tandon wrote, "if active clinical or laboratory signs of pathophysiologic conditions are still identifiable"—in other words, if the patient had any signs of schizophrenia. Not even an "absence of acute symptoms" made it safe to withdraw medication, in their view. They also objected to recommendations for seeking the lowest effective dose of medication, since it required "finding the highest dose at which symptoms occur." The strategy "appears at first glance to be safe and reasonable," but they objected because implementing it in clinical practice was "difficult and not achievable without risk." Thus, patients should "probably" receive a maintenance dose equal to "the acute treatment dosage." Finally, they dismissed targeted medication as "inferior." In general, Greden and Tandon urged a presumption against "treatment withdrawal or lowering of dosage," believing those things "should occur infrequently rather than regularly."[30]

What accounted for the enormous gap between Greden and Tandon's views and those of Carpenter and Tamminga, or Gilbert and Jeste? Greden and Tandon did question Gilbert and Jeste's "emphasis":

> Gilbert . . . chose to emphasize that "nearly half of the patients do not relapse when kept off neuroleptic therapy over a 10-month period. Maintaining medication would seem unnecessary, especially considering the risk of TD. . . . " Conversely, we are impressed that more than half the neuroleptic-free patients with a chronic (generally life-long) illness such as schizophrenia did relapse in just 10 months. The percentage of relapsers in the neuroleptic-free group increased to over 80 percent over a 2-year follow-up period. This contrasts with a 15 percent risk of relapse over 10 months and approximately 30 percent over a 2-year period in neuroleptic-treated patients.[31]

Gilbert and Jeste responded to this in their reply article: 59 percent of patients withdrawn from medications relapsed in two years, they wrote, not Greden and Tandon's 80 percent.[32]

Yet this dispute about the precise relapse figures explained little about the basic disagreements. Greden and Tandon would not change their basic recommendations because of a 59 percent, as opposed to 80 percent, relapse rate. Nor would Carpenter and Tamminga, or Gilbert if the situation was reversed. Carpenter and Tamminga acknowledged a "wide and compelling" gap between "drug and nondrug treatment"; the precise figures seemingly did not matter.

Not relapse data, but evaluations of side effects and patient preferences— indeed, everything *except* relapse data—underlay this dispute. Carpenter and Tamminga considered an increased risk of relapse manageable and worthwhile under many circumstances, in order to avoid the risks of "adverse effects, high rates of non-compliance, and patient dissatisfaction." Greden and Tandon assumed that the risk of relapse trumps almost everything else, including the problems cited by Carpenter and Tamminga, almost all of the time.

One remarkable feature of this controversy was its very existence, forty years into the medication era. Another was that so little in the research literature could influence either side's thinking. What article or result might Carpenter show Greden, or Greden show Carpenter, in the hope of changing the other's mind? Carpenter knew about relapses, Greden about tardive dyskinesia. Greden had seen innumerable patients, and their "discomfort" on medication apparently did not persuade him to withhold medication; reading articles about subjective reactions would hardly make more of an impression.

Obviously, values and attitudes powerfully affected psychiatrists' thinking about medication beyond any questions about the facts. Psychiatrists like

Carpenter may more easily tolerate disorder, or react more to a person's immediate distress, or assign a greater value to patient preferences than psychiatrists
like Greden. Relegating such differences to the realm of clinical judgment
merely obscures them. So does a focus on narrow, separate research problems.
If researchers followed patients over long periods and examined their lives—
on medication and off—in a full and naturalistic way, the results would high-
light these issues and conceivably influence the thinking of psychiatrists—and
the courts and the public—more powerfully.

On one point, however, Greden and Tandon concurred with Carpenter and
Tamminga. Each of them thought that researchers should provide strong direction to clinicians, and that clinical practice ought to accord with research
conclusions. Thus, Carpenter and Tamminga, like Gilbert and Jeste, urged clinicians to seriously consider withdrawing medication. Their conclusions differed, but Greden and Tandon's approach hardly qualified as 1980-style
balancing either. Of course, Greden and Tandon thought that clinicians had
to consider many factors. Yet Greden and Tandon deemed research conclusions
rich enough to dictate most clinical results. Classical balancing had emphasized
uncertainties; Greden and Tandon urged a "new standard of decision" for clinicians, namely, the strong presumption in favor of medication. "Treatment
withdrawal or lowering of dosage needs to be justified rather than expected,"
they concluded. Research results had not changed (the 1980 Task Force cited
relapse figures comparable to Greden and Tandon's); something else had.[33]

In fact, Greden and Tandon's approach had roots in the Study vision.
Using their proposed standard of decision making, no real distinction existed
between the needs of the public mental health system and those of the patients.
Minimizing positive symptoms and relapses made it easier to maintain patients
outside hospitals; and that counted in Greden and Tandon's standard of decision. Conversely, patients' quality of life, freedom from medication-induced distress, and neurological integrity had little bearing on whether the public health
system functioned. And those things counted for little in Greden and Tandon's
clinical calculus as well.

There was one significant difference. The Study vision imagined a perfect
harmony between patients' interests and the needs of the public mental health
system, a harmony that resulted from the supposed antischizophrenic effects and
trivial side effects of medication. Greden and Tandon could not rely on that
harmony, however; the Study had been mistaken on both points. Accordingly,
Greden and Tandon made overall relapse rates the overriding consideration and
focused on functional benefits to the exclusion of side effects in a way rarely
seen in the research literature since the era of lobotomy.

Another contributor, Richard Jed Wyatt, also abandoned Task Force–style
clinical balancing. Wyatt purported to endorse balancing, but, like Greden and

Tandon, he left little room for individualized judgment. According to Wyatt, prescribing medication required "an individual decision, one that carefully weighs the risks associated with relapse against the risks of tardive dyskinesia and other side effects." Yet he left no doubt about the end result. "The vast majority of schizophrenic patients," Wyatt concluded, "will almost certainly need to remain on antipsychotic medications indefinitely." Ironically, a foremost proponent of balancing in 1980—Baldessarini, chair of the Task Force—did not address the issue in his comment, although the theme of a deceptively complex problem surrounded by massive confounding factors ran through both his comment and the Task Force Report.[34]

Two ironies surrounded the role of classical balancing in these comments. In theory, clinicians balanced benefits and risks; in practice, they employed an overwhelming presumption in favor of medication, much as Greden and Tandon urged. Crane had identified that very presumption, and inveighed against it during the 1970s. In the guise of a recommendation, Greden and Tandon had produced a model that described actual prescribing in the supposed age of balancing.

A second irony involved Carpenter. He had urged serious reconsideration of medication strategies for fifteen years, including medication withdrawal under some circumstances. His stance had attracted criticism in the late 1970s, when he first described medication-free approaches and testified for the plaintiffs in *Rennie*. Yet in 1995, his and Tamminga's contribution was the one that adhered most closely to classical balancing. They insisted that risks surrounded every option, and that individualized consideration was imperative. They stood out in the 1990s precisely because of their adherence to the old mainstream formulas—an indication of how much psychiatric thinking had changed since 1980, when the third period began.

Why had other researchers moved away from the classical balancing formulas? It was not because of new knowledge. Relapse estimates had not significantly changed. At the same time, prevalence figures had risen for tardive dyskinesia, and new evidence had emerged about the seriousness of other side effects. If findings about medication were driving developments, researchers either should have maintained a position like Carpenter's, in favor of balancing, or—in light of the new findings—abandoned classic balancing in favor of a presumption *against* medication under various circumstances. Yet Greden, Tandon, and Wyatt had gone in the opposite direction.

How research discoveries will affect any single psychiatrist's thinking is impossible to know. Psychiatrists begin with an individual sense of the benefits and risks of medication, and with a distinctive ethical and professional orientation. As a result, psychiatrists do not all change their minds in the same way when research findings change, even if they had appeared to agree among themselves at the start. A remarkable feature of the Study period had been that so many psychiatrists did change their thinking in the same way, as if in lockstep.

On the other hand, if research is driving developments, one may assess aggregate movements in thought. Imagine one hundred psychiatrists who favored individualized clinical balancing in 1980. If subsequent research disclosed that tardive dyskinesia presented *less* risk than these psychiatrists had supposed, or that medication truly *reversed* schizophrenic processes in the brain, one would expect some of the psychiatrists—perhaps even most—to move toward a presumption in favor of medications. That had apparently happened after the Collaborative Study. By the mid-1990s, research moved in the opposite direction; and one might have expected psychiatrists to move with it. Yet the exchange over Gilbert and Jeste's article revealed the opposite.

In part, tardive dyskinesia had lost some of its former importance. Other side effects still paled beside it: that much of the older outlook had survived. Yet tardive dyskinesia now meant less. If the disorder had not existed, the 1980 and 1973 Task Forces surely would have urged a strong presumption in favor of medication. Because of tardive dyskinesia, they had hedged. Now, despite the disorder, some researchers were urging that very presumption.

Tardive dyskinesia had become less worrisome because of its familiarity. The public, as well as psychiatrists, had become accustomed to it and regarded it as an acceptable cost of medicating patients. In a process like desensitizing people to allergies, the public had first received very low prevalence estimates, then somewhat higher ones; finally even extremely high figures failed to produce a reaction. The federal courts seemed to respond in the same way. Although juries might prove unpredictable in damage cases, a psychiatrist could still reasonably suppose that tardive dyskinesia constituted far less of an ethical, political, or legal problem than it had in 1980, or in 1973. Paradoxically, as researchers reported tardive dyskinesia to be more prevalent and more serious, it became less significant.

If one focused on research results—rather than on what the public or the courts would tolerate—a presumption against medication did seem reasonable in some instances. Consider a hypothetical case that Jeste and Gilbert discussed in their reply to the comments made about their article, a case they located at the "extreme of the continuum" where withdrawal seemed most compelling:

> [A]n older patient (with a high risk of persistent or severe tardive dyskinesia) who has a first-break late-onset acute schizophreniform episode with the various reported indicators of good prognosis (e.g. short duration of psychopathological symptoms, few negative symptoms, rapid response to a low dose of an antipsychotic drug, excellent premorbid adjustment, absence of a family history of schizophrenia and a high level of psychosocial support.) After

maintaining such a patient on neuroleptic therapy for a number of months (eg [*sic*] 1 to 2 years) an attempt may be made to very slowly begin to reduce the dose. If there is no exacerbation of symptoms, it may be possible to withdraw the medication entirely at some point.[35]

Yet it seems far from obvious why this patient should receive medication in the first place. Jeste and Gilbert noted that the "*annual* incidence of tardive dyskinesia" reached 26 percent among patients over 45, their hypothetical patient's age group. If the quoted passage's reference to "1 to 2 years" of medication was not a misprint, this patient would more likely than not develop tardive dyskinesia. Even if Jeste and Gilbert meant to say "1 to 2 *months*" of medication, the patient still stood a significant chance of developing the disorder; after all, they claimed only that "it *may be* possible to withdraw the medication . . . at some point."

True, the patient's initial hospitalization probably would last longer without medication. Yet the corresponding benefits seem great. Nor does it appear that calamity would befall the patient in case of relapse. Now factor in Baldessarini and Viguera's theory that once medicated, patients will relapse more quickly than if medication had never been used. If the theory is correct, starting treatment may mean that this patient will end up receiving medication indefinitely. Thus, the initial decision may produce long-lasting consequences; as a practical matter, it might well commit this patient to a lifetime of medication.

Even so, withholding medication in this case was beyond Jeste and Gilbert's ken, and withdrawal of medication after a period of time was only "possible." More generally, their reply marked a subtle retreat from their original article. "We *do not* recommend neuroleptic withdrawal for a majority of the chronic schizophrenic patients," the reply said; "we *do* recommend a gradual reduction of the neuroleptic dose to the lowest effective level."[36] Of course, the original article had not recommended withdrawing medication from a "majority" of patients; it had specified no figures. And the reply failed to spell out what the original article had: sometimes "the lowest dose may be zero—stopping neuroleptic therapy."

Jeste and Gilbert's reply employed a rhetorical innovation. During the era's second period, psychiatrists had attempted to exaggerate, that is, overstate, the extent to which their recommendations would result in actual withdrawal of medication. Frank Ayd's "treatment of another sort" and the Task Forces' accounts of clinical balancing are examples. Now, Jeste and Gilbert used a similar rhetorical technique ("lowest effective dose") to understate the extent to which their recommendations might result in medication withdrawal. In the era of "absence of vision," even psychiatrists with serious concerns about prescribing attempted to downplay the implications of their views.

Chapter 11   Absence of Vision

History

THE NARROW FOCUS of psychiatrists produced an absence of historical as well as research vision. Hollister's 1992 letter about subjective distress represented an example, but the phenomenon was a general one. The "Overview" had focused on the existing public health system and patterns of prescribing medication, resolutely avoiding any look backward at how psychiatry had arrived at those points. Nor did the "Overview" look forward to consider other possible practices. The here and now marked the limit of its scientific and historical curiosity.

It was not hard to combine an ahistorical stance like that of the "Overview" with vague references to psychiatric progress. One could simply suppose that psychiatry had arrived at a historical plateau—a point higher than any in the past, but not on a discernible rise in slope toward the future, either. Or else one could pay little attention to the entire matter, reducing the claims of progress to mere matters of form. On the other hand, psychiatrists were keen to avoid any inference of a decline—or of a leveling off at a historic low point. Lack of historic momentum and an ahistorical stance were one thing; historic declines and low points were something else again.

The principal problem, as usual, was tardive dyskinesia. Now that psychiatry acknowledged the disorder, the question arose: why it had taken so long. The possibility of incompetence or venality appeared obvious; in various ways, the *Rennie* trial judge in 1978, Lennard and Bernstein in 1974, and Crane throughout the early 1970s had suggested it openly. Medication lost its luster because of tardive dyskinesia; would psychiatry itself suffer the same fate because of its response to the disorder?

The Task Force Report and the "Overview" attempted to sidestep this issue. Both ignored the denials of tardive dyskinesia's existence during the 1960s and

1970s and the sudden shifts in psychiatrists' thinking. The "Overview" went further, by practically excising the troublesome period of time altogether. "A quarter of a century into the neuroleptic era, drug-induced tardive dyskinesia has emerged as a significant public health problem," Gardos and Cole observed—a view that completely eliminated the period when Cole himself was offering low prevalence estimates and attributing tardive dyskinesia to preexisting brain disorders.[1]

The historical questions about tardive dyskinesia would not go away that easily; one could not forever ignore the fact that *JAMA* had editorialized about the dangers of tardive dyskinesia, and investigators—including Crane— had reported high prevalence rates long before Gardos and Cole's "quarter of a century" of the medication era had passed. To account for what had happened in those years, leading historians produced historical accounts of tardive dyskinesia and its discovery. These accounts went beyond the usual vague and unsupported claims about progress. Psychiatrists invoked a supposed historical law—the "law of the new drug"—to explain and justify the profession's response to tardive dyskinesia. Thus, the generally ahistorical third period of the era—a period of caution and careful assessment in other matters affecting medication—justified itself with breathtakingly general—and misapplied— laws of history.

The "law of the new drug" supposedly applies to all of medicine and holds that new therapies go through three stages of medical acceptance. In the first stage, overly enthusiastic physicians exaggerate the benefits and underestimate the side effects of a new treatment. In the second, physicians reverse course; overreacting to their earlier enthusiasm, they now exaggerate side effects and underappreciate benefits. Finally, in the third stage, doctors arrive at "a balanced perspective."

"The challenge," Daniel E. Casey and George Gardos wrote in 1986, "is to recognize where one stands at any particular time in this evolutionary process." They thought that psychiatry was then enduring a period of "widespread pessimism about tardive dyskinesia" that had "led some to inappropriately advocate withholding neuroleptic drugs from psychotic patients." They regarded the pessimism as a typical stage two overreaction and discounted it accordingly. Making a similar point, Dilip Jeste and Richard Jed Wyatt used the model of a pendulum. Psychiatrists had "hailed [medication] as a panacea," they observed, but "the pendulum could swing to the opposite extreme" because of tardive dyskinesia, "leading to the impression that these drugs are toxic substances with limited clinical use." Jeste and Wyatt concluded that "the truth lies somewhere between . . . [the] extremes."[2]

The "law of the new drug" fell on fertile ground in psychiatry. Perennially concerned about their profession's medical standing, psychiatrists welcomed the idea that their treatments conformed to a general medical "law." That fact joined psychiatry to the medical mainstream. And the medical law's driving forces—fluctuating optimism and pessimism—even lay within psychiatry's expertise.

Without invoking any historical "laws," earlier psychiatrists had occasionally assessed their profession's emotional state in relation to medication—and occasionally dismissed unwelcome views about medication as the products of a critics emotional imbalance. Thus, the Collaborative Study deplored unwarranted pessimism about treatment; Denber urged "sober, unemotional, objective and unbiased observations" that would discredit claims regarding side effects; and Cole cited the "optimism-pessimism balance" against Crane's views.

In retrospect, such attempts at discrediting substantive views because of their supposed emotional incorrectness appear misguided. Denber's charges of overemotionalism substituted for analysis on his part; Cole's diagnosis of pessimism resulted from his own grossly mistaken prevalence estimates for tardive dyskinesia. In these instances, the "pessimistic" and "emotional" psychiatrists proved correct, and the criticisms verged on medical demagoguery.

Despite its generality, the "law of the new drug" in psychiatrists' hands produced the same kinds of errors. Thus, Casey and Gardos simply presumed that "pessimists" about tardive dyskinesia were mistaken and that emotions explained the mistake. Denber had equated "objective" judgment with support for existing psychiatric practice and widespread use of medication; proponents of the law applied a similar definition for "balanced" judgment in an era of tardive dyskinesia. Why, for example, did Casey and Gardos regard recommendations for withdrawing medication as second stage pessimism, rather than third stage "balanced" judgment? They had simply matched positions to historical stages based on their own substantive conclusions, and then relegated psychiatrists who took a more critical view than theirs to "pessimistic" stage two.

Consider the passage that followed their description of the "law":

> Neuroleptic drugs and psychiatry have shared this cycle [the law of the new drug's] intimately over the past three decades. The remarkable effectiveness of these agents in controlling psychotic symptoms and improving the quality of life for patients overemphasized the benefits of neuroleptic therapy. A more reasoned view of these drugs evolved, but was subsequently overshadowed by the widespread pessimism about tardive dyskinesia. . . . This now looms as a near crisis.[3]

Although they did not notice, Casey and Gardos had posited a sequence that varied from that of the "law." In their account, the first period of "overemphasiz[ing]" benefits actually had arrived at accurate conclusions: medication possessed "remarkable effectiveness" at "controlling psychotic symptoms and improving . . . [patients'] quality of life." A period with a "more reasoned view" of drugs followed. (Perhaps when psychiatrists recognized tardive dyskinesia?) That, in turn was followed by "widespread pessimism." In this sequence, pessimism followed the "more reasoned" or balanced view, contrary to the law's prediction; here, pessimism came third, not second. Since Casey and Gardos rejected a dire assessment of tardive dyskinesia, however, they allocated it to the second stage. That left another stage to come, when a "balanced" view—Casey and Gardos's—would prevail. The entire scheme simply presupposed that Casey and Gardos's unexplained, undefended substantive judgments about tardive dyskinesia were correct, and that the laws of history demonstrated as much.

Casey contributed another essay to the same volume, and it demonstrated even more clearly how supposed historical laws could replace factual analysis. This essay applied the "law of the new drug" to dismiss not only recommendations about withdrawal of medication but actual research findings as well. Casey began by observing that the mean reported prevalence rate of tardive dyskinesia had increased from "less than 5 percent before 1965 to approximately 25 percent in 1980," and that "[s]ome recent studies report prevalence rates of 50 percent or more in high-risk groups, such as the elderly." "These large increases," he continued, "have led some to claim that there is an epidemic of TD. This concern may lead to inappropriate hesitation about and/or external sanctions against the use of neuroleptic medications. The outcome of either response could have profound medical and legal consequences."[4]

Turning to studies of tardive and spontaneous dyskinesias, Casey concluded that the reported prevalence of those conditions had been rising at about the same rates in the literature. That suggested psychiatrists' "increasing awareness" of dyskinesia "plays a major role in the trend toward the higher rates being reported in recent years." Thus, Casey called for "a balanced perspective."[5]

The idea of an "epidemic" implied a large number of existing cases and the prospect of future increases. Both things were true, contrary to Casey's suggestions. Incidence studies demonstrate that 4 to 5 percent of younger patients, and perhaps ten times as many older patients, develop tardive dyskinesia during each year they are exposed to medication. In all age groups, the number of new cases significantly exceeds the number of cases that remit. Thus, prevalence rises.[6]

In fact, Casey had mistakenly credited gross overestimates of spontaneous dyskinesia. More important for present purposes, he supposed that underestimates of the prevalence of tardive dyskinesia in the 1970s somehow made mid-1980s prevalence estimates too high. The natural tendency would have been to think that prevalence rates would remain steady—because current estimates were correct—or else that the rate would continue increasing, as it had in the past. Relying on the law of the new drug, however, Casey asserted that the truth had to lie between the highest and the lowest figures:

> In all likelihood, earlier studies tended to underreport TD [tardive dyskinesia], either not recognizing mild symptoms or attributing movements seen to the underlying psychiatric illness. Conversely, TD may be over-reported now, with any minor movement being called TD. This tendency should be recognized, as fears of a TD epidemic could fuel regulatory efforts to limit neuroleptic use and contribute to clinicians withholding beneficial drug therapy.[7]

From the fact that earlier psychiatrists had underreported the disorder, Casey concluded that higher figures were probably wrong. Apart from the "law of the new drug," however, that appears implausible. And apart from his imagined historical dynamic, Casey offered no evidence to support his view. Yet the supposition that "any minor movement [is now] being called TD" required argument, not general laws of history, to establish it.

Evidence available in 1986 indicated that Casey's supposition was false. For example, the 1980 Task Force relied on studies reporting rates of *moderately* severe or severe dyskinesia above 25 percent among hospitalized patients. Investigators who counted mild movements reported far higher rates, in the range of 50 percent. Casey supposed, however, that a mean rate of 25 percent *must* include mild movements. Relying on a supposed historical law, Casey used earlier findings to trump later research—exactly as Kline had done when he exalted the then existing literature and complained about a possible future "epidemic of papers."

From the fact that psychiatrists had underreported tardive dyskinesia in the 1960s and 1970s, Crane concluded that psychiatrists had defaulted on their medical obligations. From the same fact, Casey concluded that psychiatrists now overreported the disorder. His analysis was not only wrong; it left out almost everything of interest—historically, ethically, and medically.

The problem went deeper than Casey's confusion of substantive and historical issues, or other possible misapplications of supposed laws of history. The "law of the new drug" simply failed to describe the medication era. The first period—the 1950s—did not constitute a time of unrestrained enthusiasm about medication, as the "law" would predict. On the contrary, 1950s psychiatrists described side effects with more candor, and treatment benefits more modestly, than 1960s psychiatrists did. "Enthusiasm" better describes the second period, when the Study vision heralded profound drug benefits and trivial side effects—a stance that the "law of the new drug" predicts will come first. And with the sequence reversed in that way, the law's dynamic of waxing and waning physician enthusiasm simply does not work. A more familiar and nonmedical model of history fits better: the model of a classical period, when truths are discovered; a time analogous to the Middle Ages, when classical truths are lost; and a modern period, when the old truths reemerge and further advances occur.

Even if the "law of the new drug" offered a plausible historical sequence, its operative terms—"optimism," "pessimism," "balance"—often describe events and ideas too crudely. Consider, for example, the 1995 exchange about withdrawing medication. Some psychiatrists (Carpenter and Tamminga) advocated that serious consideration be given to withdrawal under many circumstances; some (Greden and Tandon) urged a nearly irrefutable presumption against withdrawal; and some (Gilbert and Jeste) took a position in the middle. Which represented the "balanced" view? Carpenter and Tamminga's, because it took seriously both the withdrawal and continued medication options? Greden and Tandon's, because it abandoned pessimism about tardive dyskinesia? Or Gilbert and Jeste's, because it stood between the others?

Or consider the 1967 reaction to Crane's findings about tardive dyskinesia. Kline suggested that Crane had invented an "epidemic"; Denber implied that Crane was professionally deranged. Yet according to Casey's version of the "law of the new drug," Denber and Kline were merely being "optimistic"—a characterization that misses everything interesting and important about their positions. Denber and Kline did not seem "optimistic" in any recognizable sense: in fact, they appeared angry and worried. Similarly, Casey's law would categorize Crane as "pessimistic" because of his accurate findings, a characterization that verges on the bizarre and parallels Cole's criticism of 1975.

Optimism, pessimism, and balance also fail as explanations of changes in the positions of individual psychiatrists. For instance, in 1975 Cole attributed tardive dyskinesia to "diagnosable and non-diagnosable" brain disorders and estimated its prevalence at 5 percent. In 1976, he and Gardos abandoned the idea of brain damage, suggested high rates of prevalence, and urged serious consideration for medication withdrawal. In 1980, they rescinded their withdrawal recommendation, ostensibly because psychiatrists had ignored it. Cole's sequence of positions roughly suits the law: optimism, pessimism, balance. Yet it seems odd to characterize his 1975 errors as "optimism," his 1976 withdrawal recommendation as "pessimism," or his 1980 retreat as "balanced." The 1975 position represented a very late and soon-to-be abandoned statement of the rejectionist position. The 1976 withdrawal recommendation rested on findings that Gardos and Cole continued to accept as valid. Their 1980 retreat hardly seems "balanced"; more aptly, one could characterize it as a pessimistic assessment about tailoring medication to an individual's needs in an era of deinstitutionalization.

For the "law of the new drug" to have any explanatory value, independent grounds must be available for deciding when physicians are exaggerating, minimizing, or fairly assessing the virtues of a treatment. One can then decide whether or not the "law" fits the facts. Psychiatrists reversed this procedure, however. They assumed the correctness of the "law" and further assumed that side effects should not significantly affect the near universal use of medication. It followed that psychiatrists who disagreed were unduly pessimistic and historically regressive. Thus, specious history—a history that, when not hopelessly vague, was false—replaced substantive medical evaluation.

Although psychiatrists misused the "law of the new drug," it describes a plausible dynamic standing alone. It may well explain numerous medical developments. Yet the law also has inherent limitations, which psychiatrists exploited. In particular, it abstracts a single factor, professional enthusiasm, from the many considerations that can prompt changes in medical thinking. Thus, it will fit events only if no other factor is operating. And in psychiatry, other factors were at work.

One such factor is medical discovery. Important discoveries about a therapy may occur at any time, not just at particular points in an emotional cycle. Psychiatric proponents of the "law" either missed this possibility or assumed that tardive dyskinesia did not qualify as a discovery.

Changes in medical economics and public health may also affect medical thinking. They did so powerfully in the neuroleptic era, yet they lay beyond the ken of the "law of the new drug." Changes in cultural attitudes, the factor that cut short lobotomy's career, also come into play. The "law" ignores them as well.

Nor does the "law" account for physicians' memories of older treatments. In the early 1950s, lobotomy spurred the idea of medication as a disease-inducing agent: it seemed "optimistic" then to suppose drugs resembled the Nobel Prize–winning brain surgery, and worked, as lobotomy did, by causing brain damage. What counted as optimism or pessimism about medication therefore depended on one's view of an older therapy as much on one's enthusiasm about a new treatment. Later, the discrediting of lobotomy led some to temper their claims about the benefits of medication.

The "law" ignores the demise, as well as the prehistory, of "new drugs." The fate of typical psychiatric treatments, like that of most therapies in medicine, is abandonment. Lobotomy, the coma therapies, and convulsive treatments for schizophrenia have all but disappeared, along with radical sleep treatment and the removal of women's ovaries. Yet the "law of the new drug" says nothing about this. Lobotomy quickly went from earning its inventor a Nobel Prize to being a procedure in disrepute; today most would agree that a "balanced" view of lobotomy is negative. That trajectory of belief, and even the possibility of a "balanced" negative view of a treatment, seem beyond the reach of the "law."

Finally, there were two ironies in psychiatrists' attempts to apply the "law of the new drug" to medication. Casey and Gardos hoped that it would help to prevent "external sanctions against the use of neuroleptic medications" from the other "law"—the one applied by courts. Yet the "law of the new drug" treated psychiatrists' waxing and waning enthusiasm as the driving force behind views of medication. And waxing or waning enthusiasm hardly qualifies as something that courts should allow free rein. Thus, if the "law of the new drug" was correct, courts actually had *less* reason to defer to psychiatrists' judgments.

The second irony also arose from the emotional dynamic behind the "law of the new drug." Since the early 1960s, psychological mechanisms had lost their place in explanations of schizophrenia or medications' modes of action. Yet the "law of the new drug" used psychological mechanisms to explain *psychiatrists'* views of medication. And although medications were no longer counted as "tranquilizers," calming down—that is, psychiatrists' calming down—was the prescription from Casey and Gardos.

Chapter 12   A Vision Restored?

THE 1995 EXCHANGES about medication withdrawal demonstrated how far psychiatry had traveled since the Collaborative Study. The contributions, particularly those that urged a presumption against withdrawing medication, were a kind of culmination of the third period of the era. The presumption made clinical judgment and public health imperatives completely harmonious. It reconciled the Task Force's clinical model with Gardos and Cole's public health approach. Other contributions to the exchange—and the very existence of a robust debate—reflected new enough elements to suggest that a fourth period of the medication era was being born during the first half of the 1990s.

That the exchange took place at all was highly significant. Not even the tardive dyskinesia controversy of the 1960sand 1970s had produced so stark an exchange of views in a major American psychiatric journal. The exchange even recalled the 1950s, when psychiatrists differed over basic issues affecting medication. Although a disjunction of research conclusions and clinical practice constituted a hallmark of the third period, withdrawing medication bore powerfully on clinical practice, and researchers here addressed the matter forcefully. Other developments of the early 1990s also suggested a major shift. For one, "atypical" medications—which differed in important ways from standard antipsychotic medications—became widely available. For another, leading psychiatrists acquired a newfound optimism and a renewed sense of progress in psychiatric history. The focus on the present and on the constraints imposed by the mental health system—the picture presented in the "Overview"—began to give way to something else. And research into the brain intensified.

The medication era was entering its fifth decade—a very long time in psychiatry. The biological therapies of the 1930s lasted only a little more than twenty years before medication appeared. In the nineteenth century, enthusiasm had waned for state mental hospitals after twenty or thirty years, although the institutions themselves endured. Was medication like mental hospitals—an intervention that hung on despite evident failures because, as Hollister said, "nothing better" was available? If Hollister was right, the answer was yes—but the same answer followed from the "Overview" or, indeed, from the ahistoric general outlook of the third period.

The fourth period of the era coincides with the writing of this book, and the lack of historical distance makes it hard to perceive what its largest features are or will prove to be. Psychiatrists' optimism may be warranted. Atypicals might truly qualify as a major advance. New knowledge about brain neurotransmitters may produce even better "designer drugs," tailored to affect particular aspects of the disease by targeting specific neurochemical processes—the Study's antischizophrenic ideal realized at last. On the other hand, perhaps psychiatrists became optimistic only through an act of will, or because some emotional dynamic—post–law of the new drug—produces optimism after forty years. Perhaps psychiatrists conjured up a sense of historical movement in an effort to conceal—from themselves and others—the facts of a tired and worn-out era.

Some things did not change. Clinical practice and public health remained on the course set by the Study vision. Much research continued to display an "absence of vision." Yet some prominent researchers again constructed large visions, visions that now included history as an integral component. The emergence of these visions affords some of the best evidence that a new period had begun.

Atypical Medications: A New Future and a New Past

During the early 1990s, "atypical" medications became available as alternatives to standard antipsychotics. Clozapine, the first atypical drug, appeared in the 1960s but had to be withdrawn from the market because it caused a potentially fatal blood disorder, agranulocytosis, in about 1 percent of patients. With clozapine available in the United States only for special cases, John Kane and a Collaborative Study group reported an impressive result in 1988: 27 percent of patients who did not respond to standard antipsychotics did respond to clozapine. Two years later, the manufacturer reintroduced the drug to the general United States market.[1]

Four features distinguished clozapine from standard medication: it produced significantly fewer extrapyramidal effects, like akathisia; it appeared to produce significantly less tardive dyskinesia; it benefited some patients who did not respond to other antipsychotics, as Kane reported; and although it affected dopamine receptors, as standard medication did, clozapine did not affect the same receptors to the same extent, and it also affected neurotransmitters besides dopamine. Together, these attributes made clozapine "atypical." By the mid-1990s, two new, apparently atypical, medications appeared that did not cause blood disorders. (Other atypicals remain under investigation and appear close to marketable.)

It was the most hopeful development since the Collaborative Study. Other post-Study developments had brought bad news: the discovery of widespread tardive dyskinesia, for example, and the disappointments of community care. Atypicals, on the other hand, suggested a bright future. In 1995, David Pickar observed that the "prospects for new . . . antipsychotics" had "created great therapeutic optimism." And "optimism" was precisely what researchers had lost when the Study vision dissolved.[2]

Psychiatrists differed in their degrees of optimism, however. A few, like Herbert Meltzer, believed that atypicals had ushered in an entirely new psychiatric era. Commenting on the Gilbert-Jeste drug withdrawal study, Meltzer recommended wholesale shifts of patients from standard medications to atypicals, even if the patients were responding to the standard treatments. Atypicals were that much better, in his view.[3]

Most psychiatrists did not go nearly that far. Because clozapine produced agranulocytosis and required expensive blood monitoring, psychiatrists largely confined its use to treatment-resistant cases. The typical annual cost for clozapine and the necessary blood monitoring equaled $5,500 according to one estimate—more than ten times the cost of standard medication. Moreover, clozapine had other undesirable side effects. A 1991 review in the *New England Journal of Medicine*—coauthored by Baldessarini—estimated that about 30 percent of patients experienced "[s]edation and fatigue"; about the same number experienced significant weight gain; 5 percent developed fevers; and as many as 4 percent developed seizures, a problem particularly associated with high doses. Moreover, the attributes of other atypical drugs remained "debatable" during the mid-1990s. Psychiatrists disagreed about whether effective dosages produced as few akathisia-like effects as clozapine did, or produced tardive dyskinesia, or afforded better relief from negative symptoms, or equaled clozapine in treatment resistant cases. These debates implicitly raised the question of how much brighter the psychiatric future actually appeared in light of the new drugs, and how confidently one should expect its imminent arrival.[4]

In fact, atypicals revealed at least as much about the past and present of psychiatry as they did about its future. These implications went largely unnoticed because of the absence of vision. Yet atypicals afforded so much hope precisely because of the shortcomings of standard medications—shortcomings that had received relatively little attention before the 1990s.

Other, more subtle implications emerged from Baldessarini's 1991 article, which skeptically reviewed claims for clozapine. Baldessarini commented on the lack of placebo-controlled clozapine trials and characterized the aggregate advantage of clozapine over standard medications in the reported trials—which included many treatment-resistant patients—as "small on average" and, indeed, below the level of statistical significance. He agreed with Kane's 1988 study "that clozapine may be superior in antipsychotic efficacy in some patients." Yet Baldessarini offered an explanation that did not suggest clozapine's superior efficacy but instead reflected badly on existing clinical practice. Kane had shifted patients from "high doses" of a medication that produced many extrapyramidal effects to "moderate doses" of clozapine, which produced "minimal extrapyramidal side effects." For that reason, Baldessarini thought "some of the apparent benefit" from clozapine "may" have resulted from "relief from side effects." Baldessarini did not spell out the implication, but it seemed obvious: merely lowering the dose of standard medication would produce at least "some" of clozapine's supposedly novel effects.[5]

Baldessarini provided a similar analysis of another supposed benefit of clozapine. Some psychiatrists thought that negative symptoms of schizophrenia—withdrawal, indifference, lack of capacity to work or relate to others—responded significantly better to clozapine than to typical neuroleptics. This supposed advantage had received considerable attention; some regarded clozapine as revolutionary because of it. But Baldessarini suggested another reason for clozapine's apparent advantage against negative symptoms, one that did not arise from the drug's effects on illness. Psychiatrists "easily confused" the side effects of medication with negative symptoms of schizophrenia, Baldessarini observed. His implication was again obvious: clozapine did not necessarily affect negative symptoms any differently; it simply failed to produce the same impairments from side effects that other medication did. Once again, a supposed positive attribute of clozapine emerged instead as a shortcoming in existing clinical practice, one that resulted from the failure of clinicians to recognize side effects.[6]

Thus, Baldessarini transformed portents of a promising future into evidence of mundane clinical lapses in the present. His argument also underscored the continuing asymmetry in views about the benefits and side effects of medication. A reduction in negative symptoms had appeared highly significant as a supposed benefit of clozapine; yet the same symptoms appeared almost insignificant as side effects of other medications. In that guise, psychiatrists largely ignored them. What happened in the realms of benefit, brain, and the future evidently mattered far more than what happened in the realms of side effects, subjective feeling, and the present. That aspect of the Study legacy had survived.

Baldessarini's review included other points that cast an unflattering light on psychiatry's present and past. He noted, for example, that the search for new medications had until recently "rested largely on narrow pharmacologic hypotheses arising from the frankly circular association of substantial central antidopaminergic action with virtually all other neuroleptic drugs." That observation portrayed dopamine imbalance theory, which had once commanded so much attention, as the result of a "frankly circular association." He also noted that clozapine was "far from ideal" even for refractory patients, and that "[i]ts reappearance 30 years after it was patented underscores the substantial lack of progress in the development of more effective and safer antipsychotic drugs." Finally, Baldessarini hoped that clozapine would spur "interest in the development of improved agents for the treatment of severely incapacitated psychiatric patients," but he did not predict research breakthroughs any time soon.[7] Instead, he focused on everyday clinical and public health responsibilities. Since "some patients" would improve on clozapine, Baldessarini wrote, "[T]here is from the clinical perspective a renewed social and medical challenge to provide additional supportive and rehabilitative services to those who can recover."[8]

Baldessarini's analysis comported with his earlier emphasis on clinical practice in the Task Force Report. That Report had made clinical judgment the foundation of psychiatric pharmacology. Eleven years later, Baldessarini suggested that clinicians were not performing well. Yet he kept his focus on day-to-day clinical practice.

In doing that, Baldessarini put himself outside the emerging currents in psychiatry. Leading figures were about to look elsewhere: to research about the brain, instead of clinical practice; to the future or the past, instead of the present. Baldessarini's place outside these currents affords more evidence that a new period of the medication era was beginning.

Progress Redux—The Future

Unlike Baldessarini, many researchers during the mid-1990s felt a renewed sense of progress. Atypicals played a part in this, but the feeling of forward momentum usually went well beyond the new drugs. In the Study vision, medication itself powered psychiatric progress; in the 1990s, atypicals represented only one manifestation of a larger process of advance. Meltzer—who thought of atypicals in nearly the same way that 1960s psychiatrists had thought of standard medications—was the exception.

Robert Michels and Peter Marzuk expressed the more widely held view in a 1993 review article for the *New England Journal of Medicine*. The article began by positing an historic change: "The field of psychiatry has undergone a profound transformation in recent years. The focus of research has shifted from the mind to the brain, one of the most exciting frontiers in biology. At the same time, the profession has shifted from a model of psychiatric disorders based on maladaptive psychological processes to one based on medical disease."[9] Thus, research and abstract models—not present therapies or patient benefits—represented the principal manifestations of progress. "[M]any of the most interesting research findings have yet to be confirmed," the authors continued, "and only a few have been translated into clinical practice." Psychiatry was "transformed" nonetheless; it had become a veritable engine of progress that would yield clinical benefits in the future.

Their concluding passage struck a tone of triumph:

> A 1975 review . . . described psychiatry as "the battered child of medicine . . . born in witchcraft and demoniacal possession, feared by the public, often scorned by the family of medical specialists, and dependent for much of its existence upon handouts from public agencies." One of the findings of research on high-risk children is that the majority do very well. Fortunately, psychiatry is in this majority. Its basic research is among the most exciting in contemporary medicine, its diagnoses are reliable, its treatments are effective, and the stigma that has long marked both its patients and its practitioners is rapidly disappearing . . . The battered child [psychiatry] . . . has been transformed by a tumultuous adolescence into a vigorous and successful young adult.[10]

Combining the opening portrait of progress with the closing metaphor of maturation, it appears that progress—particularly, in brain research—had cured psychiatry of its troubles, restoring it to the normal developmental course of a medical specialty. One might complain about transforming patients through brain interventions, but who could object to a transformation in psychiatry because of the brain?

Unlike Study-era psychiatrists, Michels and Marzuk's ideas about progress rested on psychiatry and the future more than on medication and the present—and on research more than on clinical practice. In other respects, however, they developed Study-era themes. The emphasis on the brain was one; the emphasis on "progress" was another. In both areas, Michels and Marzuk abandoned the atheoretical, ahistorical thinking that had characterized the 1980s: they produced a vision of a profession and its shimmering future. It was not exactly the Study vision, but a family resemblance seemed quite clear.

From a clinical perspective, Baldessarini saw only modest improvements for patients and little prospect for future research breakthroughs. Looking through a research lens, Michels and Marzuk envisioned huge advances. Baldessarini's approach had made him something of a conservative in 1980. By the mid-1990s, however, psychiatry was moving in a way that made Baldessarini appear a maverick.

Progress Redux: The Past

An even closer approximation of the Study vision emerged from work by Richard Jed Wyatt. A prominent researcher, Wyatt had collaborated with Jeste in studies of tardive dyskinesia during the 1980s. Taking middle-of-the-road positions, they had ranked among the leading authorities.

Their collaboration ended in the 1990s, and they proceeded in quite opposite directions. With other coauthors, Jeste published alarming findings about tardive dyskinesia and, along with Gilbert, published the 1995 review of medication withdrawal. Wyatt turned to re-creating the Study vision of antischizophrenic actions and mild side effects. The vision had unraveled because of tardive dyskinesia and the demise of claims about "antischizophrenic" effects in the brain. Wyatt revisited both issues and reached Study-like conclusions about each one.

Wyatt did not deny the existence of tardive dyskinesia or question current prevalence figures. Instead, he returned to the idea that apparent cases of the disorder did not result from medication but were instead "spontaneous"—a claim that had been made by Kline in 1967 and revived from time to time ever since. In 1991, Wyatt and Vikram Khot reviewed the literature and concluded that spontaneous dyskinesias occurred often, actually outnumbering medication-caused dyskinesias in some age groups.[11]

An even more provocative conclusion by Wyatt appeared in 1994. Along with Wayne S. Fenton and Thomas H. McGlashan, Wyatt reviewed patient charts dating from the 1950s at Chestnut Lodge in Maryland, a facility where psychiatrists had avoided using medications. Wyatt could not examine the patients described in these almost forty-year-old charts. The charts themselves, however, led him to the following conclusions: 15 percent of the patients (with a mean age below thirty) had "oral-facial dyskinesias" that the records described "with sufficient detail to be considered definite"; 30 percent suffered from a "deficit syndrome" characterized by negative symptoms such as lack of emotion and social withdrawal; 32 percent of the deficit syndrome patients, but only 8 percent of the non-deficit group, manifested dyskinesias. Wyatt went on to conclude that the deficit syndrome probably resulted from distinctive processes in the brain that produced both the negative symptoms and the dyskinesias. Thus, in "many . . . patients the emergence of movement disorders [and also the cognitive dysfunctions that some investigators linked to tardive dyskinesia] may represent spontaneous dyskinesia associated with progression of illness."[12]

The article ended with a "medicolegal caution":

> Available data regarding spontaneous dyskinesia in schizophrenia
> point to the inherent impossibility of determining the specific cause of
> a movement disorder in any particular instance. . . . [T]hose clinicians

who find the case for a significant prevalence of spontaneous dyskinesia in schizophrenia compelling may find it prudent to inform patients and families that the progression of schizophrenia (particularly the deficit and disorganized forms of schizophrenia) may be accompanied by the emergence of movement disorders. Treatment with neuroleptic agents may add incrementally to the risk of abnormal movements inherent in the illness or may hasten the appearance of such movements, but to an extent that has not been fully determined.[13]

This remarkable passage suggested that schizophrenia causes much tardive dyskinesia and that it remains unclear to what extent medication contributes to the risk. If Wyatt's proposal covered all dyskinesias, it reflected Kline's 1967 view that brain damage, not medication, caused the disorder. If it covered only dyskinesias produced by schizophrenia, it still made it virtually impossible to ascribe any particular case of tardive dyskinesia to medication. Wyatt offered a more elegant and profound confounding factor than anything the 1980 Task Force had devised. Going beyond the Task Force, Wyatt even suggested that questions about the cause of tardive dyskinesia fall within the range of clinicians' judgment.

Wyatt's article could have gone further still. If schizophrenia causes neurological damage, and if medication is effective against schizophrenic manifestations, then medication might reduce the amount of neurological harm that patients suffer. In another 1991 article Wyatt had announced just such a conclusion, without tying it to dyskinesias. Instead, he cited older studies that compared medicated to nonmedicated patients, and he suggested that a failure to receive medication early in the illness produces a worse later course of schizophrenia—even if the patient subsequently takes drugs. That happens, Wyatt theorized, because "brain damage" results from unchecked schizophrenia.[14]

Together, Wyatt's positions on tardive dyskinesia and brain damage virtually re-created the Study vision. If he was correct, tardive dyskinesia represented an overrated risk, and medication checked schizophrenia in the brain. In effect, drugs constituted a "truly antischizophrenic" therapy, although Wyatt did not use the phrase.

The Study vision unraveled because of George Crane and tardive dyskinesia, but if Wyatt was right, that should not have happened, for Crane did not just err; he actually got things backward. The salient risk of brain damage lay in withholding medication, not in giving it. As for other side effects, if they did not qualify as "trivial" standing alone, they probably did so when compared to the benefit of avoiding schizophrenia-induced brain damage. In these ways, Wyatt improved on positions that the defenders of the Study vision had advanced in the 1960s.

Wyatt did not explicitly invoke "progress," as Michels and Marzuk did. Yet his theories, like theirs, restored momentum to psychiatry and put the ahistoricism of the medication era's third period to rest. Michels and Marzuk did that by looking to the future, Wyatt by looking to the past. His claims about tardive dyskinesia rested on forty-year-old charts; his ideas about brain damage cited thirty-year-old studies. Michels and Marzuk awaited future benefits from research; Wyatt thought that past studies disclosed dramatic yet overlooked benefits in the present. Reading Wyatt, one might suppose that a treatment that conformed to the Study vision had long been available—and that the Study had identified it correctly.

Progress emerged in different ways from Wyatt's and from Michels and Marzuk's work. Michels and Marzuk posited revolutionary breakthroughs that made events before the revolution almost irrelevant. The troubled childhood of psychiatry no longer made any difference. Study-era psychiatrists had used a similar strategy in connection with standard medication, as had 1930s psychiatrists in connection with lobotomy and the coma-convulsive treatments.

Wyatt proceeded from the opposite direction. He found new significance in an old revolution, implicitly laying the foundation for a more elegant, comprehensive claim of progress. His backward-looking account solved a problem that others did not. This problem was that modern views of medication sharply differed from the Study's, yet the same prescribing practices had endured. Standard explanations were flawed: the Task Force did not really describe how clinicians balanced benefits against risks, and, in any event, its account was undermined when clinicians ignored its recommendations. Gardos and Cole made medication the "cornerstone" of the treatment, but that fact alone said nothing about progress; during other eras, mental hospitals, physical restraints, or tooth removal and coma treatments had constituted "cornerstones" too. Neither the Task Force nor Gardos and Cole had successfully justified the Study public health system and its prescribing practices in a world without the Study vision. Their failures suggested that psychiatric theory might represent little more than a set of rationalizations for the widespread use of medication.

Wyatt's theories solved these problems, and more. Wyatt made it obvious that clinicians should have prescribed medication to almost everyone through the 1990s, and that tardive dyskinesia should not have changed things. The clinicians were right because the Study itself was basically correct. With the vision restored, everything—including psychiatric history—became right again. Wyatt's account implied, contrary to Michels and Marzuk's conception, that the currents of psychiatric progress had shifted after 1980 from the research world to the clinical one.

The emergence of two such divergent views suggests that the idea of progress itself—apart from any particular reason for affirming it—was luring psychiatrists during the mid-1990s. The circumscribed, unoptimistic, and ahistorical positions of the third period had seemingly exhausted themselves. The theoretical ambition, optimism, and sense of historical progress that had marked the Study era were coming back.

Further evidence of the lure of progress lies in the weakness of Wyatt's positions—a weakness so pronounced that, like the weaknesses of the Study, it suggests something besides a scientific response to data. Wyatt's position on spontaneous dyskinesias seemingly accorded no weight to the numerous studies—including Crane's 1968 report about Turkish mental patients—that reported high dyskinesia rates among patients who had received medication and very low or negligible rates among similar patients who had not. Other studies, it was true, had reported high spontaneous dyskinesia rates. Yet a number of authors claimed the latter had erred by failing to discover patients' past exposure to medication or, as Crane suggested, by counting mild and questionable abnormal movements as dyskinesias. Since older patients develop tardive dyskinesia at rates as high as 1 percent per week while receiving medication, even brief undetected periods of treatment would explain high reported rates of "spontaneous" dyskinesia. And typical spontaneous dyskinesia studies could not detect—and did not even try to detect—possible past exposure to medication.[15]

Seemingly unimpressed by these issues, Wyatt simply averaged the results of conflicting studies, including those reporting very high rates of spontaneous dyskinesia. That yielded a statistical middle ground. Yet it was an unpromising way of rationally resolving a dispute between studies that reported virtually no spontaneous dyskinesias and those that reported very high rates. Moreover, although undetected medication exposure or misassessment of questionable movements could explain erroneous reports of high rates, it was difficult to explain away the repeated, apparently careful studies that detected virtually no spontaneous dyskinesia in never-medicated patients.

Other lines of investigation undermined Wyatt's suggestion that schizophrenia itself causes significant "spontaneous" dyskinesias. The fact that medicated people who do not suffer from schizophrenia—senile, elderly persons, for example, or those with developmental disabilities—develop tardive dyskinesia at high rates suggests that medications commonly cause it, whether or not the affected person has schizophrenia. Nor did the reported rates among patients with schizophrenia and others obviously differ. And the very fact that nonelderly patients develop tardive dyskinesia at the rate of 5 percent per year when exposed to medication, and elderly patients develop it about ten times faster, powerfully implicated medication. Given such considerations, it was hardly surprising that an incidence study by Jeste and others in 1995—a year after Wyatt's Chestnut Lodge article—found patients developing tardive dyskinesia at the same rates whether they had schizophrenia or not, a result the authors believed should "help put to rest the notion that TD is merely a symptom of schizophrenia."[16]

For all his reliance on the past, Wyatt had missed the crucial piece of research: Muriel Jones's presentation to the 1968 tardive dyskinesia workshop. With Richard Hunter, Jones had reviewed the old charts of never-medicated hospitalized patients. Unlike Wyatt, they had also examined the patients connected with charts. Jones and Hunter found a 2 percent dyskinesia rate among patients who had remained medication-free, and a 20 percent rate among patients who had received medication since the old chart entries. The charts included numerous descriptions of abnormal movements affecting patients' mouths and faces, but examination showed that these movements were not tardive dyskinesia; rather, they were the "tremors, tics and stereotypies" associated with schizophrenia. Based on chart reviews alone, Wyatt apparently considered all those movements tardive dyskinesia.

Overlooking Jones and Hunter, Wyatt instead relied heavily on D. G Cunningham Owens's decade-old reports of an association between schizophrenia and dyskinetic movements. In 1982, Owens had reported that two groups of patients—one having received medication, the other not—developed dyskinesias at the same rate, suggesting the incredible result that medication did not cause dyskinesia at all. Reviewing the same data in 1985, Owens modified his conclusions; he now reported that "[p]revious exposure to neuroleptics produced a striking increase in both the prevalence and the severity of abnormal movements." Nonetheless, he still found an abnormal orofacial movement rate of about 30 percent among patients who had supposedly never received medication, a rate high enough to suggest that schizophrenia caused many, though not all, dyskinesias.[17]

Wyatt credited that finding, but in fact Owens's work invited both of the objections noted earlier. He apparently had not explored the patients' history of treatment outside the hospital—at a time when it seems likely the patients would have received medication. And Owens apparently counted mild movements as tardive dyskinesia, a practice Crane had cautioned against twenty years earlier. Furthermore, Owens's "medicated" patients apparently received much less medication than the norm. Of 364 "neuroleptic treated" patients, 119 received only "some" medication—less than one year's worth, as far as Owens could tell. One would expect these patients to develop tardive dyskinesia at a rate close to that of the "unmedicated" group—5 percent more, perhaps. How much medication the other "medicated" patients received remains unclear; we know only that their lifetime exposure exceeded one year's worth. If they got only a little more—and this hospital obviously hesitated to use drugs—that would further diminish the expected differences between "medicated" and "unmedicated" groups.[18]

Wyatt's treatment of Owens's study and spontaneous dyskinesia compares interestingly with that of the 1992 Task Force. Obviously tempted by a Wyatt-like view, that Task Force nonetheless held back. It began by counting it as an "inescapable conclusion" from Owens's findings that "spontaneous, involuntary, orofacial movements can be a feature of chronic schizophrenia that has not been modified by the administration of antipsychotic drugs. A proportion of such movements may merely represent spontaneous orofacial dyskinesia of the elderly, but Owens . . . postulated that in some patients the syndrome reflects the pathological cerebral process underlying severe chronic schizophrenia."[19] That conclusion may have been "inescapable," but it was also hopelessly vague. The Task Force did not actually say that schizophrenia causes tardive dyskinesia or that the unmedicated patients' "involuntary, orofacial movements" were dyskinesias. In fact, the passage was so vague that it might be read to embody either Wyatt's position or Jones and Hunter's—and, given the state of the evidence, that indicated how strongly a Wyatt-like view tempted the authors.

That same temptation led the Task Force to miscite Jones and Hunter for the proposition that "abnormal involuntary movements, such as choreiform and orofacial dyskinesia, are . . . clearly described" in pre-drug era charts—a mistaken characterization of Jones and Hunter's finding that few patients had "orofacial *dyskinesia*," but one that erred in Owens and Wyatt's favor. The Task Force also asserted that spontaneous dyskinesias are "relatively more common in patients with certain psychiatric illnesses (mainly chronic schizophrenia), elderly subjects, and patients subjected to long-term institutionalization," perhaps suggesting that schizophrenia causes significant dyskinesia, as does old age—while failing to mention that all three groups commonly receive medication. A few paragraphs later, after citing a neurologist's assertions that movements in the pre-neuroleptic era differed distinctly from tardive dyskinesia in appearance (the former being "stereotyped and manneristic," the latter "irregular" and "jerky")—a conclusion that undercut Owens—the Task Force still tried to split the difference and retain something of Owens's view. It concluded that schizophrenia does *not* cause tardive dyskinesia, but added, "[I]f schizophrenic patients with motor disturbances inherent to their illnesses are more vulnerable to the neurologic side effects of antipsychotic drugs, then the two types of movement will tend to coexist in the same individuals. This seems a plausible hypothesis and is supported by the finding that both types of movement may share an association with similar clinical features."[20]

This passage cited no evidence, and its final phrase about "shar[ing] . . . an association with similar clinical features" seemed to mean only that psychiatrists had mistaken one syndrome for the other. But, however strained, the Task Force's conclusion put matters in the best possible light. Medication caused tardive dyskinesia, but its responsibility was vaguely diminished because of the "plausible" (though unsupported) hypothesis that schizophrenic mannerisms predispose patients to dyskinesia. On the basis of the same similarity of "clinical features," one could as plausibly conclude that medication makes patients "more vulnerable" to schizophrenic symptoms such as mannerisms. At the cost of coherence, the Task Force had tried to save what it could of Owens's claims.

In 1994, Wyatt had taken the Task Force's position all the way to coherence —and so to evident falsity. The next year, however, he recast his position and moved toward the Task Force's formulation. In his 1995 comment on withdrawing medication, Wyatt noted reports about a high incidence of tardive dyskinesia among older patients and described the figures as "extremely worrisome." Wyatt also noted that younger patients "have been found to have a 4% to 5% per year incidence"—a "still troubling" figure but one that "may not reflect the true risk." At that point, he described his Chestnut Lodge study as finding "a 15% prevalence of definite oral/facial or tardive dyskinesia-like movements in a group of relatively young patients with chronic schizophrenia who had never been given antipsychotic medications, indicating that some of the movements attributed to antipsychotic medications are either part of the illness or otherwise independent of medication."[21]

That phrasing represented an unacknowledged step back from Wyatt's 1994 claim that charts "documented oral-facial dyskinesias with sufficient detail to be considered definite." The "definite . . . dyskinesias" of 1994 had become "definite oral/facial or tardive dyskinesia-like movements" in 1995. The newer wording was consistent with the "movements" not being tardive dyskinesia at all.

With Wyatt's historically based positions appearing to be mistakes, the power of the past in his thinking becomes all the more remarkable. He gave the past a privileged position, supposing that answers to critical questions lay with those who suffered from chronic schizophrenia but had never received medication. Such patients no longer existed in the industrialized world; medication was too widely used. Thus, only historical investigation into the preneuroleptic period could answer the questions. And, at least until 1995, Wyatt allowed inferences from old studies and charts to overcome present lines of research, such as incidence studies of tardive dyskinesia.

No less remarkably, Wyatt seemingly overlooked important implications of his thesis. He claimed that schizophrenia causes tardive dyskinesia and conceded that medication also causes tardive dyskinesia. Combining the two claims, one concludes that medication may cause persistent schizophrenia-like changes in the brain, which result in dyskinesias—hardly a comforting idea.

That inference probably explains why Kline, Denber, and Cole never offered Wyatt's two claims simultaneously. When they claimed that George Crane saw only schizophrenic "stereotypies," they did not say that medication produced the same syndrome. When they portrayed tardive dyskinesia as the result of brain damage, they did not identify schizophrenia as the cause. The older generation of psychiatrists possessed an ability to anticipate negative inferences, if only for the purpose of avoiding them: unlike Wyatt, they did not invite the argument that medication produces schizophrenia. That capacity apparently remained lost; the "absence of vision" that had characterized the third period seemingly carried over into the fourth.

Drug Withdrawal and Brain Damage

Wyatt's other theory—that prompt treatment with medication forestalls brain damage from schizophrenia—has figured prominently in controversies about withholding medication, particularly in psychiatric research. The claim rests on studies such as one that Philip R. A. May performed during the 1970s. In May's experiment, patients undergoing a first hospitalization for schizophrenia received one of five treatments: psychotherapy, milieu therapy, electroconvulsive therapy, medication, or medication plus psychotherapy. After a patient was discharged, the study's treatment stipulations no longer applied and May no longer controlled the choice of treatment; the great majority of patients probably received medication at some point. Although May did not record the patients' posthospital treatments, he did keep track of their subsequent hospitalizations.[22]

The initial treatment seemed to make a difference later. After three years, for example, the psychotherapy-only patients had endured an average of almost four hundred days of hospitalization, and the milieu patients more than three hundred days; by comparison, the patients who received electroconvulsive therapy, or medication, or medication plus psychotherapy, each endured just over two hundred. "[T]he persistence of the favorable results of early drug treatment is impressive," May wrote.[23]

Wyatt's explanation for the difference was that brain damage had resulted from unchecked schizophrenia in the unmedicated patients. This view received sharp criticism. "We do not know of any satisfactory evidence," Jeste wrote, "that demonstrates irreversible structural brain damage as a direct result of psychotic exacerbation." Carpenter said simply: "Wyatt cites no evidence."[24]

May himself offered a very different explanation, one that cited institutional and psychological factors, not neurochemical events. He speculated that the medicated patients' advantage

> might be due to a shorter stay period in the first place and avoidance
> of the social disarticulation and institutionalization that accompany
> prolonged hospital treatment. This might also account for the
> relatively good outcome in ECT-treated patients whose
> hospitalization periods were also short and for the poorer outcome in

those treated with psychotherapy alone and milieu therapy where initial hospital stay was significantly longer and there would be a higher risk of secondary adverse effects.

Another factor could be that patients who had originally been treated with drugs might be more cooperative with subsequent treatment (particularly with drug therapy) and so less likely to relapse, whereas patients treated with psychotherapy alone may have been (unwittingly perhaps) influenced toward resistance to subsequent drug therapy.[25]

In fact, May's results did not comport well with Wyatt's thesis. True, the medicated patients subsequently spent less time in hospitals than psychotherapy- and milieu-only patients. Yet the medicated group still averaged about two hundred days of hospitalization over three years. A claim that medication prevents brain damage might have suggested a better outcome.

More importantly, the ECT patients had about the same outcomes as medicated patients. That makes it difficult to infer that medication exerts a specific effect against schizophrenia's progression in the brain—unless ECT, an utterly different intervention, somehow does the same thing. On the other hand, the similar results produced by different somatic interventions lend weight to institutional and psychological explanations like May's. And Wyatt's equation of days hospitalized with brain damage can lead to puzzling results. The psychotherapy patients endured more hospitalization than milieu patients, for example. Using Wyatt's theory, one would conclude that psychotherapy causes brain damage—or that milieu therapy prevents it.

Lobotomists made claims very like Wyatt's. They argued that surgery produced the best outcome early in the course of disease, before pathological processes had advanced. With about as much justice as Wyatt, then, they might have argued that their treatment was necessary to prevent brain damage.[26]

There was a closer analogy to Wyatt's theory. Under the sway of the Study, psychiatrists had abandoned psychological explanations of schizophrenic symptoms and hospitalizations; they theorized about brain chemical balances instead. In just the same way, Wyatt abandoned psychological and institutional explanations and turned to the brain. By making the brain effect a permanent one, however, he increased the stakes. As in the case of the Study, no compelling reason for doing so appeared, and the brain explanations were problematic in ways that psychological explanations were not.

Brains and Morals

Whatever their scientific merit, brain explanations carry a special ethical weight. May's institutional explanation of his findings had made medication seem beneficial; Wyatt's explanation of the same findings in terms of the brain made the use of medication seem imperative. This ethical effect operates in the opposite direction too, and it helps to explain tardive dyskinesia's primacy among side effects.

Brain damage does not possess a special ethical force merely because it persists, although persistence surely enters into the equation. Many patients receive medication over long periods and suffer "reversible" side effects the entire time, but tardive dyskinesia still seems to count in a different way. When Kline asserted that he could "decondition" dyskinetic patients in 1967, no one launched a nationwide crash program of deconditioning: tardive dyskinesia urgently mattered because it indicated brain damage, not because of the persistent abnormal movements as such. Even potentially reversible brain damage raises special ethical concern: tardive dyskinesia remained uniquely troubling even though it appeared reversible in a number of cases.

Why should the brain be more important in this way? Part of the answer lies in the brain's complexity and our lack of understanding. Since we cannot reliably gauge the extent of its healing or damage, every incident looms large. If one symptom improves, perhaps many others will. If a patient's tongue flutters, perhaps much else will prove wrong as well.

Even more important, brain damage constitutes "harm" to a person in a sense that reversible side effects simply do not. Someone who experiences brain damage may seem changed as a person; by contrast, reversible side effects represent mere experiences that a person has, however long and unpleasant. Mind and brain lie at the heart of human identity, as Peter Sterling has pointed out, and that makes brain damage a unique alteration of the person.[27]

This ethical reality has affected psychiatry in a variety of ways. Lobotomists took special pride in altering the brain. It seemed like wrestling with the gods and raised psychiatry's professional standing. In the 1950s, public revulsion doomed lobotomy precisely because of its connections with the brain; the public apparently wanted those gods left undisturbed by psychiatrists. The Study era posited antischizophrenic effects in the brain as the justification for widespread medication use. When tardive dyskinesia raised the specter of brain damage, it was the major crisis of the medication era.

Psychiatry seemingly weathered the storm in the 1980s, but it had no truly satisfying solution to the ethical issues posed by tardive dyskinesia. Wyatt's theories offered that solution. He marshaled the moral force of the brain for the cause of medication, rather than against it. Other psychiatrists claimed that the seriousness of schizophrenia made tardive dyskinesia an acceptable cost of treatment. Wyatt advanced a similar argument in the language of the brain. Schizophrenia equaled brain damage; avoidance of brain damage required medication. Just as Deniker's theory of medication-induced brain damage was ethically troubling, Wyatt's theory seemed ethically reassuring.

Wyatt's ideas had another ethical consequence. They placed the benefits of medication in the same scientific and ethical realm as tardive dyskinesia. With those benefits and tardive dyskinesia commensurate—both involving brain—balancing them at last became a comprehensible exercise.

According to Wyatt's critics, he offered no support for the brain damage theory. If the critics are right, the theory's moral implications may provide an explanation. Perhaps "brain damage" amounts to nothing more or less than a proposal for solving ethical problems that had loomed over psychiatry since the lobotomy era. That makes Wyatt's theory something like a linguistic proposal (for substituting "brain damage" in place of "schizophrenia" or "symptom"), even a kind of story or myth about medication and disease. It would not represent the first time a theory performed that role in the medication era.

Yet if these speculations are correct, why did Wyatt's theory attract relatively little support from researchers? And why did it fail to emerge sooner, when it was needed more? Nothing prevented this linguistic proposal—if that is what brain damage theory was—from appearing in 1967, as a response to the crisis over tardive dyskinesia. I have argued that the idea of "antischizophrenic" effects marked a linguistic proposal more than a discovery, and that it triumphed in 1964 because of the need to justify the widespread use of medication. An account is needed of why a theory like Wyatt's did not appear to answer a similar need.

The answer to such questions is speculative and complex. In 1967, Kline and Denber tried to deny that medications had *any* long-lasting brain effects; this attempt was the one consistent theme in their response to Crane. The Study posited "antischizophrenic" effects in the brain but similarly avoided any claim that the effects persisted.

The lobotomy fiasco had led many psychiatrists to place the brain off-limits. This reluctance to interfere with the brain dissipated when the "chemical imbalance" theory of schizophrenia emerged. Yet that theory, at least in its typical form, had medication affecting the brain only as long as the medication remained active in the body. Wyatt went further: he reduced the disease to the brain, and posited persistent brain effects from treatment with medication and nontreatment alike.

The fate of the chemical imbalance theory suggests that Wyatt's enhancement would not have helped, and might have hurt, psychiatry's cause. The imbalance theory did not blunt the force of Crane's attack, except among clinicians. The theory itself became a casualty as the Study vision collapsed. The inference from tardive dyskinesia to brain damage proved more compelling, ethically and scientifically, than the inference from symptom reduction to brain benefits.

Precisely why that happened is uncertain. One possibility is that lobotomy continued to influence public perception. Another is that empirical support for the imbalance theory remained too weak. Perhaps manifest symptoms of brain damage always trump weak theories about brain benefits. Or perhaps brain damage resulting from treatment always overwhelms treatment benefits, short of something like a cure. Perhaps psychiatrists overreacted during the 1970s, and the public accepted the "chemical imbalance" defense after all. The fact remains, however, that the task forces avoided this line of argument, as did Gardos and Cole.

In any case, Wyatt provided a stronger defense only if one did not examine the implications of his theory closely. By inviting attention to persistent brain changes, it might even have made a lobotomy analogy more compelling. During the third period of the medication era, most researchers had shunned deep theory, possibly fearing where it might lead; Wyatt offered such theories and, as noted, opened the door to unanticipated, negative inferences—such as the possibility that medication exacerbated schizophrenia by eliciting dyskinesias associated with the disease. If researchers looked for the persistent consequences of medication, as Wyatt seemed to want them to, they might find them. Imagine the inferences a brain-oriented researcher would draw from Baldessarini's "iatrogenic-pharmacologic stress effect" and the fact that once patients receive medication, they seem to relapse more much quickly once medication is withdrawn.

In any event, psychiatry's response to tardive dyskinesia differed from Wyatt's, and few researchers seemed inclined to follow his lead. By the mid-1990s, psychiatry's standard response to tardive dyskinesia had succeeded; the storm had passed. The disorder was attracting less public attention than it had in years, court injunctions represented no threat, and the public health system remained grounded in the use of medication. Lawsuits seeking monetary damages remained a danger, but only a modest and apparently manageable one—no greater than that faced by physicians in other medical specialties with other treatments. In that sense, at least, Michels and Marzuk were right: psychiatry had joined the mainstream of medicine.

The Future

Whatever lay on the horizon scientifically, a shift in the social and ethical landscape seemed possible during the mid-1990s. An earlier shift of that kind had doomed lobotomy. Who could say that such changes would not occur again—perhaps in the opposite direction, bringing a return of social and ethical tolerance for interventions into the brain?

During the mid-1990s there had seemed to be a growing interest in biological interventions such as castration as a punishment for sex crimes, or sterilization as a response to child abuse or as a condition of receiving public welfare. Proposals for intervention of that kind continued to evoke strong objections, but they also received more respectful attention than they had in the recent past. At the same time, interest surged in theories about the biological bases of intelligence and destructive behavior. And, as *Harper* demonstrated, courts were increasingly untroubled by the neurological side effects of medication. In many respects, the 1990s looked more like the early 1930s than like the 1960s or early 1970s.[28]

If the ethical climate changed along those lines, psychiatry might respond in numerous ways. Splintering into factions or schools was one possibility. That happened in the premedication era, when the state hospital system seemed both firmly entrenched and clearly disastrous. Numerous approaches to schizophrenia enjoyed support then, though none had seemed likely to make much difference. In the 1990s, the system of deinstitutionalization was as firmly entrenched as the state hospitals once were, and it too produced public disasters that seem beyond remedy. Psychiatrists might respond as they had before, with some taking advantage of the new social tolerance for biological interventions.

Forty years into the neuroleptic era, Wyatt's grand theories appeared unnecessary, as well as flawed, as an ethical defense of psychiatric practice. Yet because of the new ethical and social landscape, ideas like Wyatt's might again have their day—either as a dominant view or as one school of psychiatric thought among many. Like the Collaborative Study, Wyatt's theories may work best as the rallying cries for a new era.

Conclusion   Psychiatry and History

Psychiatrists frequently invoke their profession's "eras," "revolutions," and "progress." Ceremonial occasions, such as the inauguration of a president of the American Psychiatric Association, elicit frequent allusions to history. Yet psychiatrists also invoke history in connection with pivotal substantive issues —and did so repeatedly throughout the medication era.[1]

The Collaborative Study included a capsule history of twentieth-century therapies. Denber and Kline cited progress in psychiatry as somehow relevant to tardive dyskinesia's existence; they responded to the disorder as if defending a successful revolution—the medication revolution—against Crane's counter-revolutionary assault. During the 1950s, psychiatrists worried about repeating the errors of the past, especially those of the lobotomy era. During the 1980s, psychiatrists produced a "law" of history—the "law of the new drug"—to account for their response to tardive dyskinesia. During the 1990s, Wyatt returned to pre-drug-era patient charts in an attempt to trump observations about tardive dyskinesia. In each case, the past did not simply matter; it was fundamental to a basic issue in psychiatry.

These were not isolated incidents. During each period of the era, psychiatrists' views of medication included a historical component alongside the components that related to the actions of the drugs themselves, public health, and the psychiatric profession. In the first period, most psychiatrists regarded the medication era as continuous with earlier treatment eras. Medication might represent an important advance, but that did not mean that the pace of psychiatric history had quickened or that fundamentally new forces were operating. In the second period, the Study vision posited a historic revolution that transformed treatment, public health, and the very profession itself. In the third period, during the 1980s, a kind of ahistoricism emerged. Proponents of the "law of the new drug" attempted to prevent the emergence of a negative history of the medication era, but few tried seriously to connect psychiatry's past with its present. In the fourth period, a sense of progress and history returned—accompanied, however, by a remarkable tendency to avoid the present. Michels and Marzuk imparted a sense of momentum by looking toward the future; Wyatt did the same by looking to the past.

Each period's historical component cohered with the prevailing overall views. The first period's undramatic and measured view of history paralleled its undramatic and measured view of medication. The second period posited fundamental transformations both in psychiatric history and in the brain. The third period displayed an absence of vision in history, research, and public health. The fourth period showed signs of a more ambitious theoretical, as well as historical, outlook.

"Progress" remained a refrain of psychiatrists throughout the era; in the introduction to this book, I explored the reasons why. Yet each period had a different conception of progress, since each period had a different conception of history. The measured view of the first period focused on discrete improvements. How much better would patients get on medication? How much smaller would hospitals become? Progress lay in the result or sum total of such smaller advances. The second period envisioned progress as a fundamental transformation. Just as the Study turned improvement in a number of symptoms into "qualitative" or "antischizophrenic" change, the Study vision made "progress" a unitary transforming force, rather than an aggregate of smaller advances.

The third period produced a diminished concept of "progress," the result of its pervasive absence of vision. Psychiatrists still invoked progress, but in a more formal and mechanical way. Resisting negative conclusions ("the law of the new drug") became more important than drawing positive ones; in history, as elsewhere, inference—particularly negative inference—fared poorly. In the fourth period, progress revived but, as in the third period, it remained only loosely connected to the present. No longer tied to concrete developments, the idea of progress became a kind of free-floating conceptual presence.

Since the four concepts of progress were distinctive, they were open to different objections. To rebut the notion of "first period" style progress, a critic would dispute modest research findings and, perhaps, criticize psychiatry's past. To rebut the idea of progress as it was perceived during the second period, one would show the falsity of claims about antischizophrenic effects and trivial side effects, the tenets of the Study vision. The third period style of progress was almost self-contradictory, since psychiatrists generally avoided paying any attention to history. Fourth-period progress had two variants, with different vulnerabilities. Progress in identifying and pursuing important research issues—

the futurist version—is an inadequate reason for accepting current practice; it also begs the question of how we know in advance that research will prove important. Wyatt's attempt to revive the Study vision based on old patient charts—the backward-looking variant—failed because it rested on error, just as the Study vision did.

Each conception of history and progress not only fit in with other components of a period's outlook; it also comported with efforts of psychiatrists to influence the future at various points. During the first period, medication promised important—if not necessarily revolutionary—changes; naturally, psychiatrists supposed they would have a large say in what happened. Thus, they deliberated about concrete actions, which accorded with their deliberate, incremental idea of progress.

In the second period, psychiatric leaders committed the profession to government plans for deinstitutionalization. The idea of progress as fundamental transformation following a decisive event fit those events well. The decisive event, however, was more the decision of the government than the advent of medication.

Psychiatry had made a Faustian bargain. Committed to deinstitutionalization and the concomitant widespread use of medication, it could no longer choose its future. The ahistorical stance of the third period resulted. In the fourth period, with deinstitutionalization a reality beyond debate, and atypicals promising some real advance, many psychiatrists lost their sense of constraint; not a few allowed their historical imaginations to soar once again.

If history and progress represented integral components of psychiatric thought, it is tempting to consider them the least important and most ephemeral ones. How could they prove more significant than views about the actions of various medications, or about other medical matters? Yet they actually explain a great deal. In many instances, they even appear to underlie psychiatrists' purely "medical" views.

For example, the idea that psychiatrists who rejected the significance of tardive dyskinesia were defending the medication revolution against counter-revolutionary assault—an idea about history—helps explain their medical views; yet their medical views neither responded to data nor explained their ideas about progress and psychiatric history. Much the same applies to Gardos and Cole's 1980 "Overview" and to a great deal of thinking in the third period of the medication era. Earlier, the Collaborative Study's conclusions resulted in large part from a desire for change in psychiatry. Later, Wyatt's ideas about schizophrenia-caused dyskinesia seemed more closely tied to progress than to data. In these cases, and in others, psychiatrists' ideas about history loomed as large as anything else in their outlook.

Progress and Professional Autonomy

"Progress" had many shades of meaning, since every period had its own. Each afforded an argument for leaving psychiatry to its own devices, and for leaving psychiatrists free to administer treatments without interference from courts or other outside agencies. After all is said and done, however, the case for non-interference must rest on the idea that the profession of psychiatry—as opposed to just the present treatments for schizophrenia—has advanced.

The use of medication may constitute a major treatment advance standing alone; more debatably, the modern public health system may produce less misery than the old system of state hospitals. Yet if psychiatry has remained the same profession—if it approaches data, therapies, and patients in the same way that it did in the 1940s or the 1890s—the case for noninterference will fail. Medication is not so good that that psychiatrists' performance no longer matters. That might have been true had the Study vision held up; since it collapsed, psychiatry's performance and professional character have become crucial. Michels and Marzuk almost conceded as much in their metaphor of a profession that had outgrown its troubled childhood and become a responsible adult.

To appreciate psychiatry's need for such progress, consider the likely response to someone who explicitly proposed in 1953 the course that psychiatry and public health later took. "We will prescribe medication for almost everyone with schizophrenia over most of their lives," the proposal would read:

> even though many will develop persistent neurological disorders—in some cases severe ones—or endure distress and possibly anguish from medications. For much of the era, psychiatrists will ignore drug-induced neurological disorders; for almost all of it, psychiatrists will downplay patients' distress. Whether medications will enhance a person's capacity to relate to others, or to perform meaningful work is debatable; the treatment may even diminish those capacities. Nor do we know whether medications will benefit a person over the medium and long-term, at least compared with other interventions. Some patients—10 percent to 50 percent—will derive no benefit, at least over periods of two years; yet clinicians will rarely withdraw medications. Doses will be needlessly high, and researchers will usually shy away from describing the problems. The public and patients will be given a misleadingly simple and occasionally false picture of medications, in order to gain their support. We will do this because many patients who are not harmed will benefit, often substantially; because hospitalizations will become much shorter and less expensive; because relapse rates over periods of about two years will drop significantly; and because a public health system that allows patients to live outside of hospitals relatively inexpensively requires such medication and, as a practical matter, such practices.

In all likelihood, the bargain would have been refused. Concerned about psychiatric callousness and neurological side effects, the public probably would have objected. Courts, if they considered the issues, would have questioned whether neurological damage represented an acceptable cost of treatment, and perhaps insisted on real efforts to separate patients who benefited from those who did not. Always dubious about psychiatry, other physicians hardly would have cause to raise their opinion. Political figures would have welcomed cost savings, but presumably would have been influenced by their constituencies and by the other considerations.

Progress in psychiatry constituted an argument for accepting the proffered bargain. Scientists often say that they "stand on the shoulders of giants" because the discoveries of their predecessors laid the foundation for current insights. The aphorism suggests that the giants provide a higher vantage point, from which more truth can be seen. Progress in psychiatry is the giant; it suggests that psychiatrists are positioned to see more than others and that others should therefore accept their judgments.

The form of argument is familiar; the problem lies in psychiatry's past. It contains few candidates for "giant" status. Medication-era psychiatrists did not claim to stand on the shoulders of lobotomists, insulin coma therapists, or asylum doctors who removed patients' teeth and women's ovaries. State mental hospitals endured a century of decline after their founding; today the physicians who ran them are not regarded as giants either.

Only the medication era remains as a possible incubator of progress. That progress must be evident in the medium of the psychiatric profession: its quality of research, concern for patients and general professional character. Yet the claim to such progress does not match the actual history of the medication era.

Consider research. No advance in psychiatric theory produced chlorpromazine; serendipity led physicians to its psychiatric uses. Ordinary screening by the pharmaceutical industry produced other standard antipsychotics. Thus, the advent of medication alone did not render the profession more scientific.

Research developments did not play much of a role either during the medication era. Despite its methodological sophistication, the Collaborative Study reached profoundly wrong results—and did so because of an evident desire to justify the widespread use of medication, rather than because of data. The profession's response to tardive dyskinesia—within research and clinical practice alike—produced a remarkable professional default; George Crane described it as without parallel in the history of medicine. To the present day, theories about medication ignore inconvenient or negative inferences.

The salient fact is not that psychiatry erred; every science does. The character of the mistakes, not their existence, bears on the claims of progress. Tardive dyskinesia is a case in point, but similar tendencies appeared everywhere.

The identity, extent, and significance of other side effects; the nature of medications' benefits; the implications of neurological changes; the relationship of research to public mental health and clinical prescribing—on all these matters, psychiatrists' conclusions zigzagged and reversed and inverted in an apparent effort to arrive at the most convenient results for the profession and, often, the state. This process seemed uncharacteristic of science, and hardly bespoke progress.

Oliver Sacks describes a phenomenon in scientific and medical history called "scotoma." Some discoveries are so "premature," he observes, that they cannot be "integrated into contemporary conceptions." Relevant observations "fail . . . to enter the consciousness" of specialists, and "no one seems to read or remember what . . . [the discoverers] have written." "There is a historical or cultural scotoma," Sacks writes, "a 'memory hole,' as Orwell would say."[2] Thus, scotoma "involves more than prematurity, it involves the deletion of what was originally perceived, a loss of knowledge, a loss of insight, a forgetting of insights that once seemed clearly established, a regression to less perceptive explanations. All these not only beset neurology but are surprisingly common in all fields of science. They raise the deepest questions about why such lapses occur. What makes an observation or a new idea acceptable, discussable, memorable? What may prevent it from being so, despite its clear importance and value?"[3]

Sacks's own answers invoke discrete stages of scientific and medical knowledge, isolated acts of genius, and investigators' need to find meaning in their results.

Whatever produces it, scotoma is something like a side effect of long-term scientific and medical progress. If it accounts for the discontinuities in medication-era theorizing, the idea of psychiatric progress is saved. Psychiatry would become indistinguishable from other medical and scientific disciplines that suffer bouts of scotoma as they advance.

Scotoma cannot explain the medication era, however. The changes in psychiatric thought came too rapidly and too often; the forgetting came too quickly and too conveniently. Sacks describes no scientific episodes with zigzags and reversals like those of the medication era. Nor does he suppose that individual investigators could "forget" their *own* insights almost overnight. Yet that happened in psychiatry too.

For example, in 1960 Jonathan Cole cited "the absence of serious concern about adverse effects these drugs may be having upon behavior" as "the most impressive characteristic of the psychiatric drug literature." Yet in 1964, as lead author of the Collaborative Study, Cole deemed side effects "trivial" and ignored the adverse effects of medication on behavior. Scotoma does not explain how Cole forgot "the most impressive" feature of the medication literature in only four years. Again, psychiatrists unable to perceive tardive dyskinesia during the 1960s apparently had no difficulty seeing the same symptoms during the 1950s, when the movements represented desired evidence of a medication-induced, encephalitis-like brain disorder. Scotoma does not account for the disappearance of those movements from psychiatrists' awareness. Or for the near disappearance of the psychomotor indifference syndrome at the same time—the syndrome that gave medications the name "major tranquilizers."

Political, legal, and cultural factors account for such developments, which resist explanation as simple scientific mistakes. Litigation and adverse publicity preceded major changes in thinking about tardive dyskinesia. The Collaborative Study—and the fading of psychomotor indifference—were tied to a new public mental health system. Tardive dyskinesia, the medication side effect that most clearly called lobotomy to mind, became the one that psychiatrists had the hardest time recognizing after lobotomy fell into disrepute.

George Orwell described scotoma-like phenomena in political life and history as "the memory hole." Noting Orwell's phrase, Sacks found it unnecessary to point out that memory holes are associated with repressive political practices, not with science. Yet Orwell depicted the kinds of repeated and convenient changes of direction that marked the neuroleptic era.

This point should not be carried too far. Psychiatric journals remained open to dissenting views; the weight of the evidence eventually overcame 1967-style rejectionism; psychiatrists rediscovered psychomotor indifference; after a time, researchers abandoned the Study vision. Clearly, some basic scientific—or at least open—processes were operating. Yet such processes had always operated in psychiatry to a degree; they represented nothing new. By themselves, they cannot explain the shifts in thinking that marked the medication era—and the concept of scotoma does not help them do so.

Psychiatry needs and claims progress, but the circumstances that give rise to the need—the last professional default—also refute the claims. As a result, psychiatrists are forever invoking revolutions and transformations that supposedly obliterate any continuity with their past. The biological revolution of the 1930s, the medication revolution, Michels' and Marzuk's "profound transformation" in the early 1990s—all supposedly wiped the historical slate clean and produced progress from thin air. Scientists sit on the shoulders of giants; psychiatrists ride these waves of revolution.

Steven Pinker has suggestively linked "the stultification of good science by nervous authorities" with the suppression of good history by "those in power." In both instances, the authorities want "*our version* of the truth, rather than the truth itself, to prevail." Pinker was thinking of political authorities squelching the work of scientists and historians; medication-era psychiatry appears to be a special case. Here, medical authorities prevented their own field from living up to its scientific ideals, and did so in significant part by insisting on a mythical and unreal history.[4]

Psychiatry Without Progress

Many psychiatrists assume that a specific kind of historical integrity—which they call "progress"—is crucial to their standing within medicine and to their own professional integrity. Yet there is more than one kind historical integrity, and more than one relationship between the character of psychiatry and its history. In fact, some psychiatrists have always dissented from standard views.

Specifically, they have dissented from the standard claims about progress. The Collaborative Study observed that many remained unconvinced as late as the 1960s. The Study seemed to equate the lack of a belief in progress with pessimism; and the rejectionists soon equated pessimism with error, although it was almost madness to argue against the existence of tardive dyskinesia on the ground that psychiatry had made progress.

In fact, two research developments in the 1950s suggested a non-progress view. Early in the decade, Milton Greenblatt attempted to revive moral therapy. He regarded the human relationships between patients and hospital staff as the critical treatment element, and essentially called for a return to nineteenth-century methods. It followed that he did not view "progress" as the dominant motif in American psychiatric history. His hopes for improved treatment lay in a better understanding of past techniques—not in the progression of new and better biological therapies.

The second development involved research into the effectiveness of insulin coma therapy as a schizophrenia treatment. Brian Ackner, a British physician, coauthored the leading study in 1957. In Ackner's experiment, some patients received a standard course of insulin coma therapy; others received a course of treatment with a barbiturate that induced deep sleep—a sleep that to all outward appearances looked like an insulin-induced coma. Physicians told all the patients, including those who merely slept, that they had received insulin.

Over follow-up periods lasting up to two years, the insulin and barbiturate groups fared equally well. For example, Ackner reported that 40 percent of patients in each group appeared fully recovered six months after the procedure. He wrote:

> The results . . . do not demonstrate that the coma regime has no
> therapeutic effect. During insulin therapy patients are subjected to
> powerful group influence and receive increased medical and nursing
> care in a special setting. Daily they are exposed as a group to the
> threat of being rendered unconscious. Daily they are brought back to
> consciousness by doctors and nurses on whom they become
> dependent. The new relationships so built up cannot be ignored, for it
> could be that the coma regime is helping to establish that lost
> capacity for relationship with others. But the results suggest that

insulin is not the specific therapeutic agent of the coma regime as has so often been claimed.[5]

This work suggested the same conclusions about psychiatric history that Greenblatt's research did. Insulin coma treatment did not represent therapeutic progress; human relationships, not technological advance, accounted for its success.

Human relationships are not a medium for progress, at least not in any conventional sense. They do not advance as technology does, or change in the way social and economic arrangements do. One can aim to eliminate abuses in human relationships, but thinking of them "progressing" seems wrong—as odd as thinking of a major advance in the quality of human kindness or love.

Ideas like Greenblatt's and Ackner's survived into the medication era. During the 1950s, many psychiatrists thought of medications as devices to improve the quality of life and human relationships in hospitals. In 1961, the Joint Commission on Mental Illness and Health wrote that medication "might be described as moral treatment in pill form," implying both a substantive view and a view of psychiatric history like Greenblatt's.[6]

The Collaborative Study marked a turning point in views of progress and medications alike. Standing alone, however, the Study straddled the divide between progress and nonprogress. Of course, it heralded the "antischizophrenic" effects of medication, which came to be viewed as a revolutionary advance. Yet it also heralded the use of medication because it made possible a change in care arrangements from those based in hospitals to communities. That entailed more dramatic changes than any Greenblatt had contemplated, but it still represented a change in the organization of psychiatric care. Moreover, like Greenblatt, the Study portrayed psychiatrists' attitudes toward treatment—their optimism and pessimism—as a vital consideration. Read in this way, the Study approached Greenblatt's views. It proposed community care, as opposed to Greenblatt's idea of making mental hospitals more like a real community, but the nature of psychiatric history did not appear all that different in the two accounts.

To the extent it did differ from earlier conceptions, the Study's view resembled classical Marxism. In Marxism, technology determined social organization. In the Study, biological treatments made possible a new organization of public mental health. In both instances, technology underlay organization—but organization ultimately mattered.

Psychiatrists' visions did not remain focused on organization for very long. The Study linked medication to a new mental health system because, unlike the older somatic therapies, it could be administered inexpensively and safely outside a hospital. By the late 1960s, the Study vision shifted to antischizophrenic-neurochemical effects and the brain. Deinstitutionalization now seemed possible because medication counteracted disease, not because it lent itself to use outside hospitals. Thus, attention moved away from public health organization, just as it had earlier shifted from therapist-patient interactions. First the mental hospital, then the mental health system, and now the brain became psychiatrists' key concern.

These changes went hand in hand with a linear, technological view of psychiatric progress. Just as computers are superior to typewriters, and cars to animal-drawn carts, medication supposedly marked a signal advance.

Yet there have been dissenters. Most relied on older conceptions of human relationships, like Greenblatt's, and insisted on the possibility of regression, as well as of advance, in the field. Some explicitly portrayed psychiatric history as a series of cycles.

Consider four examples. The first was a letter by Stephen Fleck, a psychiatrist at Yale University, responding to Michels and Marzuk's article in the *New England Journal of Medicine*. Fleck thought Michels and Marzuk's views "should be balanced by pointing out regressive developments in psychiatry during the past two to three decades." Without questioning their "splendid review of progress in neurosciences," he lamented psychiatry's focus on "stringent lists of symptoms" and the idea that "a symptom cluster can be used to indicate specific treatment." While it was true that "certain drugs counteract neurochemical aberrations that are grossly different for different diagnostic groups," psychiatry still had "no drugs such as antibiotics that treat the specific cause" of an illness. Fleck concluded:

> Treating the patient has taken a back seat to treating the symptoms, and this development is particularly retrogressive in psychiatry, which used to be the medical specialty par excellence that dealt with people, their lifestyles, their intimate environments, and their psychological milieus. Addressing problems in these areas, whether or not they arise from the genes, was the earmark of good psychiatry until recently, and there is no indication that this tradition of holistic treatment will again became part of psychiatric education and, hence, of practice.[7]

The second example was a 1978 investigation of psychosurgery by Peter Sterling, a University of Pennsylvania neuroanatomist. Sterling ridiculed psychosurgeons' theories about the brain and found no evidence that their procedures produced any real benefits. Putting psychosurgery into perspective, he described psychiatric history as a series of "cycles" during which "somatic and 'moral' treatment" alternated. Sterling clearly preferred the periods when "successful treatment was almost exclusively psychological, without use of physical restraint or bodily interventions." Regarding medication, he said only that its effects "have not been clearly distinguished from the effects of moral therapy."

The cyclical model clearly included medications, however, and Sterling later testified for the patients in *Rennie* v. *Klein*.[8]

The third example was a 1987 article by W. A. Cramond about the history of insulin coma therapy. Cramond followed Ackner's account and ascribed the procedure's benefits to intense staff attention. Cramond reflected, "As I look with anxiety at my schizophrenic patients coping with the neurological deficits occasioned by neuroleptic drugs, I not infrequently regret the passing of insulin and wish we could use some other process to provide [the old effects]."[9]

Thus, he rejected the premise of progress and regarded human interaction as the key to treatment.

The fourth example is a 1981 article by William T. Carpenter and collaborators. Carpenter was more systematic than Cramond, more progress-oriented than Sterling and more optimistic than Fleck. He claimed that "pharmacologically oriented" researchers had focused on the symptoms of schizophrenia "most responsive to [drug] treatment," paying little attention to systems such as "long-term interpersonal functioning and deficit symptoms" that did not respond well to medication. Emphasizing the "formal correctness of [drug] outcome research"—such things as "controlled study designs and the reliable use of standardized instruments by independent raters"—psychiatrists had slighted "clinical[ly] meaningful" dimensions of outcome. The contemporary "reappraisal" of medication as "the sole and continuous treatment . . . in virtually all patients" rested on concerns about tardive dyskinesia, Carpenter observed, not on these limitations in research methodology.

Carpenter described medications as "the most significant therapeutic innovation of the past 25 years"—a phrase that suggested psychiatric advance, but not necessarily any historic transformation. Clearly, he thought the possibility of regression existed. "Continued failure to appreciate the importance of both methodologic correctness and clinical meaningfulness," Carpenter concluded, "can have serious repercussions as we accept, overgeneralize, and then retreat from therapeutic innovations." He did not identify any past "therapeutic innovations," but lobotomy clearly fit his criteria; lobotomists had failed to "appreciate the importance of both methodologic correctness and clinical meaningfulness," had announced "overgeneralized" conclusions, and had been forced to "retreat."[10]

This article suggested a complex view of history, with superimposed patterns of forward and cyclical movement. Carpenter saw cycles (acceptance, overgeneralization, retreat), but he also saw therapeutic "innovations." He subscribed to neither inevitable psychiatric advance nor inevitable decline. Sterling posited recurrent historical cycles; Carpenter saw methodologically correct and clinically meaningful research as a way to escape them. Nor did he see any conflict between psychiatric innovation and treatment of the whole person; on the contrary, he criticized researchers for ignoring clinically meaningful aspects of patients' lives. Like Michels and Marzuk, he considered research key; yet he worried that research could propel psychiatry into a vortex as well as extricate it from one.

Carpenter's example—and that of the other critics of progress—suggest that the relationship between psychiatrists' substantive and historical views holds even without a belief in progress. These critics of progress had distinctive views. They were sensitive to side effects; concerned about how treatment affected the entire person; cautious in judging benefits; and (with the possible exception of Fleck, who did not address the matter) able to contemplate the possibility of withdrawing medication. If nothing connected substantive and historical ideas, such substantive views would exist as often among the proponents as among the critics of progress. Yet that simply does not happen. The critics demonstrate something else as well: psychiatrists can still dissent, as Crane did, from the cornerstone ideas of their profession.

Causes and Implications

What made psychiatry take the course that it did in the medication era? It may be tempting to think that a single, deep cause produced all of the events—in the way that some psychiatrists supposed a single neurochemical abnormality produced patients' psychiatric problems. In fact, it remains unclear what, if anything, ultimately produced the medication era.

I have argued that often-overlooked considerations played a role. The fate of lobotomy, and psychiatrists' memory of it, was one. Another involved moral, legal, and political problems endemic to psychiatry because of the illnesses it treats, its unique responsibilities for its patients, and the limitations of its available therapies.

One can cite the possible forces behind developments and speculate about how things could have happened differently. For example, clinicians often relied on drug companies for information, researchers depended upon the companies' funding, and medication produced large profits. Perhaps, then, the pharmaceutical industry made things happen. Again, psychiatrists crave recognition for their profession; perhaps that explains their enthusiasms and lapses. Medication makes it easier to manage people; perhaps it is as simple as that.

One can only guess what might have happened in the absence of these factors. If medication was unprofitable but still promised to save public funds and produce the same medical benefits, would the public mental health revolution have taken place as it did? What if medication forestalled psychotic relapse and shortened florid psychotic episodes, but otherwise did not make people more manageable? Suppose psychiatrists felt less defensive about their discipline? Or mental hospitals had been less terrible?

Other questions arise about the influence of political and policy imperatives on psychiatric theory. Suppose psychiatrists felt confident about their autonomy, medical standing, and funding, and none of those things depended on anyone's conclusions about medication. Would Study-era psychiatrists still have exalted the benefits of medication and resisted findings about tardive dyskinesia? One can only speculate, but I believe psychiatrists would have theorized differently, and more accurately, if they had been free from those influences. That conclusion affords little comfort, however, since the same influences persist. In any case, it seems doubtful that giving psychiatrists the necessary assurances would really improve things. Psychiatry had significantly more in the way of such assurances before the medication era began, and the results were often deplorable. More accurate theories hardly compensate for more harmful practices.

A related question exists about clinical practices. If they were working within a different public health system—one that included accessible and decent hospitals and allowed longer hospitalizations—would more psychiatrists withhold medication? George Gardos and Jonathan Cole (in 1980) and George Crane (repeatedly) all answered yes. Conceivably, constant maintenance medication would represent one among many "schools" of schizophrenia treatment, just as an almost dizzying variety of psychiatric approaches to neuroses and other less severe conditions now exists.

Another conclusion, also speculative, involves other branches of medicine. Psychiatry has long had a distinctive type of responsibility for psychotic patients, unlike other physicians' responsibility. In the era of state hospitals, the responsibility was delimited by the hospitals' walls. In the era of deinstitutionalization, the same kind of responsibility is widely assumed to exist, although it is harder to see how psychiatrists can discharge it.

This special responsibility has contributed to the problems of psychiatric theory. Because of it, psychiatrists feel compelled to produce publicly defensible treatment outcomes, whatever the financial or bureaucratic restraints on their practice and however recalcitrant the disease. This need to defend outcomes provided a strong incentive for theories that exaggerated drug benefits and trivialized side effects. Wonderful medicines equaled fulfilled professional responsibilities.

Psychiatry was long unique, but the rest of medicine now may be moving in its direction. The privatized public mental health system is in many ways the first large managed care organization—unless the state mental hospital qualified for that honor first. Meanwhile, outside psychiatry, health maintenance organizations are giving physicians a new, long-term responsibility for patients. They are also forcing physicians to work within constraints and funding limits dictated by large bureaucratic organizations, just as psychiatrists traditionally have. Thus, other physicians are acquiring some of the obligations familiar to psychiatrists of defending outcomes produced by the system and are laboring with some of psychiatrists' burdens as well.

Psychiatrists have long wanted to join the mainstream of medicine. In light of these convergences, that may happen only because the rest of medicine is becoming more like psychiatry.

Notes

Introduction   Medication and Progress

1. See generally Gerald N. Grob, *From Asylum to Community: Mental Health Policy in Modern America* (Princeton, N.J.: Princeton University Press, 1991), 3 and passim. Grob observes that an apparently "stable" consensus about mental health "virtually vanished" in the years between the end of World War II and the beginning of the 1960s.
2. Judith P. Swazey, *Chlorpromazine in Psychiatry* (Cambridge, Mass.: MIT Press, 1974), 14.
3. Robert Plotkin, "Limiting the Therapeutic Orgy: Mental Patients' Right To Refuse Treatment," *Northwestern Law Review* 72 (1977): 461.
4. Stephen Jay Gould, *Time's Arrow, Time's Cycle: Myth and Metaphor in the Discovery of Geological Time* (Cambridge: Harvard University Press, 1987).
5. See, for example, Rael Jean Isaac and Virginia C. Armat, *Madness in the Streets: How Psychiatry and the Law Abandoned the Mentally Ill* (New York: The Free Press, 1990). Isaac and Armat posit "spectacular advances" in psychiatry over the preceding "fifty years" but cite grave problems with deinstitutionalization; they attribute the gap to lawyers and other opponents of psychiatry.
6. An example of this method in political philosophy is Quentin Skinner, *Reason and Rhetoric in the Philosophy of Hobbes* (Cambridge, England: Cambridge University Press, 1996), 7–8.
7. William T. Carpenter, Jr., et al., "Methodologic Standards for Treatment Outcome Research in Schizophrenia," *American Journal of Psychiatry* 138 (1981): 465.

Chapter 1   From Chlorpromazine to the NIMH Collaborative Study

1. See, for example, Albert Q. Maisel, "Bedlam 1946," *Life*, 6 May 1946, 102–118; Gerald Grob, *From Asylum to Community: Mental Health Policy in Modern America* (Princeton, N.J.: Princeton University Press, 1991), 75.
2. On the periodic mental hospital scandals reported by the press after World War II, see Grob, *From Asylum to Community*, 71–77.
3. On the notions of preventing mental illness and expanding psychiatric activities in the community, see ibid., especially 5–96.
4. See, for example, Milton Greenblatt, Richard H. York, and Esther Lucille Brown (in collaboration with Robert W. Hide), *From Custodial to Therapeutic Patient Care in Mental Hospitals* (New York: Russell Sage Foundation, 1955).
5. Ibid., 17, 167–173.
6. Ibid., 100–101.
7. Judith P. Swazey, *Chlorpromazine in Psychiatry* (Cambridge, Mass.: MIT Press, 1974), 118–184.

8. Senate Committee on the Judiciary, *Constitutional Rights of the Mentally Ill, Hearings Before the Subcommittee on Constitutional Rights*, 87th Cong., 1st sess., 1961, 37 (testimony of Dr. Winfred Overholser); Overholser had made similar points much earlier, at a 1955 symposium, *Chlorpromazine and Mental Health: Proceedings of the Symposium Held Under the Auspices of Smith, Kline & French Laboratories, June 6, 1955* (Philadelphia: Lea & Febiger,1955), 184. The "insulin of the nervous system" remark was Sigwald's; it is quoted in Lothar B. Kalinowsky and Paul H. Hoch (in collaboration with Brenda Grant), *Somatic Treatments in Psychiatry: Pharmacotherapy; Convulsive, Insulin, Surgical, Other Methods*, 2d ed. (New York: Grune and Stratton), 40. For similar characterizations of chlorpromazine, see, for example, Fritz A. Freyhan, "Immediate and Long-Range Effects of Chlorpromazine on the Mental Hospital," in *Chlorpromazine and Mental Health*, 82–83. Peter R. Breggin, *Toxic Psychiatry* (New York: St. Martin's Press, 1991), 55, surveys reports from the mid-1950s that describe the effects of medication in lobotomy-like terms.
9. Sidney Malitz, Paul H. Hoch, and Stanley Lesse, "A Two-Year Evaluation of Chlorpromazine in Clinical Research and Practice," *American Journal of Psychiatry* 113 (1956): 540, 543; Kalinowsky and Hoch, *Somatic Treatments*, 40–41. Laborit, a French pioneer who explored the use of chlorpromazine as an adjunct to surgical anesthesia, later told Swazey that the drug "made it possible to disconnect certain brain functions," with the result that "[t]he surgical patient, although conscious, felt no pain, no anxiety, and often did not remember his operation." Swazey, *Chlorpromazine in Psychiatry*, 79. The references to "disconnect[ion]" and alleviation of "anxiety" obviously suggested lobotomy.
10. Peter Sterling, "Ethics and Effectiveness of Psychosurgery," in *Controversy in Psychiatry*, ed. John P. Brady and Keith H. Brodie (Philadelphia: Saunders, 1978), 126, 135. Swazey reached similar conclusions, although she assigned more of a role to medication in the later 1950s. Swazey, *Chlorpromazine in Psychiatry*, 14. Somewhat similarly, Valenstein cited medical opposition that predated chlorpromazine and also cited the fact that medications "provided what the opposition to psychosurgery had always lacked: a viable alternative for treating the major psychoses." Elliot S. Valenstein, *Great and Desperate Cures: The Rise and Decline of Psychosurgery and Other Radical Treatments for Mental Illness* (New York: Basic Books, 1986), 254.
11. Pierre Deniker, "Experimental Neurological Syndromes and the New Drug Therapies in Psychiatry," *Comprehensive Psychiatry* 1 (1961): 92.
12. Ibid.
13. Ibid., 100. Regarding malariotherapy, see Henry J. Heimlich, letter, "Try Malariotherapy," *New York Times*, 21 February 1995, A14, national edition; for other examples of such thinking, see, for example,. Kalinowsky and Hoch, *Somatic Treatments*, 335–336, and Valenstein, *Great and Desperate Cures*, 50.
14. Pierre Deniker, "Introduction of Neuroleptic Chemotherapy Into Psychiatry," in *Discoveries in Biological Psychiatry*, ed. Frank J. Ayd, Jr., and Barry Blackwell (Philadelphia: Lippincott, 1970), 155, 161; Swazey, *Chlorpromazine in Psychiatry*, 12.
15. Deniker, "Experimental Neurological Syndromes," 99–100; Herman C. B. Denber and John H. Travis, "Chlorpromazine in the Treatment of Mental Illness V: Administrative Problems," *Psychiatric Quarterly* 32 (1958): 538, 540; Jesse L. Bennett and Kenneth A. Kooi, "Five Phenothiazine Derivatives: Evaluation and Toxicity Studies," *Archives General Psychiatry* 4 (1961): 413, 417–418; Swazey, *Chlorpromazine in Psychiatry*, 51 and 56 (discussion of remarks of George W. Brooks and Frank J. Ayd); John Denham and David Carrick, "Therapeutic Importance of Extra-Pyramidal Phenomena Evoked by a New Phenothiazine," *American Journal of Psychiatry* 116 (1961): 927–928. A frequently cited source is Hans J. Haase, "Extrapyramidal Modifications of Fine Movements—A 'Conditio Sine Qua Non' of the Fundamental Therapeutic Action of Neuroleptic Drugs," *Revue Canadienne de Biologie* 20 (1961): 425.

16. N. William Winkelman, "An Appraisal of Chlorpromazine: General Principles for Administration of Chlorpromazine, Based on Experience with 1,090 Patients," *American Journal of Psychiatry* 114 (1957): 961, 967–968; Pierre Deniker, "Psychophysiologic Aspects of the New Chemotherapeutic Drugs in Psychiatry," *Journal of Nervous and Mental Disease* 124 (1956): 371, 373; Malitz, Hoch, and Lesse, "Two-Year Evaluation," 54. In "Experimental Neurological Syndromes," 93, Deniker argued that "the characteristic neurological changes" were the "most important" defining characteristics of neuroleptic drugs.

17. G. J. Sarwer-Foner and W. Ogle, "Psychosis and Enhanced Anxiety Produced by Reserpine and Chlorpromazine," *Canadian Medical Association Journal* 74 (1956): 526, 530; L. Colonna, "Antideficit Properties of Neuroleptics," *Acta Psychiatrica Scandinavica* 89, Supplementum 77 (1994): 380.

18. The characterization of lobotomy appears in Kalinowsky and Hoch, *Somatic Treatments*, 346.

19. *Chlorpromazine and Mental Health,* discussion of remarks of Benjamin Pollack, 40; Denber and Travis, "Chlorpromazine V: Administrative Problems," 542; P. E. Feldman et al., "A Controlled, Blind Study of Effects of Thorazine on Psychotic Behavior," *Bulletin of the Menninger Clinic* 20 (1956): 25, 33; Paul H. Hoch, "The Effect of Chlorpromazine on Moderate and Mild Mental and Emotional Disturbances," in *Chlorpromazine and Mental Health*, 98; *New York Times*, 4 August 1955, 27 (quoting the New Jersey mental hospital official); Jean Delay and Pierre Deniker, "Neuroleptic Effects of Chlorpromazine in Therapeutics of Neuropsychiatry," *International Record of Medicine & General Practice Clinics* (1956): 318, 321. The views of the New Jersey official were controversial; thus, Harry Freeman, "A Critique of the Tranquilizing Drugs, Chlorpromazine and Reserpine, in Neuropsychiatry," *New England Journal of Medicine* 255 (1956): 877, 882, cautioned against "drug-shock combinations" because of the possibility of "serious complications and deaths."

20. *New York Times*, 1 April 1955; Donald Blair and Desmond M. Brady, "Recent Advances in the Treatment of Schizophrenia: Group Training and the Tranquilizers," *Journal of Mental Science* (London) 104 (1958): 625, 661.

21. Julian Abrams, "Chlorpromazine in Treatment of Chronic Schizophrenia," *Diseases of the Nervous System* 19 (1958): 20; *New York Times*, 17 January 1956 (continuation of page 1 story); Delay and Deniker, "Neuroleptic Effects," 320–322. For a general overview of the idea that chlorpromazine produced "more than 'mere pacification' of a schizophrenic's behavior—that it could effect more fundamental and long-term changes in his thought processes and behavior," see Swazey, *Chlorpromazine in Psychiatry*, 214.

22. *Chlorpromazine and Mental Health* ,48 and 94 (Bennett and Donnelly's comments); Herman C. B. Denber and Etta G. Bird, "Chlorpromazine IV: Final Results With Analysis of Data on 1,523 Patients," *American Journal of Psychiatry* 113 (1957): 972, 973; Garfield Tourney, "A History of Therapeutic Fashions in Psychiatry, 1800–1966," *American Journal of Psychiatry* 124 (1967): 92, 99; see also Sarwer-Foner and Ogle, "Psychosis and Enhanced Anxiety," 530, which denied that the new medications were "psychiatric 'specific agents' " and attributed the drugs' effects to a capacity to "chemically 'hold down' " patients.

23. Feldman, "A Controlled, Blind Study," 33. Feldman considered chlorpromazine "a useful addition to the armamentarium of the psychiatrist."

24. Freyhan, "Immediate and Long-Range Effects," 73; J. Lomas et al., "Complications of Chlorpromazine Therapy in 800 Mental-Hospital Patients," *Lancet* 1 (1955): 1144; see also Kalinowsky and Hoch, *Somatic Treatments*, 31, where they draw a similar distinction. Lomas's concept of "idiosyncrasy" would become important in later debates about tardive dyskinesia.

25. Robert A. Hall et al., "Neurotoxic Reactions Resulting From Chlorpromazine Administration," _Journal of the American Medical Association_ 161 (1956): 214, 218.
26. Deniker, "Experimental Neurological Syndromes," 94 (italics in original omitted).
27. George Paulson, "Phenothiazine Toxicity, Extrapyramidal Seizures, and Oculogyric Crises," _Journal of Mental Science_ (London) 105 (1959):7 98, 800.
28. Hall et al., "Neurotoxic Reactions," 216, 217. Interestingly, Hall either did not report or find akathisia, the restless movement syndrome that many patients deem the worst side effect.
29. Surveying the literature, Druckman's 1962 article about tardive dyskinesia cited two French-language studies that had reached conclusions like Hall's in 1956 and 1959. Ralph Druckman et al., "Chronic Involuntary Movements Induced by Phenothiazines," _Journal of Nervous and Mental Disease_ 135 1962): 69, 74. A typical statement of the prevailing view appears in Winkelman, "Appraisal," 966, which reported (in May 1957) that "nearly all . . . [drug side effects] are mild and disappear spontaneously, after modification of dosage, or after the rarely needed cessation of treatment."
30. Report of C. Quarti, as reported and translated in Swazey, _Chlorpromazine in Psychiatry_, 115–116.
31. Malitz, Hoch, and Lesse, "Two-Year Evaluation," 543; Vernon Kinross-Wright, "The Intensive Chlorpromazine Treatment of Schizophrenia," in _Pharmacologic Products Recently Introduced in the Treatment of Psychiatric Disorders: Papers Presented at a Regional Research Conference Held Under the Joint Auspices of the American Psychiatric Association and the University of Texas Medical Branch, Galveston, Texas, February 18–19, 1955_, ed. William L. Lhamon (Washington, D.C.: American Psychiatric Association, 1955), 53, 59.
32. Hoch, "Effect of Chlorpromazine," 109. This study was not especially sensitive to side effects; for example, it reported only two cases of drug-induced parkinsonism, almost certainly missing many cases. Only about half of Hoch's patients, or 67 out of 125, carried a schizophrenic diagnosis; of these, 30 had "the pseudoneurotic form of schizophrenia" and probably would not receive a schizophrenic diagnosis today.
33. Ibid., 110.
34. Winkelman, "Appraisal," 965. Hoch did note, however, that the afflicted patients were often "anxious" people.
35. In other respects, Winkelman's analysis was vague or otherwise flawed. Winkelman reported that some patients failed to become distressed when given disguised doses of chlorpromazine, but he did not specify how many, although the article supplied precise figures on a myriad of other questions. He observed that other medications produced similar distress, but he did not indicate whether they belonged to the same drug category. If they did, they should have produced similar reactions. Nor did he explain how psychiatrists elicited patients' feelings. Conceivably, if a patient failed to refuse the medications a second time—or if nursing staff failed to acknowledge the patient's refusal—Winkelman counted that as evidence of good response. He also seemed to think that if "smaller . . . dosage" produced less or no distress, that somehow demonstrated high doses did not cause distress either. The more natural inference is that distress, like other reactions, is dose related.
36. Denber and Travis, "Chlorpromazine V: Administrative Problems," 540; see _Chlorpromazine and Mental Health_, 60, for similar comments by Denber.
37. Nathan S. Kline et al., "Management of the Side Effects of Reserpine and Combined Reserpine-Chlorpromazine Treatment," _Diseases of the Nervous System_ 17 (1956): 352.
38. Douglas Goldman, "The Significance and Management of the Complications Resulting From New Drugs," _American Psychiatric Association, Psychiatric Research Re-_

port 4 (1956): 79, 88 (emphasis added). Kline had also observed that it would be "ideal" if another drug, without the side effects, became available.

39. Jonathan O. Cole, "Behavioral Toxicity," in *Drugs and Behavior,* ed. Leonard Uhr and James G. Miller (New York: John Wiley, 1960).

40. Sterling, "Ethics and Effectiveness of Psychosurgery," 150–156; quote on 151.

Chapter 2   *Public Health and Other Implications*

1. The comment about change on the wards was Charles D. Yohe's, at the 1955 symposium. *Chlorpromazine and Mental Health: Proceedings of the Symposium Held Under the Auspices of Smith, Kline & French Laboratories, June 6, 1955* (Philadelphia: Lea & Febiger, 1955), 96. Swazey's observation appears in Judith P. Swazey, *Chlorpromazine in Psychiatry* (Cambridge, Mass.: MIT Press, 1974), 216.

2. Joint Commission on Mental Illness and Health, *Action for Mental Health* (New York: Arno Press, 1961), 39; *Chlorpromazine and Mental Health,* 10–11 and 84. See generally Swazey, *Chlorpromazine in Psychiatry,* 237–245. For an account of the Joint Commission's origins and work, see Gerald N. Grob, *From Asylum to Community: Mental Health Policy in Modern American* (Princeton, N.J.: Princeton University Press, 1991), 181–227.

3. *Chlorpromazine and Mental Health,* 89; ibid., 88.

4. Daniel P. Moynihan, letter, *New York Times,* 22 May 1980, national edition. Moynihan assigned an important role to Kline and to reserpine, but the latter became associated with reports about depression in patients and quickly fell into disuse. Swazey describes each state's decision about chlorpromazine purchasing as of 1956. *Chlorpromazine in Psychiatry,* 210–213, table 5.

5. For examples of such views, see Swazey, *Chlorpromazine in Psychiatry,* 221–222 and 229–231.

6. The 60 percent figure comes from Henry Brill and Robert E. Patton, "Clinical Statistical Analysis of Population Changes in New York State Mental Hospitals Since the Introduction of Psychotropic Drugs," *American Journal of Psychiatry* 119 (1962): 20, 32–33; quoted in Swazey, *Chlorpromazine in Psychiatry,* 244. Other influential Brill and Patton studies included their "Analysis of the 1955–56 Population Fall in New York State Mental Hospitals during the First Year of Large-Scale use of Tranquilizing Drugs," *American Journal of Psychiatry* 114 (1957): 509, and "Analysis of Population Reduction in New York State Mental Hospitals During the First Four Years of Large Scale Therapy with Psychotropic Drugs," *American Journal of Psychiatry,* 116 (1959): 495. For a skeptical review of their conclusions, see Andrew T. Scull, *Decarceration, Community Treatment and the Deviant: A Radical View* (Englewood Cliffs, N.J.: Prentice-Hall, 1977), 83–85.

7. Moynihan, letter.

8. Scull, *Decarceration,* 68, table 4-2, adopted from NIMH, *Trends in Resident Patients, State and County Mental Hospitals* 1950–1968, Rockville, Maryland and NIMH, *Statistical Note* no. 114.

9. Swazey, *Chlorpromazine in Psychiatry,* 245, quoting Brill's remarks; Morton Birnbaum, "The Right to Treatment," *American Bar Association Journal* 46 (1960): 499; Joint Commission, *Action for Mental Health.*

10. See Gerald N. Grob, *The Mad Among Us: A History of the Care of America's Mentally Ill* (New York: The Free Press, 1994), 249–311; Phil Brown, *The Transfer of Care: Psychiatric Deinstitutionalization and Its Aftermath* (London : Routledge and Kegan Paul, 1985).

11. Erving Goffman, *Asylums: Essays on the Social Situation of Mental Patients and Other Inmates* (Garden City, N.Y.: Anchor Books, 1961).

12. David Rosenhan, "On Being Sane in Insane Places," *Science* 179 (1973): 250.

Chapter 3   A New Vision of Medication

1. The National Institute of Mental Health Psychopharmacology Service Center Collaborative Study Group, "Phenothiazine Treatment in Acute Schizophrenia," *Archives of General Psychiatry* 10 (1964): 246. Hereafter cited as Collaborative Study. Regarding the expectations about the effectiveness of medication, see Jesse F. Casey et al., "Drug Therapy in Schizophrenia: A Controlled Study of the Relative Effectiveness of Chlorpromazine, Promazine, Phenobarbital, and Placebo," *Archives of General Psychiatry* 2 (1960): 210, 218.
2. Gerald N. Grob, *From Asylum to Community: Mental Health Policy in Modern America* (Princeton, N.J.: Princeton University Press, 1991), 152–153.
3. Casey, "Drug Therapy"; Collaborative Study.
4. Casey, "Drug Therapy," 210–211. In addition to chlorpromazine and the placebo, the study examined promazine (another tranquilizing drug) and phenobarbital.
5. Ibid., 215, 218.
6. Ibid., 214, 216, 218, 219.
7. Ibid., 213, 219. These figures refer to patients who received chlorpromazine during the initial twelve-week period.
8. Ibid., 217.
9. Ibid., 210, 217.
10. Ibid., 213.
11. Ibid., 217–218.
12. Jesse F. Casey et al., "Treatment of Schizophrenic Reactions with Phenothiazine Derivatives," *American Journal of Psychiatry* 117 (1960): 97.
13. In an apparent lapse, the report once used the term "tranquilizer" to describe subjects' past treatment. Ibid., 98.
14. Ibid., 102–103.
15. Ibid., 103–104.
16. Ibid., 104.
17. Collaborative Study, 246, 247, and 249.
18. Grob, *From Asylum to Community*, 154.
19. For an example of the Study's continuing authority on questions about effectiveness, see American Psychiatric Association, *Tardive Dyskinesia: A Task Force Report of the American Psychiatric Association* (Washington D.C.: American Psychiatric Association Press, 1992), 122. Hereafter cited as 1992 Report.
20. Collaborative Study, 252–253.
21. On the lack of "[s]ystematic controlled data" about the long-term effects of medication see John M. Kane, "Schizophrenia: Somatic Treatment" in *Comprehensive Textbook of Psychiatry*, 5th ed., ed. Harold I. Kaplan and Benjamin J. Sadock (Baltimore: Williams and Wilkins, 1989), 777, 789.
22. Collaborative Study, 255.
23. Ibid., 258.
24. The checklists did have an entry for "Tremor of hands, arm, face." Ibid., 256 The phrase "tremor of the face" is unusual (at least I am not familiar with it). Possibly, it encompassed ticlike or dyskinetic facial movements—but, if it did, it rendered them indistinguishable from common manifestations of drug-induced parkinsonism. Writing in the same year that the Study appeared, Leo Hollister described facial dyskinesias as "rather unmistakable" and estimated their prevalence at 2 or 3 percent; he also noted early reports that dyskinesias persisted. Leo E. Hollister, "Complications from Therapeutic Drugs," *Clinical Pharmacology and Therapeutics* 5 (1964): 322, 323, 324.
25. George E. Crane, "Tardive Dyskinesia in Schizophrenic Patients Treated with Psychotropic Drugs," *Aggressologie* 9 (1967): 209, 210.

26. George E. Crane, "Risks of Long-Term Therapy with Neuroleptic Drugs" in *Antipsychotic Drugs: Psychopharmacodynamics and Pharmacokinetics*, ed. Gören Sedval, Börje Uvnas, and Yngve Zotterman (Oxford: Pergamon Press, 1976), 411, 418.
27. Jonathan O. Cole, "Behavioral Toxicity," in *Drugs and Behavior*, ed. Leonard Uhr and James G. Miller (New York: John Wiley, 1960), 168.
28. Ibid., 168–172
29. Tadashi Nishikawa et al., "Distinguishing Acute and Tardive Akathisia by Monitoring Microvibration: A Pilot Study," *Japanese Journal of Psychiatry* 46 (1992): 665; W. Wolfgang Fleischhacker, "The Pharmacological Treatment of Neuroleptic-Induced Akathisia," *Journal of Clinical Psychiatry* 10(1990):12. Psychiatrists continue to debate the relationship between the subjective desire to move and the actual restless movements; one sometimes occurs without the other.
30. Collaborative Study, 256, table 8. I have rounded the percentages to the nearest whole number. Modern estimates appear in Joseph F. Lipinski, Jr., et al., "Fluoxetine-Induced Akathisia: Clinical and Theoretical Implications," *Journal of Clinical Psychiatry* 50 (1989): 9 (citing a figure of 71 percent); Perminder Sachdev and Kityun Chee, "Pharmacological Characterization of Tardive Akathisia," *Biological Psychiatry* 28 (1990): 809 ("up to 40%"); Thomas R. E. Barnes, "Akathisia Variants and Tardive Dyskinesia," *Archives of General Psychiatry* 42 (1985): 874 (20 percent, as a widely accepted estimate). These figures include all cases; the Study tables reported only those considered "moderately severe" or worse.
31. Cole, "Behavioral Toxicity," 166, 172.
32. Collaborative Study, 257.
33. Solomon C. Goldberg, Gerald L. Klerman, and Jonathan O. Cole, "Changes in Schizophrenic Psychopathology and Ward Behavior as a Function of Phenothiazine Treatment," *British Journal of Psychiatry* 111 (1965): 120, 129–130.
34. Lester Grinspoon et al., "Psychotherapy and Pharmacotherapy in Chronic Schizophrenia," *American Journal of Psychiatry* 124 (1968): 1645, 1651. Grinspoon and his coauthors, Jack R. Ewalt and Richard Shader, were associated with Harvard; Ewalt went on to serve as President of the American Psychiatric Association.
35. Arthur Rifkin et al., "Akinesia: A Poorly Recognized Drug-Induced Extrapyramidal Behavioral Disorder," *Archives of General Psychiatry* 32 (1975): 672.
36. For a related point, see George E. Crane, "Two Decades of Psychopharmacology and Community Mental Health: Old and New Problems of the Schizophrenic Patient," *Transactions of the New York Academy of Sciences*, 2d ser., 36 (1975): 644, 648. Crane observed that standard rating scales "measure easily observable but probably peripheral manifestations" of the disease and that "what is essential" to the disease "cannot be conceptualized, let along [sic] measured, by means of standard rating instruments."
37. Collaborative Study, 253.
38. Ibid., 253 and figure 3.
39. Kinross-Wright, "Intensive Chlorpromazine Treatment," 61. Kinross-Wright reported the data in text, not tabular form.
40. Ibid., 59–60.
41. Goldberg et al., "Changes in Schizophrenic Psychopathology," 130.
42. Ibid., 131.
43. Judith P. Swazey, *Chlorpromazine in Psychiatry* (Cambridge, Mass.: MIT Press, 1974), 16.
44. Peter Breggin traces the idea of "highly specific" actions to the work of Gerald Klerman, who became director of the National Institute of Mental Health. Peter R. Breggin, *Toxic Psychiatry* (New York: St. Martin's Press, 1991), 60. Interestingly, Klerman had coauthored the 1965 article about the supposed effects of medication on "fundamental symptoms."

45. 1992 Report, 183, 184.
46. Kenneth L. Davis et al., "Dopamine in Schizophrenia: A Review and Reconceptualization," *American Journal of Psychiatry* 148 (1991): 1474.
47 Collaborative Study, 256.
48 Ibid., 257.
49. Ibid., 259.
50. Ibid.
51. Ibid. On the relationship between the report of the Joint Commission and President Kennedy's message, see Grob, *From Asylum to Community*, esp. 224–227. Grob notes that President Kennedy's proposal departed from the Joint Commission's report because, in the words of Kennedy's staff, there would be "a major effort to eliminate the State mental institution as it now exists in a generation, in favor of establishing comprehensive community-centered mental health programs." Ibid., 224.
52. Collaborative Study, 259.
53. Ibid.
54. See Elliot S. Valenstein, *Great and Desperate Cures: The Rise and Decline of Psychosurgery and Other Radical Treatments for Mental Illness* (New York: Basic Books, 1986).

Chapter 4 Tardive Dyskinesia and George Crane: 1967

1. For discussion of the early accounts, see George E. Crane, "Tardive Dyskinesia in Patients Treated with Major Neuroleptics: A Review of the Literature," *American Journal of Psychiatry* 124 (February Supplement 1968): 40.
2. William E. Fann, John M. Davis, and David S. Janowsky, "The Prevalence of Tardive Dyskinesias in Mental Hospital Patients," *Diseases of the Nervous System* 33 (1972): 182.
3. "Irreversible Side Effects of Phenothiazines," Editorial, *Journal of the American Medical Association* 191 (1965): 333. The British study was Richard Hunter et al., "An Apparently Irreversible Syndrome of Abnormal Movements Following Phenothiazine Medication," *Proceedings of the Royal Society of Medicine* 57 (1964): 758.
4. "Irreversible Side Effects," at 334; Robert A. Hall et al., "Neurotoxic Reactions Resulting From Chlorpromazine Administration," *Journal of the American Medical Association* 161 (1956).
5. George E. Crane and George Paulson, "Involuntary Movements in a Sample of Chronic Mental Patients and Their Relation to the Treatment with Neuroleptics," *International Journal of Neuropsychiatry* 3 (1968): 286. Frank J. Ayd reported on the January, 1966 conference in "Persistent Dyskinesia—A Further Report," *International Drug Therapy Newsletter*, (May 1967).
6. Crane, "Tardive Dyskinesia: A Review of the Literature," 40, 41, 47.
7. Ibid., 40, 46. For a reports of akathisia persisting in tandem with dyskinesias, see Hunter et al., "Irreversible Syndrome," 760, 759; Walter Kruse, "Persistent Muscular Restlessness After Phenothiazine Treatment: Report of 3 Cases," *American Journal of Psychiatry* 117 (1960): 152, 153; and K. Ekbom, "Oral Dyskinesia Associated with Phenothiazine Therapy," *Psychiatrical, Neturologia, Neurochirurgia* 69 (1966): 155.
8. Crane, "Tardive Dyskinesia: A Review of the Literature," 45, 46.
9. Ibid., 40 (Crane's translation from J. Sigwald et al., "Quatre cas de dyskinesie faciobucco-linguo-masticatrice a evolution prolongée secondaire a un traitement par les neuroleptiiques," *Rev. Neurol.* (1959) 751–755).
10. Crane, "Tardive Dyskinesia: A Review of the Literature," 41 (internal citations omitted).
11. George E. Crane, "Tardive Dyskinesia in Schizophrenic Patients Treated with Psychotropic Drugs," *Aggressologie* 9 (1967): 209, 212, 216. Later in the paper, he

hedged about causation, saying that the data "lend some tentative support to the hypothesis that dyskinetic phenomena are produced by neuroleptics." He also downplayed the finding that 4 percent of patients had developed tardive dyskinesia over a six-month period; later research, however, has confirmed such a result.

12. Ibid., 210, 213.
13. Ibid., 216.
14. Ibid., 217.
15. Ibid.; Nathan S. Kline, "On the Rarity of 'Irreversible' Oral Dyskinesias Following Phenothiazines," *American Journal of Psychiatry* 124 (February Supplement 1968): 48, 51.
16. Crane, "Tardive Dyskinesia in Schizophrenic Patients," 217–218.
17. Ibid., 218.
18. Ibid.
19. Ibid. It remains unclear why Denber thought Crane questioned his own data. Denber referred to a slide presentation that gave "a figure of 33 [percent] on a high dose and 24 on the placebo." Denber may have been suggesting that, if placebo patients had a high incidence of tardive dyskinesia, medication could not represent the cause. Crane's paper, however, discussed a group of placebo patients who "had been on neuroleptics before and/or after assignment to the experimental regime." Ibid., 215. Thus, if tardive dyskinesia constituted a persistent side effect of medication , it should have appeared in the placebo group.
20. Ibid., 218. Denber's phrasing was ambiguous. Did dyskinesias appear only "after" medication began, or also "after" medication stopped? In the later case, the dyskinesia would qualify as a persistent side effect.
21. Ibid. Hunter had already called the distinction between tardive dyskinesia and schizophrenic symptoms "obvious," Hunter et al., "Irreversible Syndrome," 762; Faurbye observed that tardive dyskinesia could be distinguished from "mannerisms and grimaces" because of its distinctive "rhythmic character," although he conceded that confusion could occur in some instances. A. Faurbye et al., "Neurological Symptoms in Pharmacotherapy of Psychosis," *Acta Psychiatrica Scandinavica*. 40 (1964): 10, 13 A 1980 Task Force of the American Psychiatric Association would also agree with Crane, noting that "the movements of tardive dyskinesia are much less voluntary and purposeful . . . than the stereotyped mannerisms and posturing that may occur spontaneously in schizophrenia." *Tardive Dyskinesia: Report of the American Psychiatric Association Task Force on Late Neurological Effects of Antipsychotic Drugs* (Washington, D.C.: American Psychiatric Association, 1980), 17. Hereafter cited as 1980 Report.
22. Kline's lack of attention to Crane's finding about persistence contrasts with his stance at a 1968 NIMH workshop. There, Crane and two other physicians reported on drug-induced dyskinetic movements in monkeys. These movements closely resembled tardive dyskinesia but disappeared when drugs were discontinued. "Are there residual symptoms 6 months or so after monkeys have been removed from medication?" Kline asked during a discussion period. He added, "This is crucial to my mind." By contrast, he showed little interest in 1968 when Crane reported persistence in most human patients; the point apparently did not seem "crucial" to him then. George E. Crane and Russell Gardner, Jr., eds., *Psychotropic Drugs and Dysfunctions of the Basal Ganglia: A Multidisciplinary Workshop*, proceedings of a workshop held in Bethesda, Maryland, October 31–November 2, 1968 (Chevy Chase, Md: U.S. N.I.M.H., 1969). Workshop Series of Pharmacology Section, National Institute of Mental Health, no. 3, Public Health Service publication no. 1938 (1969).
23. Hunter, "Irreversible Syndrome," 761.
24. Ibid.
25. William R. Schmidt and Leonard W. Jarcho, "Persistent Dyskinesias Following

Phenothiazine Therapy," *Archives of Neurology* 14 (1966): 369, 373; Crane and Paulson, "Involuntary Movements," 290; see also H. Edwards, "The Significance of Brain Damage in Persistent Oral Dyskinesia," *British Journal of Psychiatry* 116 (1970): 271, 275; Crane and Gardner, eds., *Basal Ganglia Workshop*. The "poisoning" observation appears in Richard Hunter et al., "A Syndrome of Abnormal Movements and Dementia in Leucotomized Patients Treated With Phenothiazines," *Journal of Neurology, Neurosurgery, and Psychiatry* 27 (1964): 219, 222; Hunter cites others who held the same view.

26. Leo E. Hollister, "Complications from Psychotherapeutic Drugs," *Clinical Pharmacology and Therapeutics* (1964): 322, 324.

27. Leo E. Hollister, "Complications from the Use of Tranquilizing Drugs," *New England Journal of Medicine* 257 (1957): 170, 176.

28. Herman C. B. Denber and John H. Travis, "Chlorpromazine in the Treatment of Mental Illness V: Administrative Problems," *Psychiatric Quarterly* 32 (1958): 540.

29. Nathan S. Kline et al., "Management of the Side Effects of Reserpine and Combined Reserpine-Chlorpromazine Treatment," *Diseases of the Nervous System* 17 (1956): 352.

30. Schmidt and Jarcho, "Persistent Dyskinesias," 373.

31. Crane, "Tardive Dyskinesia in Schizophrenic Patients," 210, 215–216.

32. Ibid., 216

33. Hunter et al., "Irreversible Syndrome," 760, 762; see also Ralph Druckman et al., "Chronic Involuntary Movements Induced by Phenothiazines," *Journal of Nervous and Mental Disease* 135 1962): 68, 76.

34. Crane and Gardner, eds., *Basal Ganglia Workshop*, 178.

35. Henry L. Lennard and Arnold Bernstein, "Perspectives on the New Psychoactive Drug Technology," in *Social Aspects of the Medical Use of Psychotropic Drugs*, ed. Ruth Cooperstock (Toronto: Addiction Research Foundation 1974), 149, 161; Phil Brown and Steven C. Funk, "Tardive Dyskinesia: Barriers to the Professional Recognition of an Iatrogenic Disease," *Journal of Health and Social Behavior* 27 (1986): 116. Brown and Funk describe Crane as a professional "maverick." See also Fann et al., "Prevalence of Tardive Dyskinesias," 182; Fann observed that "[m]ost of the literature supporting . . . [tardive dyskinesia's] existence comes from European studies" but that "these data from Europe are corroborated by well controlled studies of Crane in American hospitals."

Chapter 5   *Tardive Dyskinesia: 1967–1976*

1. Crane's statement appears in the transcript of his testimony in the *Rennie v. Klein* lawsuit; it is quoted in Sheldon Gelman, "Mental Hospital Drugs, Professionalism, and the Constitution," *Georgetown Law Journal* 72 (1984): 1725, 1754. For similar observations see George E. Crane, "Clinical Psychopharmacology in Its 20th Year," *Science* 181 (1973): 124; Phil Brown and Steven C. Funk, "Tardive Dyskinesia: Barriers to the Professional Recognition of an Iatrogenic Disease," *Journal of Health and Social Behavior* 27 (1986): 118–121; and Henry L. Lennard and Arnold Bernstein, "Perspectives on the New Psychoactive Drug Technology," in *Social Aspects of the Medical Use of Psychotropic Drugs*, ed. Ruth Cooperstock (Toronto: Addiction Research Foundation, 1974), 162.

2. Quoted in Gelman, "Mental Hospital Drugs and the Constitution," 1754.

3. William E. Fann, John M. Davis, and Davis S. Janowsky, "The Prevalence of Tardive Dyskinesias in Mental Hospital Patients," *Diseases of the Nervous System* 33 (1972): 182. The six reports are identified in Dilip V. Jeste and Richard Jed Wyatt, "Changing Epidemiology of Tardive Dyskinesia: An Overview," *American Journal of Psychiatry* 138 (1981): 297, 300, table 1. Of the six, two were by American psychiatrists.

4. George E. Crane, "High Doses of Trifluperazine and Tardive Dyskinesia," *Archives of Neurology* 22 (1970): 176; George E. Crane, "Persistent Dyskinesia," *British Journal of Psychiatry* 122 (1973): 395.

5. George E. Crane, "Pseudoparkinsonism and Tardive Dyskinesia," *Archives of Neurology* 27 (1972): 426; Crane, "High Doses," 176; Crane, "Persistent Dyskinesia," 398–401.

6. Criticisms of Crane and the idea that medication caused tardive dyskinesia appeared in John Curran, "Tardive Dyskinesia: Side Effect or Not?" *American Journal of Psychiatry* 130 (1973): 405, and Ibrahim S. Turek, "Drug Induced Dyskinesia: Reality or Myth?" *Diseases of the Nervous System* 36 (1975): 397.

7. Although the term "spontaneous dyskinesia" did not become common until later, Degkwitz had used it at the 1968 conference. George E. Crane and Russell Gardner, Jr., eds., *Psychotropic Drugs and Dysfunctions of the Basal Ganglia: A Multidisciplinary Workshop*, proceedings of a workshop held in Bethesda, Maryland, October 31–November 2, 1968 (Chevy Chase, Md: U.S. N.I.M.H., 1969). Workshop Series of Pharmacology Section, National Institute of Mental Health, no. 3, Public Health Service publication no. 1938 (1969), 24.

8. D. L. Greenblatt et al. "Phenothiazine–Induced Dsykinesia in Nursing Home Patients," *Journal of the American Geriatric Society* 16 (1968): 27.

9. George E. Crane, "Dyskinesia and Neuroleptics," *Archives of General Psychiatry* 19 (1968): 700.

10. Ibid., 701–703.

11. Crane and Gardner, eds., *Basal Ganglia Workshop*, 63 (Crane's findings); ibid., 24 and 178 (Degkwitz's results).

12. Muriel Jones and Richard Hunter, "Abnormal Movements in Patients with Chronic Psychiatric Illness," in ibid., 53. George Paulson praised their "amazing records" and "painstaking extraction" of information when he summed up the proceedings. Ibid., 173.

13. Jones and Hunter, "Abnormal Movements," 53; 58, tables 5 and 6; 63. The figures for male patients who had received medication were lower, and fewer male patients had received medications in the first place. Of eleven men who had received medication in the past, none had dyskinesia; of two currently receiving drugs, one did. Aggregating the figures for both sexes, about 20 percent of patients exposed to medications developed dyskinesias, compared with about 2 percent of those never medicated.

Jones and Hunter offered another provocative finding: many more women than men patients had received medication in the first place (sixty-nine of ninety women compared with thirteen of thirty-seven men). That dovetailed with studies that reported more women than men receiving lobotomies. Moreover, Jones and Hunter noted that women remained on medication much longer: "Whereas most of the male patients had been given drugs for less than a year, the majority of the female patients had received them continuously for several years—ten years continuous drug therapy being not uncommon." Ibid., 55.

These data suggest women may have appeared more susceptible to tardive dyskinesia during the 1960s—before universal medication of both sexes became the norm—because they received more medication. George Paulson broached that possibility during discussion, observing that "[a]pparent sex peculiarities [in the data] might be due to differences in the physician's attitudes about women." "There may be some behavior," Paulson continued, "that is more tolerable [to physicians] in males than in females, and drugs may be prescribed differently." Ibid., 64. For general discussion of the treatment of women in psychiatry, see Sheldon Gelman, "The Biological Alteration Cases," *William and Mary Law Review* 36 (1995): 1203, 1214 n. 52, 1252–1254.

14. Jones and Hunter, "Abnormal Movements," 53–54, 57.
15. Ibid., 57, 58. About female patients currently receiving medications, Jones and Hunter wrote, "Since . . . only two patients of this group had abnormal movements . . . described before starting phenothiazines, these are the only cases which can be safely termed 'non-drug induced,' however, in the majority of cases the abnormal movements were noticed for the first time after many years exposure to drugs and physical treatments and resemble those which develop spontaneously in others, which must at least call into question the part played by drugs in their aetiology." Ibid., 57.
16. Ibid., 58, table V. Confounding the problem were figures from the much smaller group of male patients. Among men, those medicated in the past had slightly *less* tremor than those never medicated. Moreover, 17 percent of never-treated men developed tics, but not a single medicated man did. (On the other hand, 10 percent of past-treated men had stereotypical movements, compared to 4 percent of never-treated men.) Further clouding the picture, some of the patients suffered from Parkinson's disease, and others had had encephalitis. Ibid., 58, 62, table VI.
    Three possible explanations exist for the general association between movement and medication: patients with spontaneous abnormal movements received medication more often, perhaps because movement made them appear more disturbed; medication caused the additional movement; or a combination of the first two—patients with movements received drugs more often and drugs produced the same kinds of movements as the disease.
17. A. B. Baker, "Clinical Manifestations of the Extrapyramidal Diseases," in Crane and Gardner, eds., *Basal Ganglia Workshop*, 36, 44 (discussion).
18. Samuel L. Liles and George D. Davis, "Permanent Athetoid and Choreiform Movements after Small Lesions in the Cat," in Crane and Gardner, eds., *Basal Ganglia Workshop*, 98; ibid., 108 (discussion).
19. Gerald A. Deneau and George E. Crane, "Dyskinesia in Rhesus Monkeys Tested with High Doses of Chlorpromazine," in Crane and Gardner, eds., *Basal Ganglia Workshop*, 12.
20. Ruthmary K. Deuel, "Neurological Examination of Rhesus Monkeys Treated with High Doses of Chlorpromazine," in Crane and Gardner, eds., *Basal Ganglia Workshop*, 15.
21. Ibid., 16, 17.
22. Ibid., 17; Deneau and Crane, "Dyskinesia in Rhesus Monkeys," 12.
23. Crane and Gardner, eds., *Basal Ganglia Workshop*, Summation, 178 (Crane), and 173 (Paulson).
24. Ibid., 177. Jones added, "It would be a pity . . . if the abnormalities of movement which occur during the natural history of mental illness were ignored or forgotten at the expense of the very striking abnormalities which occur as a result of treatment."
25. Frank J. Ayd, "Chlorpromazine: Ten Years' Experience," *Journal of the American Medical Association* 184 (1963): 173.
26. Ibid., 175; Frank J. Ayd, "Persistent Dyskinesia: A Neurologic Complication of Major Tranquilizers," *International Drug Therapy Newsletter* 1 (1966): 1,2. Ayd recast much of the text of this article into a June 1967 piece with the same title, "Persistent Dyskinesia: A Neurologic Complication of Major Tranquilizers," *Medical Science* 18 (1967): 32.
27. Ayd, "Persistent Dyskinesia" (1966), 2, 4; Ayd, "Persistent Dyskinesia" (1967), 39.
28. Ayd, "Persistent Dyskinesia" (1966), 4.
29. Frank J. Ayd, "Persistent Dyskinesia—A Further Report," *International Drug Therapy Newsletter* (1967): 18, 19.
30. Ayd, "Persistent Dyskinesia" (1967), 40 (emphasis added).

31. Ibid.
32. "A Special Report," *Archives of General Psychiatry* 28 (1973): 463.
33. Lennard and Bernstein, "Perspectives," 162. Citing Lennard and Bernstein, Brown and Funk went on to identify the manufacturer as Smith, Kline, and French (the maker of Thorazine). Brown and Funk, "Tardive Dyskinesia," 121.
34. "A Special Report," 464 (emphasis added).
35. Ibid.
36. Daniel X. Friedman, "Editorial: Neurological Syndromes Associated with Antipsychotic Drug Use—A Special Report," *Archives of General Psychiatry* 28 (1973): 465.
37. Crane, "Clinical Psychopharmacology," 127.
38. Ibid., 125.
39. Ibid., 126. The phrase "contemporary community standards" is, and was, a legal standard for medical malpractice. Crane was implying perhaps that psychiatrists should be concerned about legal liability.
40. Ibid., 125. For a similar observation, see Joseph P. McEvoy et al., "Optimal Dose of Neuroleptic in Acute Schizophrenia: A Controlled Study of the Neuroleptic Threshold and Higher Haloperidol Dose," *Archives of General Psychiatry* 48 (1991): 739, 744. McEvoy wrote that clinicians "persist in prescribing high neuroleptic dosages" in part so that the "treatment team can state that they did 'everything possible' . . . should the patient ultimately prove to be nonresponsive."
41. Crane, "Clinical Psychopharmacology," 127.
42. Ibid.
43. George Crane, "Two Decades of Psychopharmacology and Community Mental Health," Old and New Problems of the Schizophrenic Patient," *Transactions of the New York Academy of Sciences*, 2d ser., 36 (1975): 644; Jonathan O. Cole, "Discussion of Dr. Crane's Paper," *Transactions of the New York Academy of Sciences*, 2d ser., 36 (1975): 658.
44. Crane, "Two Decades," 646.
45. Ibid., 645.
46. Ibid., 645, 647–649, 655.
47. Ibid., 650–652. Describing the situation in New Jersey at about this time, Walter Sullivan, a Yale Law School graduate who was representing mental patients at commitment hearings, quipped, "It is easier to get into the Yale Law School than Trenton Psychiatric Hospital."
48. Ibid., 651, 654.
49. Crane, "Clinical Psychopharmacology," 128.
50. Crane, "Two Decades," 655–666.
51. Cole, "Discussion," 658.
52. Ibid.
53. Ibid., 659.
54. Ibid.
55. Ibid., 660.
56. Within a year, Cole would accept Crane's figure of 50 percent. See the discussion in chapter 6 of this book.

Chapter 6   *The Vision Unravels*

1. George Gardos and Jonathan O. Cole, "Maintenance Antipsychotic Therapy: Is the Cure Worse Than the Disease?" *American Journal of Psychiatry* 133 (1976): 32.
2. Ibid., 34, 35, 36 (emphasis in original).
3. Ibid., 35, 36.
4. George Gardos, Jonathan O. Cole, and Richard A. La Brie, "Drug Variables in the Etiology of Tardive Dyskinesia: Application of Discriminant Function Analysis," *Progress in Neuro-Psychopharmacology and Biological Psychiatry* 1 (1977):147. This ar-

ticle was reprinted under the same title—and, as far as I can tell, without alteration—in William E. Fann et al., eds., *Tardive Dyskinesia: Research and Treatment* (New York: SP Medical & Scientific Books, 1980).

5. George M. Simpson and Nathan S. Kline, "Tardive Dyskinesia: Manifestations, Incidence, Etiology, and Treatment," in *The Basal Ganglia*, ed. M. D. Yahr (New York: Raven Press, 1976), 432, 433. The authors referred to Kline's 1968 article.

6. Ibid., 428, 430, 431.

7. Gardos et al., "Drug Variables," 147–148.

8. Samuel Gershon, "Concluding Summary to the Neuroleptic-induced Deficit Syndrome: Proceedings of the First International Meeting on the Neuroleptic-induced Deficit Syndrome," *Acta Psychiatrica Scandinavica* 89, 380 Supplementum (1994): 83, 84; M. Wallace, "Schizophrenia—A National Emergency: Preliminary Observations on SANELINE," ibid., 33; A. G. Awad and T. P. Hogan, "Subjective Response and Quality of Life: Implications for Treatment Outcomes," ibid., 27.

9. Theodore Van Putten and Philip R. A. May, "Subjective Response as a Predictor of Outcome in Pharmacotherapy: The Consumer Has a Point," *Archive of General Psychiatry* 35 (1978): 477, 480.

10. R. H. Belemaker and D. Ward, "Haloperidol in Normals," 131 *British Journal of Psychiatry* 131 (1977): 222.

11. Gershon, "Concluding Summary," 83, 84.

12. Arthur Rifkin, Frederic Quitkin, and Donald F. Klein, "Akinesia: A Poorly Recognized Disorder," *Archives of General Psychiatry* 32 (1975): 672.

13. Arthur Rifkin, Frederic Quitkin, and Donald F. Klein, "Fluphenazine Decanoate, Oral Fluphenazine, and Placebo in Treatment of Remitted Schizophrenics," *Archives of General Psychiatry* 34 (1977): 1215, 1216.

14. T. Lewander, "Neuroleptics and the Neuroleptic-induced Deficit Syndrome," *Acta Psychiatrica Scandinavica* 89, 380 Supplementum (1994): 8, 10. Awad and Hogan noted that clinicians "have frequently observed" neuroleptic-induced changes in subjective states and found it "surprising" that neuroleptic-induced deficits and "the quality of life of schizophrenic patients on neuroleptics" receive so little attention. Awad and Hogan, "Subjective Response to Neuroleptics," 27, 28.

15. Examples include R. De Alarcon and M. W. P. Carney, "Severe Depressive Mood Changes Following Slow-release Intramuscular Fluphenazine Injection," *British Medical Journal* 3 (1969): 564.

16. Leo E. Hollister, "Choice of Antipsychotic Drugs," *American Journal of Psychiatry* 127 (1970): 104, 107.

17. Ibid., 107–108.

18. Ibid., 108.

19. Hollister later explained how the reports about "normals" on medication had influenced his thinking in Leo E. Hollister, "Neuroleptic Dysphoria: So What's New?" *Biological Psychiatry* 31 (1992): 531.

20. Theodore Van Putten, "Why Do Schizophrenic Patients Refuse to Take Their Drugs," *Archives of General Psychiatry* 31 (1974): 67, 70.

21. Ibid., 70–71.

22. Theodore Van Putten, "The Many Faces of Akathisia," *Comprehensive Psychiatry* 16 (1975): 43–47.

23. Van Putten and May, "Subjective Response," 477. Between "Subjective Response" and "The Many Faces of Akathisia," Van Putten coauthored an article that described a subgroup of "medication refusers" who seemed to prefer their grandiose form of mental illness to medication-induced contact with reality. Theodore Van Putten et al., "Drug Refusal in Schizophrenia and the Wish to Be Crazy," *Archives of General Psychiatry* 33 (1976): 1443. The thrust of this article was not that "the consumer has a point;" rather, it was that some consumers preferred to be crazy.

It is difficult to determine whether the "Wish to Be Crazy" and "Subjective Response" articles reached conflicting conclusions. They certainly differed in emphasis, but that may have been the result of differences in the populations studied as well as changes in Van Putten's viewpoint. Some or all of the variation may be due to the fact that in "Wish to Be Crazy" Van Putten thought he had eliminated side effects as a factor in drug refusal, since the "medication was adjusted so that each patient experienced either none[sic] or minimal extrapyramidal symptoms." Ibid. It seems unlikely that the Van Putten of "Subjective Response" would have been so confident about "minimal" extrapyramidal side effects having no impact on patients; indeed, in his 1974 article, Van Putten had noted that the "severity of EPI [extrapyramidal symptoms] was not related to the degree of drug reluctance" while the presence of any EPI—however mild—had a "strong association" with reluctance to take medication. Van Putten, "Why Do Schizophrenic Patients Refuse to Take Their Drugs," 70.

24. Van Putten and May, "Subjective Response," 478–479.
25. Ibid., 479–480. The authors added that their findings were "preliminary and in need of replication;" in 1985, three psychiatrists claimed to have confirmed them. T. P. Hogan, A. G. Awad, and M. R. Eastwood, "Early Subjective Response and Prediction of Outcome to Neuroleptic Drug Therapy in Schizophrenia," *Canadian Journal of Psychiatry* 30 (1985): 246, 247.
26. Philip R. A. May, Theodore Van Putten, and Coralee Yale, "Predicting the Outcome of Antipsychotic Drug Treatment from Early Response," *American Journal of Psychiatry* 137 (1980): 1088, 1089.
27. Brian G. Anderson et al., "Prolonged Adverse Effects of Haloperidol in Normal Subjects," correspondence, *New England Journal of Medicine* 305 (1981): 643.

Chapter 7   Medication and Litigation

1. A comprehensive overview of the litigation appears in Alexander D. Brooks, *Law, Psychiatry and the Mental Health System* (Boston: Little Brown, 1974), a pioneering text.
2. For a sampling of psychiatric viewpoints, see Frank J. Ayd, Jr., ed., *Medical, Moral and Legal Issues in Mental Health Care* (Baltimore: Williams and Wilkins, 1974), and Alan A. Stone, "Recent Mental Health Litigation: A Critical Perspective," *American Journal of Psychiatry* 134 (1977): 273. Psychiatrists' reactions to various legal developments are surveyed in Paul S. Appelbaum, *Almost a Revolution: Mental Health Law and the Limits of Change* (New York: Oxford University Press, 1994).
3. For the course of *Brown* and related litigation, see Gerald Gunther and Kathleen M. Sullivan, *Constitutional Law*, 13th ed. (Westbury, N.Y.: Foundation Press, 1997), 671–681, 771–793.
4. The Court reviewed these developments in *Planned Parenthood v. Casey*, 505 U.S. 833 (1992).
5. For contrasting views about extending *Brown* in these ways, see Abraham Chayes, "The Supreme Court 1981 Term—Foreword: Public Law Litigation and the Burger Court," *Harvard Law Review* 96 (1982): 4, and Paul Mishkin, "Federal Courts as State Reformers," *Washington and Lee Law Review* 35 (1978): 949.
6. Morton Birnbaum, "The Right to Treatment," *American Bar Association Journal* 46 (1960): 499.
7. Ibid., 501.
8. Ibid., quoting Sands, "Discharges from Mental Hospitals," *American Journal of Psychiatry* 115 (1959): 748.
9. Birnbaum, "Right to Treatment," 503.
10. Ibid.
11. *Rouse v. Cameron*, 373 F. 2d 451, 459 (D.C. Cir. 1966).

12. *Wyatt v. Stickney*, 344 F. Supp. 373 (M.D. Ala. 1972).
13. Brooks, *Law, Psychiatry and the Mental Health System*, 870. For a similar view, see Nancy K. Rhoden, "The Limits of Liberty: Deinstitutionalization, Homelessness, and Libertarian Theory," *Emory Law Journal* 31 (1982): 375, 402–403.
14. The figures for the Alabama hospital are reported in Ralph Reisner and Christopher Slobogin, *Law and the Mental Health System: Civil and Criminal Aspects*, 2d ed. (St. Paul, Minn.: West Publishing, 1990), 998. The Ohio case was *Rone v. Fireman*, 473 F. Supp. 92, 99–101 (N.D. Ohio 1978); according to the court, admissions fell from 1,068 in fiscal year 1975 to 393 in fiscal year 1977, and the census dropped from 957 patients to 709.
15. See, for example, Michael S. Lottman, "Paper Victories and Hard Realities," in *Paper Victories and Hard Realities: The Implementation of the Legal and Constitutional Rights of the Mentally Disabled*, ed. Valerie Bradley and Gary Clarke (Washington, D.C.: Health Policy Center, Georgetown University, 1976), 93; Jack Drake, "The Development of Wyatt in the Courtroom," in *Wyatt v. Stickney: Retrospect and Prospect*, ed. L. Ralph Jones and Richard R. Parlour (New York: Grune and Stratton, 1981), 35, 38.
16. In 1982, the Supreme Court drew the distinction between safety and treatment in *Romeo v. Youngberg*, 457 U.S. 307 (1982).
17. Crane examined the Wyatt patients as an expert for the United States Department of Justice, which was litigating the case at that point. Crane described his findings to me in a personal communication at the time. The New Jersey institution was Greystone Psychiatric Hospital; its medication practices were examined in the case of *Rennie v. Klein*.
18. *Donaldson v. O'Connor*, 493 F. 2d 507 (5th Cir. 1974), remanded on other grounds 422 U.S. 563 (1975).
19. For reviews of these issues, see Reisner and Slobogin, *Law and the Mental Health System*, 694–696, and Appelbaum, *Almost a Revolution*, 17–70. Appelbaum claims, in my view correctly, that "highly restrictive [hospital] admission policies" and "the rapid discharge of unstable persons" resulted not from changes in the law, but rather from policies of "indiscriminate deinstitutionalization." 52.
20. The commitment case was *Lessard v. Schmidt*, 349 F. Supp. 1078 (E.D. Wisconsin 1972)
21. For example, *Winters v. Miller*, 446 F. 2d 65 (2d Cir.), *cert. denied* 404 U.S. 985 (1971) held that hospitalization per se did not render a person incompetent. For surveys of the issues, see Dennis E. Cichon, "The Right to 'Just Say No': A History and Analysis of the Right to Refuse Antipsychotic Drugs," *Louisiana Law Review* 53 (1992): 283; Sheldon Gelman, "The Biological Alteration Cases," *William and Mary Law Review* 36 (1995): 1294.
22. On the earlier therapies, see Elliot S. Valenstein, *Great and Desperate Cures: The Rise and Decline of Psychosurgery and Other Radical Treatments for Mental Illness* (New York: Basic Books, 1986). The 1927 sterilization decision was *Buck v. Bell*, 274 U.S. 200 (1927); the subsequent decision that cast doubt on it was *Skinner v. Oklahoma*, 316 U.S. 535 (1942). For discussion of these and other cases, see Gelman, "Biological Alteration."
23. Alan A. Stone, "Recent Mental Health Litigation: A Critical Perspective," *American Journal of Psychiatry* 134 (1977): 273. The Massachusetts attorney general did not object to a federal court restraining order in 1975 that barred nonemergency, forced medication in state hospitals, *Rogers v. Okin*, 478 F. Supp. 1342, 1353 (D. Mass. 1979); at that juncture, the attorney general presumably considered the practice difficult to defend constitutionally.
24. Stone characterized judicial recognition of a right to refuse as "inevitable" in 1981. Alan A. Stone, "The Right to Refuse Treatment: Why Psychiatrists Should and Can Make It Work," *Archives of General Psychiatry* 38 (1981): 358. Brooks cited the four

decisions in *Law, Psychiatry and the Mental Health System*, 897. The prisoner cases were *Peek v. Ciccone*, 288 F. Supp. 329 (W.D. Mo. 1968) and *Veals v. Ciccone*, 281 F. Supp. 1017 (W.D. Mo. 1968). The Michigan case was *Stowers v. Ardmore Acres Hospital*, 191 N.W. 2d 355, 360, 362 (1971).

25. *Winters v Miller*, 306 F. Supp. 1158 (E.D. N.Y. 1969), *remanded* 446 F. 2d 65 (2d Cir.), *cert. denied* 404 U.S. 985 (1971). Ennis described his work on behalf of mental patients in Bruce Ennis, *Prisoners of Psychiatry: Mental Patients, Psychiatrists and the Law* (New York: Harcourt Brace Jovanovich, 1972). His account of the *Winters* case appears on pages 128–144, where the plaintiff, Miriam Winters, is given the pseudonym "Mary Summers."

26. I elaborate on these uncertainties in Gelman, Biological Alteration," 1728 n. 27.

27. Ennis, *Prisoners of Psychiatry*, 128–144; *Winters*, 446 F. 2d at 68.

28. *Rogers v. Okin*; *Rennie v. Klein*, 462 F. Supp. 1131(D. N.J. 1978), *class injunction issued* 476 F Supp. 1294 (D. N.J. 1979), *modified and remanded*, 653 F. 2d 836 (3d Cir. 1981), *remanded*, 458 U.S. 1119 (1982). The author was involved in *Rennie* as trial and appellate attorney.

29. *Rogers v Okin*, 1360; *Rennie v. Klein*, 1302–1303.

30. These aspects of the *Rennie* record are summarized in Sheldon Gelman, "Mental Hospital Drugs, Professionalism, and the Constitution," *Georgetown Law Journal* 72 (1984): 1756–1757, with citations to the case transcripts; for a general summary of the court record see Sheldon Gelman, "Mental Hospital Drugging—Atomistic and Structural Remedies," *Cleveland State Law Review* 32 (1983): 221.

31. Brief of the American Psychiatric Association as Amicus Curiae, *Rennie v. Klein*, No. 79–2576, 79–2577, pp. 19–20, United States Court of Appeals, 3rd Cir. (1980). Crane's testimony appears in *Rennie v. Klein*, Joint Appendix beginning at 1093a.

32. Ibid., 1300.

33. See, for example, Peter Sterling, "Psychiatry's Drug Addiction," *New Republic*, 8 December 1979, 14.

34. Thomas Gualtieri and Robert L. Sprague, "Preventing Tardive Dyskinesia and Preventing Tardive Dyskinesia Litigation," *Psychopharmacology Bulletin* 20 (1984): 346,347.

35. Henry L. Lennard and Arnold Bernstein, "Perspectives on the New Psychoactive Drug Technology," in *Social Aspects of the Medical Use of Psychotropic Drugs*, ed. Ruth Cooperstock (Toronto: Addiction Research Foundation 1974), 155; Gualtieri and Sprague, "Preventing Tardive Dyskinesia Litigation," 347.

36. George E. Gardos and Jonathan O. Cole, "Overview: Public Health Issues in Tardive Dyskinesia," *American Journal of Psychiatry* 137 (1980): 776; *Tardive Dyskinesia: Report of the American Psychiatric Association Task Force on Late Neurological Effects of Antipsychotic Drugs* (Washington, D.C.: American Psychiatric Association, 1980).

Chapter 8   *Jonathan Cole and Another Task Force*

1. Brief of the American Psychiatric Association as Amicus Curiae, *Rennie v. Klein*, No. 79–2576, 79–2577, pp. 19–20, United States Court of Appeals, 3d Cir. (1980), 19–20.

2. *Tardive Dyskinesia: Report of the American Psychiatric Association Task Force on Late Neurological Effects of Antipsychotic Drugs* (Washington, D.C.: American Psychiatric Association, 1980); hereafter cited as 1980 Report; American Psychiatric Association Task Force on Late Neurological Effects of Antipsychotic Drugs, "Tardive Dyskinesia: Summary of a Task Force Report of the American Psychiatric Association," *American Journal of Psychiatry* 137 (1980): 1163; George E. Gardos and Jonathan O. Cole, "Overview: Public Health Issues in Tardive Dyskinesia," *American Journal of Psychiatry* 137 (1980): 776. Gardos and Cole's article appeared in July, the Task Force "Summary" in October.

3. 1980 Report, 43–44 (internal citations omitted).
4. Ibid., 162 (emphasis added).
5. Task Force, "Tardive Dyskinesia: Summary," 1165. This formulation echoed George M. Simpson and Nathan S. Kline, "Tardive Dyskinesia: Manifestations, Incidence, Etiology, and Treatment," in *The Basal Ganglia*, ed. M. D. Yahr (New York: Raven Press, 1976).
6. Stewart J. Tepper and Joanna F. Hass, "Prevalence Of Tardive Dyskinesia," *Journal of Clinical Psychiatry* 40 (1979): 508, 516; Dilip V. Jeste and Richard Jed Wyatt, "Changing Epidemiology of Tardive Dyskinesia: An Overview," *American Journal of Psychiatry* 138 (1981): 302.
7. Gardos and Cole, "Overview," 776, 777; William E. Fann, John M. Davis, and Davis S. Janowsky, "The Prevalence of Tardive Dyskinesias in Mental Hospital Patients," *Diseases of the Nervous System* 33 (1972).
8. 1980 Report, 45 (internal citations and cross-references omitted).
9. Task Force, "Tardive Dyskinesia: Summary," 1164; 1980 Report, 162.
10. 1980 Report, 24–25.
11. Ibid., 101.
12. Ibid., 104–105, 170 (emphasis in original).
13. Ibid., 2, 12, 114, 115.
14. Ibid. 17, 19, 28–33.
15. Ibid., 118, 167.
16. 1980 Report,171–72. The "dilemma" phrasing appeared in Fann et al., "Prevalence of Tardive Dyskinesias," 182–183, coauthored by Task Force member Davis.
17. 1980 Report, 118, 168 (emphasis added).
18. Task Force , "Tardive Dyskinesia: Summary," 1168; 1980 Report, 169, table 16.
19. 1980 Report, 170. Davis had offered a similar recommendation in 1975. John M. Davis, "Overview: Maintenance Therapy in Psychiatry: I Schizophrenia," *American Journal of Psychiatry* 132 (1975): 1237, 1240, 1243.
20. 1980 Report, 170.
21. Ibid., 168.
22. Gardos and Cole, "Overview," 777.
23. Ibid., 779.
24. Ibid.
25. Ibid., 779, 780 (emphasis added).
26. Ibid., 780.
27. Davis, "Overview: Schizophrenia," 1240, 1244. Davis's figures suggested that 35 percent—compared with Gardos and Cole's almost 50 percent—of patients did not benefit from maintenance medication. Davis later modified his views; what matters here, however, is that his 1975 analysis supported Gardos and Cole's 1976 recommendation.
28. Gardos and Cole, "Overview," 780.
29. Ibid.
30. Theodore Van Putten et al., "Subjective Response to Antipsychotic Drugs," *Archives of General Psychiatry* 38 (1981): 187
31. Ibid., 190.
32. Ibid.

Chapter 9   *Absence of Vision: Clinical Psychiatry, Public Health, and Law*

1. Thomas Gualtieri and Robert L. Sprague, "Preventing Tardive Dyskinesia and Preventing Tardive Dyskinesia Litigation," *Psychopharmacology Bulletin* 20 (1984): 347; John Sramek et al., "Prevalence of Tardive Dyskinesia among Three Ethnic Groups of Chronic Psychiatric Patients," *Hospital and Community Psychiatry* 42 (1991): 590, 591.

2. Gerard T. Reardon et al., "Changing Patterns of Neuroleptic Dosage Over a Decade," *American Journal of Psychiatry* 146 (1989): 726, 727, 729. Arthur Rifkin, coauthor of the 1975 article that rediscovered akinesia, also coauthored this paper.
3. Julie M. Zito et al., "Pharmaco-Epidemiology in 136 Hospitalized Schizophrenic Patients," *American Journal of Psychiatry* 144 (1987): 778, 781, 782.
4. Ibid., 781. Sramek reported a similar pattern in his study: 29.4 percent of patients received lower-potency medications and 79.6 percent received higher-potency drugs. "Prevalence of Tardive Dyskinesia," 591.
5. For clinicians' views, see, for example, *People v. Bobo*, 229 Cal. App. 3d 1417,1433 (1990); according to the opinion, a Dr. Rosenthal testified that schizophrenia arose from a brain "chemical imbalance" and that people without that imbalance "cannot tolerate" the "severe side effects" of medications; see also *Guardianship of Roe*, 583 N.E. 2d 1282, 1284 (Mass. Sup. Jud. Ct. 1992), reporting the testimony of someone who wished to refuse medication that "medication is designed to correct a chemical imbalance in the brain."
6. The inpatient figures appear in Paul S. Appelbaum, *Almost a Revolution: Mental Health Law and the Limits of Change* (New York: Oxford University Press, 1994), 50. For general treatments of the subject, see, for example, Gerald N. Grob, *From Asylum to Community: Mental Health Policy in Modern America* (Princeton, N.J.: Princeton University Press, 1991), 249–311, and Ann Braden Johnson, *Out of Bedlam: The Truth About Deinstitutionalization* (Basic Books, 1990).
7. On the problems of deinstitutionalization, see the sources cited in the previous note and Rael Jean Isaac and Virginia C. Armat, *Madness in the Streets: How Psychiatry and the Law Abandoned the Mentally Ill* (New York: The Free Press, 1990). A case arising out of New York's program is *Boggs v. New York City Health & Hospital Corp.*, 523 N.Y.S. 2d 71 (1987).
8. Serious criticisms of deinstitutionalization date from the mid-1970s. Examples include Franklyn N. Arnhoff, "Social Consequences of Policy Toward Mental Illness," *Science* 188 (1975): 1277, and Stuart A. Kirk and Mark E. Therrien, "Community Mental Health Myths and the Fate of Former Hospitalized Patients," *Psychiatry* 38 (1975): 209.
9. The increased attention to nonresponding patients is reflected in works such as in Burt Angrist and S. Charles Schultz, eds., *The Neuroleptic-Nonresponsive Patient: Characterization and Treatment* (Washington, D.C.: American Psychiatric Press, 1990).
10. For an account that faults attorneys and the "political left," see Isaac and Armat, *Madness in the Streets*; for one that faults bureaucrats among others—in convincing fashion, I believe—see Johnson, *Out of Bedlam*.
11. *Rogers*, 634 F. 2d 650, 660, 661 (1st Cir. 1980).
12. Ibid., 656.
13. Alan Stone, "The Right to Refuse Treatment: Why Psychiatrists Should and Can Make It Work," *Archives of General Psychiatry* 38 (1981): 358, 362.
14. *Rennie v. Klein*, 653 F. 2d 836 (3rd Cir. 1981).
15. Ibid., 847, 848; *Rogers*, 634 F. 2d at 657. The analysis that follows is taken from Sheldon Gelman, "Mental Hospital Drugs, Professionalism, and the Constitution," *Georgetown Law Journal* 72 (1984): 1775.
16. *Parham v. J.R.*, 442 U.S. 584 (1979).
17. *Pennhurst State School and Hospital v. Halderman*, 451 U.S. 1 (1981).
18. *Youngberg v. Romeo*, 457 U.S. 307, 322–324 (1982).
19. The leading example of a decree reopened after *Romeo* is *Society for Good Will to Retarded Children v. Cuomo*, 737 F. 2d 1239 (2nd Cir. 1984), which involved long-running litigation over the Willowbrook State School in New York.
20. *Mills v. Rogers*, 457 U.S. 291 (1982); *Rennie*, 454 U.S. 1078 (1982).

21. *Rogers*, 738 F. 2d 1, 8 (1st Cir. 1984), and Rogers *v. Commissioner*, 458 N.E.2d 308, 311, 321–322 (Mass. Sup. Jud. Ct. 1983); *Rennie* 720 F. 2d 266 (3rd Cir. 1983).
22. *Rennie*, 476 F. Supp. at 1304.
23. Appelbaum, *Almost a Revolution*,140, 143. For citations to decisions upholding forcible medication when the patient suffers from tardive dyskinesia see Sheldon Gelman, "The Biological Alteration Cases," William and Mary Law Review 36 (1995): 1203, 1289–1290 n. 317.
24. Appelbaum, *Almost a Revolution*, 142–143.
25. Ibid.
26. William M. Glazer et al., "Predicting the Long-Term Risk of Tardive Dyskinesia," *Journal of Clinical Psychiatry* 54 (1993): 133, 137–138.
27. Appelbaum, *Almost a Revolution*, 150. Estimates about the number of nonresponders vary; see, for example, David Pickar, "Prospects for Pharmacotherapy of Schizophrenia," *Lancet* 345 (1995): 557. (30 to 40 percent of patients with schizophrenia "may have an inadequate or poor response to traditional antipsychotic neuroleptics"); William T. Carpenter, "Medical Progress: Schizophrenia," *New England Journal of Medicine* 330 (1994): 681 ("about 10 to 20 percent . . . have a poor response . . . and most patients have an incomplete response").
28. *Washington v. Harper*, 494 U.S. 290 (1990). For a review of the mental hospital cases and an argument that courts that apply a "professional judgment" test to medication refusal are using the functional equivalent of *Harper's* test, see Gelman, "Biological Alteration," 1267–1270.
29. *Buck v. Bell*, 274 U.S. 200 (1927).
30. *Harper* at 214.
31. Early in the *Rennie* case, the trial judge barred forced medication if a permanent side effect would result; by the end of the case, that restriction had disappeared. John Rennie received medication involuntarily, though the court found he was developing tardive dyskinesia.
32. On the lack of historical precedent for medication-caused harms see Gelman, "Biological Alteration," 1206.

Chapter 10   Absence of Vision: Research

1. George Gardos and Jonathan O. Cole, "Neuroleptics and Tardive Dyskinesia in Nonschizophrenic Patients," in *Tardive Dyskinesia and Neuroleptics: From Dogma to Reason*, ed. Daniel E. Casey and George Gardos (Washington D.C.: American Psychiatric Press, 1986), 55, 56.
2. Fred Schwartz et al., "Letter: Long-Term Outcome in Chronic Schizophrenia," *Archives of General Psychiatry* 49 (1992): 502. For an example of psychiatrists' concern with sources of funding and insurance reimbursement, and their awareness that therapeutic success might constitute a pivotal consideration, see National Advisory Mental Health Council, "Health Care Reform for Americans with Severe Mental Illnesses: Report of the National Advisory Mental Health Council," *American Journal of Psychiatry* 150 (1993): 1447.
3. Michael P. Caligiuri, James B. Lohr, and Dilip V. Jeste, "Parkinsonism in Neuroleptic-Naive Schizophrenic Patients," *American Journal of Psychiatry* 150 (1993): 1343, 1346–1347.
4. Ross J. Baldessarini et al., "Significance of Neuroleptic Dose and Plasma Level in the Pharmacological Treatment of Psychoses," *Archives of General Psychiatry* 45 (1988): 79, 80.
5. American Psychiatric Association, Tardive Dyskinesia: A Task Force Report of the American Psychiatric Association (Washington, D.C.: American Psychiatric Association Press, 1992), 236; George Gardos et al., "Ten-year Outcome of Tardive Dyskinesia," *American Journal of Psychiatry* 151 (1994): 836; R. G. McCreadie et

al., "The Nithsdate Schizophrenia Surveys—IX: Akathisia, Parkinsonism, Tardive Dyskinesia, and Plasma Neuroleptic Levels," *British Journal of Psychiatry* 160 (1992): 793; D. V. Jeste and M. P. Caligiuri, "Tardive Dyskinesia," *Schizophrenia Bulletin* 19 (1993): 303.

6. Benoit H. Mulsant and Samuel Gershon, "Neuroleptics in the Treatment of Psychosis in Late Life: A Rational Approach," *International Journal of Geriatric Psychiatry* 8 (1993):979; Dilip V. Jeste et al., "Risk of Tardive Dyskinesia in Older Patients: A Prospective Longitudinal Study of 266 Outpatients," *Archives of General Psychiatry* 52 (1995): 756, 756, 758, 763.

7. William M. Glazer et al., "Predicting the Long-Term Risk of Tardive Dyskinesia," *Journal of Clinical Psychiatry* 54 (1993): 137–138; Hal Morgenstern and William M. Glazer, "Identifying Risk Factors for Tardive Dyskinesia Among Long-term Outpatients Maintained With Neuroleptic Medications: Results of the Yale Tardive Dyskinesia Study," *Archives of General Psychiatry* 50 (1993): 723. Glazer found nonwhite patients developing tardive dyskinesia at about twice the rate of white patients; other studies either find no prevalence disparity based on race or produce inconclusive results on the question.

8. Peter F. Buckley et al., "Catching Up on Schizophrenia: The Fifth Annual Conference on Schizophrenia Research, Warm Springs, Va., April 8–12, 1995," *Archives of General Psychiatry* 53 (1996): 456 (describing a presentation by John Kane); 1992 Report, 71 (describing two studies by Glazer); Glazer et al., "Predicting the Long-Term Risk," 138.

9. Stephen M. Stahl, "Akathisia and Tardive Dyskinesia: Changing Concepts," *Archives of General Psychiatry* 43 (1985): 915.

10. Jane S. Paulsen, Robert K. Heaton, and Dilip V. Jeste, "Neuropsychological Impairment in Tardive Dyskinesia," *Neuropsychology* 8 (1994): 227, 227–232, 235, 238–239.

11. For an example, see Steven C. Dilsaver, "Antipsychotic Agents: A Review," *American Family Physician* 47 (1993): 199.

12. Perminder Sachdev and Celia Loneragan, "The Present Status of Akathisia," *Journal of Nervous and Mental Disease* 179 (1991): 381, 382, 384.

13. Ibid., 389.

14. A. G. Awad and T. P. Hogan, "Subjective Response and Quality of Life: Implications for Treatment Outcomes," *Acta Psychiatrica Scandinavica* 89 (380 Supplementum, 1994): 28.

15. Samuel Gershon, "Concluding Summary to the Neuroleptic-induced Deficit Syndrome: Proceedings of the First International Meeting on the Neuroleptic-induced Deficit Syndrome," *Acta Psychiatrica Scandinavica* 89 (380 Supplementum, 1994): 84.

16. Stephen R. Marder et al., "Costs and Benefits of Two Doses of Fluphenazine," *Archives of General Psychiatry* 41 1984): 1025, 1029.

17. Leo Hollister, "Neuroleptic Dysphoria: What's New?" *Biological Psychiatry* 31 (1992): 531.

18. Ibid., 531–532.

19. A. George Awad, "Quality of Life of Schizophrenic Patients on Medications and Implications for New Drug Trials," *Hospital and Community Psychiatry* 43 (1992): 262.

20. Patricia L. Gilbert et al., "Neuroleptic Withdrawal in Schizophrenic Patients: A Review of the Literature," *Archives of General Psychiatry* 52 (1995): 173, 182.

21. Ibid., 182, 184–185.

22. Ibid., 185, 186.

23. The comments, all in *Archives of General Psychiatry* 52 (1995) included: Ross J. Baldessarini and Adele C. Viguera, "Neuroleptic Withdrawal in Schizophrenic

Patients," 189; William T. Carpenter and Carol A. Tamminga, "Why Neuroleptic Withdrawal in Schizophrenia?" 192; John F. Greden and Rajiv Tandon, "Long-Term Treatment for Lifetime Disorders?" 197; Herbert Y. Meltzer, "Neuroleptic Withdrawal in Schizophrenic Patients: An Idea Whose Time Has Come," 200; Keith H. Nuechterlein et al., "The Early Course of Schizophrenia and Long-term Maintenance Neuroleptic Therapy," 203; and Richard Jed Wyatt, "Risks of Withdrawing Antipsychotic Medications," 205. Discussions of controversy over withholding medication in research appear in Robert Aller and Gregory Aller, "An Institutional Response to Patient/Family Complaints," in *Ethics in Neurobiological Research with Human Subjects: The Baltimore Conference on Ethics*, ed. Adil E. Shamoo (Amsterdam: Gordon and Breach, 1997), 155, and UCLA Clinical Research Center, "Statement of the UCLA Clinical Research Center" also in *Ethics in Neurobiological Research with Human Subjects: The Baltimore Conference on Ethics*, 173.

24. Gilbert et al., "Neuroleptic Withdrawal," 184, 186; Nuechterlein et al., "Early Course."
25. Baldessarini and Viguera, "Neuroleptic Withdrawal," 189, 191
26. Ibid., 189.
27. Ibid., 191.
28. Ibid.
29. Carpenter and Tamminga, "Why Neuroleptic Withdrawal," 192.
30. Greden and Tandon, "Long Term Treatment," 197, 198.
31. Ibid., 198.
32. Dilip V. Jeste et al., "Considering Neuroleptic Maintenance and Taper on a Continuum: Need for Individual Rather Than Dogmatic Approach," *Archives of General Psychiatry* 52 (1995): 209, 210.
33. Greden and Tandon, "Long-Term Treatment," 199.
34. Wyatt, "Risk of Withdrawing Medications," 208. Unlike Greden and Tandon, Wyatt favored dose reduction as a general strategy, at least if "psychosocial treatments . . . [were] provided in addition" to medication.
35. Jeste et al., "Considering Neuroleptic Maintenance," 210.
36. Ibid. (emphasis in original).

Chapter 11   Absence of Vision: History

1. George E. Gardos and Jonathan D. Cole, "Overview: Public Health Issues in Tardive Dyskinesia," *American Journal of Psychiatry* 137 (1980): 776.
2. Daniel E. Casey and George Gardos, "Introduction." In *Tardive Dyskinesia and Neuroleptics: From Dogma to Reason*, ed. Daniel E. Casey and George Gardos (Washington D.C.: American Psychiatric Press, 1986), ix; Dilip V. Jeste and Richard Jed Wyatt, *Understanding and Treating Tardive Dyskinesia* (New York: Guilford Press, 1982), 9.
3. Casey and Gardos, "Introduction."
4. Thomas E. Hansen, Daniel E. Casey, and William M. Vollmer, "Is There an Epidemic of Tardive Dyskinesia?" in *Tardive Dyskinesia and Neuroleptics*, ed. Casey and Gardos, 1.
5. Ibid.
6. Casey did not think that incidence studies necessarily explained increasing prevalence rates over time, because "they do not take into account remissions." Ibid., 8.
7. Ibid., 10–11.

Chapter 12   A Vision Restored?

1. John Kane et al., "Clozapine for the Treatment-Resistant Schizophrenic: A Double-blind Comparison with Chlorpromazine," *Archives General Psychiatry* 45 (1988):

789; Stephen R. Marder and Theodore Van Putten, "Who Should Receive Cloza-pine," *Archives of General Psychiatry* 45 (1988): 865.

2. David Pickar, "Prospects for Pharmacotherapy of Schizophrenia," *Lancet* 345 (1995): 557.

3. Herbert Y. Meltzer, "Neuroleptic Withdrawal in Schizophrenic Patients: An Idea Whose Time Has Come," *Archives of General Psychiatry* 52 (1995).

4. The cost estimates for clozapine appear in Robert Rosenheck et al., "A Compari-son of Clozapine and Haloperidol in Hospitalized Patients with Refractory Schizo-phrenia," *New England Journal of Medicine* 337 (1997): 809. Rosenheck found, however, that the total expense—including hospitalization—of treating refractory patients was slightly less with clozapine because of better patient compliance and fewer relapses. The side effect estimates appear in Ross J. Baldessarini and Frances R. Frankenburg, "Clozapine: A Novel Antipsychotic Agent," *New England Journal of Medicine* 324 (1991): 746, 751, table 3. Regarding other atypicals, the "dispute" characterization is in Samuel J. Keith, "Editorial: Pharmacologic Advances in the Treatment of Schizophrenia," *New England Journal of Medicine* 337 (1997): 851. For an example of the differing views, see the exchange of letters between Robert A. Mosqueda and Joyce E. Davidson on the one hand, and William T. Carpenter and Robert W. Buchanan on the other, *New England Journal of Medicine* 331 (1994): 275–276.

5. Baldessarini and Frankenburg, "Clozapine," 749, 750.

6. Ibid.

7. Ibid., 752.

8. Ibid.

9. Robert Michels and Peter M. Marzuk, "Progress in Psychiatry," parts 1 and 2, *New England Journal of Medicine* 329 (1993): 552 and 628. This article dealt with psy-chiatry generally, not just with schizophrenia treatment.

10. Ibid., 635.

11. Vikram Khot and Richard Jed Wyatt, "Not All That Moves is Tardive Dyskinesia," *American Journal of Psychiatry* 148 (1991): 661, 666.

12. Wayne S. Fenton, Richard Jed Wyatt, and Thomas H. McGlashan, "Risk Factors for Spontaneous Dyskinesia in Schizophrenia," *Archives of General Psychiatry* 51 (1994): 643, 648–649.

13. Ibid., 649.

14. Richard Jed Wyatt, "Neuroleptics and the Natural Course of Schizophrenia," *Schiz-ophrenia Bulletin* 17 (1991): 325.

15. Studies reporting low rates of spontaneous dyskinesia include George E. Crane, "Dyskinesia and Neuroleptics," Archives of General Psychiatry 19 (1968): 700; Greenblatt et al., "Phenothiazine-Induced Dyskinesia in Nursing Home Patients," Journal of the American Geriatric Society 16 (1968): 27; and John M. Kane et al., "Prevalence of Abnormal Involuntary Movements ('Spontaneous Dyskinesias') in the Normal Elderly," *Psychopharmacology* 77 (1982): 105, 107. For the argument that researchers overlook past medication exposure, see Stephen B. Ticehurst, "Is Spon-taneous Orofacial Dyskinesia an Artefact Due to Incomplete Drug History?" *Jour-nal of Geriatric Psychiatry and Neurology* 3 (1990): 208, 210. Crane's suggestion about minimal movements appeared in George E. Crane and Ronald A. Smeets, "Tardive Dyskinesia and Drug Therapy in Geriatric Patients," *Archives of General Psychiatry* 30 (1974): 341, 343.

16. Dilip V. Jeste et al., "Risk of Tardive Dyskinesia in Older Patients: A Prospective Lon-gitudinal Study of 266 Outpatients," *Archives of General Psychiatry* 52 (1995).

17. David G. Owens, "Involuntary Disorders of Movement in Chronic Schizophrenia in the Role of the Illness and Its Treatment," in *Dyskinesia—Research and Treatment*, ed. Daniel E. Casey et al. (Berlin: Springer-Verlag, 1985) 79, 85; D. G. Cunningham

Owens et al., "Spontaneous Involuntary Disorders of Movement," *Archives of General Psychiatry* 39 (1982): 452.

18. Regarding severity, Owens "suspended"—for unspecified reasons—the usual practice of downgrading the severity rating when the abnormal movements were elicited by some instruction of the examiner. Ibid., 453. In general, the low rate of medication use that Owens described makes his high reported dyskinesia rates even more remarkable.

19. American Psychiatric Association, Tardive Dyskinesia: A Task Force Report of the American Psychiatric Association (Washington, D.C.: American Psychiatric Association Press, 1992), 20.

20. Ibid.

21. Richard ed Wyatt, "Risks of Withdrawing Antipsychotic Medications," Archives of General Psychiatry 52 (1995): 205, 206.

22. Philip R. May, et al., "Schizophrenia—A Follow-up Study of Results of Treatment," *Archives of General Psychiatry* 33 (1976): 481.

23. Ibid., 482, fig. 1, reporting statistically adjusted results, and 486.

24. William T. Carpenter and Carol A. Tamminga, "Why Neuroleptic Withdrawal," *Archives of General Psychiatry* 52 (1995): 193; Dilip V. Jeste et al., "Considering Neuroleptic Maintenance and Taper on a Continuum: Need for Individual Rather Than Dogmatic Approach," *Archives of General Psychiatry* 52 (1995): 211.

25. May, "Schizophrenia—A Follow-up Study," 486.

26. On lobotomy, see Elliot S. Valenstein, *Great and Desperate Cures: The Rise and Decline of Psychosurgery and Other Radical Treatments for Mental Illness* (New York: Basic Books, 1986), 206–207.

27. Describing lobotomy, Peter Sterling wrote: "Although people know they are controlled in various ways through the culture, they are also aware of their power to resist unjust control. . . . They are aware that this power resides in their brains and they will not give it up in the long run. That is why psychosurgery on only 300 to 400 patients per year has caused a greater stir than the 12,000 annual deaths from more familiar kinds of unnecessary surgery." Peter Sterling, "Ethics and Effectiveness of Psychosurgery," in *Controversy in Psychiatry*, ed. John P. Brady and H. Keith H. Brodie (Philadelphia: Saunders, 1978), 157; for discussion see Sheldon Gelman, "The Biological Alteration Cases," *William and Mary Law Review* 36 (1995).

28. For a discussion of these social and legal changes, see Gelman, "Biological Alteration."

Conclusion **Psychiatry and History**

1. References to "progress" are commonplace. See, for example, Floyd E. Bloom and David J. Kupfer, eds., *Psychopharmacology: The Fourth Generation of Progress* (New York: Raven Press, 1995).

2 . Oliver Sacks, "Scotoma: Forgetting and Neglect in Science," in *Hidden Histories of Science*, Robert B. Silvers, ed. (New York: New York Review Books, 1995), 141, 150, 151, 158.

3. Ibid., 159.

4. Steven Pinker, *How the Mind Works* (New York: W. W. Norton, 1997), 305; emphasis in original.

5. Brian Ackner et al., "Insulin Treatment of Schizophrenia: A Controlled Study," *Lancet* 272 (1957): 607, 610. Ackner had suggested the same point in 1951, before medications even appeared. Ibid., 607, 609. Greenblatt had made a similar suggestion, guessing that the value of insulin coma lay in its ability to lift staff sprits and spur the staff's interest in patients.

6. Joint Commission on Mental Illness and Health, *Action for Mental Health* (New York: Arno Press, 1961), 39.

7. Stephen Fleck, "Correspondence," *New England Journal of Medicine* 330 (1994): 285–286. Michels and Marzuk replied that they saw "no conflict between a modern biomedical approach to psychiatric disorders and the humane, comprehensive care of patients with these disorders; indeed, we believe the former to be an absolute prerequisite for the latter."

8. Peter Sterling, "Ethics and Effectiveness of Psychosurgery," in *Controversy in Psychiatry*, ed. John P. Brady and H. Keith H. Brodie (Philadelphia: Saunders, 1978), 126, 128, 137; some capitalizations omitted)

9. W. A. Cramond, "Lessons from the Insulin Story in Psychiatry," *Australia and New Zealand Journal of Psychiatry* 21 (1987): 320.

10. William T. Carpenter et al., "Methodologic Standards for Treatment Outcome Research in Schizophrenia," *American Journal of Psychiatry* 138 (1981): 465, 466, 468, 470.

Index

under specific cases) 121,
123–129, 172, 176
"Right to Treatment, The" (Birnbaum)
123–124
Rogers v Okin 135–138, 140, 141, 159,
167–174, 175, 176
Romeo (see Youngberg v. Romeo)
Rosenhan, David 42–43

Sachdev, Perminder 183–184
Sacks, Oliver 228–229
schizophrenia (*see also* medication,
neuroleptic) 1, 13, 62, 63–65,
210–211, 220–221, 222
Schmidt, William R. 83, 85, 87
Science 100
scotoma 228–229
side effects (*see also* akathisia; akinesia;
blood disorders; dyskinesia;
dystonia; neuroleptic malignant
syndrome; parkinsonism;
psychomotor indifference;
subjective distress; tardive
dyskinesia)
as annoyances 19, 35, 36, 85, 117
of atypical medication 205–206
behavioral 57, 58, 93, 164
and chemical imbalance theory 69
double blind assessment of 51–52
extrapyramidal 26, 165, 205, 207
faking of, by patients 116,
135–136
fetal harm 104, 107
fever 206
heart damage 104, 107
idiosyncrasy of patients, as
responsible for 30, 33–34, 116,
135
ignoring of, by clinicians 120, 136,
207
ignoring of, by research psychiatrists
31, 32, 36, 183, 184
ignoring of, by lawyers and courts
127–129, 132–134
moral implications of 33–37, 150,
219–221
persistent 30, 31, 32–33, 36, 55–57,

104, 119–120, 141, 146, 151, 182,
219, 220
potency of medication, relationship
to 165
psychological explanation of 116
public health implications of (*see also*
tardive dyskinesia: and public
health policy) 43, 192, 226–227
and refusal of medication 115–117,
159–162
reversible 31, 94
sedation 165, 206
seizures 206
seriousness of, in general 29–30,
34–36, 49–53, 55–59, 85, 166,
178, 193
significance of, in general 33–36, 162,
202
as signs of medication-induced brain
disease 26, 27, 180
as signs of medication effectiveness
26, 29, 30, 57
setting of (community versus
hospital) 35–36, 116–117
as trivial 5, 6, 7, 55, 58, 60, 65, 181,
211, 224, 228
Simpson, George 110–111, 141–142,
144
Smith, Kline & French 24
sociological theory (*see also* Greenblatt,
Milton) 42–43
specific effects of medication (*see also*
medication, neuroleptic:
antischizophrenic effects of) 5, 66
spontaneous dyskinesia. See dyskinesia:
spontaneous
Sprague, Robert L. 138–139, 164
Stahl, Stephen M. 182
state hospitals. (*see also* mental hospitals)
2, 23, 38–47, 72, 134, 205, 227
census of 41, 126, 166
stereotypical movements. See tardive
dyskinesia: and stereotypes or
other movements related to
schizophrenia
Sterling, Peter 25, 36, 232–233
Stone, Alan M. 131, 169

About the Author

Sheldon Gelman is professor of law at the Cleveland-Marshall College of Law. After graduating from law school, he worked in private practice and at a legal aid office. Between 1975 and 1981, he represented patients in New Jersey mental hospitals.